POPE'S
EARLY CAREER

ALEXANDER POPE
From the painting by C. JERVAS in the National
Portrait Gallery

THE
EARLY CAREER

OF

Alexander Pope

By

GEORGE SHERBURN

OXFORD
AT THE CLARENDON PRESS

Oxford University Press, Ely House, London W.1

GLASGOW NEW YORK TORONTO MELBOURNE WELLINGTON
CAPE TOWN SALISBURY IBADAN NAIROBI LUSAKA ADDIS ABABA
BOMBAY CALCUTTA MADRAS KARACHI LAHORE DACCA
KUALA LUMPUR SINGAPORE HONG KONG TOKYO

FIRST PUBLISHED 1934

REPRINTED LITHOGRAPHICALLY IN GREAT BRITAIN
AT THE UNIVERSITY PRESS, OXFORD
BY VIVIAN RIDLER
PRINTER TO THE UNIVERSITY
1968

PREFACE

THIS account of the first part of Pope's career (down to about 1726 or 1727) is designed to present new facts and new interpretations of old facts in such a way as to give the reader an idea of the circumstances out of which Pope's works emerged, and an idea of the personality of the poet, which was, of course, a chief formative influence in the career. The volume contains little of literary criticism in the strict sense of the word. Few writers have suffered more from prejudiced views of their personalities than has Pope. Such prejudice has so commonly carried over into criticism that it seems worth while to examine, somewhat minutely, details of Pope's life, especially those that have through misinterpretation caused false ideas, first, as to his character, and then as to his achievement. It is certainly a tenable position that an author's personality should have no influence with a critic of his writing; but few will deny that Pope's supposed personality daily prejudices readers against his work. Although most of this book is not, then, literary criticism, it is hoped that it may serve as a preliminary to better criticism of Pope. The central purpose of the book, however, is not more to defend Pope the man than it is to show how circumstances and personal traits drove him from an early career of varied poetic composition into his true career (here untreated), which was that of perhaps the greatest of all formal satirists.

The preparation of the volume has intermittently occupied my time for a shocking number of years. As a result I am indebted to so many libraries and to so many more individuals that detailed acknowledgements are hardly possible. I must, of course, acknowledge the long-continued kindnesses of the libraries of the University of Chicago. Outside Chicago I have enjoyed the resources and courtesies of the British Museum, the Bodleian Library, the Harvard University Library, and the Huntington Library. My work on Pope was begun years ago in the Harvard Library, where, though a rank outsider,

I was permitted to use the Lefferts Collection before it
was catalogued. I finished the first draft of this book in
the Huntington Library, where I was so fortunate as to
spend the year 1929–30. Most of the work, however, was
done in the British Museum.

Assistance from individuals I have from time to time
acknowledged in my footnotes. If I were here to list the
names of all the people who have helped me, the list would
be so long that the readers would wonder if I had done
anything myself. I assure these friends that, though here
unnamed, they are remembered with gratitude. I must,
however, name my colleagues George Watson and Arthur
Friedman in gratitude for their services in revising the
manuscript for the press and in reading the proofs.

The many books, newspapers, pamphlets, and manuscripts, referred to in the footnotes, are for the most part
identifiable in such references. In the case of works very
frequently cited, economy is served by abbreviated references. Thus, 'Elwin-Courthope' is the brief form in which
I refer to the *Works of Alexander Pope*, edited by the
Rev. Whitwell Elwin and William John Courthope, in ten
volumes, 1871–89; similarly, *Anecdotes, Observations, and
Characters of Books and Men*, by Joseph Spence (edited
by S. W. Singer, 1820), is referred to simply by the author's
last name; and *Alexander Pope: a Bibliography*, by R. H.
Griffith (Austin, Texas, 1922, 1927), is cited as 'Griffith'.
I trust these and possibly a few other abbreviations will
not annoy the reader.

In Chapters VIII and IX, and elsewhere, I have made
considerable use of fragments of unpublished letters from
Pope to Jacob Tonson, and since it seemed only fair to
let the reader see how the sentences torn from these letters
fit together, a transcript of them is printed as Appendix I.
The *Odyssey* Indenture seems so difficult to interpret that
it is given entire as Appendix II.

G. S.

THE UNIVERSITY OF CHICAGO
4 *August* 1933

CONTENTS

LIST OF PLATES

INTRODUCTION: EARLIER BIOGRAPHIES

THE ill fortune that has pursued biographical work on Alexander Pope began possibly with the poet's birth; for since his parents were Roman Catholics, no official record of his birth or baptism is known. This ill fortune in any case is obvious by the time the first biographies come to be written. About 1728 the Rev. Joseph Spence had decided to collect materials for a life of Pope, whom he esteemed both as a man and as a poet. But about a decade later another Anglican priest, the Rev. William Warburton, entered Pope's career. To him was bequeathed the care of the poet's works and, so Warburton assumed, the production of an official biography. Of Spence, Christopher Pitt wrote: 'Mr. Spence is the completest scholar, either in solid or polite learning, for his years, that I ever knew. Besides, he is the sweetest tempered gentleman breathing.'[1] Warburton might have entered into competition with Spence for completeness of scholarship, but no one ever accused him of being sweet-tempered. In his 1751 edition of Pope he announced grimly: 'Together with his Works, he hath bequeathed me his Dunces.'[2] Such a spirit as this evinces helped to deter the peace-loving from Pope studies.

Long before 1751 Warburton's arrogance had scared off the inoffensive Spence, who had attempted the role of a meek and unaggressive Boswell. Some weeks before the poet's death, at a time when many friends were hovering over his arm-chair, Spence, having been approached by Warburton, set down the following memorandum, dated 7 April 1744: 'Mr. Warburton thinks of writing Mr. Pope's Life, whenever the world may have so great a loss, and I offered to give him any lights I could toward it.'[3] About

---

[1] Spence's *Anecdotes* (ed. Singer, 1820), p. xviii.
[2] *Works of Pope* (large 8vo., 1751), I. xii.
[3] Spence, p. viii.

ten years later Spence, still modest, gave Joseph Warton the following account of his yielding to Warburton:

> As they returned in the same carriage together from Twicken-ham, soon after the death of Mr. Pope, and joined in lamenting his death, and celebrating his praises, Dr. Warburton said he intended to write his life; on which Mr. Spence, with his usual modesty and condescension, said that he also had the same intention; and had from time to time collected from Mr. Pope's own mouth, various particulars of his life, pursuits, and studies; but would readily give up to Dr. Warburton all his collections on this subject, and accord-ingly communicated them to him immediately.[1]

Although Warburton's well-known belligerence kept reputable biographers from the field, it could not so easily keep out the hireling class. These authors, while of little or no importance, do have some interest for us. As early as 1720 a brief 'life' of Pope had appeared in Giles Jacob's *Poetical Register*, and this account is interesting, because the Dunces insisted that Pope wrote it himself and paid two guineas for its insertion in the volume. The scandal in this procedure lay in the fact that while practically no biographical details appeared in the account, it was ex-tremely eulogistic both of Pope's works and of his character. But when we read the letter that Jacob himself addressed to John Dennis about this 'life', we see how the Dunces could pervert facts to their own purposes. On 24 April 1729 Jacob wrote to Dennis:

> That these high Praises and Commendations of himself [Pope] were by him particularly approv'd of, in a printed Proof of his Life and Character, which I transmitted to him for his Correction, I am ready to make Oath of, if requir'd; and by his Alterations and Additions therein, he entirely made the Compliment his own. . . . whatever mean Opinion Mr. *Pope* may have at any Time conceiv'd of me, he had once some Regard for my poor Judgment, otherwise he would not have enter'd into any Correspondence with me by Letter, or subscrib'd two Guineas for one small Book in *Octavo*, to /Sir/ Your Humble Servant,/ Giles Jacob.[2]

---

[1] Spence, pp. viii–ix.
[2] John Dennis, *Remarks on the Dunciad* (1729), pp. 44–9.

Clearly what Pope did was to read and correct the proofs of this eulogy and subscribe generously for the *Poetical Register*. The compliments, one can see, were quite to his taste, or else he made them so; but Jacob's angry suggestion is scant proof that Pope's alterations really were such as to make the sentences 'his own'. In any case this first 'life' is wholly negligible as biography.

Immediately after Pope's death two pamphlet lives appeared; both were anonymous, and can best be identified by the names of their respective publishers, Weaver Bickerton and Charles Corbett. The Corbett pamphlet follows the tradition initiated by Jacob, and confines itself almost exclusively to rather perfunctory literary criticism. The Bickerton volume of seventy-six pages has slightly more interest; for it does possibly contribute something to our knowledge of Pope's childhood, because of information secured, so we are told, from an early schoolfellow, who evidently knew something of Thomas Deane's school near Hyde Park Corner. The author is also shrewd enough to use the 'P. T.' letters (that Curll had published) for details concerning the poet's father.[1] For the rest, his sources lie within the editions of Pope's works published before the poet's death or in the well-known pamphlet literature of the day. Neither of these biographers makes any pretence to personal acquaintance with Pope or with friends of Pope—except for the unnamed schoolfellow just mentioned. Possibly this friend may have been William Lewis, the Covent Garden publisher of the *Essay on Criticism*.

In general what has been said of these two authors applies to the next biographer, William Ayre, who in 1745 brought out *Memoirs of the Life and Writings of Mr. Pope* in two volumes octavo running to a total of nearly 750 pages. The bulk, however, is chiefly due to natural verbosity, to extensive quotation from the poems, and to the reprinting of various biographical or critical 'documents', chiefly letters to or from Pope. Ayre gives entire *Guardian*

---

[1] Elwin-Courthope, vi. 423–32.

No. 40 (of which he assumes Steele to be the author!); he quotes extensively from de Lyra, Donne, Dennis, Buckinghamshire, Mme Dacier, *et al.*, and reprints such things as the *Odyssey* Proposals of 10 January 1724 [1725]. There are numerous digressions, none of which is really informative, and of course Pope's will is reprinted. There is no chronological organization in the volumes: Ayre simply takes up the poems one by one in the order in which they appeared in the early collected editions. This method, especially in its total avoidance of the true business of biography, is so like that of the many lives put out by Curll's authors in this period that the work rather naturally was assumed to come from 'Curll's chaste press', or even from Curll himself. Ayre was, however, an author of known interest in Pope, and there seems to be no real reason for doubting his authorship. Curll may have been the publisher; Shiels speaks of the work as 'the Life of Pope, for which Curll obtained a patent'.[1] There is no sufficient bias against Pope to indicate a hostile provenience.

More workmanlike is the life of thirty-three duodecimo pages, written supposedly by Robert Shiels (assistant on Dr. Johnson's Dictionary) and published in volume v of the *Lives of the Poets of Great Britain and Ireland. By Mr. Cibber and other Hands* (1753). The Cibber name was purchased from Theophilus Cibber and was used by Griffiths, the bookseller, to aid sales. Shiels seems to have been the first biographer to use Spence's anecdotes, from which, as found in Warburton's footnotes, he derived details for his account of Pope's early years.

These biographers, and others unmentioned here, seem to have been quite outside Pope's circle. Their sources were chiefly the editions of his *Works*, though they sometimes quoted from his contemporaries. They used his letters and his footnotes giving biographical details; such as, for example, that to line 381 of the *Epistle to Dr. Arbuthnot*, which for a century was to be the chief source for good and bad information as to the poet's

---

[1] *Lives of the Poets* (1753), v. 226.

parentage. These early biographers made practically no attempts, so far as one can see, to gather materials; and the blunt truth is that they were third-rate literary critics with no apparent interest in biography.

Meanwhile, what was being done by Spence and Warburton, the men who had the best possible opportunities to gather first-hand materials? Spence evidently had really given up the idea of writing a life; but he still worked on the anecdotes that he had collected and placed, in part at least, at the disposal of Warburton. These he was editing and rearranging. His procedure had been to jot down verbatim on loose papers conversations that he recalled having with Pope. These were, shortly after Pope's death, digested into two octavo volumes, with a chronological arrangement. Apparently the latest Spence MS. of the anecdotes was a folio volume in which (judging from editions printed therefrom) he had suppressed much of the chronology, had grouped his anecdotes by 'centuries', and had formalized the language into a dignified style with all colloquialism effaced. Even after the folio MS. was made (one guesses), Spence carried about the octavo volumes, and read the anecdotes to such people as Martha Blount[1] (d. 1763) and the poet Young (d. 1765), who confirmed or denied the truth of the details set down.

The manuscripts from which Singer edited Spence's *Anecdotes* for their first printing in 1820 have unfortunately disappeared. The process of revision here indicated may be traced partially in Singer's Preface and for the rest in the second octavo volume of what Singer calls MS. B (the volume covering the years 1739–44, the existence of which Singer did not know). It is now in the Huntington Library. On the verso of the leaves of this octavo Spence jotted in pencil the comments of Martha Blount, or Dr. Young, or Mrs. Rackett (Pope's half-sister), as he read to them at least such anecdotes as they might be able to verify. Some of these, though not approved by such hearers, were

---

[1] Spence read the manuscript to Martha Blount, 27 May 1749. See his *Anecdotes* (ed. Singer, 1820), p. 358.

either too good to cancel, even if denied,[1] or else Spence never really finished revision of the folio MS.

Since these anecdotes represent the one extensive 'original' attempt to portray Pope directly from the personal side and not indirectly, as most others must do, through the poet's works, their permanent value is inestimable. Yet questions as to their accuracy are bound to arise. It is frequently assumed, in case of manifest error, that Spence was simply setting down misinformation, which Pope intentionally or accidentally gave him wrong. It is quite possible that Pope did this. Clearly, if Pope told Spence that the 'Atticus' lines were written and sent to Addison in 1716 and that Gildon's *Memoirs of Wycherley* (which appeared in 1718) were a cause of the lines, he was telling an impossible story. It is clear, on the other hand, that while Spence pretends to give us the exact words of Pope, he habitually revises those words, sometimes in a fashion such as to make the two versions flatly contradictory.[2] Again, Spence, according to the Huntington Library MS., set down in August 1742 the fact that Pope's dog Bounce was buried in the garden of Pope's villa[3]; but we learn from Pope's authentic correspondence with the Earl of Orrery that Bounce was sent to his Lordship's estate in Somersetshire in July 1742, and died there early in April 1744. There are other examples of misstatement that can hardly be set down to Pope's duplicity. Spence was honest, but his methods of recording, expanding, and

[1] In the Huntington Library MS., page 410 contains the well-known stories (a) that the Duke of Wharton gave Young £2,000 upon the publication of the *Universal Passion* and (b) that Wharton used to set up a human skull with a candle in it to serve as light while Young was composing. On the blank verso of page 408, opposite the first of these anecdotes, Spence has pencilled 'Not true', and opposite the second, 'No such thing. Dr. Yg.' Yet these anecdotes were printed. See Singer's ed. (1820), p. 255.

[2] See the statements as to the first Earl of Oxford's relations with the Pretender: Singer ed., p. 313.

[3] This anecdote of Bounce is given in Singer's ed. (1820, p. 269) as coming from Mrs. Rackett, with only slight modifications in the diction which in the manuscript is ascribed to Pope. Significantly Mrs. Rackett is made to say that her brother 'had some thoughts of burying him [Bounce] in his garden'. For the Orrery letters see Elwin-Courthope, viii. 503 and 518.

revising what pretends to be Pope's exact language would not make for perfect accuracy. In the case of complicated stories, such as the origin of the lines on Addison, error of detail might creep in without intention on any one's part.

The real value of Spence's work lies partly in the fact that he has preserved specific personal information for us, which he gathered from Pope himself and from Pope's friends and relatives. In this information error obviously may and does appear. But Spence's value lies not merely in this specific information; he has a general aim—to give an interpretation of the poet's character by one who knew him well. On the first leaf of his manuscript he summed up this purpose in words that should always be remembered by any one who writes about Alexander Pope:

All the people well acquainted with Mr. Pope, looked on him as a most friendly, open, charitable, and generous-hearted man;—all the world almost, that did not know him, were got into a mode of having very different ideas of him: how proper this makes it to publish these Anecdotes after my death.[1]

Spence allowed Warton and others to see and use his *Anecdotes*; yet, intimidated by Warburton (and possibly by the difficulty of the task), he wrote no formal biography, but left his collected materials to be published imperfectly long after his death.

If it was Pope's misfortune that Spence did not write his life, it was doubtless good luck that Warburton had small interest in biography. Warburton loved romances, controversy, and what must, I fear, be called ratiocinative virtuosity. He had not the sound love of human nature that characterized many of his contemporaries. He loved to juggle ideas as a vaudeville 'artist' juggles billiard-balls; and he was an expert in this art. The ideas themselves were of secondary importance: it was the tricks one could make those ideas perform that delighted the author of *The Divine Legation of Moses*. His interest in juggling with the

---

[1] Spence, p. xiii.

ideas in the *Essay on Man* is well known; his lack of interest in the details of Pope's life can be seen by any one who reads his notes to Pope's satires. As annotator he continually prosecuted his own quarrels and perpetuated Pope's ancient animosities as well; but when a non-controversial problem of biographical nature presented itself, Warburton adopted a magisterial tone or said nothing. There is one classic example in a note to line 88 of the *Imitation of the Sixth Epistle of the First Book of Horace*. On the couplet

> Or if three ladies like a luckless play,
> Takes the whole house upon the poet's day,

Warburton comments:

The common reader, I am sensible, will be always more solicitous about the names of these *three Ladies*, the unlucky *Play*, and every other trifling circumstance that attended this piece of gallantry, than for the explanation of our Author's sense, or the illustration of his poetry; even where he is most moral and sublime. But had it been in Mr. Pope's purpose to indulge so impertinent a curiosity, he had sought elsewhere for a commentator on his writings.[1]

Warburton had little of that 'impertinent curiosity' that makes a thorough biographer, and yet he had announced as early as 1745 his intention of writing Pope's life. On a leaf at the end of his 1745 octavo edition of the *Essay on Man* he advertises:

There is preparing for the Public
The LIFE of Mr. *POPE*,
with a
Critical Account of his Writings,
By Mr. *WARBURTON*.

And in 1751, in the first volume of his edition of Pope,[2] he again talks in considerable detail of this project. The life will contain 'a large account of his writings, a critique on the nature, force, and extent of his genius, ... a vindication of his moral character ... his reverence for the constitution of his country, his love and admiration of VIRTUE, and ...

---

[1] Pope's *Works* (large 8vo, 1751), iv. 134–5.   [2] pp. x–xi.

his hatred and contempt of VICE, his extensive charity to the indigent, his warm benevolence to mankind, his supreme veneration of the Deity, and, above all, his sincere belief of Revelation. Nor shall his faults be concealed. . . . In a word I mean not to be his Panegyrist, but his Historian.' With such a life, 'to be printed in the same form with this and every future edition of his works, so as to make a part of them', Warburton might have changed the face of Pope criticism, but probably his own personal unpopularity would have defeated his good intentions. In any case, years passed, and no life appeared from this self-constituted official biographer.

Presently another critic interested himself in Pope. Joseph Warton was a friend of Spence's, and while visiting him in 1754 copied such of the *Anecdotes* as he wished to use in his forthcoming *Essay on the Genius and Writings of Pope* (published in 1756). This essay, like Ayre's *Memoir*, is organized as a general commentary on the standard edition of Pope's *Works* (then Warburton's), and biographical anecdotes appear only casually. But Warton was allowed to print from Spence's *ana*, and this fact as well as Warton's temerity in venturing to write on Pope's genius after the official editor had staked out a claim to that field annoyed Warburton. In spite of the cordial reviews that welcomed the first volume of Warton's *Essay* the publication of the second volume was long delayed. In the early 'sixties Warton was estranged from Dr. Johnson, and Johnson, who had welcomed the first volume as a 'just specimen of literary moderation', began to see (doubtless in the somewhat unfortunate Dedication to Young) an attempt to undermine Pope's reputation. Warton's second volume appeared, shortly after Johnson's life of Pope, in 1782, and it is perhaps significant that Warton ranked Pope just above Dryden, while Johnson in his Life had ranked him just below. Warton, like Spence, was somewhat sensitive, and, in spite of what historians have said, he had little, if any, disposition to minimize Pope's achievement. He was genuinely grieved that some critics should regard

him as Pope's enemy, and as late as 1795 he said in a letter
to Hayley:

> I thank you for the friendly delicacy in which you speak of my
> Essay on Pope. I never thought we disagreed so much as you seem
> to imagine. All I said, and all I think, is comprehended in these
> words of your *own*, 'He *chose* to be the Poet of reason rather than
> of fancy.'[1]

His Dedication hardly does more than reaffirm the commonplace of neo-classical criticism that ranks the epic,
tragedy, and great ode as the higher poetry, and the *genres*
written by Pope as the lesser poetry. There is little that is
revolutionary or 'romantic' in the position, nor was it total
damnation in Warton's day or in his eyes to be called a
'poet of reason'. In his essays prefixed to Pitt's *Virgil* in
1753 Warton is tolerant of didacticism in poetry and not
at all 'advanced'. It is perhaps true that in his observations
on Pope's 'Pastorals' and other descriptive poems he shows
a love of particularity at a moment in the eighteenth
century when abler men like Hume, Johnson, and Reynolds
were insisting more strongly than ever English critics had
done on the doctrine of universality. In any case, Warton's
Essay became, justly enough, the first 'standard' treatment
of Pope, and it is significant that the work was only slightly
biographical.

The chief biographical services of Warton's first volume
were the inclusion, from Spence, of accounts of Pope's
childhood, education, and juvenilia. We have an account
of Walsh's services to Pope, and a detailed explanation of
the hostilities between Pope and Addison. In the second
volume he reprints the well-known summary of the evidence on this quarrel drawn up after Ruffhead's life
appeared. The biographical portions of the first volume
of the *Essay* are not extensive.

Warton's work stimulated one W. H. Dilworth to bring
out in 1759 a small *Life* in 150 duodecimo pages. Dilworth
probably belongs to the class of needy biographers. One
assumes his character of hack from his bold plagiarisms of

---

[1] J. Wooll, *Biographical Memoirs of Warton* (1806), p. 406.

Warton. His other sources are equally obvious. His flamboyance and his amusing revelation of the attitude of would-be biographers towards Warburton may be seen in the following passage:

> Few among the poets, ancient or modern, deserve to be wreathed by Apollo, so well as Alexander Pope, whose life we are going to write in a clear and succinct manner; which the public has been long desirous of, not satisfied with that crowded farrago which already hath been imposed on it [by Ayre]; and having quite exhausted its patience in waiting for the so-long-promised one by the Colossus-bully of literature, as the mis-estimator of the principles and manners of the times calls him.[1]

The 'colossus-bully' realized that an official life must be produced. Very likely, when he thought of the magnificent promises he had made and realized how little interest he had in Pope as a man, he decided that he himself was not to be the biographer. One guesses that he did not encourage Spence because they were not intimate and because Spence would know more about Pope than his supervisor would. It was evidently Warburton's idea that the life should be such a commentary on Pope's works as might fit the interpretation given in the Warburton editions of Pope. We know that the bishop desired his disciple Hurd to help on the book; but finally in 1767 Warburton, now aged and infirm, persuaded an able lawyer named Owen Ruffhead (1723–69) to undertake the volume under his supervision and according to his plan. It appeared early in 1769, and Ruffhead died within a few months thereafter. This life must have been widely read; for four editions are said to have appeared within a year. The reviewers were not too kind: possibly they saw a chance to wound the truculent Warburton through his shield, Ruffhead.

---

[1] p. 2. The last is an allusion to John Brown's (1715–66) *Estimate of the Manners and Principles of the Times* (1757), in which the author says, ' "amidst this general decay of taste and learning," one great writer . . . Warburton, "bestrides the narrow world like a Colossus." ' Brown's 'Essay on Satire' was published in Warburton's edition of Pope.

The 'advertisement' prefixed to the volume announced:
'The following History hath been chiefly compiled from
original manuscripts, which the writer had the honour to
be entrusted with by the reverend and learned prelate, the
Bishop of Gloucester, the intimate friend of Mr. Pope.'
The reviewer in the *Gentleman's Magazine* (May 1769)
comments on this statement:

> ... there is scarce a single event related ... that may not be found
> either in the notes and commentary with which the bishop has
> illustrated his works, or in the Epistolary Correspondence of Mr.
> Pope and his friends, with which the publick is well acquainted;
> there are, however, many events relative to Mr. Pope's life scattered
> about in various publications which Mr. Ruffhead has not brought
> together.

The truth is that Warburton, controversialist to the end,
was as anxious to reply to Warton's *Essay* as he was to
present the world with a just life of Pope. The title-page
had called the work a 'life of Alexander Pope, Esq. . . . with
a critical essay on his writings and genius', and much space
in the 'essay' parts of the volume is devoted to refuting
Warton. Dr. Johnson preferred Warton and said of Ruffhead, 'He knew nothing of Pope and nothing of poetry.'[1]
And of Ruffhead's criticism the reviewer in the *Gentleman's
Magazine*, who certainly sounds like Dr. Johnson, remarked: 'Mr. Ruffhead says of fine passages, that they are
fine, and of feeble passages that they are feeble; but recom-
mending poetical beauty, is like remarking the splendor
of sunshine; to those who can see, it is unnecessary, and to
those who are blind, absurd.' The reviewer reprints as the
principal novelty of the work the summary of Pope's pro-
jected epic on Brutus, and in an earlier article (February
1769) had reprinted several of the anecdotes embedded in
the volume. This belated 'official' biography can only be
disappointing to readers. Ruffhead used certain letters
that have never been printed entire, but he hardly related
a single event, as his reviewer said, for which there is not
a better source than his own relation.

[1] Boswell's *Johnson* (ed. Hill, 1887), ii. 166–7.

The publication of the volume doubtless stimulated the printing of brief biographies or anecdotes about the poet and of letters and verses by him.[1] The period for gathering first-hand materials from Pope's friends was now largely past, but letters by him and his friends or enemies were printed not infrequently in newspapers or magazines —from which they have since been somewhat casually gleaned. They were not printed too carefully; for addresses and postmarks are practically never given, and these details have extreme value in the case of Pope, who was very negligent in dating letters. The anecdotes printed in the later part of the century are frequently of value, but must always be used cautiously. The account of Pope's health, for example, that is given in the *Gentleman's Magazine* for September 1775 has been generally accepted; but a careful scrutiny of its details will convince a reader that much, if not most, of the information was supplied by the preconceptions of 'D' in his questions to the person whom he was interviewing, an aged woman, formerly a domestic in the household of the Earl of Oxford—which Earl does not clearly appear. Obviously, Pope could never have meant much in her existence, and her memories over a period of fifty years or more can have no primary importance or real authority.

In this later part of the century came one work of first importance. Johnson's life of Pope was published in 1781, and in the opinion of the present writer it is easily the most satisfactory of the lives of the poet yet written. Johnson, granting always something to idiosyncrasy, had a sound sense of Pope's merits as a poet; he understood Pope's personality better than any one else has seemed to do; and if his assemblage of biographical facts is not so large as those of his successors, or so accurate as they ought to have been, the facts lacking or mistaken do not leave the total portrait of man or artist much distorted. A life of Pope was evidently felt by Johnson to be one of his most difficult

---

[1] In *Additions to the Works of Alexander Pope, Esq.* (2 vols., 1776) are collected many of Pope's letters. The second volume contains an early, if not the first, printing of some of the letters preserved in the Homer MSS.

and important attempts, and so he left it to be written last of all his series, in the summer of 1780. It is easy to discredit his 'scholarly method' by retailing the amusing story of Boswell's attempt to arrange an interview for him with Pope's friend Lord Marchmont. Boswell's announcement that Marchmont 'will call on you to-morrow at one o'clock, and communicate all he knows about Pope,' offended Johnson, who ill-humouredly replied: 'I shall not be in town to-morrow. I don't care to know about Pope'. And when Mrs. Thrale remarked that one might well expect him to wish to know about Pope's life, the retort came: 'Wish! why yes. If it rained knowledge I'd hold out my hand; but I would not give myself the trouble to go in quest of it.'

There is less than half a truth in this retort. A year later Johnson went cheerfully to Marchmont for facts, and came away grateful. Earlier he had known many of Pope's acquaintance, notably, of course, Richard Savage. He had conversed with Henry Lintot, 'son of Bernard', and doubtless with others of Pope's publishers and printers. In general his information is wisely used. The account of the publication of Pope's letters—gained probably from the publishing trade—is a great advance over the earlier biographies. Spence usually is his primary source, and when he depends on Spence he seldom goes far wrong. Where he leaves Spence (as in the case of Pope's alleged attack on the Duke of Chandos) he is less reliable than Spence. Johnson's career in Pope's time was of course associated with Grub Street rather than with the aristocratic circles in which Pope moved. One sees traces of Savage throughout the account of Pope: the details concerning the *Dunciad* acquire much of their interest from Savage's equivocal position as a friend to Grub Street and a protégé of Pope. Towards Pope's more illustrious and equally trustworthy friends Johnson is likely to be hostile. He even goes so far as to say that 'except Lord Bathurst, none of Pope's noble friends were such as that a good man would wish to have his intimacy with them known to posterity'. This is the quite unwarranted effect of class and party prejudice. Thus the account of Halifax's patronage of Pope's *Iliad* is to be discounted as the attitude of a 'respectable Hottentot' towards a type thought pernicious to letters. From his interview with Lord Marchmont Johnson probably got dissuasives (badly needed) from attacks on Bolingbroke, and possibly some encouragement to speak slightingly of Martha Blount, whom Marchmont and Bolingbroke, as well as the Allens, seem to have disliked.

In comparison with the earlier biographies Johnson's life adds a wealth of fact material. The strength of his work, however, lies in his admirable treatment of Pope as poet, and especially (for present purposes) in his ability to present a balanced picture of a mixed character. He sees something of ostentation in Pope's manifestations of moral quality; he had known Savage. On the other hand, Savage (and others) had taught him not to expect perfection in men; and he can admire the artist even when he deprecates the man. In his lives of those two curious friends, Savage and Pope, Johnson, hardly taking a step out of his way to do so, showed a human wisdom in dealing with human instability that all biographers must envy. Possibly he was severe upon Pope's usually harmless chicanery, but one feels that on the whole Johnson understood Pope both man and artist better than any one can ever understand him now that he has been dead nearly two centuries.

Since the publication of Johnson's life, contributions for the most part to understanding Pope have been made by editors, antiquarians, and bibliographers, rather than by biographers. Of these, the editors (who must be antiquarians, bibliographers, and biographers all in one) naturally come off with most service and least credit. They steadily increased the bulk of annotation, but the increase did not always illuminate the reader's mind. The best service of the editors has been the accumulation of additional letters by Pope. In the octavo *Works* of 1742, which was Pope's latest edition of his correspondence, 344 letters are indexed. Warburton contented himself with adding only 33 (written to himself and Allen). Warton in 1797 raised the total to something like 500 by including the correspondence of Pope to Aaron Hill (printed in 1751), the letters of Pope to Lady Mary Wortley Montagu, and, among others, something like 60 letters from the Homer MSS. already in the British Museum. Bowles made slighter additions in 1806, but included 57 letters to or from Fortescue, 19 to Mrs. Newsham or her friends, 12 'To a Lady' (Judith Cowper),[1] and over a dozen from miscellaneous sources. Bowles first went to the manuscripts at Mapledurham for a text of the letters to Teresa and Martha Blount; but in so doing he caused some confusion because he retained forms of these letters as printed by Pope addressed to 'Several Ladies'. This seemed to indicate that possibly Pope sent the same letter to different ladies—and indeed there is still some obscurity on this point. In 1807 a group of booksellers brought out a 'Supplementary Volume' designed to include all additions to the *Works* by Warton and Bowles. This volume contains 257 letters; but many of these, the 37 Mapledurham letters, for example, are not strictly new to editions of Pope's *Works* before 1797. The Elwin-Courthope edition (1871–89) contains almost twice as many letters as Bowles printed; in other words, slightly over a thousand.

Warton as an editor had two outstanding faults: he was 70 years old, too old for the study and labour necessary to the task; and his mind had always been discursive and anecdotal. Much of his annotation is irrelevant, and yet most of it (Pope aside) is interesting and entertaining. Neither his edition nor that of Bowles is so unfriendly to Pope as historians have assumed. Warton had been intimate or at least had talked with numerous friends of Pope, and consequently he is the last editor who can claim the authority of contact with Pope's circle. The details that he adds to our knowledge of Pope are small and come too often in the guise of gossip; but one is interested in such gossip as the statement reported from the third Duke of Chandos

---

[1] First published by Dodsley in 1769.

that his grandfather was thought to be not 'perfectly satis-
fied' with Pope's asseverations that Chandos was not
'Timon' in the Epistle to Burlington. This is a typical
Warton addition to our knowledge.

William Lisle Bowles, who next (1806) edited Pope, was
less happy in his results than Warton. He added only a
few easily obtainable letters to his edition of the correspondence, and he had no thorough acquaintance with the
career of Pope or with the society in which Pope moved.
He erroneously thought Edward Blount was the brother
of Martha Blount, and that the Moore who corresponded
with the Blount sisters was James Moore [Smythe], which
last error all his successors have followed.[1] He mistook the
identity of Pope's friend Caryll. He made easily such errors
as the idea that Burlington and Bathurst would be pleased
to see Chandos attacked, not knowing of their intimacy
and regard for the owner of Cannons. His statements
concerning the contemporary reputation of Chandos have
slight basis in fact. He also lacked any adequate imaginative
intuition for the period. He examined the manuscripts of
the Mapledurham letters; but his more than Victorian
prudishness and his ignorance of the epistolary manners of
Pope's day led him to a squeamishness in interpreting
phrases in these letters that reflects on himself rather than
on the recipients of the letters. His imagination is most at
fault when he imputes motives to Pope himself. The
alleged loneliness of the establishment at Binfield is supposed by him to have stimulated the composition of Pope's
Ode to Solitude—a Horatian glorification of retired life.
'Mortified pride' (for which no good evidence is forthcoming) led to the attack on Dennis in the *Essay on
Criticism*, so he tells us. He has been most blamed for
applying to Pope's work Wordsworthian criteria of literary
excellence, and of course the chief result of his edition was
the well-known Byron-Bowles controversy, which, not

---

[1] See J. T. Hillhouse, 'Teresa Blount and "Alexis" ', in *Modern Language
Notes*, xl (1925), 88–91. The gentleman was H. Moor of Fawley Hall (or Court),
twenty miles from Mapledurham.

being biographical, need hardly concern us here. To judge Pope by romantic criteria is of course to condemn him by the laws of a country in which he was no citizen. The controversy certainly strengthened the affection which the anti-Wordsworthians felt for Pope, and among the romantics it tended to undermine the position of Pope so much that the mid-nineteenth century was the readier to think badly of Pope as a man because they were accustomed to think him no great genius as a poet.

In the edition of Pope supervised by William Roscoe (1824) there is evident reaction against the critical opinions of Bowles, just as in Warton's edition there had been animosity to the views of Warburton. A person with Roscoe's knowledge of renascence literature might naturally sympathize somewhat with the aesthetics of Pope, but Roscoe more than any other of Pope's editors was ignorant of both Pope and his period. His annotations are the genteel observations of a man whose taste doubtless seemed old-fashioned in his own day. His addition to our biographical knowledge is slight. He adds a few new letters, chiefly from Pope to the Bethels and to Fortescue. He uses the printed *Anecdotes* of Spence, but adds little to Johnson or Warton from this source. From the start Roscoe's edition was severely criticized, and it surely might have been better; for while the critics had been worrying over the good or bad art of Pope's work, the antiquarians had been digging up factual detail that should have been illuminating.

Works that might have been used by Roscoe were numerous. Of Spence nothing more need be said. The documents printed by John Nichols as *Literary Anecdotes of the Eighteenth Century* (9 vols., 1813–15) and his *Illustrations of the Literary History of the Eighteenth Century* (8 vols., 1817 ff.) were of the first importance, and even to the present day must serve the student of Pope as original source material. The elder D'Israeli's *Quarrels of Authors* (3 vols., 1814) contains an elegant account of Pope's enmities—perhaps the most readable account even to this day. D'Israeli had gone through more of the attacks on

Pope than some of Pope's editors, but he had a conception of Pope's character that is hardly warranted. 'Pope's literary warfare', he tells us, 'was really the wars of his poetical ambition, more, perhaps, than of the petulance and strong irritability of his character.' This is true, but the warfare is even more due to the political and religious animosities of the time than to Pope's thirst for fame. 'His retired life', we are told on the next page, 'was passed in the contemplation of his own literary greatness.' Again, this is somewhat less than half the truth. Pope doubtless had a good conceit of himself, but his life (except in illness, or in occupation on the *Iliad* or on his gardens) cannot be called 'retired'; and to picture him as a secluded literary Narcissus is as far from the truth as one could get. Even in such retirement as was granted him for translation or gardening he had always friends at hand; he was never in any sense solitary. The suave phrases of D'Israeli doubtless had much influence in forming the nineteenth-century notion of Pope's personality.

More thorough, yet less elegant, were the pages of Pope's most painstaking and least fortunate biographer, Robert Carruthers. This energetic Scot brought out in 1853 a life of Pope that in factual content far surpassed those of all his predecessors—and perhaps even his successors as well. And yet he had the mortification to find his 'facts' supplanted almost as soon as they were printed. In 1858 he brought out a 'second edition, revised and considerably enlarged', in an endeavour to bring the work up to date. Carruthers settles rightly many details uncertain in his predecessors, but the known data about Pope were at the moment changing and increasing so rapidly that it was a most unfortunate time at which to publish a biography.

These rapid changes were due not merely to the work of writers like John Wilson Croker, who in 1831 agreed with the publisher Murray to undertake an edition of Pope, but also to the labours of men whose names are not popularly connected with lives or editions of the poet, but who are the only men who make satisfactory lives and editions possible. Two such were Charles Wentworth Dilke and W. J. Thoms, who, chiefly in the pages of the *Athenaeum* and *Notes and Queries*, began about this time to publish highly valuable notes and comments on Pope, which naturally stimulated others to do likewise. Thoms is responsible for enormously important beginnings of bibliographical work, most useful now in the field of Popiana. Fundamental study of Pope's quarrels must continue to start in the pages of *Notes and Queries*, at least until Professor Griffith publishes his promised bibliography in this field.

The contributions of Dilke were chiefly concerned with the authenticity of various of Pope's correspondences, though his criticisms of biographical detail evince an incisiveness that may be the ideal and the despair of any biographer. That neither Spence nor Dilke should have written a life of Pope is a major catastrophe to this field of scholarship. They were complementary types of mind, and between them should have given a clear conception of Pope's personality as it affected his work. Dilke, to be sure, shows some of the bias of his century. His discovery of the Caryll correspondence and consequent discovery that Pope 'cooked' some of his letters—that is, more specifically, that Pope revised letters to Caryll and printed them as letters to Addison or Wycherley—seemed a last blow to Pope's honesty and led Dilke to be dominated by an attitude of suspicion with regard not merely to Pope's self-edited letters but also to other phases of the poet's career. Critical suspicion should exist in the mind of any one studying Pope, but such a state of mind should not dominate one's whole attitude. The essential point to keep clearly in mind is Pope's motives in 'cooking' these letters. In Dilke's day it was assumed that Pope wished to emphasize his intimacy with Wycherley and Addison—perhaps even his ascendancy over one of them, and that he wished to put his own conduct towards them 'in a good light'. It is possible that this second motive may have operated, but it is doubtful if Pope has so falsified his letters as to change the story fundamentally. He had a superfluity of letters that he had written to Caryll, who was a person of no interest to the public. He probably had none of those that he had addressed to Addison, though he must have written several if he answered those from Addison, the covers of which he used as paper on which to translate the *Iliad*. The Homer MSS. are perfect evidence that in the days of 1713–19 Pope was not 'saving' letters. His public would have considerable interest in letters to Addison, and if none appeared they would wonder why. Such ideas as these probably occurred to Pope and led him to undoubted and inexcusable impropriety with regard to these letters, but there is no need to impute darker motives. It had been known or suspected ever since 1735 that Pope had edited his own letters even for the Curll editions, but Dilke proved that Pope transferred letters from one correspondent to another, that he combined two or three letters into one, that he consequently misdated events intentionally or unintentionally, and that he changed the phraseology of letters when printing them—though usually, if not always, such revision had no other purpose than literary effect. Dilke failed to realize at times that a letter containing facts impossible for the date of a letter is not necessarily a complete forgery but may be merely a unification of parts of two or more letters of different dates. He failed to realize that most letters printed in the eighteenth century were revised for publication. Without warning the reader, Warburton, Bowles, Elwin, and Courthope all made intentional as well as unintentional changes in Pope's phrasing, and *they* at least should hesitate to blame Pope for doing likewise. Dilke, very likely, would have been a more scientific editor.

At any rate it was in these suspicious days when Pope's letters—the chief source for biographers—seemed a Serbonian bog that Carruthers's life appeared and that work was begun on the edition of Pope that is still 'standard'—the so-called Elwin-Courthope edition. At the start (1831) this work was under the supervision of J. W. Croker, and it is impossible to tell how many people worked on parts of it. After Croker's death in 1857 the Rev. Whitwell Elwin took charge, an event which recalls Byron's battle-cry in a letter that is (I think) unpublished: 'We must rescue Pope from the priests!' When finally in 1871 and 1872 the first, long-awaited volumes appeared (i and ii of the poetry and i, ii, and iii of the letters), the outcry against the religious and aesthetic bias shown in the editing was such that Elwin retired, and W. J. Courthope took over the completion of the work. A reviewer in the *Saturday Review* for 8 April 1871 (said to be Sir Leslie Stephen) was most caustic, and Elwin's treatment of Pope and especially of the *Essay on Man* caused Mark Pattison to burst forth in the *British Quarterly Review* in 1872:

> We are made to feel from beginning to end that the object had in view in editing Pope was to induce us to desist from reading him. Pope is a liar, a cheat, and a scoundrel, and his so-called poetry is ungrammatical, ill-rhymed, unmeaning trash.

Using the accumulated materials of his predecessors (and it is by no means easy to work well with data collected by others), Courthope brought out the remaining five volumes of poems, letters, and biography, in the years 1881–9; so that the edition was completed almost sixty years after it was begun, and under the care of at least three successive editors.

Considering these facts and the more important fact that really scholarly editing of English masterpieces was almost unknown in the Victorian period, it is small wonder that this edition, with its mass of new letters and its usually informative footnotes, cannot be regarded as consistently authoritative. The texts of the poems are unreliable, and in spite of the castigation the editors give Pope for his 'cooking' of letters, there are cases where they err likewise.

A single such example may prove illuminating. After having read in the Public Record Office the Bill Pope presented to the Lord Chancellor on 16 February 1742/3 complaining of Lintot's infringement of the author's rights in the copy of the *Dunciad*, I was surprised to find in Courthope's volume ix that in a letter dated 28 December

1742 Pope writes to Warburton saying, 'My law-suit with
Lintot is at an end.' Obviously there was something wrong
about these dates; for the suit began six weeks after Pope
said it was over. Courthope's footnote to the letter: 'First
appeared in Warburton, 1751. Collated with the MS. in
the British Museum', seemed to make the matter darker.
Upon examining the MS. (Egerton 1946), however, it soon
appeared that if Courthope had collated the text printed,
he had not thought it essential to tell the reader that
Warburton had made up this letter out of parts of four;
that the first half of the letter (MS. fol. 69) was actually
of December 1742; that the third quarter of it (fol. 68)
was from a letter postmarked on 15 December (no year);
that the last two paragraphs (fol. 75) date properly 21 May
[1743].[1] This amalgam is probably typical of what Pope
himself did in fabricating letters: the rhetorical effect is
improved, tactless remarks are omitted—but as historical or
biographical source material the printed letter is worthless
and even misleading. But what shall we say of such editorial
carelessness? Apparently we must distrust not Pope alone
but all of his editors, from Warburton to Courthope.

   In 1880, while the Elwin-Courthope edition was un-
completed, Sir Leslie Stephen brought out a life of Pope
for the English Men of Letters Series. It is a useful biography; but some pages at least are marked by excessive
prejudice. It may well be that one can write judicious
aesthetic criticism of an author's works when one does not
respect the author; but one is unlikely to write a just
biography of a man whom one can stigmatize (so Stephen
does Pope) as 'the most untruthful man of his age'. Stephen
knew Pope's period well, though even in his great work on
English Thought in the Eighteenth Century he can hardly
be accused of excessive sympathy for its mental processes.

   The Elwin-Courthope edition was completed in 1889
when volume v appeared, containing Courthope's bio-

---

[1] Without remarking on the fact Courthope omits the third paragraph of the
letter printed by Warburton. This paragraph still exists on fol. 84 of the manuscript, and cannot possibly be a part of this letter.

graphy of Pope. In view of the vicissitudes of this age-long edition, Courthope did the wise thing and stuck largely to literary criticism—by far the safest tradition in biographies of Pope, but, apart from Johnson and Courthope himself, not a very distinguished tradition. It remained for the resources of his edition to be applied to a detailed biography by 'George Paston' (Miss E. M. Symonds) in her *Mr. Pope* (2 vols., 1909). This work uses a first-hand study of various manuscript letters and embodies really new facts. Unfortunately the facts of the volume are mixed with inaccuracies of a sort quite inexplicable save to one who has himself been at times lost in the maze of detailed and self-contradictory 'fact' that exists about Pope, and it may be added that such a perplexed though understanding soul, bewildered by strange new inaccuracies in such a field, is likely to cry out:

This is the wandring wood, this Errour's den!

More recently (1930), Miss Sitwell has used Pope as a sort of canvas upon which to display the brilliant colouring of her wit. She has given us no new facts about Pope's life, but has been more sympathetic than any one for a century with regard to his much abused personality. She accepts but somewhat gaily defends his supposed preference of lying to truthfulness, and makes unwarranted twentieth-century assumptions that Pope at heart hated moralizing. Apart from such misconceptions of his psychology, Miss Sitwell has written brilliantly of Pope's art, concerning which she is doubtless a competent and interesting witness. Her approval of some of his personal traits or actions, while ungrounded in fact by her, can be so grounded, and it is probable that in days to come her volume will be cited as a notable correction of false nineteenth-century ideas.

The best contribution to the study of Pope that has been made for many a year is the two-volume *Alexander Pope. A Bibliography* (1922, 1927), by Professor R. H. Griffith. When this work is completed by a third volume, dealing with early Popiana, it will bring us far from the fogs of biographical misconception that have prevailed. The idea that Pope is furtive or malignant has frequently been based on ignorance of the simplest bibliographical facts. Witness, for example, the malicious comment of Elwin and Courthope on the word *venal* in line 150 of the *Epistle to Dr. Arbuthnot*, all based on the assumption that the word was not in the earliest editions. We know now that it was in the first known edition, and that the chicanery in this case existed largely in the editorial mind. This point was settled before Professor Griffith's work appeared, but he has exploded many a so-called plot or trick on Pope's part. Without Professor Griffith's bibliography, the writing of this present volume would have been practically impossible.

A word may perhaps be added concerning the scope of the present work. There are at least two things that it clearly is not. First, it is in no sense an attempt at a definitive treatment of Pope's early life. That will not be expected by any one possessing even the cursory information here given in this survey of what has been done by editors and biographers. One of Dilke's incisive thrusts is to the effect that before writing Pope's life one should edit his letters. The remark is as true now as it was a hundred years ago. We need a critical text of Pope's poems, and an edition of *all* his letters, based so far as possible upon the manuscripts that exist. Editors habitually have been content to reprint Pope's letters from earlier editions, and have not collated the printed texts carefully with the manuscripts. This is no time to talk of definitive lives of Pope. Secondly, this book, in spite of its title, has practically nothing in common with the aims of that admirable *genre* of French critical writing, titles of which frequently begin *La jeunesse de.* . . . In other words, only remotely and partially, if at all, does this volume analyse the formation of Pope's genius in terms of his reading or aesthetic theory.[1] It does seek to show the influence of his environ-

---

[1] This method of approach has been adopted by Professor Austin Warren in *Alexander Pope as Critic and Humanist* (Princeton, 1929). Fortunately Professor Warren plans to continue his study of Pope's reading.

ment on the direction of his genius towards satire. It is
at sharp issue with a conception of Pope as a solitary whose
days were passed 'in the contemplation of his own greatness'
and in the concoction of new schemes to blacken worthy
rivals. Pope was one of the busiest poets that ever found
time to write. He lived 'among the great' and worked with
them on their houses, monuments, epitaphs, or family
papers. A retired merchant's son, he achieved this position
by force of natural ability. His success, his brilliance in
caustic utterance, his religion, and his political activities
all brought attack. His energy led him to retorts; he presently acquired the notion that he was being persecuted,
and hence probably he justified his deviations from honesty,
which are much less serious than our morally expert but
bibliographically untrained grandparents used to imagine.

I do not expect to revolutionize the conceptions that
have been current concerning Pope's character. I do hope,
however, to correct them by placing him in a more detailed
environment than he has yet been seen in. The new facts
and interpretations here presented are based on a fairly
wide reading in the quarrel literature of Pope's day and a
rather fuller reading of the newspapers of the time than
has been the lot of most biographers. (I have here imitated
the methods of T. R. Lounsbury in his *Text of Shakespeare*
—though I do not share his conclusions!) In addition I
have used some unpublished letters of Pope—notably those
to Jacob Tonson; and have tried to read widely in the
correspondence of Pope's contemporaries. To my regret
I seem to have gone beyond Carruthers in being ploddingly
factual. I should have liked to let in a breath of fresh air
to dissipate the atmosphere of fetid suspicion that sur-
rounds Pope; but the multiplicity and complexity of the
facts are such that quite possibly no ventilation will be
apparent.

I

FAMILY AND CHILDHOOD

NEAR the top of the High Street, Andover, still stands the 'Angel' Inn, which at the beginning of the seventeenth century was kept by Richard Pope, great-grandfather of Alexander Pope the poet.[1] This Richard was very likely son of another Richard, who had been a well-to-do blacksmith in Andover. It is certain that the innkeeper was one of the leading men of the town: he served as churchwarden; was four times bailiff; and he died in office, April 1633. His son Alexander (1599–1646) had an even more interesting career. He was educated at Oriel College and Gloucester Hall (now Worcester College), Oxford, and as an Anglican priest secured the patronage of the Paulett family. He was for a time chaplain to a fellow Oxonian, Lord John Paulett, who in 1629 became Marquess of Winchester, and who in the years 1643–5 distinguished himself by his loyal defence of Basing House during the long siege by the Puritans. From Lord John and his father young Pope got written promises of various livings, but at least one of the promises was later fulfilled only upon legal compulsion.[2] By the University of Oxford the Rev. Mr. Pope had in 1631 been preferred to the Rectory of Thruxton, worth £120 a year. (The University had the gift of the living because of the recusancy of the Philpots, who at the time held the manor of Thruxton.)[3] In 1633 the

---

[1] In this chapter details concerning the Pope family are chiefly drawn from the registers of the parishes of Andover, Thruxton, Micheldever, and Pangbourne, or from various Chancery Bills. Especial thanks are due to the Rev. H. E. Clatworthy, rector of Thruxton; to the Rev. A. B. Milner, vicar of Micheldever; to the Rev. J. W. Brennan, rector of Pangbourne; and to Arthur C. Bennett, and E. Parsons of Andover. Articles by F. J. Pope in *Notes and Queries*, 11 S. vii (1913), 281–3 and 441, and by Lucius Fitzgerald ('Pope at Binfield') in the *Home Counties Magazine*, ii (1890), 53–61, have proved invaluable.

[2] The following details come from Chancery Proceedings, Charles I, W 88/61, P 59/5, and P 50/59.

[3] *Victoria County History of Hampshire*, iv. 388.

rector secured from John Paulett, then Marquess of Winchester, the prebend of Middleton (worth over £200 a
year) in exchange for advowsons which he already had from
his lordship. It is probable that by this time the Marquess
was, perhaps secretly, reconciled to the Church of Rome.
Apparently before getting this living the rector of Thruxton had lost his lordship's favour by 'having married Lord
Henry Paulett [the Marquess's brother] unto a Recusant
[Lucy Philpot] out of his Lo^{pps} howse & converted her
unto our Church of England'.[1]

At any rate in 1638, when the prebend of Itchen Abbas,
long since promised to Pope, fell vacant, it was only by
a suit in chancery that his lordship was brought to fulfil
his promise, and the rector acquired a third living, worth,
this time, £120. As the Marquess complained, Pope had
'about four years since applied himself to Walter, then and
now Bishop of Winchester, and without notice or regard
of this defendant, whose chaplain he was, then became
chaplain to the Bishop of Winchester'. Thus had ended a
friendship with the Marquess, probably begun at Oxford
twenty years earlier. Within a decade thereafter his lordship, after heroic but futile service in the cause of Charles I,
was to go to the Tower; the Bishop was to be driven from
his diocese; and in February 1645/6, at a moment when
probably he would have been driven from his hard-won
pluralities, the Rev. Alexander Pope unexpectedly died.
One would like to know if he had Puritanical leanings: for
his joy at having converted Lucy, daughter of Sir George
Philpot, from Romanism to 'our Church of England' time
was to bring its revenge.

Upon the death of the rector of Thruxton, Mrs. Dorothy
Pope, his widow, with her surviving children—Dorothy
(1635–95), Mary (1636–94), and William (b. 1643), found
shelter in Andover, possibly at the 'Angel', though with
her brother-in-law, John Pope, who was then in charge of
the inn, she speedily quarrelled.[2] In the parish register of

---

[1] Chancery Proceedings, Charles I, W 88/61. For the names see Collins's
Peerage (1812), ii. 387.   [2] See Chancery Proceedings, Charles I, P 19/48.

Andover there is the following entry concerning the posthumous birth of the poet's father:

Allickzander sonne to Dorathy Pope widow of M[r] Allickzander Pope late deceased paptized in y[e] p[ish] Church of Andev[r] Aprill 22 1646

Mrs. Pope was the daughter of the Rev. William Pyne of Micheldever, who held his parish under the Commonwealth till his death in 1658.[1] The widow and (now) four children presently removed to Micheldever, where her father and her husband's friend of the days at Oriel, Richard Stansby,[2] guided her somewhat litigious widowhood. Her two sons completed apprenticeships in the cloth trades during the last year of her life.[3] In November 1669 she divided £1,000 equally between them, probably to give them a start as merchants trading in linens; and upon her death in January 1670 her will divided a somewhat larger amount of property between her two daughters. Mary had for some years been the wife of the Rev. Ambrose Staveley, who since about 1651 had been rector of Pangbourne (Berks.). Sometime after her mother's death Dorothy removed either to Reading or to Pangbourne, where she died unmarried in 1695. The property of the two sisters eventually descended to Mary's daughter, Dorothy (b. 1664), who became the wife of Nicholas Pottenger and the mother of Judge Richard Pottenger, M.P. (d. 1739), of Reading.[4]

The careers of William and Alexander Pope are obscure. Where they served their apprenticeships we do not know. It is certain that they were partners in a profitable commerce in linens, at times with the American colonies, until the Revolution of 1688, when the poet's father, at the age of 42, retired from business. About William we

---

[1] But Pyne must have had his troubles: see John Walker, *Sufferings of the Clergy* (1714), pp. 421–2.

[2] On the Stansbys see A. B. Milner, *History of Micheldever* (Paris, 1924), p. 57.

[3] Her will, made 28 January 1668/9 and proved 18 February 1669/70, is to be found in the District Probate Registry at Winchester.

[4] See A. B. Milner's *History of Micheldever*, p. 144, for a map of Weston in 1730. Two plots of ground are marked 'Pottinger's Closes'.

hear nothing after 1684, when he was in chancery trying to get a rascally factor to pay for a valuable cargo which he had received in Virginia from the Pope brothers.[1] A remark in the poet's *Letter to a Noble Lord* implies that William predeceased his brother, and that the two may have been estranged.[2]

The poet's father is an impressive but shadowy figure. He has, indeed, always been the object of much misstatement. Nothing annoyed the poet more than to have his father called a farmer or a hatter, and in revulsion from such descriptions and with encouragement, perhaps, from Oxford friends he annotated line 380 of the *Epistle to Dr. Arbuthnot* (1735), saying that 'Mr. Pope's father was of a gentleman's family in Oxfordshire, the head of which was the Earl of Downe. . . . Mr. Pope died in 1717, aged 75.' The poet may have believed all this, but only the date of his father's death is correctly stated. The Andover Popes were not apparently related to those of Oxfordshire; and the father of the poet was 71 years old when he died. Since even the inscription on his tomb says 75, the mother as well as the son may have been mistaken in the elder Pope's age. One wonders if, when he married his second wife, the father added four years to his age so that Editha Turner (b. 1642) might seem still to take an elder to herself as husband.

The legend develops further when we come to Warton, who in 1782 reported[3] that the Dean of Carlisle told him that Judge Pottenger, a cousin of the poet's, wondered at this fine pedigree and 'corrected' it, saying: 'Mr. Pope's grandfather was a clergyman of the church of England, in Hampshire. He placed his son, Mr. Pope's father, with a merchant at Lisbon, where he became a convert to Popery.' This remark gives a proper clue to the poet's grandfather; but since the poet's father was born after the death of the rector of Thruxton, evidently the rector did not choose his

---

[1] Chancery Proceedings, Reynardson 86/84. The Bill is dated 27 May 1684, and was drawn and signed by Nich. Potenger.

[2] Elwin-Courthope, v. 433.

[3] *Essay on the Genius and Writings of Pope* (ed. 1806), ii. 255–6 n.

son's career. An incomplete but extensive search through
various files of documents fails to show the presence of any
Englishman by the name of Pope in Lisbon in the third
quarter of the seventeenth century. 'P. T.' (probably the
poet himself), in one of his letters to Curll, calls the father
'a modest and plain honest man,—a posthumous son, and
left little provided for, his eldest brother having what
small estate there was, who afterwards studied and died
at Oxford. He was put to a merchant *in Flanders*, and
acquired a moderate fortune by merchandise, which he
quitted at the Revolution, in very good circumstances,
and retired to Windsor Forest, where he purchased a small
estate and took great delight in husbandry and gardens.'[1]
This account contains certain strikingly authentic facts—
the posthumous birth would not be remembered outside
the family—and certain equally striking bits of fiction:
William Pope shared alike with his brother in the family
fortune, and so far as is known he neither studied nor died
at Oxford. But in view of these remarks of 'P. T.', and
since both Mrs. Pope and Martha Blount told Spence[2]
that Mr. Pope's father 'dealt in Hollands wholesale', it
seems probable that Flanders and not Lisbon may have
seen the beginnings of the merchant's career. If a Catholic
at the time of his first wife Magdalen's death, he might
have hesitated to entrust his two children to the household
of the rector of Pangbourne. At any rate, we do not know
when, where, or why he became a Roman Catholic.

The known facts in the early life of the merchant are as
follows: He was born in April 1646; he completed his
apprenticeship about 1669, when his mother gave him and
his brother William each £500 as their shares of the paternal
estate; and by 1677, when their troubles with John
Durant,[3] the Virginia factor, began, the two brothers were
partners in a considerable trade in linens with persons in

---

[1] Elwin-Courthope, vi. 423–4.   [2] Spence, pp. 8 and 357.
[3] The name recalls the fact that one of the poet's pamphleteering enemies was
John Durant Breval, who used the pseudonym of J. Gay, or sometimes Joseph
Gay.

Virginia. The brothers were properly merchants,[1] not linen-drapers, and 'Alexander Pope of London Merchant' is the habitual legal description of the poet's father. Unfortunately there was another Alexander Pope, who died intestate in the parish of St. Mary le Bow and whose widow, Sara Pope, was given letters of administration for the estate, 3 August 1700,[2] and this namesake makes details in the London life of the poet's father somewhat uncertain. Thanks, however, to the preservation[3] of the churchwardens' books of the period for the parish of St. Bennet Fink, we know that the poet's father lived in that parish at least during 1678 and 1679, and that his wife Magdalen was buried there on 12 August 1678. This was the mother of the poet's half-sister Magdalen, who later married Charles Rackett and resided at Hall Grove, Bagshot. Concerning another child the Rev. Ambrose Staveley made the following entry in the parish register of Pangbourne:

Alexander Pope a childe of my Brother in law Alexander Pope a Merchant of London was buried September y ͤ first 1682.

This child was probably born of Magdalen Pope; for in the death notices of Editha Pope, the poet is called 'her only child'.[4] It seems plausible that upon the death of Magdalen Pope her children were entrusted to their aunt Mary Staveley, and that Alexander died in Pangbourne in 1682. Presently the father found a second wife, perhaps in Pangbourne or in Reading, where the Turners were intermarried with the Pottengers, who were friends of the Popes.

Editha Turner,[5] the poet's mother, who was baptized in Worsborough (Yorkshire) on 18 June 1642, was of somewhat more ancient and gentle blood than the Popes were.

---

[1] *Notes and Queries*, 11 S. vii. 283.
[2] P.C.C. Entered among the Admon. of the year 1700 (fol. 171).
[3] In the Guildhall Library, London.
[4] *Gent. Mag.*, June 1733, p. 326: reprinted from the *Grubstreet Journal*, 14 June 1733.
[5] Details concerning the Turners, unless otherwise specified, are all drawn from Robert Davies's *Additional Facts concerning the Maternal Ancestry of Pope*, 1858.

For at least four generations before Editha, the Turners had been a family of some means in the city or county of York. Her father, William Turner, was the heir of a rich uncle, who may have been secretly a Roman Catholic. Her brothers and sisters (she had according to the poet three brothers and fourteen sisters, all of whom she survived) were almost evenly divided as to religious faith. Two of the brothers died in the Civil Wars, and William, the third, died 'a general officer' in Spain.[1] Some of the sisters deserve mention. Christiana (1623–94), who was a Roman Catholic, married the well-known painter Samuel Cooper (1609–72), who made a lovely miniature[2] of her. Alice (b. 1626) married Richard Mawhood, and kept the Anglican faith. Mrs. Cooper was godmother to the poet, and some of his Mawhood cousins—there were at least eight—aided him and his father in transfers of real estate. It was an unmarried aunt, probably Elizabeth, who taught the poet to read. He entered her name in his 'Memorial List of Departed Relations and Friends'[3]:

> Anno 1710, Jan. 24, Avita mea piissimae mem., Eliz. Turner, migravit in coelum, annum agens 74.

She is the only relative apart from his parents whose death was thus remembered. The poet's mother has ordinarily been thought of from the image of her, drawn after death, by the painter Richardson.[4] The drawing and the ladylike bad spelling of her letters have given her a meaner regard than she probably deserves. By family and training she was the sort who might well win friends for her son among the wits and nobles who later flocked to his villa, although she seems to have been more remarkable for kindness and good sense than for love of fashionable society. Pope's friends frequently indicate their pleasant remembrances of his mother in letters to the poet, and a probably typical estimate of her is that of Lord Harcourt's daughter-in-law,

---

[1] Elwin-Courthope, iii. 271 n. Cf. *Gent. Mag.* iii (1733), 326.
[2] Reproduced in the *Walpole Society*, iv (1916), facing p. 86.
[3] Elwin-Courthope, I. ix.
[4] Ibid., viii, frontispiece.

who wrote to her mother Mrs. John Evelyn, 16 August 1718:

. . . Mr. Gay has left us; Mr Pope and his mother being come to Stanton Harcourt; she is a very good sort of woman, and will make a very good neighbour whilst she stays, which I believe will be about a month or six weeks longer, by that time I sopose they will be weary of theyr solitude.[1]

Since both parents of the poet were Roman Catholics, we have no record and consequently no date for their marriage. Tradition says that they lived during their early married life in Lombard Street, London, in a house that then closed the bottom of Plough Court.[2] Here on 21 May 1688 was born the poet. Of the life of the family between that date and 1700 we know very little. The father had done well financially; for he seems to have retired from business in 1688, at the age of 42. Carruthers quotes from the *Weekly Journal* the death notice of the poet's father, which concludes: 'He passed twenty-nine years in privacy.'[3] From 1688 to 1717, the year of his death, would be twenty-nine years. Judging from various investments of which mentions survive (for Warburton's account, so often repeated since 1751, of taking to Binfield a chest containing the family gold, which for the rest of the elder Pope's life was uninvested, is of course absurd),[4] he must have been worth at least ten thousand pounds—and such a fortune was the modest desideratum of heroes of fiction in the days of *David Simple*. Warburton placed the fortune of the retiring merchant at fifteen to twenty thousand pounds,[5] but that seems a large estimate.

Whatever the poet's father did after removing to Binfield, we may be sure that three influences operated

---

[1] *Harcourt Papers*, ii. 184.

[2] Spence, pp. 203 and 259. See *London Topographical Record*, ii (1903), 38–9, for a picture of the house. The date has been variously given, but Spence is clearly the safest authority.

[3] Carruthers, *Life of Pope* (1857), p. 160 n.

[4] Elwin-Courthope, vi. 165, 189, &c., and the will of the poet's father: P.C.C. 218 Whitfield (dated 9 February 1710 [1709/10?] and proved 12 November 1717). This will is printed by Carruthers (1857), pp. 463–4.

[5] Pope's *Works* (large 8vo, 1751), iv. 212 n.

constantly in determining his conduct. First, he loved gardening. 'P. T.' informs us that he 'took great delight in husbandry and gardens'. His neighbour Sir William Trumbull was most appreciative of the Pope 'Harti-chokes',[1] and we may also recall the frequency with which the Dunces spoke of our gardener as a farmer. Secondly, the welfare of his son would be his preoccupation. And lastly, there was the fact that they were Roman Catholics. This third fact would be the most obvious external influence. The poet spoke feelingly when he said,

> Hopes after hopes of pious Papists fail'd
> While mighty William's thund'ring arm prevail'd.

One of the early Acts (1688) in the reign of William and Mary was 'for amoving papists and reputed papists from the cities of London and Westminster, and ten miles distance from the same'. This law like most of the other anti-Catholic laws was not generally enforced, but like all such laws it kept Catholics uneasy and fearful. In 1696 a royal proclamation seemed to insist on the enforcement of this Act of 1688, and curiously enough at the very end of the poet's life the activities of the Young Pretender brought this ten-mile limit again into prominence, and made it advisable for the poet to remain at Twickenham, in spite of the fact that there the best medical care was less easy to procure. The first and last civic lesson he had to learn was submission to

> . . . certain laws by suff'rers thought unjust.

Obedience was practically impossible in the case of laws that began by requiring attendance at Anglican services and abstention from the sacraments of the Roman Church; that continued by demanding anti-Roman oaths such as to-day many of the Anglican clergy might hesitate to take, and that ended in double taxation and in prohibiting the acquisition of real estate or the possession of 'any arms,

---

[1] Elwin-Courthope, vi. 2. From Add. MS. 4807, fol. 169ᵛ.

weapons, gunpowder, ammunition'—or a horse worth more than five pounds. Subterfuge and secretiveness were the inevitable results of such oppression.

Our merchant of London apparently gave such obedience as his conscience required, and he was more strict than many Catholics. He seems to have removed to Hammersmith, which, if not ten miles from Hyde Park Corner, was remote enough from the City to show his good intentions. He is described as 'of Hammersmith aforesaid merchant' in the deed conveying to him in 1698 a property at Binfield comprising 'all that messuage or tenement called Whitehill House, with five closes of arable or pasture land, containing by estimation fourteen acres'[1]. . . . The acquisition of this place marks the emergence of the family from documentary obscurity. The property had been purchased by Charles Rackett of Hammersmith—then or later son-in-law to the merchant—in 1695 for £445, and in 1698 was sold by him to the elder Pope for the same sum. The family may not have occupied the place, which was leased to a tenant, before 1700, in April of which year the poet's father, perhaps because of the technical illegality in a Catholic's acquiring real estate, conveyed the property to Mrs. Pope's nephews, Samuel and Charles Mawhood, 'in trust for his only son Alexander Pope'. A further reason for believing that the family moved to Binfield about 1700 (Pope's remark to Spence[2] is of course sufficient) is the fact that in May 1701, for the Visitation at Reading, the Binfield churchwardens' presentments include the statement: 'We present as Reputed Papists in our parish Allixander Poope gent. and his wife.'[3] Not before 1698 and not after 1701, then, the Popes moved to Binfield. In addition to the father and mother and the young son, the family included the boy's nurse, Mary Beech, and his aunt Elizabeth Turner, who had taught him to read.

---

[1] For details concerning Whitehill House see Lucius Fitzgerald, 'Pope at Binfield', in the *Home Counties Magazine*, ii (1890), 53–61.

[2] Spence, p. 193.

[3] The Berks. Archdeaconry Papers (in the Bodleian Library): Berks. c. 105. Churchwardens' Presentments for Binfield, fol. 22.

Binfield must have been a delightful spot for one seeking retirement. The house was small—

> A little house with trees a-row
> And like its master very low,

was the memory the poet had of it, and there can be no doubt that in his letters, if not in his poetry, Pope shows a pleasure in outdoor life acquired 'in the Forest' and felt to his last years. Apart from the peace of the countryside, there was the added attraction of the social environment. There were numerous friendly neighbours to whom the father sent presents of artichokes, cauliflowers, and 'the earliest melons of the year'. Many of these neighbours would be Roman Catholics.[1] The manor of Binfield was owned by a Catholic, John Dancastle (d. 1740), whose brother Thomas (d. *c.* 1727) transcribed for the press the poet's 'foul copy' of the translation of the *Iliad*. Nine miles away was Whiteknights, the home of Anthony Englefield[2] (*c.* 1637–1712), also a Catholic, who was grandfather of Teresa Blount (b. 1688) and her sister Martha (1690–1763) of Mapledurham. In 1676 a religious census of Berkshire[3] showed 24 Catholics at Binfield, 16 at Cookham, 16 at Inglefield, and 28 at Upton. Since there were in some of these villages also numerous separatists, it seems fair to infer that the region had a reputation for tolerance, and that this reputation helped to bring the Popes there. The presence of the Racketts at Hall Grove near Bagshot, seven miles from Binfield, and of relatives and friends of the elder Popes at Pangbourne and Reading, would also be influential.

Of the life of the small boy we know nothing except what Joseph Spence later collected by way of anecdote. Mrs. Rackett told him of various escapes the child had—once

---

[1] Lucius Fitzgerald, 'Alexander Pope's Catholic Neighbours', in *Month*, cxlv (1925), 328–33.

[2] Englefield after his death in 1712 was described by the poet as 'vir facetissimus, juventutis meae deliciae'. Elwin-Courthope, I. ix.

[3] Walter Money, 'A Religious Census of the County of Berks in 1676', in the *Berks, Bucks, and Oxon Archaeological Journal*, iv (1898), 112–15; v (1899), 22–6, 55–9.

from a wild cow, which when 'driven by the place where he was at play, struck at him with her horns; tore off his hat, wounded him in the throat, . . . and trampled over him'.[1] Life at Binfield was doubtless not too adventurous, but Courthope perhaps stressed the isolation of the poet's childhood excessively.[2] We have no information as to what he found thereabouts in the way of playfellows when at the age of 12 he settled there with his parents.

Lack of educational advantages for the boy would seem perhaps a more inevitable problem than the possible lack of companions of his own age. It is certain that, for various reasons, attendance upon schools formed but a small part of his education. Our source of information, again, is almost exclusively Spence. There are, to be sure, a passage or two in Pope's later Imitations of Horace that might seem illuminating; but the fact that they are, in part, versions of Horace makes them of doubtful authority. Such a couplet as

> Bred up at home full early I begun
> To read in Greek the wrath of Peleus' son,

may be autobiography, or Horace, or merely Pope answering half-forgotten critics who had said he knew no Greek. From Spence[3] we learn that the poet had been early trained at home by a priest named Banister, alias Taverner. His first schooling away from home, and before 'home' was Binfield, had been in the excellent but (for those days) remote school at Twyford, near Winchester.[4] Placed here at the age of 8, he apparently was unhappy; at least it is said that 'he wrote a satire on some faults of his master', for which he was 'whipped and ill-used', so his sister told Spence, 'and taken from thence on that account'. Next he was placed under Mr. Thomas Deane, formerly of University College, Oxford, but *non-socius* after 1688.

---

[1] Spence, p. 5.
[2] Elwin-Courthope, v. 9–10.
[3] Spence, pp. 259 and 192–3, for this and succeeding details.
[4] The school was in a house now known as Segar's Buildings. See *Victoria County History of Hampshire*, iii. 339.

Pope must have lived for a time in Deane's establishments in Marylebone and near Hyde Park Corner.

A few interesting details concerning Deane's school have come down to us, independent of Spence, in the 1744 *Life* of Pope published by Weaver Bickerton.[1] The anonymous author of this biography asserts that he has secured various bits of information from 'one who was School-fellow with Mr. Pope', and such a statement gives this *Life* possible authority concerning Pope's school-days. He informs us that Deane, because of the hostile activities of 'a busy Justice in that neighbourhood', removed from Marylebone

to a House near *Hyde-Park Corner*, on the very Spot where *Down-street* was afterwards built, which having till then belonged to a Nursery-Garden, and consequently having a large open Space adjoining thereto, was not only pleasant and healthy, but perfectly convenient; and the fittest imaginable for the Use for which he designed it.

To this agreeable Abode Mr. *Pope* removed with his Master . . . where how long he continued is uncertain, though we are credibly inform'd he staid there some Years; as we are likewise of this particular and remarkable Circumstance, that at the Hours of Recreation, whilst the Rest of his School-fellows were diverting themselves at such Games and Sports, as was usual with Boys of their Age, Mr. *Pope* used to amuse himself with Drawing, and such like improving and rational Accomplishments.

With regard to the school experience at Twyford this biographer seems untrustworthy; for he dates it after the residence in Deane's school, and locates it at Sylstead [Silkstead?], which while near Twyford need not have been confused with it.

In spite of the fact that he later spoke slightingly of Deane's tuition, Pope had gratitude enough as late as 1727 to contribute to a pension for his former master, who was then in prison for a 'seditious' pamphlet.[2] Pope says:

[1] *The Life of Alexander Pope, Esq; with Remarks on his Works. . . . London: Printed for Weaver Bickerton, in the Temple-Exchange Passage, in Fleet-street.* 1744. Pp. 10–14 are here used.

[2] Elwin-Courthope, vi. 296. One may guess from this letter that Pope is writing to the fathers of his fellow students under Deane. Among these would

With the two latter masters [I] lost what I had gained under the first.—About twelve years old, I went with my father into the Forest, and there learned for a few months, under a fourth priest. —This was all the teaching I ever had, and, God knows, it extended a very little way.[1]

The Rev. William Mannock, who possibly was this 'fourth priest'[2] (he was in the family of the Racketts), gave Spence further details of Pope:

He set to learning Latin and Greek by himself, about twelve; and when he was about fifteen he resolved that he would go up to London and learn French and Italian. We in the family looked upon it as a wildish sort of resolution; for as his health would not let him travel, we could not see any reason for it. He stuck to it: went thither; and mastered both those languages with a surprising dispatch. Almost every thing of this kind was of his own acquiring. He had had masters indeed, but they were very indifferent ones; and what he got was almost wholly owing to his own unassisted industry.[3]

These details are not all thoroughly consistent, but it is apparent that the poet had very little formal schooling, and it is obvious that he must have done wonders by himself. Spence and others liked to consider Pope as a striking example of the force of nature or of natural genius: untrained, he seemed to them to equal in scholarship men from the universities. Except for the sojourn in London to work on French and Italian, his education was apparently continued at home in Binfield. Whether he was in London

be, then, John Caryll, Jr., Webb (who married the widow of Pope's friend Henry Englefield), and Charles Dormer, who being a Catholic priest did not assume the title of Baron Dormer when his father died in 1728. There was also a Robert Dormer who was a comrade in mischief of the younger Caryll (Add. MS. 28237, fols. 62, 63). Nichols in his *Literary Anecdotes*, iii. 646, and viii. 168, mentions William Lewis the bookseller as a schoolmate of Pope's, and Lewis might well be the informant, already quoted from the Bickerton *Life* of Pope. In one of Curll's volumes of *Mr. Pope's Literary Correspondence* (iii. 6–7) is still another story of a school kept by a priest named Bromley in Bloomsbury, which Pope attended with 'the late Duke of Norfolk and others'. The story, while very specific, has never been accepted. [1] Spence, pp. 192–3.

[2] Another possibility is Father Philips, of whom Pope writes to Thomas Dancastle, 18 February [1716], and to John Dancastle, 30 May 1717. These letters are in the Huntington Library. [3] Spence, pp. 25–6.

long enough to master any language one may doubt: evidently he had some training and did much reading in the four that he attempted—Latin, Greek, French, and Italian. Of the last two he probably tried to acquire only a reading knowledge. Voltaire[1] exaggerated Pope's ignorance of French, which the poet read, though he could neither speak nor understand the spoken language. It would be interesting to know what Scipio Maffei thought of Pope's Italian when he called upon the poet in 1736, and found him in the gesture of translating *Merope* from the Italian.[2] Shortly after 1709, when George Berkeley, the philosopher, came to London and became Pope's friend, he spoke with great respect of the poet's wit *and learning*.[3] Spence always regarded Pope's attainments in archaeology with surprising seriousness. Probably Pope's masters were hardly so incompetent as he thought them: it is customary for geniuses to disparage their teachers; but in any case he seems to have done astonishingly well by himself.

The urge to read and study probably came largely from within. Much must be assumed on the part of his father's intellectual interests, and Banister, Deane, and the other priest may deserve more credit than they have had. It is probable, however, that Sir William Trumbull, the former Secretary of State, whose life both intellectual and political had been rich and varied and who settled at Easthampstead Park shortly before the Popes came to reside a mile or so away at Whitehill House, may have afforded both stimulus and guidance. It seems so, indeed, from Pope's remarks to Spence:

It was while I lived in the Forest, that I got so well acquainted with Sir William Trumbull, who loved very much to read and talk of the classics in his retirement. We used to take a ride out to-

---

[1] Elwin-Courthope, ii. 291, note 2, and, to more purpose, E. Audra, *L'Influence française dans l'œuvre de Pope* (1931), pp. 116–38, &c.

[2] See *La Merope*, Verona, 1745. (Italian text with French and English translations, the latter by William Ayre.) On p. 180 Maffei tells of his visit to Pope and says, . . . 'quel bravo Poeta mi fece vedere, che lavorava alla versione della mia Tragedia in versi Inglesi: se la terminasse, e che ne sia divenuto, non so'.

[3] Benjamin Rand, *Berkeley and Percival* (1914), p. 110 (7 March 1712/13).

gether, three or four days in the week, and at last, almost every day.[1]

It seems quite possible that Sir William's guidance through something like a decade might well have replaced the formal training of the university, over his escape from which Pope affected to rejoice.[2]

Sir William's interest in his young companion must, from the habit of riding so often, have extended wisely to the boy's health. As a small child the poet was attractive and apparently not deformed. Father Mannock gave Spence the following account:

He was a child of a particularly sweet temper, and had a great deal of sweetness in his look, when he was a boy. This is very evident in the picture drawn for him when about ten years old: in which his face is round, plump, pretty, and of a fresh complexion.—I have often heard Mrs. Pope say, that he was then exactly like that picture.—I have often been told that it was the perpetual application he fell into, about two years afterwards, that changed his form and ruined his constitution.[3]

Too much study was the usual explanation of the increasing fragility, recurrent headaches, and final curvature of the spine that ruined the poet's physique. Pope himself gave Spence the following details concerning his health between the ages of 12 and 16:

. . . his perpetual application (after he set to study of himself) reduced him in four years time to so bad a state of health; that, after trying physicians for a good while in vain, he resolved to give way to his distemper; and sat down calmly, in a full expectation of death in a short time. Under this thought he wrote letters to take a last farewell of some of his more particular friends; and among the rest, one to the Abbé Southcote. The Abbé was extremely concerned, both for his very ill state of health, and the resolution he said he had taken. He thought there might yet be hopes; and went immediately to Dr. Radcliffe, with whom he was well acquainted, told him Mr. Pope's case; got full directions from him and carried them down to Mr. Pope in Windsor Forest. The

[1] Spence, p. 194.   [2] Ibid., pp. 259, 279.   [3] Ibid., p. 26.

chief thing the doctor ordered him, was to apply less; and to ride every day: the following his advice soon restored him to his health.[1]

This picture of the young Pope calmly sitting down to inform 'some of his more particular friends' of his 'full expectation of death in a short time' may be the result of progress of the tubercular infection (Pott's disease) that eventually deformed him, or the result of some particular illness. It is obviously tinged with a half-conscious cast of adolescent melancholy that evokes a smile as well as pity. Very likely this organic affliction is what gave the feverish energy to the young man's efforts in educating himself, as it later gave a certain glow to his mind and eloquence to his style. It also lent an animation to his voice and manner that attracted many friends. The disease would not in its early stages limit his activities except as his physical fragility made him a prey to headaches and chance illnesses. Years later Arbuthnot expressed his opinion that Pope's great trouble was that he lived on equal terms with persons of superior vitality and thus exhausted his own health.[2] It is safe to say that *usually* Pope did not allow his health to interfere with his activities except when to do so suited his convenience. Certainly the report of his health in 1705 (?) as he gave it to Spence has not at all the tone of the valetudinarian: it ends with an easy and sanguine restoration of health. Pope was exuberant and active as well as peevish and ailing. In 1715 he called himself

> The gayest valetudinaire,
> Most thinking rake, alive.[3]

As a young man he was possibly not unattractive in appearance, though his smallness (he was only about four feet six

---

[1] Spence, p. 7. Note also Pope's grateful remembrance of Southcote twenty years later, when he led Walpole to secure for Southcote an abbey near Avignon. Spence dates Pope's illness in 1705; but this is uncertain, since Pope's memory for dates in his career is frequently faulty. It should possibly be noted further that a letter (Add. MS. 28237, fols. 23, 24) from Southcote to Caryll, dated from Cambray, 30 April 1740, shows him in jurisdiction over a religious house in that town.

[2] Letter of Arbuthnot to Swift, 13 January 1733. In Swift's *Correspondence*, ed. E. Ball, iv. 379.　　　　[3] Elwin-Courthope, iv. 483.

inches in height when grown up) made him seem like a toy to his elders.

Amongst the giants of his day he must have felt inferior; and though the amusement that such myrmidons as Wycherley got from his 'little, tender, and crazy carcass'[1] was almost always affectionate, there would always be on Pope's part a forced effort to meet such friends on equal terms in eating and drinking, and to surpass them, where he could, in witticism. That he succeeded in building up a reputation as a gardener, a *gourmet*, and a conversationalist is evidence of his genius for the externals of friendship. For the sound sympathy and helpfulness that are also essential we have already evidence in his kindness to Deane and Southcote.[2] There were numerous other similar cases.

[1] Wycherley to Pope, 19 February 1708/9. Elwin-Courthope, v. 396.
[2] Spence, pp. 7–8.

II
MAKING FRIENDS, 1705–15

IN many respects the most interesting fact concerning
Pope's life at Binfield is that in this retired spot he acquired a circle of friends both numerous and distinguished.
From the extreme of obscurity he 'arrived' at the pinnacle
of fame in less than a decade, and his friends as well as his
genius aided this success. Pope certainly had notable social
as well as literary gifts: his incisiveness of wit, together with
his attractive features and voice, would combine to make
him an agreeable companion. He was more attractive
physically as a young man than when older, but even in his
last years his features seemed pleasing to Sir Joshua Reynolds, though his back had by this time become distressingly
curved. Reynolds says:

He was about four feet six high, very hump-backed and deformed.
He had a very large and very fine eye, and a long handsome nose;
his mouth had those peculiar marks which are always found in the
mouths of crooked persons, and the muscles which run across the
cheeks were so strongly marked as to appear like small cords.[1]

Lord Orrery, writing also of Pope's later years, speaks with
characteristic Hibernian 'flow' of the poet's social graces:

His voice in common conversation was so naturally musical, that
I remember honest Tom Southerne used always to call him *The
little nightingale*. His manners were delicate, easy, and engaging:
and he treated his friends with a politeness that charmed, and a
generosity that was much to his honour. Every guest was made
happy within his doors. Pleasure dwelt under his roof, and elegance
presided at his table.[2]

These qualities of distinction are, of course, in part a
reflection of Pope's literary fame, and while they doubtless
attest his natural social graces, it is evident that these graces

---

[1] Elwin-Courthope, v. 345.
[2] Orrery, *Remarks* (2nd ed., 1752), pp. 145–6.

(the voice excepted) might not have existed when Pope was only 16 or 18—the period when he was making friends. Southerne's fondness for calling Pope 'the little nightingale' shows that for elderly persons Pope, as a youth, had a considerable charm. Such charm, indeed, is evident from the fact that most of Pope's early friends were elderly.

On slighter evidence we may guess that younger or hostile men found the youth from Binfield at times somewhat rustic. Chevalier Charles Wogan, whose presence in Binfield is probably somehow due to Catholic connexions, and who is one of the few recorded youthful intimates of Pope's own age,[1] spent two or three summers in Binfield, and later boasted to Swift (27 February 1732/3) concerning Pope as one 'whom I had the honour to bring up to London, from our retreat in the forest of Windsor, to dress à la mode, and introduce at Will's coffee-house'.[2] That Pope needed this fashionable refashioning is evident from reminiscences of his first appearance in London by less friendly people. Gildon, for example, in his *Memoirs of William Wycherley* (1718), writes:

I remember I was once to wait on Mr. *Wycherley*, and found in his Chamber this little *Æsopic* sort of animal in his own cropt Hair, and Dress agreeable to the Forest he came from. I confess the Gentleman was very silent all my stay there, and scarce utter'd three Words on any Subject we talk'd of, nor cou'd I guess at what sort of Creature he was, and shou'd indeed have guess'd all the Pretences of Mankind round before I shou'd have imagined him a Wit and Poet. I thought indeed he might be some Tenant's Son of his, who might make his Court for continuance in his Lease on the Decease of his Rustick Parent, but was sufficiently surpriz'd when Mr. *Wycherley* afterwards told me he was Poetically inclin'd, and writ tolerably smooth Verses.[3]

---

[1] The *D.N.B.* (queried) date for Wogan's birth (1698?) is clearly too late. He was old enough to be a notable rebel in 1715, and, if born in 1698, would hardly in 1719 have been delegated the task of choosing a wife for the Pretender. He must have been about as old as Pope.

[2] Swift's *Works*, ed. Sir Walter Scott, xviii. 21. Cf. also Swift's *Correspondence*, ed. E. Ball, iv. 390-3.

[3] P. 16. The gibe about the 'Rustick Parent' is an envenomed reference to the recent death of Pope's father.

Such a picture from Pope's rival in the love of Wycherley
is not to be accepted too readily as truthful, but taken with
Wogan's remark, and with admissions by Pope himself that
at about the age of seventeen he 'first came up to town . . .
with short rough hair, and that sort of awkwardness which
one always brings up at first out of the country',[1] the picture
acquires authenticity. This awkwardness, however, must
be ascribed (as Pope ascribes it) to a youth spent in a retired
residence with elderly persons as intimates, and not to bad
breeding. Pope's early friends—Wycherley, Cromwell,
Rowe, Gay, and Parnell—were constantly being invited to
Binfield, and later references to his aged mother by noble
friends are affectionate as well as respectful. In spite of
whatever 'rusticity' may have marked the young poet, it is
true either that his elderly friends had unusual perspicacity
in choosing young men to patronize or that from the first
Pope's social and literary talents were arresting.

His friends may be variously grouped according to
political and religious faith or according to their dominant
interests in literature, painting, gardening, or politics.
Here, in order to show how gradually they were acquired
in the days when Pope was just becoming 'a fool to fame', it
seems well to group them chronologically, as they came into
his life. This, of course, can be done only imperfectly, for
the documents concerning his early friendships are meagre,
and, in the case of some of his own letters, unreliable. We can
conveniently distinguish four groups—all of which will
overlap to some extent. The first includes the friendships,
mainly non-literary, formed at Binfield itself. The second
includes the wits of Dryden's day, found in their autumnal
years at Will's coffee-house. The third, only briefly attached
to Pope as friends, is Addison's little Senate, at Button's
coffee-house; and the last includes his most famous and
dearest friends, associated in the Scriblerus Club. These
groups include only friends known by the poet before the
translation of Homer, which achievement opened all doors,
and increased his circle of acquaintance as well as his fame.

[1] Spence, pp. 59-60.

The first group of friends has been mostly introduced already. In it were the Englefields and the Dancastles, who by religious faith and propinquity were naturally friends of the Popes, and who remained humble admirers of the poet's genius in the later years of their lives. Sir William Trumbull, as we have seen, read and rode with the poet, and we shall presently find him suggesting themes for verses and correcting the poet's efforts as well. Pope must early have met Sir William's relatives, the Rev. Ralph Bridges and Sir Clement Cotterell. Sir Clement was related to the Dormers, and the sixth Lord Dormer had perhaps been a schoolfellow of Pope's. Through Sir William, possibly, Pope met Wycherley and other friends of the outside world. Sir William and Bridges usually maintained an air of superiority in their friendship: to them the young man was 'little Pope', and in Pope's youth 'littleness' was a bane that deformity could only embitter in later years. In a letter to Caryll he speaks of himself as 'the little Alexander the women laugh at' (25 January 1711). He does not mean 'ladies', and coming from one associating with 'men about town', most of whom had their mistresses, there is a wry pathos in the remark.

Pope seems not to have objected to the patronage of Bridges,[1] though the two were not intimate. With older men he got on better. It is possible that among these older men, first known on their visits to Binfield, Thomas Southerne, at the height of his fame in Pope's childhood, should be mentioned as a visitor at Trumbull's: there is little known of such acquaintance, and very likely it began later. Anthony Englefield of Whiteknights, an elderly neighbour, was—so his granddaughter declared—'a lover of poetry and poets', and he as well as Trumbull may have introduced the poet to literary men. At Whiteknights Pope would occasionally see his friend John Caryll, who was a relative of the Englefields. Pope's letters to Caryll as printed from Caryll's copies constitute one of the most

---

[1] For Bridges' attitude see *Hist. MSS. Comm.: Report on the MSS. of the Marquess of Downshire*, i. ii (1924), 853. See also Elwin-Courthope, vi. 11-14.

valuable records we have for much of his career. At Whiteknights also, at some undetermined date, Pope doubtless
met the Blount sisters from Mapledurham; for Englefield
was their grandfather. Martha Blount told Spence[1] she
met Pope after the appearance of the *Essay on Criticism*
(1711) and before that of the *Iliad* (1715). She also remarked that it was when she was 'a very little girl', and
since she was born in 1690, her statements leave us
guessing.

So far we can with some assurance trace the friendships
formed in the Forest. With regard to two other persons,
both important because of literary connexions, there is less
certainty. The first is Edmund Smith (1672–1710),
author of *Phaedra and Hippolytus* (1707) and a friend of
Pope's later enemies of the 'Little Senate'. Some one told
Spence that 'Captain Rag', as Smith was called by his
friends, 'after being in Mr. Pope's company when about
fourteen', announced: 'Igad that young fellow will either
be a madman or make a very great poet.'[2] If authentic,
this anecdote has real interest as an early impression, however casual, of the boy's precocity; but it seems improbable
that Smith should know Pope in 1702. As pure hypothesis
one may suggest that since Tenbury, the residence of
Smith's foster-parents, is close to Abberley, the seat of
William Walsh, Smith and Pope may have met in 1707
when the latter spent some time at Abberley. Captain
Rag's judgement of the young poet's genius would be just
as valuable and more plausible if made when Pope was
nineteen. The second of these persons whose acquaintance
with the poet is obscure is the great tragic actor, Thomas
Betterton. Pope told Spence: 'I was acquainted with Betterton from a boy.'[3] This seems probably true; for Betterton died in 1710, and the two were well acquainted
at that time. Pope painted, or copied after Kneller,

---

[1] Spence, pp. 356, 357 n. Pope's letter to Cromwell, 21 December 1711, was
evidently composed to be shown to the Misses Blount. Does it express an
enthusiasm of first acquaintance?

[2] Spence, p. 25 n.

[3] Ibid., p. 25. Cf. pp. 5, 275–6, and 293.

Betterton's portrait,[1] and it is probable that he aided in revising and publishing some modernizations of Chaucer that Betterton had made.[2] Bolingbroke said to Pope, 'You and I knew Betterton and Mrs. Barry off the stage as well as on it.'[3] The remark leads one to suspect that Betterton's 'small farm near Reading'[4] was the scene of the acquaintance; for Bolingbroke after his first marriage (1700) lived for a time at Bucklebury, near Reading, from which town Binfield is not far distant. These details fit together so plausibly that one is inclined to credit Pope's 'from a boy'. It is of course possible that only after he began frequenting Will's coffee-house did he know the actor. If the 'farm near Reading' happened to lie towards Binfield, unsuspected channels are at once opened for the poet's transition to the great world of the London coffee-house.

By whatever channels, during the years 1705-11 Pope was becoming acquainted with the literary celebrities of his day in London. We may pass over such acquaintances as Brocas, Fowler, Baker, and Cheek, but must examine more closely his relations with the remaining members of Dryden's circle—Wycherley, Walsh, Congreve, Granville, and Henry Cromwell—who were all his friends during this period and who, except Congreve, passed from recorded intimacy with him shortly after 1712.

'Wycherley', so Father Mannock said, 'was Mr. Pope's first poet-friend, and Walsh his next.' In entering the death of Wycherley in his Virgil, Pope added the comment: 'ille meos primus qui habebat amores'.[5] The poet's letters to Wycherley and Walsh, as edited by himself, have been

---

[1] Spence, p. 336. Cf. Elwin-Courthope, vi. 95, 193.

[2] In Lintot's Miscellany (1712, 1720, 1722) appeared modernizations as if by Betterton, which Pope's friend Harte told Warton were really by Pope. See Pope's *Works*, ed. Warton (1797), ii. 166. See also Caryll's letter to Pope, 23 May 1712, on Betterton's literary remains.

[3] *Philosophical Works* (8vo, 1754), ii. 325.

[4] So Aston called it. See R. W. Lowe, *Life of Betterton* (1891), p. 145. Lowe wrongly thought the place was sold in 1692. Gildon in his *Life of Betterton* (1710), p. 11, writes: 'The Year before his Death being at his Country House in Reading . . . I call'd to see him.'

[5] Spence, p. 25, and Elwin-Courthope, i. ix.

viewed with suspicion. He is thought to have 'edited' frequently in such a fashion as really to fabricate letters that were never sent. Usually, to be sure, he fabricated from materials that had been sent, but he rearranged and recombined in a fashion that throws doubt on all correspondence edited by him. We can, however, at times check his 'edited' letters with others not published until after his death and with facts quite outside his correspondence. Proceeding in this fashion, we find that possibly as early as the end of 1704 and certainly in 1705 Pope and Wycherley were friends. One may doubt if before he was twelve Pope had visited Will's coffee-house and seen Dryden there, though he is explicit in saying that he did. At any rate he pretty certainly visited Will's in October 1705, dressed *à la mode* and conducted thither by Charles Wogan. It is possible that he found there Wycherley, with whom he already had acquaintance, or Betterton, or even Walsh, who, if we may believe Pope's letters, had seen the youthful poet's 'Pastorals' in April.[1]

Pope now felt himself definitely launched on a career. In April 1706 he received a most flattering letter from Jacob Tonson, the leading publisher of poetry at the time. Pope did not have to seek a publisher; his friends had shown Tonson his poems, and Tonson wrote to offer his services:

Gray's-Inn-Gate, April 20, 1706

Sir,—I have lately seen a Pastoral of yours in Mr. Walsh's and Mr. Congreve's hands, which is extremely fine, and is generally approved of by the best judges in poetry. I remember I have formerly seen you at my shop, and am sorry I did not improve my acquaintance with you. If you design your poem for the press, no person shall be more careful in the printing of it, nor no one can give greater encouragement to it than, sir, your, &c / Jacob Tonson.[2]

---

[1] Arguments against the authenticity of Walsh's letter to Wycherley (20 April 1705), based on the fact that Walsh was reading the 'Pastorals' a year later, are unsound. Walsh clearly read the poems more than once, and 'Autumn' he had not seen at all as late as September 1706. See Elwin-Courthope, vi. 49.

[2] Elwin-Courthope, ix. 545, with corrections from the original in Add. MS. 4807, fol. 172ᵛ.

The impatient publisher added in a postscript: 'Pray give me a line per post', and on the whole must have given Pope as much pleasure by his note as ever a bookseller did. Most young poets would have saved that letter, and Pope did so until he began to translate the *Iliad*, and then its clean verso was used as paper on which to translate part of Book IX.

Probably about the same time he got this letter he made the acquaintance of George Granville, who presently made occasion to introduce both Wycherley and Pope to an unidentified friend 'Harry', as the following letter by Granville testifies:

In short, Sir, I'll have you judge for your self: I am not satisfied with this imperfect Sketch: Name your Day, and I will bring you together; I shall have both your Thanks. Let it be at my Lodging. I can give you no *Falernum* that has out-liv'd twenty Consulships, but I can promise you a Bottle of good old Claret that has seen two Reigns: *Horatian* Wit will not be wanting when you two meet. He shall bring with him, if you will, a young Poet, newly inspir'd, in the Neighbourhood of *Cooper's-Hill*, whom he and *Walsh* have taken under their Wing; his name is *Pope*; he is not above Seventeen or Eighteen Years of Age, and promises Miracles: If he goes on as he has begun, in the Pastoral way, as *Virgil* first try'd his Strength, we may hope to see *English* Poetry vie with the Roman, and this Swan of Windsor sing as sweetly as the *Mantuan*. I expect your Answer. Dear Harry, Adieu, &c.[1]

The circle was widening fast, and while some of these persons mentioned as of it seem now of slight importance, they were all in their day people of some distinction, whom a retired merchant's son from Binfield might well be proud to number among his friends. On the fly-leaf opposite the first page of the original manuscript of his 'Pastorals', a first page so carefully written in a 'printing' hand that it looks like typography, Pope made the following memorandum:

This Copy is that wch past thro ye hands of Mr Walsh, Mr Congreve, Mr Mainwaring, Dr. Garth, Mr Granville, Mr Southern, Sr H. Sheers, Sr W. Trumbull, Ld Halifax, Ld Wharton, Marq. of

---

[1] Lansdowne's *Works* (1732), i. 436–7.

Dorchest.ᵗ D. of Bucks. &c. Only yᵉ 3ʳᵈ Eclog was written since
some of these saw yᵉ other 3. wᶜʰ were written as they here stand
w.ᵗʰ yᵉ Essay, anno 1704.—Ætat. meae, 16.—
The Alterations from this Copy were upon yᵉ Objections of
some of these, or my own.[1]

There may be some doubt if Pope knew all these men as
early as 1706, but he must have made their acquaintance
not many years thereafter, and it is an astonishing list. Of
Wycherley's reputation there is no need to speak. His
services in presenting Pope to his friends were doubtless
very great. He wrote some lines on Pope's 'Pastorals',
which, Pope's enemies asserted, he had composed in praise
of himself.[2] Various misfortunes thus attended this friendship, especially in Pope's attempts to revise the older man's
verses, which occupied the younger poet's leisure intermittently for some years. Most of Pope's biographers have
thought these revisions led to an estrangement, possibly
even to a quarrel, but there is not much evidence of this
last event. The final letter which we have from Wycherley
to Pope is submissive so far as the matter of revision goes
and is cordial in expressing Wycherley's hope that he may
visit Binfield at once.[3] The correspondence did not cease
with this letter, and though Wycherley cooled towards
Pope in 1709 and 1710, Cromwell represents him as quite
friendly in October 1711. Pope, Cromwell, and later even
Edmund Curll[4] seemed to think that Charles Gildon caused
trouble between Pope and Wycherley; but the estrangement was probably slight in any case.

One of the less creditable things about this friendship
is the artificial tone of the letters that passed between the
two. Of course the relations between an unknown youth
of seventeen and the most famous dramatist of the day, a
man of sixty-five, not given to paternal airs, must at best

---

[1] From the facsimile printed in Sotheby's catalogue for the sale of the Burdett
Coutts Library, 15–17 May 1922 (facsimile faces p. 56).
[2] Elwin-Courthope, i. 22 n., and Dennis's *Reflections upon An Essay upon
Criticism* (1711), pp. 29–30.
[3] Elwin-Courthope, v. 405–7 (27 April 1710).
[4] Ibid., vi. 87 n.

be somewhat unnatural. This situation accounts in part
for a lack of directness and easiness of tone. But the real
reason for this artificiality—and both men seem equally
artificial and effusive—is not the falseness or insincerity of
the feelings expressed but rather the fact that both writers
are conscious that this is a 'literary' correspondence; and
hence they write in the elaborate and literary tradition of
letter-writing that the French had evolved in the seventeenth century. This tone of high compliment, common
in the day, deceived even 'the fair' but seldom, and it is
certain that Wycherley and Pope knew perfectly that they
were merely playing an old-fashioned game of 'courtly'
compliment. Once at least Wycherley pricks the bubble
with the statement, 'Very fine, Mr. Pope, by Gad (as Bays
wou'd say).'[1] And Pope might have retorted in kind had
he wished. The game, however, was old, and the pace set
by these rivals in compliment was excessive, and had to
stop. Pope admitted that friendship was made difficult by
Wycherley's total lack of memory, but they kept, he says,
'pretty well' together, and the younger poet saw Wycherley twice when the old dramatist lay on his death-bed
in December 1715.[2] There is no evidence of infidelity
on Pope's part or of permanent doubt on the part of
Wycherley.

It is natural that Pope should have been flattered by the
praise of his second 'poet-friend', William Walsh (1663–
1708). Had not Dryden recently called Walsh 'without
flattery . . . the best critic of our nation'?[3] In addition
to being a critic and poet Walsh was a Whig member of
parliament and gentleman of the horse to Queen Anne.
'He loved to be well dressed', we are told by Dennis,[4] who
evidently thought that position and foppishness rather than
ability had given Walsh reputation. Perhaps Dennis resented Dryden's compliment; for he himself was regarded
by some as the head of English criticism. Walsh was cer-

---

[1] Elwin-Courthope, v. 404 (1 April 1710).   [2] Ibid. vi. 366.
[3] In his 'Postscript to the Aeneis' (1697).
[4] Reflections upon An Essay upon Criticism (1711), p. 28.

tainly elegant, formal, and facile, rather than vigorous and
independent; in consequence, his works, prose and verse
alike, are now forgotten, but through his connexion with
Pope he exercised a notable influence on English poetry.

There is some doubt as to the exact moment when the
acquaintance began. Elwin, with characteristic truculence,
does more than distrust the letter from Walsh to Wycherley
(20 April 1705), which Pope printed, and which shows that
Walsh had read some of Pope's 'Pastorals' and wished to
meet the author. Elwin is sure the letter is fabricated.[1]
His argument is mainly drawn from Walsh's first printed
letter to Pope, dated fifteen months later, which seems to
him to show that the friendship was only beginning in June
1706. He may be right; but Tonson was soliciting the
publication of the 'Pastorals' in April 1706, and had seen
them before then in the hands of Walsh and Congreve.
It is surely quite possible, therefore, that Walsh had had
them as early as April 1705. He may have taken as long
to revise Pope's work as Pope did Wycherley's, and it would
be strange if he recommended to Tonson early drafts of the
poems before he had overseen revision of them. The slow
progress of the friendship in 1705 could easily be explained
by the fact that soon after April 1705 Walsh went to the
north to stand for his new seat in the general election of that
year. He was during the summer returned as member for
Richmond (Yorkshire), and may have been fairly busy with
politics during the year. Pope's statement that he spent
the summer of 1705 with Walsh at Abberley[2] seems clearly
wrong. When, thirty years later, Spence began to ask questions about early dates, it is probable that Pope answered
mistakenly rather than mendaciously; one can hardly be
sure of his intention to deceive, and indeed on such a matter
any wrong intention seems less probable than does carelessness. Much of the summer of 1707 Pope did spend at
Abberley. Walsh was daily expecting him in late July,[3]
and Trumbull in a letter of 5 August notes that 'our little

[1] Elwin-Courthope, i. 240–1.   [2] Spence, p. 194.
[3] Elwin-Courthope, vi. 59.

poet is gone a dreadful long journey into Worcestershire
to Mr. Walsh', and under date of 18 September writes that
'Little Pope is returned from Mr. Walsh's'.[1]

By this summer the 'Pastorals' should have been in toler-
able form, and there seems to be no reason why Walsh may
not have revised Pope's version of a part of Statius and even
have seen portions of the *Essay on Criticism*. Pope and
Walsh, if we may judge from their correspondence, habitually discussed problems in literary technique, and the *Essay*
certainly grew out of such interests on Pope's part. Most
of the poem was, to be sure, written after Walsh's death
(16 March 1707/8); but the very fact that in its conclusion
it is dedicated to Walsh's memory suggests that it was in
part inspired by his teaching and that some of it may, as
Pope said, have been shown to him.[2] Pope's laughable
multiplicity of contradictory statements concerning the
early history of the poem is a very clumsy attempt to deceive,[3] if deception is its intent. If one works on a poem
through a period of years, which year is one to choose as
that in which the poem was written? And is it strange if
in various statements one does not always choose the same
year? It is accurate but unfashionable to confess to having
laboured on a poem for a period of years.

The friendship with Walsh was cut short by Walsh's
death. Since Pope always spoke with respect of Walsh's
guidance and teaching, it is important to ask what he
learned from 'the best critic of our nation'. What he told
Spence about it is well known:

He [Walsh] used to encourage me much, and used to tell me, that
there was one way left of excelling: for though we had several great
poets, we never had any one great poet that was correct; and he
desired me to make that my study and aim.[4]

But just what correctness meant it is difficult to say, beyond

---

[1] A footnote in Dilke's *Papers of a Critic*, i. 224, and manuscript notes by Dilke
in his copy of Carruthers (now B.M.: press-mark 12274 i 13), supply these two
mentions of the visit by Trumbull. They are not in the *Hist. MSS. Comm.:
Report on the MSS. of the Marquess of Downshire* (1924).

[2] Spence, p. 194.   [3] Elwin-Courthope, ii. 10-12.

[4] Spence, p. 280.

Courthope's explanation of it as 'propriety of design and justice of thought and taste', which after all is merely propriety or decorum.

It is possible to reconstruct tentatively some of Walsh's views from his scanty remains in prose, though never did a 'best critic' leave less written criticism than did this author. One or two of his letters to Pope, though some may doubt their authenticity, will help; and there are interesting pronouncements in the Preface of his *Letters and Poems Amorous and Gallant* (1692). The author of the biographical sketch in Curll's edition of Walsh's *Works* (1736) would find two periods in Walsh's career: in the first he was the amorous, sparkish gentleman; in the second he 'left Cupid in the Lurch, wholly gave himself up to a *Literatum Otium*, became one of the best Subjects to his Sovereign, King William',[1] and' later to Queen Anne. Whether Walsh really recovered from the foppishness of taste implicit in the early phase of his career one may doubt. His urging Pope to enter the field of pastoral drama hardly sounds like it.[2] And yet with this taste for artificiality he combined certainly a clear perception of the demands of life upon literature. He can see that while Donne, Suckling, and Waller have written pleasing love poetry, their poetry betrays the fact that they were in no true sense great lovers.

I am satisfied [he writes], that *Catullus, Tibullus, Propertius,* and *Ovid,* were in love with their Mistresses. . . . I confess I cannot believe *Petrarch* in Love with his, when he writes Conceits upon her Name, her Gloves, and the Place of her Birth.[3]

He is against conceit and 'glaring thoughts', and professes a belief in nature and in Horatian simplicity of style. He is firmly for the Ancients as compared with the Moderns.

The Occasions upon which the [Love] Poems of the former are written, are such as happen to every Man almost that is in Love; and the Thoughts such as are natural for every Man in Love to

---

[1] p. 124.   [2] Elwin-Courthope, vi. 50.
[3] *Works* (1736), p. vi.

think. The Moderns, on the other hand, have sought out for Occasions, that none meet with but themselves; and fill their Verses with Thoughts that are surprizing and glittering, but not tender, passionate, or natural, to a Man in Love.[1]

He holds the sensible, moderate view of his day towards 'the rules', and instructs Pope:

... a man may correct his verses till he takes away the true spirit of them, especially if he submits to the correction of some who pass for great critics, by mechanical rules, and never enter into the true design and genius of an author.[2]

In fact, the only 'rule' that he commonly invokes is that of propriety, though his Preface suggests metrical formalities for stanzas somewhat in the fashion of those in Pope's letter to him (22 October 1706).

Such teaching seems to have little connexion with Pope's 'Pastorals', and in fact those poems fall far short of telling the whole story of Walsh's influence. On them he strove to bestow, with Pope's aid, the height of smoothness in melody and of propriety in language. It is probable that the general plan of the 'Pastorals' was fixed before the poems reached him. His ideas of the pastoral, as expressed in the Preface to his *Letters and Poems* (1692), do not at times agree with Pope's structural or stylistic concepts. He does not quite insist that the Golden Age is to be depicted: 'The Design ought to be the representing the Life of a Shepherd, not only by talking of Sheep and Fields, but by shewing us the Truth, Sincerity and Innocence that accompanies that sort of Life.'[3] He would bar the wantonness of some ancient pastorals, and expresses disapproval of the homosexual touches in Virgil's *Alexis*, which Pope notwithstanding copied in the first edition of the pastoral dedicated to Wycherley. Humility, modesty, and innocence are the traits that he thinks essential to the pastoral. It is a 'lower' type of love poetry than the elegy. 'The Numbers of the first [former] ought to be looser, and not so sonorous, as the other; the Thoughts more simple, more easie, and

[1] *Works* (1736), p. v. [2] Elwin-Courthope, vi. 54.
[3] *Letters and Poems* (1692), p. ix.

more humble.'[1] Walsh's own pastorals achieve a simpler, plainer, and far less musical style than Pope's.

In the process of rephrasing various passages of Pope's 'Pastorals' Walsh would be able to inculcate his favourite doctrines, which might well reappear in Pope's later works. These doctrines would be nothing strikingly original; they would be the good sense of French and Italian writers which in his travels Walsh had come to value. They would have an elegance that would counteract the rough contempt for finish that Wycherley preached at times. That dramatist regarded himself as a disciple of Donne, and thus Pope wrote to him (10 April 1706): 'Donne, like one of his successors, had infinitely more of wit than he wanted versification; for the great dealers in wit, like those in trade, take least pains to set off their goods, while the haberdashers of small wit spare for no decorations or ornaments.'[2] Walsh disparaged Donne, preached the value of form, and praised a controlled and precise workmanship that strove to produce effects of simplicity, though of a simplicity somewhat artificial. It is probable, furthermore, that Walsh did not diminish Pope's fondness for the genteel and superficial pedantry in criticism that marked his generation. One can see it in Sir William Temple as well as in Walsh. Pope with his limited education was naturally dazzled with the brave show of learning such men made, and he strove to emulate their fashionable air of erudition.

This sort of pedantry adorns much of the correspondence that passed between Pope and his third coffee-house friend, Henry Cromwell. With it occasionally are blended jocose remarks about their mistresses such as were to convey the impression that Pope was genuinely a man about town. From Cromwell Pope learned little except perhaps wisdom as to the ways of the literary world. Cromwell was of service in healing whatever breach there was between Pope and Wycherley, but did no similar service later between Pope and Dennis.[3] This friendship began in the days

[1] Ibid.   [2] Elwin-Courthope, vi. 28.
[3] Ibid. vi. 125, 191, 197.

of Pope's early appearances at Will's, but their correspondence really throve only in the years 1709–11. After
that Pope doubtless felt too obviously his superiority to
this elderly rhymester; and Cromwell's friendliness with
Dennis, who in 1711 became gall and wormwood to Pope,
may have curtailed his friendliness with Pope. Pope and
he remained casual friends after 1711, but apparently
corresponded no further. The value of their letters lies in
the facts of Pope's career that chance to emerge; for these
letters still exist in manuscript. If there was, as Pope told
Spence,[1] any hidden design in these letters to Cromwell, it
would seem to have been that of practising his learning so
as to see if it could pass muster. The results were encour-
aging, apparently, for throughout his life Pope indulged
in this harmless parade of his wide but superficial reading.

Granville and Garth, though less influential friends,
were persons of importance in Pope's early work. Granville very possibly introduced him to Cromwell, and later,
when Secretary at War, led the poet to turn *Windsor Forest*
into a poem on the Peace of Utrecht. The fall of the
Tories in 1714 brought the ruin of Granville, who in 1712
had become Lord Lansdowne. He spent about two years
(1715–17) in the Tower, and after 1722 lived mainly abroad.
Sir Samuel Garth, famous in his own day as author of *The
Dispensary* and as one of the best-natured of men, touched
Pope's orbit for a rather longer time. It is indeed doubtful
if Pope, as he said, knew Garth as early as 1703;[2] but it is
certain that their friendship was early, and lasted until
Garth's death in 1719. Pope's *Autumn* (1709) is dedicated
to Garth, and because of a bit of defence of Garth in the
Essay on Criticism, the Preface to *Claremont* praised in
return *Windsor Forest* over *Cooper's Hill*. This praise from
Garth, coming in April 1715, when the wits at Button's
coffee-house were showing hostility to Pope, is evidence
of Garth's partiality to the young poet. In 1716 we shall
see Garth trying to make peace between Pope and Tom

---

[1] Spence, p. 167. Cf. Elwin-Courthope, x. 5; and Carruthers (1857), pp. 43-4.
[2] Elwin-Courthope, i. 276.

Burnet.¹ One source of Garth's attraction for Pope was his free-thinking, which was of the witty brand that Pope might be expected to love. In his 'Farewell to London' (1715) Pope calls Garth

> the best good Christian he
> Although he knows it not.

It is impossible to estimate how far the good-natured deistic tolerance of Garth and others of his sort may have taken our young poet. There is extant a letter from him to Ralph Allen (8 September [1736?]) in which he tells how he had written and given 'twenty years ago' to the Duke of Shrewsbury (d. 1718) the 'first state' of a poem which he is sending to Allen with the title 'A Prayer to God (1715)',² and which he published in 1738 as *The Universal Prayer*. Other evidence of an early tendency to think for himself in religious matters is found in some verses inserted in Lintot's miscellany *Poems on Several Occasions* (1717), which Professor A. E. Case has shown to have been supervised by Pope.³ This poem, 'On the River Danube', is evidently a quaint warning to the young man against such influences as Garth and others had been exerting:

> See how the wandring *Danube* flows,
>   Realms and Religions parting;
> A friend to all true christian foes,
>   To *Peter, Jack*, and *Martin*.
>
> Now Protestant, and Papist now;
>   Not constant long to either,
> At length an infidel does grow,
>   And ends his journey, neither.
>
> Thus many a youth I've known set out
>   Half protestant, half papist,
> And rambling long the world about,
>   Turn Infidel or Atheist.

Many of Pope's good friends must have feared the results

---

¹ *Infra*, p. 155.
² Sotheby Sale catalogue for 18 April 1932, lot 198.
³ *London Mercury*, x (1924), 614-23.

of the open-mindedness on religious matters which he exhibited as early as the *Essay on Criticism*. The intimacy of Garth and Pope found literary manifestations of another sort again in 1717, when Garth brought out through Tonson a most elaborate edition of Ovid's *Metamorphoses* 'translated by several hands', of which Pope's was one. Apparently interest in the venture led Pope to compose his ballad of *Sandys' Ghost*. At the end of 1718, within three months, Pope lost three of his most congenial friends —Parnell in October, Nicholas Rowe in December, and in January 1719 Garth, whom he had delighted to call 'the best natured man alive'.

The rest of the group whom Pope probably first met at Will's, are, with the exception of Congreve and Addison, negligible. They are the sort of rakish persons that the careful father of the poet might not welcome as friends of his son. Parental control obviously had weight if we may judge from Wycherley's remark (11 November 1707): 'I am sorry your Father is averse to your coming to Town at this time',[1] and from Pope's own account to Henry Cromwell of the restrictions placed upon him at home in Holy Week:

I had written to you sooner, but that I made some scruple of sending profane things to you in Holy Week. Besides, our family would have been scandalised to see me write, who take it for granted I write nothing but ungodly verses; and they say here so many prayers that I can make but few poems.[2]

Similarly he felt it appropriate to discontinue work on Wycherley's papers till Easter Monday.[3] This atmosphere of the home was not that of Will's, where one was at the same time disgusted and diverted by the filth of General Tidcombe, who in turn valued Pope for his 'pretty atheistical jests'.[4] (Tidcombe, it may be noted, was intimate with the novelist Mary Manley, who later lived with another of Pope's acquaintance, Alderman Barber.)[5] Control

---

[1] Elwin-Courthope, v. 389.   [2] Ibid. vi. 91 (10 April 1710).
[3] Ibid. vi. 44.   [4] Ibid. vi. 84 and ix. 255.
[5] *Biographia Dramatica* (1812), i. ii. 488-9.

from the Forest, together with the crazy condition of
Pope's carcass, to borrow Wycherley's phrase, probably
saved the poet's genius from the rakishness and roughness
to which the myrmidons of Will's were impelling it.
Various small pieces composed throughout his career show
the natural affinity Pope had for tavern companions. His
'Imitation of Chaucer', his (or Rowe's) epigram 'On the
Lady who shed her Water at *Cato*' (1713), his 'Farewell
to the Town' (1715), and the much-disowned 'Version
of the First Psalm' (1716), are striking results of such
contacts.

The examples of Congreve and Addison led him in the
opposite direction, but it seems doubtful if with either of
these correct and admirable gentlemen Pope was ever on
terms of closest intimacy. He knew Congreve from the
early years at Will's. According to Tonson, Congreve was
one of the first to approve of the 'Pastorals'. But if intimacy
came, it probably came later, when both Congreve and
Pope were flattering Lady Mary Wortley Montagu. Congreve aided Pope in his efforts with the *Iliad*, and presumably took Pope's side in the 1715 campaign made by the
Buttonian wits against the first volume of the translation,
facts which led Pope to dedicate the translation to Congreve in 1720 when the last volume of the *Iliad* appeared.
It is hard to believe Lady Mary's statement, made after
Congreve's death, that he consistently made fun of Pope
and his wit.[1] Lady Mary's veracity was not greater than
that of the average angry woman of her day. Congreve's
sense of decorum may have been shocked at Pope's satire on
Addison; and he may, as the Dunces after his death asserted,
have sighed at the lines and said: 'From this Day forward
I number him among the Incurables.'[2] But this again is
possibly a post-mortem bit of gossip that its anonymous
author thought safe to utter, since Congreve would probably not rise from the grave to contradict it. The influence

---

[1] Elwin-Courthope, iii. 251-2; and *Letters of Lady Mary Wortley Montagu*
(ed. Thomas, 1893), ii. 21.

[2] *Ingratitude to Mr. Pope* (1733), pp. 8-9.

of Congreve, in conjunction with that of Walsh, Lansdowne, and even of Addison, would be marked in teaching that literary achievement is less important than one's position as a gentleman. These men all were elegant amateurs in the tradition of the *grand siècle*. The worst thing they had to teach was snobbery, which Pope on occasion exhibited; the best thing that they could teach was artistic conscience, of which he seldom later forgot the importance. At least some of the credit for this fact must go to the wits at Will's coffee-house.

Pope and his Tory friends continued to frequent Will's after Button's new coffee-house was opened in 1712. Some Whigs as well, notably Congreve, Garth, and Rowe, probably stayed on. Addison's 'Little Senate' of Whigs moved to Button's, and by 1713 Addison had a definite following among rising literary men, due in part to the reputation which he, with Steele, had acquired from the *Tatler* and *Spectator*, and also from the fact that after the death of Arthur Maynwaring (November 1712) Addison may have succeeded to his influence in doling out such 'loaves and fishes' as went to party writers. Addison's friendliness to Pope was very likely in part due to a desire to control his pen for the Whigs. This Addison, and even Lord Halifax, who presently offered a pension, failed to do. The political relations of Pope and Addison were never friendly, and party violence was a dominant force in making the two men finally quite hostile to each other. But Addison and Steele combined had a notable formative influence on Pope, quite apart from the elegant amateurism which Addison exemplified. They were practical moralists, apostles sent to elevate the taste of the English public; and from them Pope inherited ideas and attitudes concerning taste and morals that governed his whole career.

Probably Caryll introduced Steele to Pope.[1] In any case

---

[1] Dilke was, I think, the first to point out that at the time (1696) when Caryll was repurchasing the confiscated family estates from Lord Cutts, Steele was Lord Cutts's secretary, and as such must have formed Caryll's acquaintance. Pope's letters to Caryll show that the latter recommended the poet to Steele. See Dilke, *Papers of a Critic*, i. 250-3 (from the *Athenaeum*, 8 May 1858).

they were corresponding in the summer of 1711, and Pope then promised to write some words for Steele's friend Clayton to set to music. What he produced, if anything, is unknown. When in December 1711 the *Spectator* No. 253 indulged in high, if qualified, praise of the *Essay on Criticism* Pope naturally thanked Steele for the praise. The fact that the paper was written by Addison led to an introduction and to friendly relations—for a time. It was doubtless easier to be friendly with Steele than with Addison. Steele had the warmer, more human nature, though he lacked the stability of Addison. The cold and complete correctness which Addison habitually exhibited was more admired as a personal trait in his day than it is nowadays. The present century perhaps underestimates the achievement of true decorum, the ability always to do the correct thing and to say the correct thing; to reprove without heat or malice and to praise justly, elegantly, and —here is the danger—with no surplusage of effusiveness. Who but must be amazed if such an ideal became actual? And who (if the realized ideal became somewhat conscious of his achievement) would not laugh? And if the ideal became a surface achievement merely, with cold and partisan malice corrupting the highest possibilities of magnanimity, all the world must see the tragedy. It is easy to praise Addison overmuch, Macaulay and Thackeray have done so; but it is at present even easier to be unjust to him. It was hard for Pope to know Addison in his most genial state; for the many cups required to bring on that blissful thaw (love and drinking were no sin in Queen Anne's days!) would render Pope incapable of appreciation. And yet he speaks more than once of Addison's conversational powers with highest praise.[1] No one, in fact, has spoken more highly.

After the kindness of *Spectator* No. 253, a kindness evenly mixed with reproof, Pope sent Steele the 'Messiah', which appeared in the *Spectator*, 14 May 1712. The poem made the issue for that day one of the most esteemed in the course

---

[1] Spence, pp. 50, 195; *Epistle to Dr. Arbuthnot*, line 196.

of the paper, and must have pleased a whole class of readers untouched by the 'Pastorals' or the *Essay on Criticism*. It must also have served as a sop to the family at home, who had begun to suspect his muse of ungodliness. Pope may have contributed to a number of other *Spectator* essays, which escape identification;[1] at any rate in his valedictory on 6 December 1712 Steele mentioned Pope second in a list of helpers less important to the periodical than Addison and Budgell had been. About a month before this, Steele had approached Pope asking his assistance in a new design.[2] Late numbers of the *Spectator* had really announced that after an interval the paper would be resumed with Mr. Spec. no longer taciturn. This project was dropped, but when on 12 March 1713 the *Guardian* first appeared, Pope was a chief assistant, and Addison was not of the enterprise.

For the *Guardian* Pope wrote at least eight essays of considerable excellence, Nos. 4, 11, 40, 61, 78, 91, 92, and 173. Of these the most interesting is probably the last, which is an early announcement of Pope's views on gardening. No. 78 contained the 'receipt' for an epic poem, which was really a part of the *Memoirs of Martinus Scriblerus* (1741), and No. 40 is the famous ironical paper on the pastoral, which infuriated pompous Ambrose Philips and according to tradition made it unwise for Pope to visit Button's coffee-house. Collaboration with so ardent a Whig as Steele annoyed Pope's Tory and Catholic friends, and when the *Guardian* was dropped and the political *Englishman* begun, he amicably ceased working with Steele.

The year 1713 saw Pope's best and most unlucky attempts to be non-partisan in the political struggle then so

---

[1] For *Spectator* No. 457 (14 August 1712) an unidentified correspondent (probably Pope) sent Addison the Scriblerus proposal for a periodical to be called 'An Account of the Works of the Unlearned'. If Pope sent this, the first sentence of No. 457 identifies him as author of the letter in No. 452. Addison's publication of the letter in No. 457 probably is the ground for alleging his interest in the Scriblerus Club, as Spence does in his *Anecdotes*, p. 10.

[2] Elwin-Courthope, vi. 395.

bitter. Passivity was seldom a good role for Pope, and consequently it is characteristic of him that he should try to seem impartial by allying himself with friends of both factions. In March, for example, he published *Windsor Forest*, which praised the approaching Tory peace and which was dedicated to Lord Lansdowne, one of Queen Anne's new peers. At the same time he was collaborating with Steele, who was constantly the object of violent political attack, and when Addison's Whig tragedy of *Cato* was acted, beginning 14 April, the Prologue was by Mr. Pope. He was by now of course the friend of Gay, Swift, Arbuthnot, and Parnell, at least two of whom were writing numerous and invaluable pamphlets for the Tories. On 27 April appeared the offensive *Guardian* No. 40, on the pastorals of Philips and Pope; thereafter the minor members of Addison's group would have it that Pope was a Tory, and as such to be shunned. Swift and Steele were raging at each other, and even Swift and Addison were estranged. 'All our friendship and dearness are off: we are civil acquaintance, talk words of course, of when we shall meet, and that's all', writes Swift with a touch of weariness.[1] It was inevitable that Pope like the rest of the world must choose between the two groups, and it was inevitable which group would be chosen. The friends at Will's had regarded literature primarily as an art, and Pope had mastered their doctrine; Steele and Addison in the days of the *Tatler* and *Spectator* had regarded literature chiefly as a corrective of morals—and of taste, which was in a sense the basis of a gentleman's morals. Pope from them acquired similar views. The *Rape of the Lock* is a laughing satire on the foibles of women which would have been almost impossible before the raillery on the fair sex made popular by Steele and Addison. Even the later epistle *On the Characters of Women* departs from Juvenal and Boileau to adopt the *Spectator*'s tone, and scattered through the poet's work are other notable traces of ideas and indeed a whole way of thinking that came from his admiration of these essayists.

[1] *Journal to Stella* (Bohn Library ed.), p. 101.

But, after all, their 'fair-sexing it to the world's end' was
not a solid and staple diet: they could not hold him; and
when Addison saw this, he advised Pope to be non-partisan
—'not to be content with the praise of half the nation',[1]
and let him go. It would have been hard for any keen
genius to be non-partisan at that moment: for Pope it was
impossible.

[1] Spence, p. 195. Cf. Elwin-Courthope, vi. 402.

III

THE SCRIBLERUS CLUB

BY 1712 or 1713 Pope's intimacy with his group of elderly friends at Will's had ceased or had become for the most part casual. Walsh and Betterton were dead, and while Pope was at least outwardly on friendly terms with Wycherley and Cromwell, they were not corresponding with him any more and were not so cordial as formerly. Probably the reason is that as Pope's reputation and circle of acquaintance grew, he naturally attached himself to persons who were more active and prominent in literature at the moment. Hence the connexion with Steele and Addison. But evidently this connexion annoyed his Roman Catholic friends, who wondered at his association with such Whigs; for Pope's letters to Caryll in 1712 and 1713 are frequently apologetic. The passages on the monks and on Erasmus in the *Essay on Criticism* had astonished good Catholics, who were further made sensitive by certain lines in the *Rape of the Lock*. Thus a considerable, if quiet, pressure must have existed, which would tend to make the poet defer to Catholic scruples when such deference would not incommode him. Most Catholics, though not active Tories, preferred the Tory party to that of the Whigs. And from the other side, there developed in 1713 an opposition to Pope among Addison's followers that was not quiet, and that made Button's coffee-house less hospitable to Pope.

It was chiefly this Addisonian 'senate' of Whig writers that Pope began to avoid. Charles Jervas, the painter, who was an ardent Whig, put his house at Pope's disposal as a place of residence when the poet was in town, and so Cleveland Court was for years Pope's London address.[1]

---

[1] The address was Bridgewater House, Cleveland Court, by St. James's (Elwin-Courthope, viii. 31); or, as indicated in advertisements to subscribers to the *Odyssey*, 'next Door to the Right Hon. the Lord Viscount Townshend's' (*Evening*

There were also at least two men among the literary Whigs whom it was not necessary to sacrifice. Congreve, the first, was almost the only man among the poets of the day who either by ill health or by natural dignity was able to keep above party broils. He has been named as a member of the Scriblerus Club, but probably by error. Nicholas Rowe, the second of these Whigs, was a violent partisan and cared to converse with no Tories, but he remained to his death (1718) a friend of Pope. For some reason Rowe was not fond of Addison or his little circle, and this may have brought him closer to Pope. The intellectual relations between these two editors of Shakespeare would be interesting to study if there were means. They seem to have met usually in coffee-houses or taverns—though at least once, in September 1713, Rowe visited Binfield with Pope.[1] The friendship at times must have taught Pope tolerance; for partisan vehemence at a moment when Catholics, threatened with added land-taxes, were selling their estates and moving to the Continent—the painful moment when the house at Binfield was sold—had led Rowe to insert the following lines in his Prologue to Cibber's *Non-Juror* (1717), a play that Pope for various reasons abominated:

> Ship off, ye Slaves, and seek some passive land,
> Where tyrants after your own hearts command.
> To your transalpine master's rule resort,
> And fill an empty, abdicated court:
> Turn your possessions here to ready rhino,
> And buy ye lands and lordships at Urbino.

Catholics were used to this sort of thing, and these particular lines apparently did not affect Pope's friendliness with Rowe. But a similar attitude towards Catholics, underlying most Whig policy and much Whig utterance, helps to explain why it was advisable in 1713 to cease collaborat-

---

Post, 15 April 1725). Of course at times Pope stayed elsewhere: with Lord Peterborough in Bolton Street, in August 1723 (Elwin-Courthope, ix. 496); or with Lord Bathurst in St. James's Square, in September 1724 (ibid. viii. 197).

[1] Elwin-Courthope, vi. 194.

ing with Steele and to hold aloof from the group at Button's.

Other friends were available. Before the end of 1712 Pope was acquainted with Gay, Swift, Arbuthnot, and Parnell. One assumes that he met them at Will's or at other places where the wits of the day forgathered. Pope's reputation as based on his contributions to the miscellanies of Tonson and Lintot and on the *Essay on Criticism* would doubtless make him sought after. Gay's mixture of genius and diffidence must have been charming in itself as well as in contrast with the heavy pretentiousness of people like Philips. With Gay Pope must have become friendly in 1711. Gay is mentioned in that year in the letters to Cromwell, and he comforted Pope after Dennis's attack on the *Essay on Criticism*;[1] later, in January 1713, he printed his delightful *Rural Sports* 'inscrib'd to Mr. Pope'. In May 1713 Gay's comedy the *Wife of Bath* had been damned: possibly Pope's modernization of her Prologue (published December 1713) was suggested by Gay's attempt with the lady. Pope helped to revise the *Fan* for Gay, and inspired him to write the *Shepherd's Week* in burlesque of Philips.

In 1712 Swift was of course at the height of his career. As the confidant of the Lord Treasurer (Oxford) and the ablest writer for the Oxford ministry, he was influential with almost every one except Queen Anne, the Archbishop of York, and the Somersets. His brilliance of wit and astounding directness in social relations made him a most amusing companion. We do not know just how Pope made the 'advances' that Swift always expected from would-be friends. It may be that Lansdowne, the Secretary at War (whom Swift disliked), arranged all that. When in March 1713 *Windsor Forest* appeared, dedicated to Lansdowne and to the cause of a Tory peace, Swift must have rejoiced at this accession to the ranks of Tory writers. His friendship with Pope, however, probably dates from at least some

---

[1] Elwin-Courthope, vi. 124 and 155. See *infra*, p. 93, on the *Critical Specimen* (1711).

months earlier. Swift became in the autumn of 1713 about the most active promoter of the subscription to Pope's *Iliad*, and the friendship proved to be lifelong.

Another member of the group was that *'vir doctiss., probitate ac pietate insignis'*,[1] Dr. John Arbuthnot, the favourite physician to the Queen. He was not merely one of the best scientists of his day but also a literary man of surprising and delightful inventiveness. He was respected as an adviser in musical matters, was an agreeable hand at the card-table; he was, all told, a charming companion, a tender-hearted father, and a most caustic satirist. At the time when Pope probably first knew him (1712), he was amusing the public with a series of pamphlets that, when collected, became the *History of John Bull*. 'John Bull' as an epitome of British traits dates from Arbuthnot's work.

The last important Scriblerean to be introduced is the Rev. Thomas Parnell (1679–1718), who came to England from Ireland after the death of his wife in 1711. Parnell was evidently a sympathetic soul, whose own personality as well as his present sorrow won him many friends. Pope and he both wrote *Guardian* essays, and thus perhaps the two were brought into intimacy. During a visit to Binfield in 1714, he endeared himself greatly to the poet's parents. His knowledge of Greek made him indispensable to Pope during the process of translating Homer and of excavating notes on Homer from the earlier commentators. He rendered further assistance by his *Life of Zoilus*, finally published in 1717, which had been prepared largely as a defence of Pope against possible attacks from Dennis. Parnell's transference of friendship from Whig to Tory writers parallels that of Pope and is due to exertions in his behalf by Swift, who introduced him to various chief ministers, and worked for his ecclesiastical preferment.

These men—including the head of the ministry, Robert Harley, Earl of Oxford, and his chief rival within the ministry, Henry St. John, Viscount Bolingbroke—became for the rest of their lives Pope's most intimate and famous literary

[1] Elwin-Courthope, I. x.

friends. Swift was perhaps at the moment the most active and compelling of the group, but Bolingbroke as a finished man of the world would be a thrilling acquaintance for Pope, and in charm of amiability and in resourcefulness of wit no one could surpass Arbuthnot. Swift was eager to serve his newly chosen patron (Oxford) with his pen and to attract other writers to his service. As early as 1711, in his absence, the Brothers Club had been founded[1] as a rival to the Whig Kit-Kat Club. There were at the start twelve 'brothers'—lords and wits—and later there were more. They met in various places, usually on Thursday, dined together, and frequently after dinner the printer ('Alderman' Barber?) would be brought up with the newest pamphlets ready for the morrow. Sometimes on a Friday after such a dinner Swift took to the printer curious compositions. On 4 January 1711/12 he writes to Stella:

I was in the City to-day, and dined with my printer, and gave him a ballad made by several hands, I know not whom. I believe Lord-Treasurer had a finger in it; I added three stanzas; I suppose Dr. Arbuthnot had the greatest share.

Collaborate authorship was established before the Scriblerus project. The Brothers Club was purely political, and encouraged humble writers by occasional gratuities raised by levy on the society. These levies and the expensive dinners that came to be expected were disliked by Swift, who for a time was Secretary of the Club as well as its moving spirit, and by the end of 1712 his blunt verdict was: 'We do no good.'[2] It may very well be that the size of the Club imperilled the essential anonymity of pamphlets, and caused Swift himself, for example, to worry about his connexion with the *Conduct of the Allies* and other things. With another group, somewhat smaller and more responsible, Swift dined on Saturdays at the Lord Treasurer's, but even here he found 'a rabble' intruding.

Along with Swift's weariness of these dinners came at times a weariness also of politics, due to the lack of forceful

[1] *Journal to Stella*, 9–20 June 1711 (Bohn Library ed.), p. 194, &c.
[2] Ibid., 18 December 1712.

leadership on Oxford's part. There developed increasingly a fatal rivalry between Oxford and Bolingbroke; and Swift, who had gathered literary friends about him partly in the hope of aiding Oxford, must have begun to doubt the possibility of sustaining a house divided against itself. Neither Swift nor these his closest literary friends would be interested in party-writing alone, and gradually their interests shifted from politics to the old topic of pedantry.

The love of satirizing pedantry is first seen in this group in Swift's *Tale of a Tub* and *Battle of the Books* (1704); Pope's *Essay on Criticism* had slight manifestations of this attitude. In March 1712 a well-known periodical called the *History of the Works of the Learned* had gone out of existence, after having reviewed for a dozen years (1699–1712) outstanding English or continental learned works chiefly in the fields of science and theology. On 14 August 1712 *Spectator* No. 457 published a long letter suggesting two possibilities for burlesque journals. The second was as follows:

I need not tell you, sir, that there are several authors in France, Germany, and Holland, as well as in our own country, who publish every month, what they call *An Account of the Works of the Learned*, in which they give us an abstract of all such books as are printed in any part of Europe. Now, sir, it is my design to publish every month, *An Account of the Works of the Unlearned*. Several late productions of my own countrymen, who many of them make a very eminent figure in the illiterate world, encourage me in this undertaking. I may, in this work, possibly make a review of several pieces which have appeared in the foreign *Accounts* above mentioned, though they ought not to have been taken notice of in works which bear such a title. I may likewise take into consideration such pieces as appear from time to time under the names of those gentlemen who compliment one another, in public assemblies, by the title of the *Learned Gentlemen*. Our party authors will also afford me a great variety of subjects, not to mention editors, commentators, and others, who are often men of no learning, or what is as bad, of no knowledge. I shall not enlarge upon this hint; but if you think anything can be made of it, I shall set about it with all the pains and application that so useful a work deserves.

Subsequent events seem to indicate that Pope must have contributed to the *Spectator* this letter with its proposal for a burlesque on pedantry. When it was printed by Addison, Swift was at Windsor Castle, doubtless as guest of Arbuthnot. He saw and approved the proposal, perhaps before it was published, and presently we find Pope writing to Gay on 23 October [1712][1]:

Dr. Swift much approves what I proposed, even to the very title, which I design shall be, The Works of the Unlearned, published monthly, in which whatever book appears that deserves praise, shall be depreciated ironically, and in the same manner that modern critics take to undervalue works of value, and to commend the high productions of Grub-street.

Parnell evidently was also well disposed to the whim; for in this same letter Pope tells Gay that Parnell 'enters heartily into our design'.

The first production[2] in this scheme came from the pen of Arbuthnot, and it came so soon after the letter to the *Spectator* that it may possibly have been independent of Pope's proposal. Swift wrote to Stella on 9 October 1712:

Arbuthnot has sent me from Windsor a pretty discourse upon Lying, and I have ordered the printer to come for it. It is a proposal for publishing a curious piece, called The Art of Political Lying, in two volumes, &c. And then there is an abstract of the first volume, just like those pamphlets which they call 'The Works of the Learned'.[3]

[1] Elwin-Courthope, vii. 412. The date suggested for the letter by these editors is [1713]. It should certainly be changed to [1712]. The appearance of Pope's proposal in the *Spectator* is alone sufficient evidence; but there is additional proof. The letter to Gay speaks of Pope's illness, and in 1712 he had been ill: we have no information as to his health in 1713. Gay's *Fan*, which Pope in the letter wishes to take into the country for further revision 'a month hence' (i.e. 23 November), was published on 8 December 1713 [the *Daily Courant*, 9 December 1713, advertises it as 'Yesterday was published']. On 23 October 1713, consequently, the poem was far too near publication for Pope to be talking of revisions to be made 'a month hence'. If the letter had been written in October 1713, it is probable that Pope would have mentioned to Gay the proposals for the subscription to the *Iliad*, which were just out at that time.

[2] The attack on Dennis called the *Critical Specimen* (1711), which possibly came from some member of this group, antedates the *Art of Political Lying* as a satire in this type by over a year. See *infra*, p. 93.

[3] *Journal to Stella* (Bohn Library ed.), p. 386.

The probability is that this pamphlet is an example of what the group early meditated as a pattern for their satire. They might naturally have in mind also, one imagines, such things as Dr. William King's *Useful Transactions in Philosophy and other Sorts of Learning* (1708). Evidently, however, the project languished and died: it demanded more learning than some of our authors had, and it gave too little scope for the burlesque narrative in which they excelled. Swift spent the summer of 1713 in Ireland, and very likely only after his return to England another design—possibly also Pope's originally—appealed to the group: that of writing burlesque memoirs of a many-sided pedant, whose name was early determined as Martinus Scriblerus. From this hero the Club has taken its name. Pope's comment to Spence on this last project is worth attention:

The design of the Memoirs of Scriblerus was to have ridiculed all the false tastes in learning, under the character of a man of capacity enough; that had dipped into every art and science, but injudiciously in each. It was begun by a club of some of the greatest wits of the age. Lord Oxford, the Bishop of Rochester, Mr. Pope, Congreve, Arbuthnot, Swift, and others. Gay often held the pen; and Addison liked it very well, and was not disinclined to come in to it. The Deipnosophy consisted of disputes on ridiculous tenets of all sorts: and the adventure of the Shield was designed against Dr. Woodward and the Antiquaries. It was Anthony Henley who wrote 'the life of his music master Tom Durfey'; a chapter by way of episode.—It was from a part of these memoirs that Dr. Swift took his first hints for Gulliver. There were pigmies in Schreibler's travels; and the projects of Laputa.—The design was carried on much farther than has appeared in print; and was stopped by some of the gentlemen being dispersed or otherwise engaged (about the year 1715.) See the memoirs themselves.—*P*.[1]

Inasmuch as we are here primarily concerned with Pope's connexion with the Club and its influence on him, we need not, perhaps, argue all the dubious points in this account, set down by Spence as material communicated to him by Pope in the early years of their acquaintance (1728–30).

[1] Spence, pp. 10–11.

It seems unlikely that Congreve or Addison, particularly the latter, had any part in the Club. The appearance of Pope's letter in *Spectator* No. 457 may very likely explain the remark that Addison 'liked it very well'. The prime movers in it were Arbuthnot, Swift, Gay, Parnell, and Pope. Lord Bathurst and the Rev. George Berkeley,[1] who was in London in 1713, have been mentioned as members, but the connexion, if actual, must have been slight. Anthony Henley and others doubtless had only small shares in it also.

The substitution, in place of the *Works of the Unlearned*, of the *Memoirs of Scriblerus* was a happy idea. The central theme or purpose of Scriblerus was to illustrate the misapplication of talents in the person of a 'man of capacity enough; that had dipped into every art and science, but injudiciously in each'. This was a more concrete and dramatic device, and it gave a specious unity to a personality sufficiently diverse to allow each satirist to work in his own art or science. Swift says Pope first had the idea of Scriblerus, but obviously Arbuthnot, apart from Swift, was best qualified to carry on the jest. Swift writes justly when he tells Arbuthnot:

> To talk of Martin in any hands but yours, is a folly. You every day give better hints than all of us together could do in a twelve-month; and to say the truth, Pope who first thought of the hint has no genius at all to it, in my mind. Gay is too young; Parnell has some ideas of it, but is idle; I could put together, and lard, and strike out well enough, but all that relates to the sciences must be from you.[2]

Pope's genius apart, he was presently so busy with his translation of the *Iliad* that it is hard to see how he could find time for another project. But Arbuthnot must have been worried and occupied by the ill health of Queen Anne and by politics, so that it is astonishing if he could find time

---

[1] Warton's *Essay on Pope* (1806), ii. 199 n. The anecdote here narrated about Berkeley and the Club must date later than 1713. The years 1726, 1727 might be appropriate, but the anecdote is the puzzling sort that Lord Bathurst seems to have loved.

[2] Swift's *Correspondence*, ed. Ball, ii. 162–3 (3 July 1714).

for such work. In the period after the invention of Scriblerus, the Club as a whole can hardly have met often except for the brief period from February 1714, when the Queen's (and consequently Arbuthnot's) removal from Windsor to Kensington became possible, to the first of June, when Swift retired to Letcombe. The only meetings that we can specifically date took place in 1714 on 20 March, 14 April, 5 and 12 June.[1] Since three of these four fell on Saturdays, we may assume that the Club was designed to assemble the Lord Treasurer's poets and leave to the cabinet his dinners of Saturday. One also assumes that by preference the Club met in Arbuthnot's apartments in the palace, and that the ritual of meeting included a doggerel invitation to the Lord Treasurer to join them.[2] Even after Swift had gone to Letcombe, Oxford attended at least one meeting of the Club. The last recorded meeting (12 June), Arbuthnot informed Swift, was to be held at the Pall Mall coffee-house at one o'clock.[3] Two days after this date Gay left London on his thankless journey to Hanover.

> I sold my sheep and lambkins too,
> For silver loops, and garment blue,[4]

as he later wrote of his efforts to please the Court; but he dedicated the poem to Bolingbroke, and that fact precluded patronage from George I and Walpole. Pope and Parnell retired to work on Homer at Binfield, whence they visited Swift for a few days at Letcombe in early July. Pope, after this visit, agreed with Swift as to Scriblerus:

This is not a time for us to make others live, when we can hardly live ourselves; so Scriblerus (contrary to other maggots) must lie dead all the Summer, and wait till Winter shall revive him.[5]

The work of the Club as such was ended.

It is doubtful if any of the group, except Swift, recognized the critical state of affairs just before the death of

---

[1] Elwin-Courthope, viii. 225 n.; Swift's *Correspondence*, ed. cit. ii. 145, 151, 417.
[2] Arbuthnot's *Works*, ed. Aitken, pp. 56–7 n., and Swift's *Correspondence*, ed. cit. ii. 416–17.   [3] Swift's *Correspondence*, ed. cit. ii. 151.
[4] Prologue to the *Shepherd's Week*.
[5] Elwin-Courthope, vii. 468 (11 July 1714).

Queen Anne on 1 August 1714. Swift certainly foresaw stormy days ahead, and withdrew to a quiet corner to endure as best he could his chagrin at the tragic lack of leadership in the Tory cause. An Irish deanery was to be the bound of his ambition, and in a sense he realized that much of the rest of his career was to be wrapped in defeat. Arbuthnot, who was perhaps at fault in concealing from the Tory leaders the true state of the Queen's health, was left at her death amidst what looked like the ruins of a career. While reorganizing his life he perhaps found solace in planning and writing the *Memoirs*. On 7 September he wrote to Pope (and Parnell), taking to himself the name of Scriblerus, as they had applied it:

Martin's office is now the second door on the left hand in Dover Street, where he will be glad to see Dr. Parnell, Mr. Pope, and his old friends. . . . I have seen a letter from Dean Swift: he keeps up his noble spirit, and though like a man knocked down, you may behold him still with a stern countenance, and aiming a blow at his adversaries. I will add no more, being in haste, only that I will never forgive you if you do not use my foresaid house in Dover Street with the same freedom as you did that in St. James's.[1]

But Pope and Parnell were bound for Bath, and when in December Pope again reached London, his settled efforts were devoted to the *Iliad* and to worries over the welcome it might receive. The death of Queen Anne had been a terrific blow to the hopes of all his friends: to him it was almost nothing. He had in 1713–14 substantially become a Tory partisan—though what he loved was certain Tory friends and not the lost cause of a party. He had not yet learned to think ardently, as he later did in the days of the Patriot group, in terms of party, and though he was already accused of Jacobitism by Whig writers, the accusation was intended as general abuse rather than as a serious charge. Early in the summer of 1715, only Gay, Arbuthnot, and Pope were left 'at large' in London. Parnell had followed Swift to Ireland. Oxford was in the Tower accused of high treason. In March Bolingbroke had fled to France in the belief that only flight could save his life.

It is in every way natural that the publication of the works of the Scriblerus Club should appear a considerable time later than the recorded meetings of the Club. What those meetings did, in all probability, was to make preliminary drafts of individual episodes.[1] They did not evolve any new fundamental ideas as to satire on scientific or literary pedantry. Satire on scientific topics had been a commonplace of the time since the founding of the Royal Society; and satire on pedantry with regard to classical literature had existed long before the *Battle of the Books*, which 'battle' the Scriblerus Club more or less inherited. But Pope knew nothing of science, and while he might have been imbued with hostility to literary pedantry by contacts with Wycherley, Walsh, and others, it seems probable that his animosity to textual and other pedantic criticism came from association with Swift and this group. His personal prejudice against such scholarship came in part, of course, from unfortunate contacts with such men as Dennis, Bentley, and (later) Theobald; but his reaction to these men, if personal, found utterance through channels made familiar by the thought of Swift and Arbuthnot. Their methods of thinking colour obviously much of Pope's work after his period of translation and even some of the incidental work of that period.

It goes without saying that the only works of first importance that are due to the stimulus of the Club are *Gulliver's Travels* (1726), the *Dunciad* (1728), and the *Memoirs of Martinus Scriblerus* (1741). There are, however, smaller pieces of importance that may at least be mentioned here. Pope's *Key to the Lock*, 'a treatise proving beyond all contradiction the dangerous tendency of a late poem entituled *The Rape of the Lock* to government and religion. By Esdras Barnivelt' (1715) may be placed in this tradition;

---

[1] A half-leaf of manuscript from the Scriblerus story is preserved in the Homer MSS. (Add. MS. 4808, fol. 13ᵛ). This is in the hand of Arbuthnot, revised much by Pope. It is a preliminary draft of part of the episode of the double mistress.

for the mind of Barnivelt (drawn perhaps from an actual apothecary) certainly works much like that of Scriblerus. Another piece would be *Three Hours after Marriage*, the farce which three club members confederated to write in Gay's name. This was staged in 1717 amidst much opposition. In it Arbuthnot satirized the geological studies of Dr. Woodward in a Scriblerean manner, and Pope similarly carried on his quarrel with Dennis. In 1723 appeared the *Memoirs of Scriblerus*, by 'Dr. S—t', advertised as 'reprinted from the Dublin copy'.[1] The substance of this pamphlet differs largely from the authentic *Memoirs of Martinus Scriblerus* published by Pope in 1741. The 1723 *Memoirs* are not satirical of pedantry in science, but deal only with that of literary critics. The work was perhaps organized to annoy Dennis, and since in 1723 Pope and Dennis were trying to be polite to each other, the chances are that the work is a piracy, composed by some one who had slight knowledge of the Club's *Memoirs*. It is probable that *The Memoirs of P. P. Clerk of this Parish* designed by Pope and Gay as a satire on Bishop Burnet was composed shortly after (if not before) that prelate's death in 1715. It is a piece to be compared with the *Notes and Memorandums* of the last days of the bishop, ascribed to Arbuthnot. Certainly the *Peri Bathous; or the Art of Sinking in Poetry* was under way in June 1714, when Arbuthnot wrote to Swift: 'Pope has been collecting high flights of poetry, which are very good; they are to be solemn nonsense.'[2] This remark explains the generally neglected fact that the 'high flights' in the *Peri Bathous* as printed in 1728 come mainly from a much earlier period. That the work was placed in the 1728 volume of poetic *Miscellanies* instead of being placed in one of the prose volumes is due to a natural decision to print separately the *Dunciad*, which had been designed to complete the poetic volume of 1727 8. The *Peri Bathous* was a substitute. It is interesting to note

---

[1] See Griffith, *Pope Bibliography*, i. 108. Professor Griffith very kindly allowed me the use of his copy of this rare work.
[2] Swift's *Correspondence*, ed. Ball, ii. 160 (26 June 1714).

the large collections made from the solemn nonsense of Blackmore, who before 1717 was not embroiled with Pope, although he had been offensive to Swift and Arbuthnot. If the critical doctrines of this work were overvalued by Pope and some of his contemporaries, they have been undervalued in more recent times. Upon publication the work was a sensation mainly because its illustrations were taken largely from Pope's enemies, though some came from his own juvenile verses. The examples are not unjustly cited, and they must have served as warning guides to poets. They show the true bent of Pope's genius, exemplified best in his works written after the *Dunciad*; it was a bent towards the rational plainness of common sense and away from the strained floridity of his baroque predecessors. The *Bathos* was translated into French at least as early as 1749,[1] and thus may have had an international influence on the art of the eighteenth century. It is, in any case, one of the more serious and purposeful Scriblerean pieces, most of which, especially such small works as *God's Revenge against Punning* (1716) and *Annus Mirabilis* (1722), are holiday efforts. The Club was far from originating a satirical bent in Pope, but it helped to fix in him habits of satirical thought and expression.

[1] *Traité des dissensions entre les nobles et le peuple. . . . L'Art de ramper en poësie, et L'Art du mensonge politique.* La Haye, 1749. Reprinted in vol. iii of *Le Conte du tonneau* (La Haye, 1757).

IV

EARLY POEMS

CONCERNING many of his juvenilia Pope adopted
the wise procedure of talking—and destroying. Consequently we have a list of boyish efforts, no one of which
has survived in its juvenile form. His father early set him
to making English verses, so Mrs. Pope told Spence: 'He
was pretty difficult in being pleased; and used often to
send him back to new turn them. "These are not good
rhimes;" for that was my husband's word for verses.'[1]
Pope himself told Spence practically all we know of these
early things:

I began writing verses of my own invention, farther back than
I can well remember.—Ogilby's translation of Homer was one of
the first large poems that ever Mr. Pope read; and he still spoke
of the pleasure it then gave him, with a sort of rapture, only in
reflecting on it.—'It was that great edition with pictures, I was
then about eight years old. This led me to Sandy's [sic] Ovid,
which I liked extremely; and so I did a translation of part of
Statius, by some very bad hand.'—*P.*

When I was about twelve,' I wrote a kind of play, which I got
to be acted by my schoolfellows. It was a number of speeches from
the Iliad; tacked together with verses of my own.—The epic poem
which I begun a little after I was twelve, was Alcander, Prince of
Rhodes: there was an under-water scene in the first book, it was
in the Archipelago.—I wrote four books toward it, of about a
thousand verses each; and had the copy by me, till I burnt it,
by the advice of the Bishop of Rochester, a little before he went
abroad.—*P.*

I endeavoured, (said he, smiling), in this poem, to collect all the
beauties of the great epic writers into one piece: there was Milton's
style in one part, and Cowley's in another; here the style of Spenser
imitated, and there of Statius; here Homer and Virgil, and there
Ovid and Claudian.—'It was an imitative poem then, as your other
exercises were imitations of this or that story?'—Just that.—*P.*

[1] Spence, p. 8.

Mr. Pope wrote verses imitative of sounds so early as in this epic poem.—

> 'Shields, helms, and swords all jangle as they hang,
> And sound formidinous with angry clang.'

Was a couplet of this nature in it?—There were also some couplets in it which I have since inserted in some of my other poems, without any alteration. As in the Essay on Criticism;

> 'Whose honours with increase of ages grow;
> As streams roll down enlarging as they flow.'

Another couplet, inserted in the Dunciad already mentioned,[1] and I think he said the same of that simile—

> 'As clocks to weight their nimble motion owe;
> The wheels above urg'd by the load below.'

In the scattered lessons I used to set myself, about that time, I translated above a quarter of the Metamorphoses, and that part of Statius which was afterwards printed with the corrections of Walsh.—*P.*[2]

This passage tells most of the story, though one should add a mention of the complete tragedy (not preserved) on the legend of St. Genevieve and various smaller pieces.[3] The most notable of the smaller pieces would be those printed in a very obscure Miscellany published under Pope's editorial care by Lintot in 1717.[4] Here first appeared the lines 'On Solitude', later revised to make one of Pope's best short poems. The lines may originally have been written when the poet was aged 12, but they did not attain their final form before 1730. Another interesting short poem is Pope's first published satire, the lines 'To the Author of a Poem, entitled Successio', which a note to *Dunciad*, Book i, line 181, announced as written when the poet was 14. The author attacked is Elkanah Settle, whose long career in anti-Catholic pamphleteering may have made him a bugbear of the Pope household.

---

[1] *Dunciad*, Book iii, lines 56–7.   [2] Spence, pp. 276–8.

[3] Ibid., p. 197. In the early, unprinted manuscript of Spence's *Anecdotes*, now in the Huntington Library, we read on fol. 358: 'Mr. Pope finish'd his Tragedy on the pretty story of St. Genevieve when he was about 13.'

[4] *Poems on Several Occasions*. . . . London: Printed for Bernard Lintot. . . . 1717. In the Yale Library (Z 78. 88h).

Received ten Guinea's for ye
Tale of Chaucer, and the Eclogues, amounting to abt one
thousand and 2 hundred lines,
of Mr Tonson,

march 4th: 1708/4   A: Pope.

Jan. 13. 1708/9.
Received of Mr Tonson 3 Guineas for
a Translation of the Episode of Sarpedon, printed in ye 6th pt of miscellany
Poems.
                        A. Pope.

POPE'S FIRST POETICAL EARNINGS
Original document in the Pierpont Morgan Library

It is thus apparent that the young poet began experimenting early with attempts in the noblest genres, in translation, and in themes of interest to the family group; such as retirement, saint's legends, or satire on anti-Catholic writers. The first published of these early efforts were a modernization of Chaucer's 'Merchant's Tale', the 'Episode of Sarpedon' from the *Iliad*, and, more important, the 'Pastorals'. These pieces appeared in volume vi of Tonson's (or, as it is sometimes called, Dryden's) Miscellany.[1] The 'Pastorals' were a frank imitation of classical models in accord with seventeenth-century theories of the genre. There was a popular notion among critics that the pastoral is a natural mode for a young man to use in his first wooing of the muses: Virgil had begun that way, and possibly Milton too, among other moderns.[2] The exact date of composition of Pope's 'Pastorals' is difficult to determine; there were four of the poems, and they were not all written at once. We know that in April 1706 Tonson had seen and wished to publish at least one of them which had been approved already by Walsh, Congreve, and 'the best judges in poetry'. 'Autumn' was not circulated among these judges before the end of the year,[3] but it is probable that all four were waiting for the press[4] before Tonson was ready (1709) to bring out his Miscellany. When the poems appeared, 'Spring', 'Summer', and 'Autumn' were respectively inscribed to Sir William Trumbull, Dr. (later Sir Samuel) Garth, and Wycherley. 'Winter' was inscribed, at Walsh's request, to the memory of his friend Mrs. Tempest, whose death had been the occasion of more than one poem. Such publication certainly constituted a dignified and assured entry to the world of letters; but it is possible that the poet's distinguished friends had commended excessively these youthful efforts. Their praise

[1] *Poetical Miscellanies: The Sixth Part.* . . . London, Printed for Jacob Tonson. . . . 1709.
[2] Spence, p. 278.   [3] Elwin-Courthope, vi. 55.
[4] Bridges writes to Sir William Trumbull (28 October 1707), 'He [Pope] designs in the spring to print . . . his Pastorals.' See *Hist. MSS. Comm.: Report on the MSS. of the Marquess of Downshire,* i. ii (1924), 853.

before publication, coupled with the preference which writers for periodicals expressed for the Pastorals of Ambrose Philips (also published in Tonson's Miscellany), eventually gave Pope some uneasiness and, as we shall see, led to overt animosities in 1713 and thereafter.

Probably before the 'Pastorals' were in print Pope had started work on a more important and quite different poem, his *Essay on Criticism*. Under the influence of Walsh and other friends he had become interested in the problem as to what constituted a good critic. Since the battle between the Ancients and the Moderns, and since Blackmore's *Satyr against Wit*, .nere had been in London a quite vocal group of wits that abhorred the critic and all his works. Wycherley's preface to his *Miscellany Poems* (1704) shows his sympathy with this position, and it was of course the attitude of the popular *Tale of a Tub*. In his *Essay* Pope aimed not to be abusive but to be corrective. He wished to expose the misleading idols of the critic and to state the traits of mind essential to the true critic. The pastoral may be an easy and harmless genre for a young poet, but clearly the attempt to educate one's critics less befits the novice. On the other hand, Pope was not beguiled by any itch of originality; his method was scientific and inductive: the experience of the past could be codified into guiding rules and could show the proper temper and behaviour for the critic. In general, his object was to restate accepted wisdom (or commonplace), but to restate it in that compelling form which is the magic of true wit.

The poem was for the most part composed, if we may trust the author, in 1709. But since he acknowledged the influence of Walsh upon it, and once said the poem was shown to Walsh,[1] it may be that parts of it were written before or during the visit to Walsh at Abberley in 1707. According to tradition the poem when published in May 1711 attracted little attention;[2] but it may well be that

---

[1] Spence, p. 194.

[2] This tradition finds late expression in Warton's edition of Pope's *Works* (1797), i. xviii. The Lewis-Warton story would be more convincing if Warton

such tradition dates from the time when Addison's friends wished Pope's reputation to date from the praise of the *Essay* in *Spectator* No. 253. Walsh had died in 1708, and Wycherley was perhaps temporarily estranged; but with such sponsors as Congreve, Garth, and others, anything by Pope should not have gone entirely unobserved. The neatness of his epigrammatic couplets alone would and doubtless did win quotation; but the sort of vogue that is shown by popular quotation of a poem on literary criticism seldom develops overnight. Addison's praise seven months after publication was without doubt a great help.

If the general doctrine of the poem was inoffensive, certain specific lines were not so. One passage was the small beginning of great woes. In urging that the critic should give helpful advice freely in spite of the danger of giving offence, Pope inserted an incautious personal illustration:

> Fear not the anger of the wise to raise;
> Those best can bear reproof, who merit praise.
> 'Twere well might critics still this freedom take:
> But Appius reddens at each word you speak,
> And stares tremendous, with a threatening eye,
> Like some fierce tyrant in old tapestry.[1]

'Appius' was easily recognized as John Dennis (1657-1734). His tragedy *Appius and Virginia* had failed in 1709, and he was notorious for his frequent use of the word *tremendous* as well as for his fierce scowling. Dennis's retort, published less than six weeks after Pope's *Essay*, fully justified the truth if not the wisdom of Pope's illustration. It was called *Reflections Critical and Satyrical, upon a late Rhapsody, call'd An Essay upon Criticism*. The style of Dennis's satirical muse was not—to borrow a phrase from himself—'like the faint Eagerness of Vinegar decay'd';[2] it was vitriol and boiling lead, served generously. Never in his long career of violent disapproval does Dennis seem to have been more

had not frequently shown a predisposition towards thinking that poems win their way slowly. Pope had excellent and active 'backers' in 1711.

[1] Lines 582–7.

[2] *An Essay on the Genius and Writings of Shakespear: with some Letters of Criticism to the Spectator* (1712, published November 1711), p. 51.

enraged; and the reasons for this superlative fury (another of his nicknames was *Furius* or *Furioso*) as well as for Pope's original attack are obscure.

The two had barely met. In his *Remarks upon Mr. Pope's Dunciad* (1729) Dennis tells us:

> At his [Pope's] first coming to Town, he was very importunate with the late Mr. *Henry Cromwell* to introduce him to me: The Recommendation of Mr. *Cromwell* engaged me to be about thrice in Company with him; after which I went into the Country, and neither saw him nor thought of him 'till I found myself most insolently attack'd by him, in his very superficial Essay upon Criticism, which was the effect of his impotent Envy and Malice, by which he endeavour'd to destroy the Reputation of a man who had publish'd Pieces of Criticism, and set up his own.[1]

Suspicion as well as irascibility was a quality from which Dennis suffered often, and his theory as to Pope's purpose does not convince one. It is, in fact, notable that Pope does not satirize Dennis as a critic, but as a playwright who cannot endure criticism. The explanation ordinarily given for the attack is that Dennis had spoken ill of Pope's 'Pastorals'. This may be true, but there is no evidence that he did so except his calling Pope in the *Reflections* 'an eternal writer of amorous pastoral madrigals'—which, coming after the fact, is hardly evidence. Lines from the *Epistle to Dr. Arbuthnot* have been cited frequently as evidence:

> Soft were my numbers; who could take offense,
> While pure Description held the place of Sense?
> Like gentle *Fanny's* was my flowery theme,
> A painted mistress, or a purling stream.
>
> .   .   .   .
>
> Yet then did Dennis rave in furious fret.[2] . . .

But these clearly refer to Belinda in the *Rape of the Lock* as the 'painted mistress' and to the Lodona episode of *Windsor Forest* as the 'purling stream'. On these two poems Dennis made attacks; concerning the 'Pastorals', so far as

[1] p. 39.   [2] Lines 147–50, 154.

we know, he said nothing before 1711; and whatever unpleasant things one may say about Dennis, one must say
that he was honest (except when too blind with rage to
be himself) and brave, and that he did not talk obscurely
behind one's back. He put his name on his title-pages.

The truth is that before his 'Pastorals' were printed,
Pope was one of those who saw the uncouth and eccentric
qualities of Dennis, and did not see the good qualities. In
1707 in a rhyming epistle sent to Cromwell,[1] Pope made
a casual uncomplimentary mention of Dennis, and he may
have learned from others to think lightly of Dennis's
abilities.

Dennis was a critic of the school of Rymer, and on the
whole a distinguished member of the school. It was his
misfortune to be a despondent critic: in his days England
was not being 'Americanized' by the cinematograph, but
it was being 'Italianized' by the opera. Through this vagary
Dennis arrived at the axiom that opera had so far destroyed
taste in England that such a quality was practically non-
existent. The despondent attitude is not uncommon
among critics, but the courage with which Dennis sprang
to attack any work that the taste of his day notably commended is almost unparalleled. There is an honesty of
effort and, above all, a vigour and directness of style that
one must now admire. In a sense he was an inferior Dr.
Johnson born before his time. He had much of Johnson's
eccentricity, but lacked his good nature and most of his
good sense. Personal eccentricity had won him notoriety
before he came to be attacked by Pope. In *A Comparison
between the two Stages* (1702) his excessive fondness for the
word *tremendous* is noted,[2] and Swift had attacked him in
1704 in *A Tale of a Tub*.[3] The classic anecdote about the
'stolen thunder'[4] as well as the later story Swift printed
about the French privateer[5] may be unauthentic, but they

---

[1] Elwin-Courthope, vi. 64.   [2] p. 37.

[3] In the 'Digression concerning Critics'.

[4] Elwin-Courthope, iv. 332.

[5] Swift's *Works*, ed. Hawkesworth (1766), xii (or xxii), 272. The anecdote is
perhaps first printed here. It was evidently current as early as 1711 when the

passed current, and with dozens of others helped to make Dennis ridiculous. Steele had been an early friend, but by the time he began the *Tatler* he probably had ceased to be such. Dennis at least imagined himself frequently attacked in these essays, and he was definitely mentioned in No. 42 (16 July 1709). If he was attacked in *Tatler* No. 246, as he said[1] he was, it must be as the 'fat fellow . . . wearing his breast open in the midst of winter, out of an affectation of youth'. There were apparently many slurs on critics that he took to himself,[2] some of which seem definitely personal and caustic. In July 1710 he wrote to Steele[3] complaining of Steele's unfriendly failure to reply to a letter, and from then they ceased to expect civility from each other. Although Addison wrote most of the papers in the *Tatler* and *Spectator* which Dennis found offensive, Steele took and was allowed to take such blame as Dennis bestowed. The critic's reaction to *Spectator* No. 47 (24 April 1711), in his *Essay on . . . Shakespear*, printed seven months later, is sufficient to show how insanely sensitive and suspicious he was.[4] His fury at Pope's lines in the *Essay on Criticism* is to be viewed in the light of his belief that there was a conspiracy to destroy his reputation as a literary man. The poem appeared on 15 May, and coming apparently independent of the subversive attacks of the *Tatler* and *Spectator* increased Dennis's rage and suspicion.

Pope may have thought Dennis a popular person to illustrate poetic touchiness. If so, he probably got the idea from current talk about Dennis based on slurs in the *Tatler*. It may have come to him earlier from Walsh, whose elegance contrasted with the slovenliness and roughness of Dennis. In his *Reflections* Dennis speaks of Walsh's relations

anonymous *Critical Specimen* [of the History of the Renown'd Rinaldo Furioso] appeared. See p. 15. It is reprinted in later editions of Swift; e.g. Temple Scott ed., i. 284. For other anecdotes of Dennis see *Joe Miller's Jests* (1739), p. 47 and *passim*.

[1] *Essay on . . . Shakespear*, p. 50.

[2] *Tatler*, Nos. 29, 42. 165, 246; *Spectator*, Nos. 47, 70, 74. See Dennis's *Essay on . . . Shakespear*, pp. 38–66, or his *Original Letters* (1721), pp. 166–93, 407–16.

[3] See *Original Letters* (1721), pp. 28–9 (28 July 1710).

[4] pp. 52–61.

with Pope, and his conception of Walsh seems not too complimentary:

I had the good Fortune to know Mr. *Walsh* very well; who was a learned, candid, judicious Gentleman. But he had by no means the Qualifications which this Author reckons absolutely necessary to a Critick; it being certain that Mr. *Walsh* was like this Essayer a very indifferent Poet; but he was a Man of a very good Understanding, in spight of his being a Beau. He lov'd to be well dress'd, as *Dorimant* says, and thought it no Disparagement to his Understanding; and I remember a little young Gentleman, with all the Qualifications which we have found to be in this Author [i.e. the anonymous author of the *Essay on Criticism*], whom Mr. *Walsh* us'd sometimes to take into his Company as a double Foil to his Person, and his Capacity.[1]

Obviously there are various grounds on which Pope's attack on Dennis can be explained, but since the passage is so perfectly in the line which Swift, Steele, and Addison had taken, one judges that Pope, substantially unacquainted with the critic, merely stated the hearsay reputation of the man. Dennis's response is evidence that Pope had spoken justly but mildly.

No more cruel review ever greeted a young beginner than these *Reflections upon an Essay upon Criticism*. It is true that they enabled Pope to improve various lines of the poem, but considered as an intellectual product the *Reflections* are Dennis at his worst. He finds Pope's poem bad beneath contempt: and he stoops to say so in thirty violent pages. Pope's ability is thought unequal to his rashly undertaken task; while he 'affects the Dictatorian Air', he plainly shows himself a mere schoolboy. Like a schoolboy he borrows 'both from the Living and Dead'. He frequently contradicts himself, doesn't know his own mind, and is 'almost perpetually in the wrong'. In more specific charges the critic is equally rigorous. So innocent a commonplace as

Let such teach others who themselves excel;
And censure freely who have written well—

[1] pp. 28–9.

which Addison had stated in *Tatler* No. 239, is elaborately
and contemptuously refuted. The apostrophe to the
Ancients (lines 181–200) is said to pay servile deference to
them. One need not admire *every* ancient poet, so we are
told, and Pope's *each* in the line

> Still green with bays each ancient altar stands

makes him servilely fond of all, including Lycophron,
Nonnus, Apollonius Rhodius, and others, whom Dennis
names, and thinks inferior to Milton! The confused and
ambiguous expression of various passages is castigated,
properly enough at times, but the tone is never that of a
critic but always that of a man in a rage. This rage bursts
forth when Dennis remarks: 'As there is no Creature in
Nature so venomous, there is nothing so stupid and so
impotent as a hunch-back'd Toad.' The last paragraph of
the pamphlet indulges the full-organ tones of personal
abuse—justified, Dennis said, by Pope's having begun the
personalities:

And now if you have a mind to enquire between *Sunning-Hill*
and *Ockingham*, for a young, squab, short Gentleman, with the
forementioned Qualifications, an eternal Writer of Amorous Pastoral Madrigals, and the very bow of the God of Love, you will
be soon directed to him. And pray as soon as you have taken a
Survey of him, tell me whether he is a proper Author to make
personal Reflections on others; and tell him if he does not like my
Person, 'tis because he is an ungrateful Creature, since his Conscience tells him, that I have been always infinitely delighted with
his: So delighted, that I have lately drawn a very graphical Picture
of it; but I believe I shall keep the *Dutch* Piece from ever seeing
the Light, as a certain old Gentleman in *Windsor-Forest* would
have done by the Original, if he durst have been half as impartial
to his own Draught as I have been to mine. This little Author
may extol the Ancients as much and as long as he pleases, but he
has reason to thank the good Gods that he was born a Modern.
For had he been born of *Graecian* Parents, and his Father by consequence had by Law had the absolute Disposal of him, his Life
had been no longer than that of one of his Poems, the Life of half
a day. Instead of setting his Picture to show, I have taken a keener
Revenge, and expos'd his Intellectuals, as duly considering that let

the Person of a Gentleman of his Parts be never so contemptible, his inward Man is ten times more ridiculous; it being impossible that his outward Form, tho' it should be that of downright Monkey, should differ so much from human Shape, as his immaterial unthinking part does from human Understanding.[1]

Lintot had shown Pope the *Reflections*, so we are told,[2] before they were printed. Thus warned, he went to the Forest, and did not face the town at their publication. He naturally enough pretended to feel only amusement at Dennis's fury and only contempt for his personalities. Of course it was mere pretence: being human, Pope must have been enraged at the unjust brutality of the attack. Most people of that day would have agreed with Dennis when he wrote to Steele that 'no Man can have an Obligation strong enough laid on him to make him pass by a Box on the Ear, or the being expos'd in Print, without returning each of th' Affronts in Kind'.[3] Certainly a man of Pope's alleged irritability would not be likely to suffer patiently in silence; but so far as is known Pope himself made no immediate reply.

Pope decided, so he told Caryll,[4] not to retort; but there did appear a neglected and possibly negligible reply in a sixteen-page octavo entitled the *Critical Specimen. . . . London: Printed· in the Year, 1711.* This is a pretended advertisement of a forthcoming work to be called 'The Mirror of Criticisme: or, The History of the Renown'd Rinaldo Furioso, Critick of the Woful Countenance'. The pamphlet alludes once or twice to the *Reflections Critical and Satyrical upon... An Essay upon Criticism*, but it is a burlesque upon Dennis and his career in general rather than an obvious retort to the attack on Pope. In its biographical aspects it foreshadows in some details the *Memoirs of Scriblerus*, and in invention it has also a remote relationship to the *Art of Political Lying*. It stresses the failures of Dennis as a dramatist, and alludes casually to remarks in the *Tatler* and *Spectator* in such a way as to suggest, perhaps

[1] p. 29.
[2] Elwin-Courthope, vi. 123.
[3] *Essay on . . . Shakespear*, p. 66.
[4] Elwin-Courthope, vi. 154.

intentionally, that Steele is the author. On the other hand, it makes deft use of bits from *A Tale of a Tub*, and contrives at times, perhaps intentionally, to sound like Swift. *Aut Pope aut diabolus* was likely the verdict of Dennis, but there seems to be no sufficient evidence to determine the award of the pamphlet either to Pope or to any one of his friends.

The immediate consequence of the vehemence of Dennis was that Pope gained new friends and supporters. Old friends seemed to choose him rather than Dennis, where choice was necessary. Cromwell spent some time with Pope at Binfield; in the autumn Wycherley was again writing to Pope, and throughout the year Caryll was most kind. Steele, who could sympathize as a fellow sufferer, did Pope the compliment to request him to write some verses for Clayton to set to music; and in December, probably under Steele's influence, Addison wrote *Spectator* No. 253, which gave the *Essay* its due meed of praise and possibly a super-flux of blame. In the same month Gay, another recent friend, sent Pope a poem containing a compliment to him,[1] and four months later with exquisite irony Gay dedicated his piece the *Mohocks* to Dennis in a fashion doubtless pleasing to Pope. The dedication in part reads as follows:

There are several Reasons which induce me to lay this Work at Your Feet: The Subject of it is *Horrid* and *Tremendous*, and the whole Piece written according to the exactest Rules of Dramatick Poetry, as I have with great care collected them from several of your elaborate Dissertations.

The World will easily perceive that the Plot of it is form'd upon that of *Appius* and *Virginia*, which Model, indeed, I have in great measure follow'd throughout the whole Conduct of the Play. . . .

As we look upon you to have the Monopoly of *English* Criticism in your Head, we hope you will very shortly chastise the Insolence of the *Spectator*, who has lately had the *Audaciousness* to show that there are more Beauties than Faults in a Modern Writer.

I am not at all concern'd at this *Tragedy's* being rejected by the Players, when I consider how many of your immortal Compositions have met with no better Reception. . . .

---

[1] 'Verses to be prefix'd before Bernard Lintot's New Miscellany', lines 80–5. See Elwin-Courthope, vi. 130.

The latter half of 1711 was spent in the Forest. Pope declined invitations to London, and was, as he wrote to Cromwell in December, charmed by 'two of the finest faces in the universe':[1] interest and ambition could not tempt him from them. The Misses Blount were probably as efficacious as Gay's compliments in helping the poet to forget Dennis.

The retirement from London during these months had placed Pope in a world quite removed from Will's, in one that was occupied with Catholic hopes and fears and gossip. Apparently from Caryll and Thomas Southcote he learned that the *Essay on Criticism* contained passages offensive to certain Catholics. The praise of Erasmus, following the disparagement of the medieval monks as ignorant, naturally displeased;[2] and it even to-day makes one wonder how widely the poet had read in the books of polemic divinity which his father had inherited from Anglican parents. Pope felt it wise to change 'dull believers' in line 428 to 'plain believers', and he argued (in the face of evident obscurity) against a heterodox interpretation of lines 394–407. It is an interesting passage:

> Some foreign writers, some our own dispise;
> The ancients only or the moderns prize:
> Thus wit, like faith, by each man is apply'd
> To one small sect, and all are damn'd beside.
> Meanly they seek the blessing to confine,
> And force that sun but on a part to shine
> Which not alone the southern wit sublimes,
> But ripens spirits in cold northern climes;
> Which from the first has shone on ages past,
> Enlights the present, and shall warm the last;
> Though each may feel increases or decays,
> And see now clearer and now darker days.
> Regard not then if wit be old or new,
> But blame the false, and value still the true.

The passage may seem to demonstrate Dennis's contention that the young poet did not know his own mind. Pope in combating the idol of provincialism intends to assert that

---

[1] Elwin-Courthope, vi. 128. [2] Ibid. vi. 145–54.

true wit, like true faith, has a universal and eternal validity; but, as frequently happens, his mind is caught by an analogy, and he follows it until he seems to say that just as no one nation or climate can engross to itself all wit, so no one religious body can claim a monopoly of true faith. His language certainly smacks of deism. His defence of the passage is also somewhat typical of his mental processes. He first writes to Caryll (18 June 1711) that there is a period after line 397, and that 'they', being plural, must refer back to 'some'. The objections, however, continued, and on 19 July 1711 he wrote Caryll a somewhat formal defence, in which, while reasserting the dead stop at line 397, he also asserts that his charge against the Roman Catholic Church has, after all, justice in it and that nothing is gained by denying incidental errors not inherent in the constitution of the Church. Since this is almost Pope's first statement of the 'native moderation' of which he was to be so proud—and justly proud—throughout his career, one paragraph at least deserves quotation:

I have ever thought the best piece of service one could do to our religion was openly to expose our detestation and scorn of all those artifices and *piae fraudes* which it stands so little in need of, and which have laid it under so great a scandal among the enemies. Nothing has been so much a scarecrow to them as the too peremptory and seemingly uncharitable assertion of an utter impossibility of salvation to all but ourselves, invincible ignorance excepted, which indeed some people define under so great limitations and with such exclusions, that it seems as if that word were rather invented as a salvo or expedient, not to be thought too bold with the thunderbolts of God (which are hurled about so freely almost on all mankind by the hands of the ecclesiastics) than as a real exceptive to almost universal damnation. For besides the small number of the truly faithful in our church, we must again subdivide, and the Jansenist is damned by the Jesuit, the Jesuit by the Jansenist, the strict Scotist by the Thomist, &c. There may be errors, I grant, but I cannot think them of such consequence as to destroy utterly the charity of mankind—the very greatest bond in which we are engaged by God to one another as Christians.[1]

[1] Elwin-Courthope, vi. 150.

But Pope's preoccupation during these months was not defence of poems already printed; he was busy preparing for the press various small pieces and one masterpiece, the *Rape of the Lock*, and early in 1712 these various poems began to appear. In Tonson's *Ovid's Epistles* (18 March 1712) was included Pope's excellent version of *Sappho to Phaon*,[1] a forerunner of *Eloisa to Abelard* and the *Unfortunate Lady*. From the days of his self-education Pope had a fondness for translation, of which his friends could not cure him. In December 1711, Cromwell urged him to 'Leave elegy and translation to the inferior class, on whom the Muses only glance now and then'.[2] He wished Pope to essay tragedy, 'the greater poetry', and thus foil Dennis in drama as in criticism. Pope, however, lacked dramatic gift, but he had the imitative abilities necessary for a successful translator. These gave him an even more brilliant success than *Sappho to Phaon* in his next publication, *Messiah*, which appeared in the *Spectator* for 14 May 1712. This, one imagines, was hastily executed in the design of pleasing Steele and perhaps such Catholics as had begun to regard Pope's gifts as heterodox if not ungodly. The poem is certainly one of the best to be printed in the *Spectator*, and it must have aided Pope's reputation for virtue and piety as much as it did his fame as a poet. The eloquent and, at times, too grandiose style is an interesting contrast with the elegiac softness of his version of Ovid.

A week after *Messiah* appeared, Lintot published a volume entitled *Miscellaneous Poems and Translations*, which contained, scattered through it, seven new pieces by Pope. The volume began with his translation of the First Book of the *Thebais*, as they then called the poem. Statius had been an early favourite with Pope, and to excuse his taste he at times said this version was 'made almost in his childhood'.[3] Much of it, however, was done after 1709,

---

[1] *Ovid's Epistles Translated by Several Hands* . . . Printed for Jacob Tonson. 1712. The manuscript of 'Sappho to Phaon' was inscribed by Pope, 'Written first in 1707'; but of course he polished it later. Elwin-Courthope, i. 90.

[2] Ibid. vi. 128.   [3] Ibid. i. 43; vi. 73. Cf. Spence, p. 278.

when he submitted the earlier parts to the criticism of Cromwell. In its finished form it presents, after *Sappho to Phaon* and *Messiah*, a third tone in versification and style that is experimentally interesting. A second piece of translation by Pope in this volume is the *Fable of Vertumnus and Pomona* from Ovid. This fable is followed by Pope's first printed epistle in verse, *To a Young Lady* [Martha Blount] *with the Works of Voiture*. It was very likely finished in December 1711, when in a letter to Cromwell, as in the poem, Pope seems affected by the celebrated blue eyes of Miss Patty.[1] The poem seems for Pope relatively unpolished, but it reflects to some extent the elegant and artificial effect of Voiture's letters, not merely on the literary style of Pope and his generation but upon their lives and manners. The epistle is from the same world as the *Rape of the Lock*, to which it has parallels in ideas and phrasing. The first form of the *Rape*, in two cantos, without the sylphs, is also found in this Miscellany, and it is an interesting product of this period of abstention from town life after Dennis's attack, a period when he was influenced by Caryll and other Catholic friends rather than by his coffee-house companions. Caryll's relative, Lord Petre, had caused a quarrel between his family and that of Mrs. Arabella Fermor by cutting off a favourite curl of the lady's. Caryll wished Pope to burlesque the episode so that all concerned would see it as too trivial to quarrel over. Pope was, perhaps naturally, kinder to the Caryll faction than to Miss Arabella and her friends, and the poem, according to tradition, was not well received by the lady. Its public reception was doubtless enthusiastic.

Three smaller pieces by Pope in Lintot's Miscellany were a poem *On Silence* (in imitation of the Earl of Rochester's *On Nothing*), *Verses design'd to be prefix'd to Mr. Lintot's Miscellany*, and twenty-four lines *To the Author of a Poem entitled 'Successio'* [Elkanah Settle]. The imitation of

---

[1] Elwin-Courthope, vi. 128. This same letter foreshadows the lines 'To a Lady with the *Temple of Fame*', which were probably sent to Miss Blount in 1715, and first printed in 1727.

Rochester is distinctly inferior to the famous lines *On Nothing*, but it is amusing. It shows Pope's struggle for faith in the wisdom of silence in the months after Dennis's fulminations. Curiously enough it fails just where Pope is usually strongest—in versification: the sustained strength and dignity of Rochester's triplets become flatly monotonous in Pope. The lines on Settle are a rather dull satire on dullness; their interest now lies in the possible inference from them that Pope was ready to publish his hostility to the Hanoverian succession. None of these pieces published by Lintot was discreditable, but only the exquisite *Rape of the Lock* was destined to add materially to his fame.

The rest of the year 1712 was a very quiet one for Pope. Indeed, his health in the spring, while the Miscellany was in the press, seems to have been bad, and in November, after cold weather set in, he spent his days 'lolling on an arm-chair, nodding . . . over a fire, like the picture of January in an old Salisbury Primer'.[1] His whereabouts in the preceding summer are less certain because of probable changes in plans not set down in his published letters. Caryll's son was to be married in July, and Pope was to accompany the young couple to Ladyholt when they returned to that parental roof. It is quite possible, however, that he visited Ladyholt in June and returned thence to London in July. Caryll's uncle, the Jacobite baron and Secretary of State to the Pretender, had died in September 1711, and sometime during the latter part of the summer of 1712 Caryll went to France to settle the estate. Such journeys were naturally matters of suspicion to Hanoverians, and the *Flying Post*, which was violently Hanoverian, apparently commented on Caryll in a fashion that irritated Pope almost to the point of a reply. Throughout this year and later Caryll and Pope were allies in the cause of a Mrs. Weston,[2] who was, as they thought, badly treated by her husband and by her guardian. Doubtless they meant well,

---

[1] Ibid. vi. 173.

[2] *Athenaeum*, 15 July 1854, pp. 876–9. Reprinted in C. W. Dilke's *Papers of a Critic*, vol. i. See esp. pp. 130–4.

but no real good seems to have come from their inter-
ference, except the possible inspiration the unfortunate
woman gave Pope for a later elegy. Pope's relatives and
neighbours disapproved heartily of his concern in Mrs.
Weston's affairs.

It had been a year of great political turmoil. From the 1st
of January when the twelve new peers were named to make
a majority for peace, and when it was announced that 'His
Grace the Duke of Marlborough is remov'd from all his
Places', on to a November made thrilling by the 'band-box
plot' on the 4th and the Hamilton-Mohun duel on the
18th, there was plenty of excitement. The lions in the
Tower died—sure presage of revolution! Prince Eugene
came and went, with nothing gained for the Allies by his
visit. Young Whigs as Mohocks terrorized the streets
by night—at least the Tories said they did—and on
3 October, the birthday of the Electress Sophia, crowds
in Bloomsbury Square and elsewhere made night hideous
with their song of 'Over, over, Hanover over!' Pope's
newer friends of the Tory persuasion were engrossed in
political writing. Addison and Steele, their party out of
power, were mainly engaged in the one great literary
achievement of the year, the *Spectator*. Even the *Spectator*
was not entirely free from politics; but it was almost
entirely free, and it represented the best and the ablest
literary achievement at the moment. It is then natural that
Pope, even if Addison and Steele hardly hated the *Flying
Post* as he did, should frequent the newly opened coffee-
house of Daniel Button with these authors. He contributed
to the *Spectator*, No. 378, his *Messiah*, and in No. 532 a letter
concerning Hadrian's verses in apostrophe of his soul. Mr.
Spectator in return made Pope and Lintot's Miscellany a
compliment on 30 October, and in the valedictory number
of 6 December gave him rather surprising thanks as a chief
helper in the periodical. He is thought to have contributed
unidentified essays.[1]

[1] Probably his unidentified contributions consist of letters sent to the editors
(Steele and Addison); used by them, sometimes with only brief introductions, and

During the year 1712 Pope also prepared for the press certain literary remains (*Chaucer's Characters*) of his friend Betterton, and worked on his own adaptation of the *Hous of Fame* and on *Windsor Forest*. The poem last named was remade to fit the political situation. A part of it had been written, so Pope said, as early as 1704.[1] This section, suggested by Sir William Trumbull, was an imitation of Denham's *Cooper's Hill*. Another part was now added at the suggestion of Lord Lansdowne, the Secretary at War, in honour of the Peace of Utrecht. The negotiation of this peace was completed in September, and as early as November poems on the subject began to appear. On 30 October the *Spectator* ordered the expectant poets to avoid on this occasion the cant of classical mythology, and took the chance to compliment the poem *On the Prospect of Peace* by Thomas Tickell, just then published. Perhaps because it came early, perhaps because of Addison's praise or of its own merit, Tickell's poem sold probably better than any of the others written on this theme. It averaged almost an edition a month for the early months of its existence: its fourth was advertised on 13 March 1713,[2] a week after *Windsor Forest* first appeared. Pope's poem had only two editions in its first year. Sewell, Trapp, Tate, Settle, and some modestly anonymous bards were among those who sang the praises of peace during the later months of 1712 and the earlier ones of 1713.

The publication of *Windsor Forest* in March to celebrate the conclusion of a Tory peace and the presentation to the public of Pope's Prologue to *Cato* in April may symbolize the essential activities of Pope for 1713. He aspired to be non-partisan and yet to please both parties. At the early

---

signed with initials that might seem to indicate that the editor was the author. So the issue that consists of nothing but the *Messiah* has Steele's signature, 'T'; and Nos. 452 and 457, which contain letters almost certainly Pope's, are signed 'C' in the original sheets. See *supra*, pp. 74–5.

[1] It is mentioned in 1707 in a letter from Ralph Bridges to Sir William Trumbull. See *Hist. MSS. Comm.: Report on the MSS. of the Marquess of Downshire* I. ii (1924), 853. See also Pope's *Works*, i (8vo, 1736), 67 n.

[2] Adv. in the *Guardian*.

performances of *Cato* 'the prologue writer . . . was clapped into a staunch Whig, sore against his will', so Pope wrote to Caryll. George Berkeley, who on the first night was present in a side box with Addison, some friends, and 'two or three flasks of burgundy and champagne,' wrote to Percival: 'Some parts of the prologue, which were written by Mr. Pope, a Tory and even a Papist, were hissed, being thought to savour of Whiggism, but the clap got much the hiss.'[1] At this time, though known evidently as a Tory, Pope seems to have been much closer to the Whig literary men than to the Tories. Up to October he worked with Steele on the *Guardian*, to the displeasure of his Tory, Jacobite, and Catholic friends. During most of the year also he lived with a Whig, the painter Jervas, in Cleveland Court, though he doubtless made frequent journeys to Binfield.

Probably his excuse for living in London was his desire to study painting. His interest in this art may go back to childhood and to a possible attraction to it through the influence of his Aunt Cooper (his godmother), widow of Samuel Cooper the painter, whose pictures and objects of art were bequeathed first to her sister Elizabeth (who lived with the Binfield Popes till her death in 1710) and secondly to the poet. If we may trust a letter dated 1 March 1705, in Pope's self-edited correspondence,[2] Pope was at that time copying a portrait. By January 1711 he had sent the Carylls a Madonna,[3] but much of his painting seems to have been a matter of pastime for his mornings in 1713. At the end of August of that year he reports to Caryll:

They tell us, when St. Luke painted, an angel came and finished the work; and it will be thought hereafter, that when I painted, the devil put the last hand to my pieces, they are so begrimed and

---

[1] *Berkeley and Percival*, by B. Rand, pp. 113–14. In quoting I have ventured to emend *favour* to *savour*. Evidently Berkeley intended to say 'the hiss got much the clap'.   [2] Elwin-Courthope, x. 258.

[3] Ibid. vi. 140. This is certain evidence that Pope was painting, and making presents of his work, as early as 1710. The Bickerton *Life* (1744), it will be recalled, said that in Deane's school while the other boys 'were diverting themselves at such Games and Sports, as was usual with Boys of their Age, Mr. *Pope* used to amuse himself with Drawing' (p. 14).

smutted. It is, however, some mercy that I see my faults; for I have been so out of conceit with my former performances that I have thrown away three Dr. Swift's, two Duchesses of Montague, one Virgin Mary, the Queen of England, besides half a score Earls and a Knight of the Garter. I will make essays upon such vulgar subjects as these, before I grow so impudent as to attempt to draw Mr. Caryll; though I find my hand most successful in drawing of friends and those I most esteem, insomuch that my masterpieces have been one of Dr. Swift, and one of Mr. Betterton.[1]

The last known surviving work of Pope's brush is a copy of Kneller's portrait of Betterton.[2] Spence had seen 'of Mr. Pope's drawing, a grave old Chaucer, from Occleve; a Betterton; a Lucius Verus, large profile; two Turkish heads; a Janizary from the life; Antinous; and St. John praying'.[3] Pope's pleasure in painting was apparently keen, but experience of the art affected his poetry hardly more than in the occasional use of technical terms from painting.[4]

Pope must have led an active life in London; for in addition to painting and spending time with his rapidly increasing circle of acquaintance, he was working on the *Guardian*[5] and on various things of his own as well. The first of these to be printed was the *Ode for Musick* (July 1713), one of Pope's least successful poems. In an edition of his *Works* published in 1736 there appeared under the title of the poem the date 1708. Pope told Spence that it was written at the request of Steele, and he was almost certainly unacquainted with Steele in 1708. If these were the words Pope wrote for Clayton upon Steele's request of 26 July 1711,[6] they may well have been completed in a first form before 1713. Even later (1730), when the poem was revised and set to music for the Commencement at Cambridge, it seems not to have evoked much comment.

---

[1] Ibid. vi. 193.

[2] W. T. Whitley, in his *Artists and their Friends in England from 1709–1799* (The Medici Society, 1928, i. 42–3), thinks this copy from Kneller is too skilful to be Pope's work; but Whitley much underestimates the time Pope gave to painting.   [3] Spence, p. 336.

[4] *Spectator*, cxxxiii (1919), 364–5, 'Pope and the Technicalities of the Arts.' The subject deserves further study.

[5] Elwin-Courthope, vi. 183.   [6] Ibid. vi. 387.

In July, two years after Dennis's attack on the *Essay on Criticism*, Pope found his chance for a counter-attack. Pope loved to work under advice, and with allies. In 1711, when every one had advised him to leave Dennis alone, he had subsided—though his instinct then as later prompted retort. In the summer of 1713 came a good opportunity, with probable encouragement from an ally. Dennis's disbelief in the taste of his day had found grounds for rage in the excessive praise Addison (whom he did not love) got for *Cato*. In certain respects—poetic justice, for example —the tragedy did not accord with the rules, and most of these heterodox details had, so Dennis and others thought, been quietly defended in advance in the *Tatler* or *Spectator*. Somewhat naturally Dennis thought the whole business of bringing on the play was tinged with private cabal and the spirit of political party, and he was genuinely revolted at hearing the piece called a *literary* success. Consequently, after urging by friends, he wrote and allowed Lintot to publish on 11 July his *Remarks upon the Tragedy of Cato*. He was keenly alive to the unwisdom of his course. He says, 'I pass for a man who is conceitedly resolved to like nothing which others like',[1] and certainly his attack on *Cato*, though restrained and quiet in tone, must have cost Dennis much of whatever esteem the public had previously kept for him as a critic. The Duke of Buckinghamshire, and possibly Congreve, had tried to dissuade Dennis from publication, but Lintot was solicitous to print. Dennis said later that Pope teased Lintot to act in the matter; at any rate Lintot's arguments, probably monetary, and Dennis's conviction in his opinions outweighed the advice of the Duke. On 19 June Dennis had written His Grace that he had 'never yet resolved to publish those Remarks',[2] but a week later Lintot concluded one of his newspaper advertisements thus: 'And in a few days will be Published, Remarks on the Tragedy of Cato, written by Mr. Dennis.'[3]

---

[1] *Remarks on Cato* (1713), p. 3.   [2] *Original Letters* (1721), p. 55.
[3] *Daily Courant*, 26 June 1713. Advertised ibid., 11 July 1713, as 'This Day is Published'.

It is quite possible that Pope, having heard the critic's tremendous oral fulminations against *Cato*, had been convulsed with mirth, and had exclaimed, 'If only the old fool would put them in print, all the world would see how absurd and mad he is!' And he may have suggested to Lintot (who had printed the *Reflections* of Dennis on the *Essay on Criticism*) that Dennis's observations on *Cato* would have a good sale. The only 'evidence', however, came from Dennis himself when again in a rage with Pope: in his *True Character of Mr. Pope* (1716) Dennis hints at such a 'conspiracy' and amplifies the charge in a fashion that all the Dunces were later to adopt. Addressing himself to an unidentified 'Friend', Dennis expresses his apprehension that it was Pope

who endeavour'd to expose you in a *Billingsgate* Libel, at the very time that you were doing him a Favour at his own earnest Desire, who attempted to undermine Mr. *PHILIPS* in one of his *Guardians*, at the same time that the *Crocodile* smil'd on him, embrac'd him, and called him Friend, who wrote a Prologue in praise of CATO, and teaz'd *Lintott* to publish Remarks upon it; who at the same time, that he openly extoll'd Sir *Richard Steele* in the highest manner, secretly publish'd the Infamous Libel of Dr. *Andrew Tripe* upon him.[1]

Let us pass for the moment all these indictments (except the one concerning the *Remarks*) with the statement that the accusation with regard to Steele is false and that the others at least slightly misrepresent the facts. Pope may have 'teaz'd Lintot to publish Remarks' by Dennis. If he did so, it was with no idea in the world that Dennis's frothings would in any way injure Addison or that Pope could get Addison attacked and then, seeming to come to his defence, vent his own spleen on Dennis. This is what Dennis wished to imply and what some writers on Pope have accepted as the truth. There is no evidence that Pope teased Lintot except in Dennis's charge, coupled with other charges, some of which are clearly false. But if Pope did, it was because he had what he thought was a clever idea of

[1] p. 6.

advertising to the world the insanity of Dennis as a critic. There is no evidence that by July 1713 Pope and Addison were so hostile that Pope would enjoy seeing Addison attacked; and Pope had no reason to fear that Dennis's attack would hurt the high repute of *Cato*. If Dennis had written more excitedly against *Cato*, the jest would have been better; but whatever he wrote, his reputation for rage would be adequate for the retort that was *possibly* planned in advance.

Pope's idea—if it was his—came from an advertisement that had been appearing intermittently in the newspapers for some time. It appeared, for example, as follows in the *Postman* of 25 December 1711:

> Robert Norris at the Pestle and Mortar on Snow Hill, having been many years experienc'd in the Care of Lunaticks, hath Conveniencies and suitable Attendance at his own House for either Sex; any Person applying themselves to him as above, may have unquestionable satisfaction that the Cure shall be speedily and industriously endeavour'd and (by God's Blessing effected) on reasonable Terms.

This unctuous morsel had been often reprinted and so had been long in the eye of the public, and of Alexander Pope. During the ten days after Dennis's *Remarks upon the Tragedy of Cato* were published, the advertisement is significantly printed twice in the *Guardian*.[1] This should mean that Steele was in the plot. At any rate, after having recalled to the minds of the public the cures which could by Robert Norris be 'speedily and industriously endeavour'd and (by God's Blessing effected) on reasonable Terms', the conspirators advertised in the *Post Boy* for 28 July 1713:

> This Day is Publish'd.
>
> The Narrative of Dr. *Robert Norris*, concerning the strange and deplorable Frenzy of Mr. *John Denn-s*, an Officer of the Custom House; being an exact Account of all that pass'd betwixt the said Patient and the Doctor, till this present Day; and a full Vindication of himself and his Proceedings from the Extravagant Reports

---

[1] For 18 and 20 July. It was later printed there on 13 and 14 August and 18 and 19 September.

of the said Mr. *John Denn-s.* Printed for J. Morphew, near
Stationers-Hall. Price 3d.

The only retort one could make to Dennis when he wrote
as he had done about the *Essay on Criticism* was: 'The
man's a lunatic!' But this was now to be said in much the
same method as that used by Squire Bickerstaff when telling
John Partridge that he was a quack. Pope had no great
gift for such dramatic narrative: Steele and some of Pope's
Tory friends had, and some of them must have helped to
produce this pamphlet. Many critics, to be sure, have
regarded the piece as malignant and dull, but these cannot
have read it in relation to its background. The *Narrative*
may be brutal, but when did John Dennis shun brutality?
Charles Lamb enjoyed the pamphlet,[1] and hence the rest
of us need not feel that we lay ourselves open to charges of
being unduly malicious if we confess enjoyment of it. If
Pope is the sole author, it is one of the liveliest pieces of
prose he ever wrote. The mind may be that of Pope, but
the voice is that of some friend. Of Pope's friends Steele
had best grounds of grievance against Dennis; he might
plausibly assist in inserting Norris's advertisement in the
Guardian; and he, as we shall presently see, was requested
by Addison to apologize for the pamphlet. But this is not
conclusive proof of his collaboration.

The story of the *Narrative* is as follows: On 20 July an
old woman (much after Mistress Quickly of earlier fame)
called Dr. Norris to attend her master, 'one Mr. Dennis,
an officer of the custom-house', who since April had been
ill of violent, though intermittent, frenzies.

Alas! sir, says she, this day fortnight in the morning, a poor
simple child came to him from the printer's; the boy had no sooner
entered the room but he cried out, the devil was come. He often
stares ghastfully, raves aloud, and mutters between his teeth the
word Cator, or Cato, or some such thing. Now doctor, this Cator
is certainly a witch, and my poor master is under an evil tongue;
for I have heard him say Cator has bewitched the whole nation. . . .
Upon this I went and laid out a groat for a horse-shoe, which is

[1] In 'On the Melancholy of Tailors'.

at this time nailed on the threshold of his door; but I don't find my master is at all the better for it; he perpetually starts and runs to the window when any one knocks, crying out, S'death! a messenger from the French King! I shall die in the Bastile.

Dr. Norris tells us he hastened to Dennis's lodgings 'near Charing-Cross, up three pair of stairs', where in an apartment worthy the brush of Hogarth, he found the critic in company with his printer, Mr. Lintot, and 'a grave elderly gentleman' (thought to represent Henry Cromwell). The Doctor is treated to some rant about Democritus and Aristotle and is assured that Dennis has no other ailment than a swelling in his legs.

Dr. Pray, sir, how did you contract this swelling?

Denn. By a criticism.

Dr. A criticism! that's a distemper I never heard of.

Denn. S'death, sir, a distemper! It is no distemper, but a noble art. I have sat fourteen hours a day at it; and are you a doctor, and don't know there's a communication between the legs and the brain?

Dr. What made you sit so many hours, sir?

Denn. Cato, sir.

Dr. Sir, I speak of your distemper; what gave you this tumour?

Denn. Cato, Cato, Cato.

Old Wom. For God's sake, Doctor, name not this evil spirit; it is the whole cause of his madness: alas! poor master is just falling into his fits.

Mr. Lintot. Fits! Z—— what fits! a man may well have swelling in his legs, that sits writing fourteen hours in a day. He got this by the Remarks.

Dr. The Remarks! what are those?

Denn. 'Sdeath! have you never read my remarks? I will be damned, if this dog Lintot ever published my advertisements.

Mr. Lintot. Z——! I published advertisement upon advertisement; and if the book be not read, it is none of my fault, but his that made it. By G—, as much has been done for the book, as could be done for any book in Christendom.

Dr. We do not talk of books, sir; I fear those are the fuel that feed the delirium; mention them no more. You do very ill to promote this discourse. . . .

Denn. Is all the town in a combination? Shall poetry fall to the ground? Must our reputation be lost to all foreign countries! O destruction! perdition! Opera! Opera! As poetry once raised cities, so when poetry fails, cities are overturned, and the world is no more.

Dr. He raves, he raves; Mr. Lintot, I pray you pinion down his arms, that he may do no mischief.

Denn. O I am sick, sick to death!

Dr. That is a good symptom, a very good symptom. To be sick to death (say the modern physicians) is an excellent symptom. When a patient is sensible of his pain, it is half a cure. Pray, Sir, of what are you sick?

Denn. Of every thing, of every thing. I am sick of the sentiments, of the diction, of the protasis, of the epitasis, and the catastrophe.—Alas! what is become of the drama, the drama?

Old Wom. The dram, sir! Mr. Lintot drank up all the gin just now; but I'll go fetch more presently.

Denn. O shameful want, scandalous omission! By all the immortals, here is no peripætia, no change of fortune in the tragedy; Z—— no change at all!

Old Wom. Pray, good Sir, be not angry, I'll fetch change.

Dr. Hold your peace, woman; his fit encreases; good Mr. Lintot hold him.

Mr. Lintot. Plague on 't! I'm damnably afraid, they are in the right of it, and he is mad in earnest. If he should be really mad, who the devil would buy the Remarks? (Here Mr. Lintot scratched his head.)[1]

Soon Dennis's ravings become so violent that after locking the grave gentleman in another room the Doctor binds his patient and claps a half-dozen cupping glasses on his head. The supposed apothecary bursts from the closet, cuts the critic's bandages, and in a battle of volumes in folio that ensues, the cupping glasses are broken with attendant bloodshed, and the good Doctor, Lintot, and the servants are put to utter rout—in the best farcial tradition.

Lintot imparts various anecdotes to the Doctor concerning Dennis's earlier manias, the best of which are:

That the said Mr. John Dennis, on the 27th of March 1712, finding on the said Mr. Lintot's counter a book called An Essay

---

[1] Elwin-Courthope, x. 454–7.

on Criticism, just then published, he read a page or two with much frowning, till coming to these two lines,

> Some have at first for wits, then poets past,
> Turn'd critics next, and prov'd plain fools at last.

he flung down the book in a terrible fury, and cried, By G—d he means me.

That being in his company on a certain time, when Shakespear was mentioned as of a contrary opinion to Mr. Dennis, he swore the said Shakespear was a rascal, with other defamatory expressions, which gave Mr. Lintot a very ill opinion of the said Shakespear.[1]

Norris supposedly is writing the *Narrative* to state the falsity of the various reports that Dennis circulates concerning him: that he entered Dennis's room to steal 'a new play called Coriolanus,[2] which he has had ready for the stage these four years,' or to steal other manuscripts, or that Norris is a French spy, &c. The paper concludes gravely with an implied threat that these matters might be brought into the courts, though Norris is piously forgiving and prays 'that the Lord may restore him [Dennis] to the full enjoyment of his understanding'.

On the whole the pamphlet is not bad fun. It is much lighter and defter in its malice than anything Dennis ever wrote—in fact, most of it is written in a mood of tolerant good humour which contrasts with the rage so characteristic of Dennis's *Reflections*. While the old critic is shown as thoroughly absurd, he is not shown really as an ill-natured or unlikeable person: he is simply and truly the victim of his own eccentricities. It is doubtless brutal, and unscriptural, to call any one, especially a critic, a fool; but most of us win the appellation at some time. Dennis won it often, but he was never called a fool more artistically than on this occasion.

---

[1] Elwin-Courthope, x. 459.

[2] Ibid. x. 460. Dennis's reworking of Shakespeare's play was finally performed three times in November 1719. It failed, so the managers said, to make expenses for those three performances. The failure of the play highly incensed Dennis against the managers, especially Steele, who thereupon became for two or three years Dennis's favourite object of attack. See Dennis's Preface to the *Invader of his Country* [Coriolanus] (1720) and his various attacks on the *Conscious Lovers*, &c.

Consequently Pope was, we may assume, pleased with the pamphlet. He might, one thinks, have had qualms over the treatment of Cromwell, if indeed Cromwell is the 'grave elderly gentleman' present as friend and supporter of Dennis. We can only guess that at some time after his visit to Binfield in the summer of 1711 Cromwell had offended Pope by turning partisan of Dennis. Pope's explanation to Cromwell of Dr. Norris's *Narrative* can hardly have been convincing. He wrote Caryll:

As to the whim upon Dennis, Cromwell thought me the author of it, which I assured him I was not, and we are, I hope, very far from being enemies. We still visit, criticise, and drink coffee as before. I am satisfied of his merit in all respects and am truly his friend.[1]

We must believe that Pope had at least a hand in this whim. Some of the medical details suggest Dr. Arbuthnot, of course. The *Narrative* was included in the volume of the *Miscellanies* published in 1732, and the authorship was implicity confessed by Pope in a note to a forged (?) letter to Addison dated 20 July 1713.[2] If we try charitably to assume that Pope's collaborator wrote the parts dealing with Cromwell, the assumption will hardly excuse Pope's attitude as seen in his letter to Caryll just quoted. It may be that the 'grave elderly gentleman' was never intended to represent Cromwell: it is certainly a fact that most satirists have at times felt it wise to be tactful and not truthful in disowning their literary progeny. Pope certainly denied his offspring more than once.

Another person whose reaction to this whim on Dennis was fully as important as that of Cromwell was Joseph Addison. As author of the tragedy, the success of which had occasioned the *Remarks* by Dennis and the counterblast by 'Dr. Norris', he might be suspected of conniving at this treatment of Dennis. He desired to avoid any such suspicion. The result was the following letter first printed

[1] Ibid. vi. 197.
[2] Ibid. vi. 398.

by Dennis in his *Remarks on several Passages in the Prelimi-naries to the Dunciad* (1729):

August 4, 1713

Mr. Lintot,—Mr. Addison desired me to tell you that he wholly disapproves the manner of treating Mr. Dennis in a little pamphlet by way of Dr. Norris's account. When he thinks fit to take notice of Mr. Dennis's objections to his writings, he will do it in a way Mr. Dennis shall have no just reason to complain of. But when the papers above mentioned were offered to be communicated to him, he said he could not, either in honour or conscience, be privy to such a treatment, and was sorry to hear of it. I am, sir, your very humble servant.[1]

This letter, written by Steele, is in many ways a curious performance. Why, in the first place, should Addison feel obliged to express any disapproval at all when he had himself been responsible for more than one sharp slur on Dennis in the *Spectator*? He evidently did feel desirous of being circumspect where Dennis was involved: witness his reservations in his praise of the *Essay on Criticism* in *Spectator* No. 253. One may best assume perhaps that Dennis's value to the Whig party made it inadvisable for Addison to come under suspicion of creating dissension in the ranks of party writers. But with regard to the letter under consideration one must note further that it is addressed, not to Dennis himself, as one might expect, but to Lintot, who had published the *Remarks on Cato*. And why did Addison not write the letter himself? Possibly because Steele was concerned in the authorship of the piece, though in such a case the apology could hardly seem particularly sincere. A further curious detail is the fact that Addison had knowledge of the pamphlet before it was printed. He had even then expressed disapproval. One wonders how strenuously? The highest standards of conduct would certainly demand from him either remonstrance sharp enough to prevent publication altogether, or (if after the sharpest possible decorous remonstrance, publication ensued) a severance of friendship with the offending authors. Possibly one might

---

[1] Here quoted from Elwin-Courthope, vi. 400.

before publication tell the authors that one disapproved and then after publication remain frigidly silent and take any censure that might come. But to protest formally, permit the insult, and then apologize indirectly after the fact, is hardly 'correct'. It results in something very like the behaviour of those who 'without sneering teach [at least *permit*] the rest to sneer'.

Pope was doubtless a sore trial to Addison in 1713 and Addison was the model of good form often enough, so that some lapses are humanly essential. He was astonishingly tolerant of Pope in this year, and the reason again is probably political rather than personal. Many Whigs valued Pope's abilities and wished to keep them from the Tories: Addison could help, and he tried, though the task must have been at times as unpleasant as it was eventually unprofitable. Pope and Steele were friendly enough so that Pope must have known of Steele's letter: it is rather surprising, therefore, that he and Addison remained on such terms that when in October (1713) Pope announced his intention of translating the *Iliad*, Addison was among the supporters of the project.

V

ADDISON, THE LITTLE SENATE, *ET AL.*

IN considering the decline of the friendship between Addison and Pope, it is well to keep in mind the two facts that they were never really intimate and that they never openly quarrelled. Few people in fact were truly intimate with Addison, though most people had a very high esteem for his personal and literary qualities. To close friends he was a charming companion. Pope told Spence:

Addison was perfect good company with intimates; and had something more charming in his conversation than I ever knew in any other man: but with any mixture of strangers, and sometimes only with one, he seemed to preserve his dignity much; with a stiff sort of silence.[1]

This shyness and consequent restraint not only kept him from making friends but at times from keeping them. Dignity was promptly assumed at sight of deviations from correct conduct. Even Swift, who of all Addison's contemporaries seems best to have appreciated his fine and sure sense of decorum and who was genuinely and greatly pained by the thought that a mere difference in politics had estranged them, could not brook the later cold reserve of Addison's manner. He should not have been a 'difficult' person, but more than one man found him so. In his later career he must by his increasing aloofness have hurt Steele even more than he had grieved Swift. The 'little Dicky' passage in the *Old Whig*[2] is hard to explain away. It is natural that political hangers-on, expectant place-seekers, should be irked by his coolness. Oldmixon was doubtless the most furious of this type; for Oldmixon had been a favourite of Maynwaring's, and when Addison succeeded Maynwaring as a sort of literary whip for the Whigs,

---

[1] Spence, p. 50.   [2] No. II, p. 4 (2 April 1719).

Oldmixon felt a chilling change. Even Ambrose Philips was not content with what Addison did for him; and young Thomas Burnet, though he had no right to complain, was positively brutal in his impatience and in expressing his belief that Addison kept him out of a place. Among others Dennis, Rowe, and Tonson seem to have respected but disliked the man. His chosen protégé and later editor, Thomas Tickell, was the truest and most discreet friend Addison had. About some things, as we shall see, Tickell found it best to remain silent, and it would be hard to find a period in literary history when silence was rarer or more difficult than in the early eighteenth-century days of gossip.

Addison seems to have been one of those who, perhaps from shyness or from sensitiveness to criticism, prefer to associate with intimates at least slightly inferior in position or ability. In 1712 he set up Daniel Button, a former servant, as keeper of a coffee-house in Rose Street, Covent Garden, not far from Will's. Whatever the design in this may have been, Button's coffee-house became the resort of Whig literary men or 'party writers', with Addison as the presiding genius of the place. Here he could

Like Cato give his little Senate laws,

and receive his reward in feeling free from the embarrassment of strangers. His preference of Button's to Will's probably helped him to avoid Tories, but it must have limited his intercourse with Wycherley, Congreve, and Garth, as well as with Swift, Arbuthnot, Gay, Pope, and other wits whom we now consider greater geniuses than the frequenters of Button's. At Button's the ablest poets were Philips, Tickell, Carey, and John Hughes. Budgell, Addison's cousin, who was at times mentally unbalanced and who ultimately committed suicide, was perhaps, after Addison and Steele, the best prose writer of the group. Leonard Welsted as a young man showed promise in both verse and prose; but later years did not see his genius improving. Charles Johnson was famous for writing a play a year and for being at Button's coffee-house every day in the year. The inseparable collaborators, Thomas Burnet, youngest son of the bishop, and George Duckett, were the keenest of the pamphleteers. Col. Brett, the husband of the notorious countess who insisted she was not the mother of Richard Savage, may stand as a representative courtier and man about town. Pope gave Spence the following account of Addison's manner of life in the years under consideration:

> Addison's chief companions, before he married Lady Warwick (in 1716), were Steele, Budgell, Philips, Carey, Davenant, and Colonel Brett. He used to breakfast with one or other of them, at his lodgings in Saint James's Place, dine at taverns with them, then to Button's, and then to some tavern again for supper in the evening: and this was then the usual round of his life.[1]

With these men Pope, and doubtless Gay, who was more of a Whig, mingled on friendly terms during 1712 and much of 1713. When we are surprised that Addison endured the doubtful good taste of some of Pope's escapades during this period we must remember that it was his duty as a leading Whig to attract young writers to the cause. He must have suffered more from Thomas Burnet and probably from others than he did from Pope. Burnet in his invaluable letters to Duckett has left us a caustic comment on the later stages of the Pope-Addison friendship:

> It has very often made me smile at the pitifull soul of the Man, when I have seen Addison caressing Pope, whom at the same Time he hates worse than Belzeebub & by whom he has been more than once lampooned.[2]

Such a picture need not surprise us if we recollect the basis of the friendship. It was built on no similarity of tastes or common ideals of conduct. For Pope, in his earlier years, London was an escape from the somewhat rigorous Catholic background of Binfield. One imagines that Addison and

---

[1] Spence, p. 196.
[2] 1 June 1716. Add. MS. 36772, fol. 121. In the *Letters of Thomas Burnet to George Duckett, 1712-1722* (edited by David Nichol Smith, The Roxburghe Club, 1914), p. 99.

Pope's father might have got on excellently; but Pope was impulsive and unsteady in word and deed: he was not intentionally malicious, cruel, or underhanded, but his utterance was brilliant and rash in cases when Addison's would be elegant and composed. The two had in common only their genuine interest in literature (though Pope's self-acquired knowledge of the classics must have amused the scholarly Oxonian) and their knowledge that each could be of service to the other. It is most important to remember that Addison as a party whip was not always free to cut loose from a friendship which personally he might dislike.

It seems probable also that they could have got on together except for the Little Senate. It could not be of service to Pope; and though he seems to have enjoyed some of its members and to have admired their work, he was accustomed already to more distinguished friends. The wits at Button's in turn saw Pope more and more friendly with Swift and Arbuthnot; they also saw in Lintot's Miscellany lines 'To the Author of a Poem entitled *Successio*', which darkly had Jacobite tendencies, and in 1713 *Windsor Forest* confirmed their suspicions that Pope was 'disaffected'. They doubtless wondered at Addison's preference of the little Papist. Pope, on the other hand, must have felt their growing hostility; for at first he had been ready to praise the 'Pastorals' of Philips; but by the spring of 1713 he noted the frequence with which the group praised Philips's work excessively, while they were almost totally silent as to his own 'Pastorals', which, after all, better men, such as Walsh, Wycherley, and Congreve, had found most charming.

At this juncture Pope's mind apparently began to work like that of Dennis. The Little Senate seemed to be conspiring against his reputation as a poet, or at least as a pastoral poet. We do not know what remarks on this score may have been made at Button's. Pope had in 1710 praised Philips's 'Pastorals' to Cromwell, and as late as December 1712 quoted Philips with approval to Caryll. In 1710

Philips's eclogues attained[1] (as Pope's had not done) a second edition. In the last paragraph of the Preface Philips says:

> Theocritus, Virgil, and Spencer, are the only Writers, that seem to have hit upon the true Nature of Pastoral Poems. So that it will be Honour sufficient for me, if I have not altogether fail'd in my Attempt.

Such a remark made only once should not wound; for if Pope was excluded from consideration, he was excluded amongst a large number of reputable shepherds. Apparently an excessively dignified soul, Philips was (until he became 'Namby Pamby') nicknamed 'Pastoral Philips',[2] and his poems continued to have vogue. His *Winter Piece* appeared in the *Tatler*, and his 'Pastorals' had been promptly commended in No. 10 of that periodical. Addison complimented them in *Spectator* No. 223. Philips received notice also in Nos. 229, 336, 400, and 578 of the *Spectator*. Welsted praised Philips's 'Pastorals' in his *Remarks on the English Poets* (1712); Tickell in *The Prospect of Peace* (1712) called Philips 'a second Spenser'; and Gildon later in his *Complete Art of Poetry*[3] said bluntly that in the pastoral 'most of our young Dablers in Rhime have try'd their Strength; but alas! not one besides Mr. *Philips* has hit the Mark'. Gildon further ranked Philips as 'beyond Controversy the third at least' in the *genre*. The matter had become really annoying when in the spring of 1713 the *Guardian* ran a number of papers[4] on pastoral poetry written by an unidentified contributor, possibly Tickell, who in the fashion of Philips's friends praised the pastorals of Philips and omitted to mention Pope's. For this critic only Philips counted. In No. 30 the *Guardian* says: 'It is easy to be observed that these rules are drawn from what our countrymen Spenser and Philips have performed in this way.' And in No. 32 we read: 'His

---

[1] This edition was 'Printed and Sold by H. Hills', and hence was probably a piracy.

[2] John Jortin, *Works*, xii (1790), 448.   [3] Ed. 1718, i. 157.

[4] Nos. 22, 23, 28, 30, 32. Cf. also No. 40 (by Pope). There is some evidence that the first five of these were written by Thomas Tickell. See J. E. Butt in the *Bodleian Quarterly Record*, v (December 1928), 302.

heir was called Theocritus, who left his dominions to Virgil; Virgil left his to his son Spenser; and Spenser was succeeded by his eldest-born Philips.' If English writers other than Spenser and Philips had written pastorals, this critic had apparently never heard of them.

A poet need not be excessively sensitive to criticism to be hurt at such biased neglect of his work. Pope's 'Pastorals' had been overpraised by the best judges of the day, but for the Little Senate they did not exist. His resentment at perceiving this was natural; his manifestation of the resentment was, to say the least, indecorous. He wrote anonymously a *Guardian* paper (No. 40) which purported to come from the same hand as the earlier papers on the pastoral and which ironically compared the rival eclogues and continued the preference for those of Philips, but on grounds palpably absurd. The irony is deft but obvious, and it lacks modesty—for example, in its concluding paragraph:

> After all that hath been said, I hope none can think it any injustice to Mr. Pope that I forebore to mention him as a Pastoral writer; since, upon the whole, he is of the same class with Moschus and Bion, whom we have excluded that rank; and of whose Eclogues, as well as some of Virgil's, it may be said, that (according to the description we have given of this sort of poetry) they are by no means Pastorals, but something better.[1]

Warburton has left us an account of this incident, which is interesting, though one suspects the details of it may have been elaborated by Pope or by Warburton himself in the passage of time:

> The sycophancy of A. Philips, who had prejudiced Mr. Addison against Pope, occasioned those papers in the Guardian, written by the latter, in which there is an ironical preference given to the Pastorals of Philips above his own, in order to support the profound judgment of those who could not distinguish between the rural and

---

[1] Elwin-Courthope, x. 514. The irony seems obvious now, but it should be noted that the author of the Bickerton *Life of Pope* (1744) and Ayre in his *Life* (1745) both assume that the paper is by Steele, and unfriendly to Pope.

the rustic, and on that account condemned the Pastorals of Pope for wanting simplicity. These papers were sent by an unknown hand to Steele, and the irony escaping him, he communicated them to Mr. Pope, declaring he would never publish any paper where one of the club was complimented at the expense of another. Pope told him he was too delicate, and insisted that the papers should be published in the Guardian. They were so. And the pleasantry escaped all but Addison, who, taking Pope aside, said to him in his agreeable manner, 'You have put your friends here in a very ridiculous light, as will be seen when it is understood, as it soon must be, that you were only laughing at the admirers of Philips'. But this ill conduct of Philips occasioned a more open ridicule of his Pastorals in the mock poem called the Shepherd's Week, written by Gay. But though more open, the object of it was ill understood by those who were strangers to the quarrel. These mistook the Shepherd's Week for a burlesque of Virgil's Pastorals. How far this goes towards a vindication of Philips's simple painting, let others judge.[1]

Evidently Warburton was, as usual, writing recklessly. One sees no reason to think *Guardian* No. 40 due to Philips's 'sycophancy,' and only one paper was written by Pope on this occasion. Spence, who is fully as trustworthy as Warburton, says that 'Addison did not discover Mr. Pope's style' in this paper.[2] These stories cannot then be reconciled. It seems evident, however, that the irony is so obvious that there could be no general concealment in the matter, but that Pope's authorship must have been speedily known. Possibly the supposed subterfuge on his part has been exaggerated.

Philips was very angry. According to a post-Dunciad story, found in a pamphlet called *Pope Alexander's Supremacy*, he bought a rod which he 'stuck up at the Bar of Button's Coffee-house' and which Pope 'avoided by his usual Practice after every Lampoon, of remaining a close Prisoner at Home'.[3] The story sounds apocryphal, but an Irish friend of Philips, signing himself 'H. B.', contributed to the *Universal Visiter* for July 1756 reminiscences of

[1] Elwin-Courthope, i. 233–4.   [2] Spence, p. 168.
[3] p. 16 (4to ed., 1729).

Philips with similar details. He represents Philips as saying:

that, notwithstanding all the scurrilous treatment he had received from Mr. *Pope*, he always acknowledged him for the best poet of the nation, and ever treated him with respect; except one particular time at *Bolton's* [Button's] when he brought a little switch there on purpose to chastise Mr. Pope, for what Mr. *Phillips* called a false and insolent paper, wrote by Mr. Pope against Mr. *Phillips* and Mr. *Tickel*.[1]

Pope's account of Philips's attitude towards him was sent to Caryll in a letter of 8 June 1714, which, it will be noted, does not mention a whip:

Mr. Philips did express himself with much indignation against me one evening at Button's Coffee-house, as I was told, saying that I was entered into a cabal with Dean Swift and others to write against the Whig interest, and in particular to undermine his own reputation and that of his friends Steele and Addison: but Mr. Philips never opened his lips to my face, on this or any like occasion, though I was almost every night in the same room with him, nor ever offered me any indecorum. Mr. Addison came to me a night or two after Philips had talked in this idle manner, and assured me of his disbelief of what had been said, of the friendship we should always maintain, and desired I would say nothing further of it.

Philips acted irritatingly, so Pope goes on to say, with regard to money given him by the Hanover Club (of which he was Secretary) for their subscriptions to Pope's *Iliad*, and Pope tells Caryll: 'It is to this management of Philips that the world owes Mr. Gay's Pastorals.' The *Shepherd's Week* by Gay was of course due to the overpraise of Philips as well as to Philips's 'management' of the Hanover Club subscriptions.

The publication of Gay's poem in April 1714 marks a period of open animosity between Pope and his rival shepherd. About this same time Parnell wrote his 'Bookworm', which stigmatizes Dennis and Philips as 'mortal bards'. In 1714 Pope very likely quit Button's; but there

---

[1] p. 310. 'H. B.' is *possibly* Henry Brooke. The mention of Tickell may be additional evidence of his authorship of the offending *Guardians*.

is no evidence that he ceased to go there as early as April
1713. It is worth noting that his *Guardian* paper appeared
about a fortnight after *Cato* was first acted, with a Prologue
by Pope, that is, at a moment when Pope and Addison were
publicly associated. The paper would not necessarily affect
his relations with Addison. Pope continued to contribute
to the *Guardian*, and his letters to Caryll show him in the
company of Addison and Steele later in the summer of
1713. The *Narrative of Dr. Robert Norris* (July 1713), as
we have seen, was a strain on the friendship of Addison and
Pope; but it is certain that Addison later countenanced the
beginning of Pope's project of translating the *Iliad*, which
was formally announced in October 1713. When the first
volume of his *Iliad* appeared in 1715, the Preface contained
the statement: 'Mr. Addison was the first whose advice
determined me to undertake this task.' It may be that
Sir William Trumbull had given equally early advice on
the matter, but no one arose to deny that at the start
Addison encouraged Pope.

Until the end of 1713 Addison had little reason to complain of Pope unless he had a genuine and not merely a
politic disapproval of 'Dr. Norris's' *Narrative*. Pope had
at least some reason to believe the Little Senate were unjust
to his poetic abilities, and probably in a later search for
grounds of grievance against Addison himself he came to
think that the essayist had jealously advised against the
proposed enlargement of the *Rape of the Lock*. According
to Warburton, Pope communicated this plan for revising
the poem to Addison,

who he imagined would have been equally delighted with the improvement. On the contrary, he had the mortification to have his
friend receive it coldly; and more, to advise him against any alteration; for that the poem in its original state was a delicious little
thing, and, as he expressed it, *merum sal*. Mr. Pope was shocked for
his friend; and then first began to open his eyes to his Character.[1]

One can now see that what happened was probably that
Pope came upon Addison in one of his reserved moments.

[1] Pope's *Works* (large 8vo, 1751), iv. 26 n.

Addison himself was not greatly given to revisions, and his advice is quite comprehensible without assuming on his part any *arrière pensée*. The episode hardly would seem important in the relations of the two.

There can be no doubt, however, that about the time when Pope's proposals for translating the *Iliad* began to circulate (October 1713), Addison perhaps not too openly began to turn against Pope. It will be remembered that in 1716 Burnet said Pope had 'more than once' lampooned Addison. The statement is probably accurate; it is certain that in 1713 Addison had better reasons for being critical of Pope's conduct than Pope had for being critical of Addison's—unless, of course, the latter encouraged, or too freely permitted, his followers to gibe at Pope. Two epigrams relating to *Cato*, and possibly by Pope, have been found; and Addison seems to have been very sensitive concerning such things. In the *Diary of Viscount Percival* (6 October 1730) is preserved the following relevant anecdote. Gyles Earl, who told Percival the story, was a friend of Addison and Burnet, and doubtless a frequenter of Button's Coffee-house.

Talking of several matters and persons with the Speaker, Gyles Earl, of our House, etc.; the latter gave an instance of Mr. Addison's excessive jealousy of his reputation. He said that after his fine play of Cato appeared in print, Tom Burnet (the same who died Governor of New York)[1] took it into his head to burlesque a celebrated passage in it, not with design to ridicule the poet, by exposing that idle pastime to the world, but only to satisfy an instant thought of his own, and to try his skill that way; he therefore showed this piece to very few. But Mr. Addison (however it came) got knowledge of it, and gave no rest to Mr. Earl till he obtained a promise from Burnet to give no copy of those verses, but to burn them.[2]

Addison was not so fortunate with other levities concerning his tragedy. The first of the two epigrams men-

---

[1] This is Percival's error: it was Sir Thomas's eldest brother William who had been transferred from New York to Massachusetts and had died, governor of the latter province, in 1729.

[2] *Hist. MSS. Comm.: MSS. of the Earl of Egmont*, i (1920), 105.

tioned (and to it Pope at least gave circulation) is found in
the manuscript copy of Pope's letter to Caryll, 30 April
1713.[1] In the printed letter it should follow the remark
about Cato's daughter; but a Victorian delicacy in some
ways creditable to the Rev. Whitwell Elwin led him to drop
the epigram, silently, from his edition. The verses point
out, crudely enough, some obvious differences between the
morals and physiology of Cato's daughter and those of
Mrs. Oldfield, who acted the role. There is no evidence
that Pope was the author of the epigram, but he gave it
circulation, though Addison may not have known that.

The second epigram in question was very probably by
Pope. It also was a squib on *Cato*, and it was unhesitatingly
ascribed by Tom Burnet to Pope and Rowe.[2] It was
printed anonymously in the *Poetical Entertainer*[3] No. V
under the title 'Upon a Tory Lady who shed her Water at
Cato'. Since it was in 1727 included in the 'last' volume
of the *Miscellanies*, one may assume that Burnet was
probably right and that Pope had a hand in its composition.
What Burnet knew or suspected, the *Grande Société* at
Button's would know; and very likely it was this epigram
that caused Pope to be gazetted as an enemy to the society.[4]
While the epigram reflected neither on Addison nor on his
play, unless the curious expression of contempt by the
Tory Celia was a reflection, the lines were exactly the sort
of vulgarity that Addison would find intolerable.

Another piece in which, later, *Cato* was lightly treated
was Gay's farce the *What D'ye Call It* (1715). Of this the
wits at Button's[5] seem to have believed Pope the principal
author, and they resented the burlesques of Philips's
Distress'd Mother as well as that of the scene in *Cato* where
the great Roman is discovered reading Plato. These were

---

[1] Add. MS. 26618, fols. 14–16. Printed (except the epigram) in Elwin-
Courthope, vi. 183–5. The epigram belongs at the very bottom of p. 184.

[2] Burnet's *Letters*, ed. cit., p. 57. Letter of 18 March 1714.

[3] Advertised as 'this day published' in the *Post Boy*, 18 February 1713/14.

[4] Elwin-Courthope, vi. 202. The 'Gazette' mentioned in the manuscript copy
of the letter is the *Leyden Gazette*, and not the *London Gazette* (as printed).

[5] And others also. See Spence, p. 348.

burlesqued, to be sure, along with the best known passages of Shakespeare, Dryden, and Otway; but apparently the popularity of the farce in February and March gave Philips great offence. What Addison thought we do not know, but two such animadversions on *Cato* supposed to come from the writer of its Prologue were naturally something to think about. By the time of the appearance of the epigram (February 1713/14) Addison had begun to cool towards Pope.

It is likely that they now met seldom. Pope was concerned with the Scriblerus Club and with his translation of the *Iliad*. By-products of his genius such as the 'Receipt to make a Cuckold', published in Oldmixon's Miscellany (April 1714), probably without Pope's consent, would hardly meet with Addison's approval. Addison was not, according to Pope's story, inclined to enthusiasm over the more important employment of revising the *Rape of the Lock*, which upon publication in March 1714 was a great success, though it was speedily (6 April) attacked by Charles Gildon in a pamphlet called the *New Rehearsal*. It is worth noting that this work by Gildon is apparently the first to represent Addison as hostile to Pope. Gildon also sneers at Pope's scholarship[1] when he makes the poet assert the possibility of translating a Greek author without knowing any Greek.

At the moment Homer was the major task. In May[2] the proposals for the *Iliad* were republished with a list of subscribers to date; and Pope was already with Parnell at Binfield, where he remained all summer (except perhaps for brief journeys) working on the *Iliad*. He was at Bath for a month in the early autumn but probably was remote from the Little Senate from May to November. When he came up to town at the beginning of November 'to set Homer forwards in the press', he had reasons for suspecting that a malicious attempt was also 'forwards' to injure his chances of success. He now began to have good grounds for being suspicious of Addison.

---

[1] pp. 41–2.　　　　[2] *Evening Post*, 15 May 1714.

The story, with its culmination in the 'Atticus' portrait, finally placed in the *Epistle to Dr. Arbuthnot* (2 January 1735), has often been told. In 1779 no less a person than the great Blackstone summarized the evidence[1] and adjudged Pope the more guilty. Since that time his verdict has been generally accepted. But Blackstone did not know many of the important facts, and while even now there are many details uncertain or unknown, those that we do have seem to point to a quite different judgement in the case. This is perhaps distressing, for Pope cannot be presented as an ideal or even as a decorous sufferer of injustice; and Addison has been so thoroughly idealized by such men as Macaulay and Thackeray that it is a pity to spoil the picture with no great gain to another's reputation.

The energy with which Pope's acquaintances aided the subscription to his *Iliad* made such activity a sort of test of friendship. By the end of June, Pope wrote Caryll to this effect and added:

... I find I have at least six Tory friends, three Whig friends, and two Roman Catholic friends with many others of each who at least will do me no harm. I have discovered two dangerous enemies whom I might have trusted, besides innumerable *malevoli*, whom I will not honour so far as to suppose they can hurt anybody.[2]

Two months earlier he had recognized the support of Caryll and Edward Blount (Roman Catholics) and had said people called him a Whig 'because I have been honoured with Mr. Addison's good word, and Mr. Jervas's good deeds, and of late with my Lord Halifax's patronage'.[3] Apparently Addison's 'good word' was all that he had; for in answering charges of ingratitude brought by the Dunces, Pope denies that Addison got him any subscribers or friends: 'But if there be living any one nobleman whose friendship, yea any one gentleman whose subscription Mr. Addison procured to our author let him stand forth. . . .'[4] If one wishes to

---

[1] *Biographia Britannica*, i. 55–8. Cf. Joseph Warton's *Essay on Pope* (1806), ii. 237–9.   [2] Elwin-Courthope, vi. 212.

[3] Pope to Caryll, 1 May 1714. See Elwin-Courthope, vi. 208.

[4] 'Testimonies of Authors' prefixed to the *Dunciad* in 1729; see Elwin-Courthope, iv. 62–3.

question the sincerity of this challenge by stressing the word *living*, one may do so; but no Dunce ever did it, and there seems to be no evidence that Addison was active in the subscription. Inactivity would be no crime of course.

But somehow and at some time early in 1714 Addison deviated into activity. His servant in the matter was Thomas Tickell (1686–1740), Fellow of Queen's College, Oxford, a well-trained classical scholar and an admirable young poet. How far responsibility must be divided between Addison and Tickell it is difficult to say. Pope had no real quarrel with Tickell, who in his poem *On the Prospect of Peace* had written:

> Like the young spreading laurel, Pope, thy name
> Shoots up with strength, and rises into fame.

The poem associates Pope with Congreve, Rowe, Addison, Prior, Garth, Philips, and others. In later years after Addison's death Tickell was a friend to both Swift and Pope.[1] There is nothing more admirable than the silent discretion with which Tickell met attempts to win from him after Addison's death admissions that would fix upon Addison and remove from himself responsibility for the events concerning the early history of Pope's first volume of the *Iliad*. Tickell seems to have enjoyed in days of detraction a reputation for integrity that leads one to believe that if he erred in trying to spoil Pope's triumph in the *Iliad*, he erred because an older and highly influential friend urged him into error. Addison could aid Tickell to a career: in fact, he was doing so. Meanwhile it behooved

---

[1] On his relations to Swift see R. E. Tickell, *Thomas Tickell and the Eighteenth-Century Poets* (London, 1931), pp. 95–101, &c. With Pope, Tickell was naturally less intimate since after 1724 he lived chiefly in Ireland; but such acts as his acceptance of Pope's prefatory poem for Addison's *Works* (1721) and his sending to Pope his sympathy or 'services' in letters of A. Corbiere (Homer MSS.: Add. MS. 4809, fol. 63ᵛ: Corbiere to Pope, 28 February 1723–4) and of Swift (Elwin-Courthope, vii. 338, 7 February 1735–6) indicate a friendly understanding after Addison's death. One suspects that the lines in answer to Pope's 'Atticus' portrait printed as by J. Markland in *Cythereia* (1723) had been written some years earlier, and were published by Curll without Tickell's knowledge. See J. E. Butt in the *Bodleian Quarterly Record*, v (December 1928), 301.

Tickell to do nothing of which Addison could possibly disapprove.

We know that at the end of 1713 Tickell was in Oxford, actively at work on an edition of Lucan.[1] Apparently in May 1714, just as Pope was leaving town, he came up to London, and he may have remained there most of the year.[2] In May 1715, if not earlier, Tickell had on foot a subscription for his Lucan, and Jervas and Pope were aiding Addison to get subscribers.[3] Their activity was probably stimulated by somewhat hypocritical kindliness; for by this time Pope knew that Tickell was preparing to print a translation of the first book of the *Iliad*. Tickell went presently into a public career, and the edition of Lucan never appeared. That he actually did much work on the edition appears from notebooks of his still preserved by his descendants. It is somewhat surprising to find that at a moment when he was beginning an edition of Lucan, he also planned a translation of the *Iliad*. On 31 May 1714 he signed with Jacob Tonson, the publisher, an agreement still preserved by his descendants.[4] In it Tickell agreed to translate twenty-four books of the *Iliad*, and Tonson was to pay twenty guineas for the copy of each book, except the last, for which he was to give forty. Since Tickell contracted to deliver the copy of four books a year, one assumes that one volume a year was to be published. If a subscription was promoted, Tickell was to have for his subscribers books on royal paper at the price of ordinary volumes. 'Cutts' might be subscribed for to Tickell's sole advantage. There was an interesting proviso for possible abrogation: 'provided nevertheless That in Case the first four Books shall not Succeed & Sell off according to the Expectation of the

---

[1] R. E. Tickell, *Thomas Tickell*, pp. 28–34. Cf. Add. MS. 3781, fols. 169–75.

[2] He was not in Oxford on 31 October 1714. See Thomas Hearne's *Collections*, iv. 422.

[3] Elwin-Courthope, viii. 10.

[4] This agreement is reproduced in facsimile and transcribed by R. E. Tickell, op. cit., pp. 38–9. Mr. Tickell is of course in error when he assumes (p. 38) that in May 1714 his ancestor could have been ignorant of Pope's intended translation of the *Iliad*. Pope's subscription had been noisily under way for six months before the Tonson-Tickell agreement was signed.

s^d parties then the Agreem^t for the future Twenty Books
to be void or else to remain in full force.'

What is the meaning of this agreement? One is surprised
at its existence, which, except for a brief mention by Miss
Aiken in her *Life of Addison*, has been unnoticed by biographers. Ozell and others had begun (1712) to publish a
version of the *Iliad* in blank verse, printed as prose; Pope
had, since October 1713, been pushing an astonishingly
successful subscription for a metrical translation. In fact,
Pope's agreement with his publisher, Bernard Lintot,
signed on 23 March 1714,[1] seems to have served as a model
in some respects for the Tonson-Tickell agreement of two
months later. Pope's translation was to appear in six annual
volumes of four books each, but since his subscription had
been so phenomenally successful, Lintot could give him
far better terms than Tonson gave his poet.[2] Did the publishers anticipate an astonishing demand for the *Iliad* in
English, a demand that would justify one prose and two
poetic translations in the same decade? Or did certain persons believe that a demand had been demonstrated by
Pope's subscription but disbelieve that Pope could satisfy
the demand? The worst possible interpretation of the
Tickell-Tonson agreement would be that the intention
was to publish a rival volume each time Pope published a
volume; but such a procedure would be so obviously and
childishly malicious after the unparalleled popularity of
Pope's subscription that no one will believe that such an
intention existed.[3] The most plausible explanation is that
Tickell and his supporters believed, as they easily might,

[1] The original document I have not seen. The date is found in a subsidiary
agreement, Egerton MS. 1951, fols. 2 and 3.

[2] Malice might suggest another interpretation; namely, that Tonson paid less
because he intended to undersell Lintot's expensive volumes of Pope's translation.

[3] Of course the popularity of Pope's subscription may post-date May 1714.
About the middle of May (*Evening Post*, 15 May 1714, adv.) Pope's proposals
were republished with 'a List of those who have already Subscrib'd'. If a copy
of this publication still exists, the point could be settled; but one assumes the
list would not have been printed had it not contained a great many distinguished
names from all political groups. Incidentally, could Pope have been pleased to
have Tickell soliciting subscribers for Lucan while Pope was still in the market
for subscribers to the *Iliad*?

that Pope was totally incompetent to translate the Greek; that his first volume would burst the bubble, and that a competent translator might then profitably step forward. But considering the fact that Pope and Tickell were from rival political camps and that the fashionable world was all on Pope's side, one can hardly refrain from suspecting a certain amount of malice against Pope in this agreement. It is well to remember also that a metrical translation of twenty-four books of Homer is a task that no man undertakes lightly, and one that Tickell, considering his other engagements, would certainly not undertake at all without the encouragement and support of considerable persons.[1] Tonson and Addison must have been among those persons.

Very likely Pope never knew the details of this Tonson–Tickell agreement. He does not indicate any knowledge that Tickell planned to translate the entire *Iliad.* Of course it is desirable in such matters to use only evidence, as so far we have done, from 'uninspired' sources, but in telling how Pope came to know of Tickell's translation of the first book we naturally have to depend upon him for evidence. In any case, the details are few but curious. Since they come from Spence they are, of course, 'inspired' by Pope.[2] One may note, however, that Spence made attempts to verify the story;[3] so that it is not entirely uncorroborated. Stripped of most of its dubious details the story is that after a period of some coldness between Pope and Addison, probably in the autumn of 1714, Addison informed Pope that Tickell had translated the first book of the *Iliad* and now designed to publish it. Addison consequently begged to be excused from correcting Pope's first book, 'because if he did, it would have the air of double dealing'. This excuse of Addison must come into the class of dubious details: it has pretty certainly been given a malicious turn. Addison, Pope says, read and highly commended the second

---

[1] If Tickell, as 'H. B.' hinted so many years later—see *supra*, p. 121 n.—was the author of the *Guardian* papers on pastoral poetry that Pope had made light of, he would possibly have a personal grievance; but it still remains true that such a grievance would hardly inspire one to translate the whole *Iliad.*

[2] Spence, pp. 146–8.   [3] Ibid., pp. 148, 348.

volume [i.e., book]; he was also present when Pope read
parts of his version of the first four books to Lord Halifax.[1]

At any rate Pope came to know that Tickell had a version
of the *Iliad* I, which he designed to publish. The knowledge came in such a way as to imply no malice or rivalry
in the publication, and it came apparently with no implication that Tickell had (within the year) signed an agreement
to do the whole *Iliad*. In fact, one must conclude that as
Tickell's friends came to realize not only the popularity
of Pope's project but also the conscientious efforts that he
and all his friends were putting into the translation, they
could not advise Tickell to proceed beyond Book I.

Of course it has been said that the translation was not
Tickell's at all, but Addison's. A surprising number of persons in the eighteenth century believed this; but since 1800
practically no one has done so. Young, who was intimate
with Tickell, expressed early doubts.[2] Steele, when angry,
printed the charge,[3] and (in Spence's presence) Tickell
himself did not deny it.[4] Warton says: 'Dr. Young, Lord
Bathurst, Mr. Harte, and Lord Lyttelton, each of them
assured me that Addison himself certainly translated the
first Book of Homer.'[5] Three of these men were perhaps
prejudiced in Pope's favour; but Young certainly would not
be. Cibber[6] believed the charge, but doubtless only on
gossip, which would be the basis of 'Hesiod' Cooke's repeti-
tion of it in his *Battle of the Poets*,[7] and other similar
repetitions. The printer Watts 'declared that the copy of
the translation . . . was in Tickell's handwriting; but much
corrected and interlined by Addison.'[8] It seems clear that
both of them were in some degree concerned in it.

Sir Leslie Stephen in his *Life of Pope*[9] shows much irritation that Pope should have ventured to be annoyed because
some one other than himself dared to translate Homer
while he was doing it. The reason for the annoyance was

[1] Spence, p. 134.   [2] Ibid., p. 147.
[3] In his Dedication to the *Drummer*, 1722.   [4] Spence, p. 148.
[5] In his edition of Pope's *Works* (1797), iv. 34 n.
[6] Spence, p. 348.   [7] p. 19 (folio ed., 1725).
[8] *Addisoniana*, i. 167.   [9] pp. 56 ff.

not total depravity, as Sir Leslie seems to have thought, but
a trait almost as common: Pope wanted to make money;
and while his subscription-list seemed to assure that result,
it was still true that the subscribers had paid in only two
guineas in advance, and that if the translation were in its
first volume discredited by a rival translation made by two
former Oxford dons, the subscribers would have sense
enough not to waste four more guineas on later volumes.
It is pretty certain that the Lintot-Pope contract would,
like that of Tonson and Tickell, contain a proviso for
abrogation in case the first volume proved a failure. The
financial success of the whole subscription seemed to Pope
crucial. He wished to frequent the most fashionable
society, to which his talents had now won him access. For
such a career money was essential. At the very moment
when his translation was announced the family income,
none too large, apparently, had been diminished by an
edict of the French king which reduced by one-fourth the
interest on French annuities granted between 1702 and
1710.[1] 'This misfortune will go near to ruin me', Pope
wrote Caryll in January 1714, and since £8,250 of the
family fortunes (very likely the better part of them) was
so invested, his anxiety is understandable.[2] Indeed, the
competition of two thoroughly trained classicists and excellent poets with the relatively ignorant Pope might well
prove a serious matter, and any annoyance on his part
would have warrant.

But, some one will ask, why should two translations
necessarily 'compete'? A sufficient reply might be that
whenever two translations of the same work have appeared
at the same time, comparisons have resulted. And when
the authors of the two translations belong to unfriendly
groups of writers, rivalry is inevitable.

That, however, is not the end of the story. If you put
yourself in Pope's place and consider the problem of what
to do when an abler rival is about to publish a translation
of the same book of the *Iliad* that you are about to publish,

---

[1] Elwin-Courthope, vi. 201.   [2] Ibid. vi. 189.

you will see that it would be very agreeable if he would publish first, and let you cancel pages, if corrections seemed necessary in order to eliminate errors or infelicities that a comparison might expose. Evidently Pope wished his rivals to lead the way. It seems fairly evident, however, that they wished as nearly as possible a simultaneous publication: they courted comparisons. If Tickell's *Iliad* I was translated at Oxford earlier than 1714,[1] there seems to be no reason why it might not have been published before June 1715; and if it was made after Pope and he signed their respective contracts (March and May 1714), one would, even so, normally expect that Tickell's translation of one book could be finished and published more quickly than Pope's translation of four books, with an elaborate critical preface and copious footnotes. By the end of 1714 Pope evidently suspected or knew that simultaneous publication was the aim of his rivals, and he tried to defeat their purpose by announcing an early and probably false date of publication. His first volume had been expected to appear about the beginning of May 1715; but in the *Post Boy* for 25 December 1714 it was advertised that 'whereas it was proposed that the first volume of the Translation should be published by the beginning of May next, the Editor intends it shall be delivered two months sooner than the time promised';[2] but when March came it was not published.

If Pope's Christmas advertisement was calculated to 'draw fire' from the group at Button's it was hardly successful. The rival translation did not appear, but Thomas Burnet in his *Grumbler* No. 1 (24 February 1715) advertised:

There is now in Press, and will be speedily publish'd, HOMERIDES: Or, a Letter to Mr. *Pope* occasion'd by his intended Translation of *Homer*. By Sir *Iliad Doggrell*. Sold by *J. Roberts* in *Warwick-Lane*. Price 6d.

After repetitions of this advertisement the pamphlet appeared on or about 7 March. It was written by Burnet and George Duckett in collaboration, and from Burnet's letters

---

[1] Spence, pp. 146–7. [2] Nichols, *Literary Anecdotes*, i. 77 n.

we learn that it was originally to have had a name something like *A Specimen of the Hump Conference* and was to be 'sharp on Pope's person'. On the 2nd of February Burnet wrote Duckett urging him to send at once the trunk in which they exchanged papers (Burnet was in London and Duckett in Dorsetshire): 'for if it comes next Saturday I shall be able to put the *Conference* out just a fourtnight before his first Volume when all the Town will be full of expectation & when London will be twice as full as it is now.'[1] A letter of a fortnight later (19 February) has also an interesting passage:

As to our *Specimen*, I shewd great part of it to Mr. Addison, who advised me in two things, first to convert the Dialogue into a Narrative Letter and secondly to strike out all the Reflections upon the poor fellow's person; all this I have done, but his Homer is so speedily to appear that I cannot have time to wait for your second Approbation, but have put the Press to work already, and with all the haste I shall make *mine* won't be publishd above a week before his. The Title of it, I have altered much for the better, and it is *Homerides* . . . and that Pope may see I cou'd be sharp on his Person if I wou'd, I have placed the Greek Sentence at the head, but have not translated it; and so much for Homer.[2]

It is notable that, departing from his precedent in the episode of the *Narrative of Dr. Robert Norris*, Addison 'when *these* papers were offered to be communicated to him' did not refuse to be privy to the attack, and while he softened the details concerning Pope's deformity, he may have done so to make the pamphlet effective rather than to make it mild. At the time Burnet writes, 'Addison is so outwardly fond of me, that you wou'd be amazed at it, and we often drink together; the last time we met, I never was in a better cue, and we did not part till after four in the morning.'[3] Duckett evidently thought *Homerides* tame in its printed form, and Burnet on 26 March writes to defend his and Addison's changes:

I can assure you *Homerides* notwithstanding your anger at it, is universally approved, and although much of the Humour is lost

---

[1] *Letters*, ed. Nichol Smith, p. 80.   [2] Ibid., p. 81.   [3] Ibid., p. 82.

by the Exchange, yet I wou'd not have printed the *Hump Conference* for any money. For *Pope* as he is a fellow of a Contemptible figure is the object of the Town's Pity; and all they blame in *Homerides* is the motto. What then wou'd they have done if the whole *Hump Conference*? I will acknowledge to you that I believe you guess right, that Addison did this out of no manner of good will to me; but till you give me some farther Reasons, I shall think I was wise in following his Advice.[1]

This first *Homerides*—of which a second edition appeared two months later—was hardly a strong pamphlet. Its burden is one of reproach to Pope for his presumption in thinking himself competent to translate Homer. Except as the first drop in a shower it was negligible; but the shower now came on apace.

By the 1st of February had appeared Pope's *Temple of Fame* (which he had had by him since 1712), and not later than April he published his allegorical interpretation of the *Rape of the Lock*, a delicious burlesque on the political pamphleteering of the day. He called it *A Key to the Lock. Or a Treatise proving, beyond all Contradiction, the dangerous Tendency of a late Poem entituled The Rape of the Lock, to Government and Religion. By Esdras Barnivelt.* These two works came under the lash of Burnet in his *Grumbler* No. 14 (6 May 1715), and towards the end of May he began advertising there a second edition of *Homerides*. About the 30th this appeared, and it proved to be not a second edition but a new attack. Two pages jeer at Pope's audacity and eagerness for cash; the rest contain mainly doggerel specimens of passages from various books of the *Iliad*. One jest was the ironical project of Sir Iliad to aid Pope's subscription by getting Powell, the puppet-show man, to turn the *Iliad* into a puppet-show. In line with this Duckett contributed to the volume 'An Epilogue for Punch to speak, at the Representation of the Siege of Troy for Mr. Pope's Benefit, in Mr Powel's Theatre at Bath.' At the end, we have a parting jeer about exchanging brass for gold: the subscribers give Pope the gold.

[1] Ibid., p. 84.

Pope's advertisement of December 1714 appointing
1 March 1715 as the date of the appearance of the first
volume of his *Iliad* may be responsible in part for the
appearance on 5 March of another attack. This was entitled *Aesop at the Bear-Garden: A Vision. By Mr. Preston.
In Imitation of the Temple of Fame, a Vision, By Mr. Pope.*
The authorship of this pamphlet is obscure. Mr. Preston
was, as a note in the volume explains,[1] the 'bear-marshal'
at Hockley in the Hole, and hence his name is used as a
pseudonym. The attack is mainly concerned with burlesquing Pope's *Temple of Fame*, which it does with considerable skill. Pope's diction in his re-working of Chaucer
easily lent itself to ridicule in passages, and of course the
parallelism between Fame's Temple and Preston's bear-
garden would in itself be a reduction of the poem to
absurdity. At the beginning of the volume, however, is
placed an advertisement that may well mean that the
author of *Aesop at the Bear-Garden* was one of the conspirators watchfully awaiting the publication of Pope's
Iliad. It is a burlesque of Pope's advertisement of the
previous December:

> The first book of *Tom Thumb*, transform'd from the original
> Nonsense into *Greek* Heroicks, is so near finished, that the Under-
> taker hopes to be able to deliver it to the Subscribers by the first
> of *April* next.
>
> This is therefore to desire all Gentlemen and Ladies, that have
> not yet paid in their Subscription-money according to the Proposal,
> that they would be pleased to do it on or before the said first of
> *April*, either to the Undertaker himself, or Monsieur *Lewis le
> Pedant* in *Covent-Garden*, or they'll be excluded the Benefit, &c.
>
> N.B. There will be fine Cuts, and learned Annotations; and to
> prevent the Destruction of Paper, there will be no more printed
> than the Exact Number that are subscrib'd for.

A third pamphlet, also inspired by the animus at Button's

[1] p. 34: '*Preston* the present Marshal, was the Son of *Preston* the Great, the
first Founder of the rough Game, who unhappily falling into the Paws of his own
Bear, was cruelly slain, and almost devour'd before he was discover'd by his Son,
who immediately slew the Bear, and so Succeeded his Father in Honour, Post
and Authority.'

against Pope, was *A Complete Key to the last New Farce The What D'ye Call It.* Of this, Gay wrote to Caryll, probably in April:

There is a sixpenny criticism lately published upon the tragedy of the What d'ye Call it, wherein he [the author] with much judgment and learning calls me a blockhead, and Mr. Pope a knave. His grand charge is against the Pilgrim's Progress being read, which, he says, is directly levelled at Cato's reading Plato.[1]

The 'blockhead-knave' charge is found in the Preface of this pamphlet, which, as attack, is the most interesting part of the work. In this Preface the author (later Pope ascribed the pamphlet to Griffin, a player, and Theobald) represents himself as an outsider listening to a coffee-house discussion as to the lengths to which authors will go for the sake of novelty. Among the speakers was 'a certain tall, well-dress'd Modern of great Gravity and much Politeness', apparently Ambrose Philips. He attacks the farce of Gay and Pope in part as follows:

For my own part, I freely forgive their Impotence in attempting to Sacrifice my Name to their Mirth; but I cannot with the like Patience hear the venerable *Names* of *Shakespear, Otway,* and *Dryden* abused upon the same Stage, where they have shone to so great an Advantage. . . . the *Satyr* runs all the way on the finest Passages in the most Celebrated Plays. . . . I own, that I despise the Composition horribly, and look on it as the most unnatural, ill-affected Wit that the Age has produc'd. But we could expect nothing less from the baseness of a busy Pen, which is now attacking all the Reputations that rais'd its own, and skreens it self behind a borrow'd Name. For give me leave to quote *Virgil* for once; and I think I may say of the *skreening Friend,*

————Nihil ille nec ausus
Nec potuit;————

But this *malevolent Critick* fights like *little Teucer,* behind the shield of *impenetrable Stupidity.*

This is probably the first time the oft-repeated charge of ingratitude to those who gave him reputation was laid at Pope's door, and it must be one of the few times any one

---

[1] Elwin-Courthope, vi. 227.

ever accused John Gay of stupidity. Evidently Philips—
and Addison?—lacked a sufficient sense of humour to see
that parody might be good fun and not mere malice.

The authors of the *Key*, whoever they were, believe in
the joint authorship of the farce. In the Preface they say:

However you lovely Yoak-mates, Joint Fathers of a poor Jest,
your equally laborious Commentators, who have endeavour'd to
trace your Allusions, hope for your Pardon and Patronage . . . .
A late *gentle* Author, famous for his *Madrigalls*, took the pains to
comment upon his own Writings;[1] and this Farce, having an equal
right to his Esteem, ought at least to be favour'd with the same
Indulgence. . . . One would naturally presume that the *Corpulent
Writer*[2] had the largest Share in the Machinery of this Motley
Banter; but that (as Dr. *Bentley* once observ'd on a subject of more
Weight) 'tis currently reported, *that every Line was writ when he
was in Bed and Asleep.*

The text of the *Key* itself is not so hostile to the authors
as this Preface might lead one to expect. A passage on
page 22 mildly accuses Pope of irreligion, but in general
the text is a serious attempt to point out what is being
parodied in each passage. Probably because of the apparent
knowledge shown here, Burnet in the *Grumbler* No. 14
(6 May) accused Pope of writing this *Key* as well as the
Key to the Lock. The passages just quoted from the Preface
are a sufficient reply to this imputation. It may, however,
be noted that when Pope had the 'Libels on Pope' bound
up,[3] the *Key to the What D'ye Call It* was included in the
first volume[4] of attacks on himself that he wished to preserve. The true authors were very likely persons connected
with the stage, who could easily point out parallels from
plays that they knew by heart. Why Theobald, who in
1717 was friendly to Pope, should be joined to Griffin as
author, unless through malice *ex post facto*, is hard to say.

The year 1714–15 saw Pope and Rowe or Pope and Gay

---

[1] This is an allusion to Pope's *Guardian* No. 40, in defence of his own pastorals,
or to the recent *Key to the Lock*.

[2] Gay.

[3] About 1735? See Elwin-Courthope, ix. 554.

[4] British Museum, press-mark 1421 g 6.

(so the Buttonians said) burlesquing *Cato.* In retort we have at least three major pieces—*Homerides, Aesop at the Bear-Garden,* and this *Key* to Gay's farce. There were other things possibly, but these three show a considerable amount of sensitiveness on the part of the Little Senate as well as a woful lack of sense of humour; for the Pope-Rowe epigram and the *What D'ye Call It* are both harmless, and the farce was then, and still is, very amusing. It is possible that the attacks by the Little Senators indicate something like an organized effort to discredit Pope upon the appearance of the first volume of his *Iliad*; for they were concentrated about the date on which its publication had been promised.

Pope's announcement that Homer was to appear early in March[1] had brought on these showers of attack, but had not 'drawn' the rival translation of the first Book—which, after all, was the great affair. There followed a period of waiting on both sides. On 18 March Gay writes to Parnell that 'Homer will be published in three weeks'.[2] Somewhat later (April) Gay and Pope in a letter to Caryll speak of the work as 'retarded by the great rains that have fallen of late, which cause the sheets to be long a-drying'.[3] Their grief

---

[1] In the Letterbooks of the first Duke of Chandos (asserted by Pope's enemies to be the 'Timon' of the fourth 'Moral Essay') is preserved a copy of a most curious letter by His Grace to Pope's friend the Hon. Simon Harcourt, who was active in getting subscriptions for the *Iliad.* The letter seems to indicate that printed copies of Book I, or at least specimens of Book I in print, were circulated early in 1715 among prospective subscribers. If so, it is strange that no surviving examples of such a piece of printing have been noted by collectors or bibliographers. The letter to Harcourt (preserved among the Huntington Library MSS. in the Letterbooks of James Brydges, Duke of Chandos, xi. 210–11) is as follows:

9 Jan 1714/5

S^r I was at y^r door whilst I was in town to return you my humble thanks for y^r oblidging present of Mr Pope's translation of ye first book of Homer. A Genius like his can never fail of performing what he undertakes to ye satisfaction of true Judges. Nor c^d he have given a more certain proof of it than in making you sensible, how much he deserves ye hon^r of y^r approbation.

As I desire to oblidge some friends as early as I can with this great work, I entreat you will subscribe for ten sets for me. I think ye subscription money is 2 Guin. each, & I enclose a Note for ye sum on Mr Zollicoffre who will wait upon you to take it up. I am with ye greatest respect &c.

[2] Elwin-Courthope, vii. 455.   [3] Ibid. vi. 227.

over this last delay is tinged with a facetiousness that leads one to believe them reconciled to a postponement. They joke at Lintot's uneasiness in the matter. At the time of publication Lintot writes as if he feared Pope might cause further delay.[1] His worry also because of the inopportune moment chosen for publication, a moment when political excitement kept attention from Homer, may be based on a notion that an earlier publication would have avoided such distraction of interest. There is some reason, at any rate, for thinking that Pope moved the date of publication from 1 May to 1 March, and then postponed the actual appearance of the work, seemingly to Lintot's discomfort, until 6 June. The *Post Boy* for Tuesday, 31 May, carried the following announcement:

This is to give Notice to the Subscribers for Mr. Pope's Translation of Homer, that the first Vol. is now finish'd, and will be ready to be deliver'd to them, upon producing their Receipts, or paying the Subscription Money, on Monday the 6th Day of June next, by Bern. Lintott, Bookseller, at the Cross Keys between the Temple Gates in Fleetstreet; where the several Pieces Mr. Pope has publish'd, may be had.

Thereupon the next *Gazette* (Saturday, 4 June) announced:

On Wednesday next will be published. The First Book of Homer's Iliad. Translated by Mr. Tickell. Printed for Jacob Tonson at Shakespear's Head against Catherine-Street in the Strand.

And so, on Monday and Wednesday the 6th and 8th of June, the watchful waiting ended. The minute Pope's volume was actually published, his rivals announced in the *Post Boy* of 7 June, 'Tomorrow will be publish'd The First Book of Homer's Iliads translated by Mr. Tickell.' After all that had passed it was now somewhat naïve of Tickell and Addison to disclaim rivalry with Pope. To his volume Tickell prefixed a statement 'To the Reader', which said:

I Must inform the Reader, that when I begun this First Book, I had some Thoughts of Translating the whole *Iliad*, but had the

---

[1] Elwin-Courthope, ix. 540. This letter is genuine.

pleasure of being diverted from that Design, by finding the Work was fallen into a much abler Hand. I would not therefore be thought to have any other View in publishing this small Specimen of *Homer's Iliad*, than to bespeak, if possible, the Favour of the Public to a Translation of Homer's Odysseis, wherein I have already made some Progress.

This declaration did no good; for apparently there was a blunt tendency to disbelieve it. Hardly more than a month later appeared a pamphlet called *Homer in a Nut-shell; or, The Iliad of Homer in Immortal Doggrel*, by 'Nickydemus Ninnyhammer, F. G.,' which contained a doggerel version of the first three books of the *Iliad* and which had prefixed to it, as the advertisements said,[1] 'an unaccountable Dedication, after the Buttonian Manner, a whimsical Ode, and an odd kind of Preface'. This prefatory material contains a brutal attack on Gilbert Burnet, the recently deceased Bishop of Salisbury, done in burlesque of Tickell's dedication of his *Iliad* to the recently deceased Lord Halifax. What interests us at the moment is the further parody of Tickell's address 'To the Reader':

> This is to certify all whom it may concern, that I had a Maggot come into my Head some time ago to Translate all *Homer's* Works, but had the *Pleasure of being* Mortified, *by finding* the Iliad so incomparably done by Mr. *Pope*, and the *Odysseis* design'd to be infinitely better Translated by Mr. *Tickell*, alias *Jo.* Addison. *I would not therefore be thought to* endeavour to prejudice Mr. *Pope, or to have any other View in publishing this small Specimen of* Homer's *Iliad, than to bespeak, if possible, the Favour of the Publick to a Translation of* Homer's *Batrachomuomachia*, to the Tune of *Chivy-Chase*, so justly applauded by the *Spectator*.

Since Pope was about this time urging Parnell to send from Ireland his version of the *Batrachomuomachia* for publication, it seems apparent that Pope or one of his 'gang' was masquerading as Mr. Ninnyhammer. Such echoes of the struggle were to last long.

Pope's choice of a day of capitulation had not been altogether happy. The interest of the town was at the moment

---

[1] *Weekly Packet*, 23 July 1715.

focused on politics. Tom Burnet's over-violent pamphlets against the fallen Tories were beginning to bring results. On the 10th of June Bolingbroke (who had escaped in disguise to France on 28 March) and Oxford were impeached for high treason. On the 16th Oxford went to the Tower. Pope had dedicated his first volume to no one, but the Preface had daringly joined praise of his Whig patron, Halifax, who was recently dead, with encomium of Bolingbroke. Lintot's comment was, 'The noise the report[1] makes does me some present harm.'[2] As for Pope the moment was too much for him to face: he had fled to Binfield, where he remained until the middle of August. Then he, with Arbuthnot, Jervas, and Colonel Disney, set out for a month at Bath.

There is plenty of evidence that the simultaneous publication had done Pope no real harm, and that 'the malice and juggle at Button's', as Lintot called it, recoiled upon its perpetrators. Even before the books were out the *Weekly Journal. With fresh advices foreign and domestick,* had on 4 June printed the following item:

> The Discourse at present among the Learned, is upon the Publication of the first Volume of *Homer*, done by the most Ingenious Mr. Pope, who has already given us as Many Testimonies as he has written Poems, that he alone is equal to so great an Undertaking; and this Pleasure is heightened by a Consideration, that those Enemies of Wit who would get a Name by finding Fault with any Perfection that they cannot attain to, are like to meet with as much Discouragement as Mr. Pope will with Honour and Applause: We are however advised from *Button's*, That as their Party have engrossed to themselves the whole Art of Politicks, so they will now advance with Vigour and will continue to make violent Incursions into all the Provinces of Literature, till they have laid waste all good Sense as well as Honesty. But as the Fort of *Homer* is the first Place they set upon, and seems impregnable by Art and Nature, 'tis believ'd the Siege will be razed [sic], and the Besiegers quit with Shame, so heedless a Project, and so unpromising an Undertaking.

---

[1] Of the committee of the House of Lords.

[2] Cf. a letter of 1716 in which Arbuthnot tells Parnell that politics injured the sale of the first volume. Elwin-Courthope, vii. 460.

A week later (11 June) the same paper printed further support of Pope:

According as we advised in our last, a Poetical War was openly declar'd on Wednesday, by Mr. *Tickel*, (supported on one Hand by Sir R . . . . . St . . . le, and on the other by a Person who made his Fortune by one *Campaign*) whose Translation of the first Book of HOMER's Iliad was then publish'd, in Opposition to the first Volume of the same Author translated by Mr. *POPE*: These Gentlemen have gain'd great Reputation by the Parts they have already perform'd of this Work; for as HOMER was accounted the most ingenious among the Greek Authors, so Mr. *POPE'S* Translation has the Reputation of coming next to it: And as all Authors agree that HOMER was Blind, so Mr. *Tickel* is said to have imitated him in that Respect, which occasion'd the following *Epigram*:

> As some harsh Criticks, who are too severe,
> And verse, by Judgment try, as well as Ear,
> 'Gainst *Tickel* as a *Rhiming Falstaff* plead
> For Murth'ring HOMER, after he was dead;
> And say, our *Isle* could for no Pardon hope,
> Were not th'absolving Words bestow'd by POPE:
> So by more *Civil* Judges it is said,
> That not ev'n POPE could without *Tickel's* Aid,
> Have rais'd *entire*, HOMER from the Dead.
> 'Tis plain to reconcile the Difference,
> *This* Bard his *Blindness* shews, and *that* his *Sense*.

One would like to know the authorship of this, almost the only printed support of Pope in the newspapers of the year. But if the public press was thus reserved, Pope's friends made amends in their letters. Parnell, Jervas, Caryll, Gay, Berkeley, Arbuthnot, and doubtless others were most cordial and satisfactory in their praise. Swift found fault with the rhymes, but said of the book, 'If it pleases others as well as me, you have got your end in profit and reputation.' Curiously enough, Swift does not mention the Tickell version. The attitude of those at Button's is expressed in a fragment of a letter by Gay printed by Pope under date of 8 July 1715:[1]

---

[1] Of course Pope's editing makes the letter of questionable authenticity, but it seems genuine.

I have just set down Sir Samuel Garth at the opera. He bid me tell you that everybody is pleased with your translation, but a few at Button's; and that Sir Richard Steele told him, that Mr. Addison said Tickell's translation was the best that ever was in any language. He treated me with extreme civility, and out of kindness gave me a squeeze by the fore-finger. I am informed that at Button's your character is made very free with as to morals, &c., and Mr. A[ddison] says, that your translation and Tickell's are both very well done, but that the latter has more of Homer. I am, &c.[1]

The last sentence probably expresses the exact attitude of Addison and his group. Since Burnet has left us his opinion in a letter of August 1715 it may be well to let him speak for the group, as he originally wrote at Addison's suggestion:

And by Mr. Addison's direction I have enclosed in the Trunk aforesaid . . . Mr. Tickel's Translation of the first Book of the Iliad, which I dare say you will approve of; to me it seems to have all the Beauty and Majesty which Homer's loose way of writing carryes with it: whilest Pope's, if you were extravagant enough to buy it, woud appear only like a smooth soft Poem, rather of Dryden's than Homer's Composing.[2]

They had a just sense of Pope's limitations but not of Tickell's. Meanwhile, Oxford as well as London declared for Pope. On 28 June Edward Young, the poet, wrote Tickell a letter that shows how widely the design of the Buttonians was regarded as malicious:

. . . To be very plain the University almost in general gives the Preference to Popes Translation. They say his is written with more Spirit Ornament & Freedom & has more the air of an Original.

I inclined some, Harrison &c, to compare the Translations with the Greek, which was done; it made some small alteration in their opinions, but still Pope was their Man. The Bottom of the Case is this, they were strongly prepossest in Popes Favour, from a wrong Notion of your Design, before the Poem came down & the Sight of yours has not had Force enough upon them, to make them willing to contradict themselves. . . . [Young adds that many desire Tickell to proceed with the Odyssey, and continues:] I seriously

---

[1] Elwin-Courthope, vii. 417–18.   [2] *Letters*, ed. Nichol Smith, p. 92.

believe your first Piece of that will quite break this Partiality for Pope, which your Iliad has weakened & secure your Success.[1]

In spite of the soothing praise, which must have come in quantities, it was natural that Pope should feel great irritation towards the Buttonians and towards their master, Joseph Addison. In fact, the success of his translation may well have strengthened his resentment. Even he himself must have doubted his ability to succeed in such a rivalry: they might be right, he might be incompetent. But the event had proved them conclusively wrong and perverse in their preference of their own work; and all the pent-up emotion of six months or more of doubt and angry strain may have found vent at about this time in the satire on Addison, later so famous as the 'Atticus' portrait.[2]

So far as is now known, the lines were first printed, probably without Pope's consent, in *St. James's Journal*, 15 December 1722,[3] where they seem to have attracted practically no attention. They were reprinted various times, very likely again without Pope's consent, until he owned them, with something like an apology to Addison,[4]

---

[1] R. E. Tickell, *Thomas Tickell*, p. 43.

[2] Evidence of Pope's excitement at the moment is seen elsewhere also. His copy of Tickell's first book of the *Iliad*, now in the Hurd Library at Hartlebury Castle, was annotated fully in the margins by Pope with the evident purpose of attacking the translation. Professor Conington published an account of these marginalia in *Fraser's Magazine*, lxii (1860), 260–72. One of the more interesting of the ideas that emerge from Pope's mind in these jottings is the fact that the pre-publication circulation of his first book, in manuscript or in print, gave Tickell the chance to borrow some good phrases from it for his own version. Among the parallels that Pope marked, and that Conington published, one or two are so striking that an angry man in Pope's position would certainly come to the same conclusion as he did. The parallels, though striking, are probably astonishing coincidences. Pope was wise in not publishing this charge of plagiarism. It may be noted that before 1720 Pope revised his own translation, and in so doing felt free to borrow several good phrases from Tickell

[3] Nichols, *Literary Anecdotes*, iv. 273–4, errs in asserting that they were printed in 1717; and the *D.N.B.* errs (s.v. 'Pope') in dating the first edition 1723. On other early editions see the *Curliad* (1729), p. 30.

[4] In the Preface to vol. i (1727) they say: 'In regard to two Persons only, we wish our Raillery, though ever so tender, or Resentment, though ever so just, had not been indulged. We speak of Sir *John Vanbrugh*, who was a Man of Wit, and of Honour; and of Mr. *Addison*, whose Name deserves all Respect from every Lover of Learning.'

and placed them among his and Swift's *Miscellanies* in
1727. The fact that they were first printed in 1722 naturally
gave the Dunces a chance to spread the scandal that they
were written after Addison's death.[1] There can be no doubt
that they were written before Addison died, however; for,
among several others, even Lady Mary Wortley Montagu
in the days of her hatred of Pope said she had seen them
before that event.[2]

It is probably impossible to fix the exact date for the
composition of these lines, concerning which Pope's nineteenth-century editors were needlessly unkind in their
comments. An important indication, however, is seen on
a leaf in the Homer MSS.[3] that contains a few lines, half-
lines, and phrases that are evidently the 'Atticus' portrait
in early embryo. The writing on this leaf must date about
July 1715. Pope's well-known economy in the use of paper
—'paper-sparing Pope' Swift called him—led him, as every
one knows, to translate much of the *Iliad* and the *Odyssey*
on sheets that had been used on one side, chiefly for letters
from friends or for covers for such letters. Book VIII, of
which this leaf (fol. 118) is a part, is written on letters that
can be dated by one means or another as received in June
or July 1715, and that fact supports a natural supposition
that the portrait had been begun on folio 118 shortly after,
if not in one of those months.[4] Almost everything that

---

[1] (Mist's) *Weekly Journal*, 8 June 1728. Cf. *Dunciad* (4to, 1729), p. 11, among
the 'Testimonies of the Authors', where Pope refutes the charge.

[2] Spence, p. 237.

[3] Add. MS. 4807, fol. 118.

[4] The rectos of the leaves near 118 contain, of course, Pope's first draft of
Book VIII of the *Iliad*; the versos contain the following materials:

108 Letter from Lintot to Pope, 20 June 1715.
109 The end of Lintot's letter begun on 108.
110 Letter from Pope to Jervas (Elwin-Courthope, viii. 15).
111 Draft of a letter in Pope's hand (4 lines, undated).
112 Address of a letter to Pope at Binfield in the hand and with the frank of
    'Joseph Addison', postmarked 2/IY (though the IY is not clear).
113 The end of Pope's letter to Jervas begun on 110.
114 The address of a letter to Pope at Binfield, also franked by Addison and
    postmarked 2/— with the month undecipherable.
115 Address of a letter to Pope at Jervas's house, postmarked clearly 2/IY.
116 Letter of Ralph Bridges to Pope, 2 July 1715.

Pope tells us supports the probability that the lines in question were composed shortly after the appearance of Tickell's
Iliad; but, in his anxiety to justify the satire by stating his
full grievance against Addison, Pope told a story that does
not perfectly 'hang together'. In support of the early
composition of the lines, one may cite his letter (15 July
1715) to Craggs, in which are embodied phrasal echoes or
anticipations of the satire. Unlike the leaf in the Homer
MSS., to which Pope never referred, this letter is suspect
as evidence since it is a letter printed by Pope, and so
possibly manufactured by him for purposes of publication.
There is no especial ground for suspecting the authenticity
of this letter more than that of others printed by Pope
from originals that he destroyed, and, in any case, the letter
is of interest as showing either the actual date or the date
which Pope wished to establish as that of the composition
of the lines. There is no evidence against the belief that
the lines were sketched in 1715 and sent to Addison in 1716
except Pope's statement to Spence[1] involving Gildon's
Memoirs of Wycherley and the Earl of Warwick's gossip
about it. This episode cannot date earlier than May 1718
when the *Memoirs* appeared.[2] Evidently Pope, as usual,
confused facts recklessly rather than subtly, or else Spence
set them down awkwardly. The hypothesis that seems best
to explain all the details is that the portrait of Addison was
sketched in the summer of 1715, and sent to Addison not

117 The address of Bridges's letter.
118 The lines of the satire in question.
119 The address of a letter to Pope, postmarked 30/IV.
120 Caryll's letter to Pope, 29 June [1715] (Elwin-Courthope, vi. 230).
From folio 121 to the end of the Book we have the *Iliad* on both recto and
verso, a frequent sign that Pope was away from home and using the paper of his
host. The fact that all these leaves came into Pope's hands certainly in a very
limited period leads one who knows how waste paper accumulates to assume that
it was all prepared for translation purposes (i.e. written on, torn or cut to size,
&c.) at about the same time.

[1] Spence, pp. 148–9.
[2] These *Memoirs* were regarded as non-existent by Sir Leslie Stephen and
others; but several copies are now known: there is one in the British Museum,
and still others in the New York Public Library, the Huntington Library, and
the library of the University of Michigan.

later than May 1716; for on 1 June 1716 Burnet writes
Duckett 'that Addison and the rest of the Rhiming Gang
have dropt their Resentment against the Lordlike Man
[Pope]'. Addison himself in the *Freeholder* of 7 May 1716
tried by compliment to make amends for former errors
concerning Homer. According to Pope[1] this change of
front was due to his sending Addison an expostulating letter
with the first sketch of this satire subjoined. Pope adds:
'He used me very civilly ever after; and never did me any
injustice, that I know of, from that time to his death, which
was about three years after.'

Pope's story emerges, then, with only one obvious flaw:
the *Memoirs of Wycherley* appeared two years after the
event of which he alleges they were a partial cause. Two
explanations are possible. First, he wrongly swept the
Memoirs into the story as a ground of grievance which
seemed very real and seemed to give additional justification
to the portrait. If the lines were sent to Addison after the
Memoirs appeared in 1718, Addison, who died in 1719,
could not have used Pope well for 'three years' before his
death, as Pope said he did. According to the second possible
explanation, however, we have to disregard this statement
concerning the three years of good treatment and assume
that the portrait was written and sent (if sent at all) to
Addison after May 1718, when the *Memoirs* appeared.
The line about 'meaner Gildon's venal quill' must, of
course, have been written after May 1718; but it is not
a vital part of the fragment.[2] The first alternative hypothesis seems to explain more of the facts and explain them
better than does the second. In any case Pope was much
wronged by his nineteenth-century editors and biographers
in the matter of his relations with Addison. Perhaps the
great error in Addison's career, of which the printed pages
were so nearly spotless,[3] was his failure to be firm in his
restraint of his Little Senate and to keep himself clear of
connivance in the affair of Tickell's translation.

---

[1] Spence, p. 149.   [2] See *infra*, p. 273 and note.
[3] *Epistle to Augustus*, ll. 215–16.

VI

ENTER EDMUND CURLL: 1716

W E have now seen Pope passing through some early skirmishes and through a serious campaign directed against the success of his *Iliad*. Before we plunge farther into this morass of attack and counter-attack, it may be well to pause and analyse the situation.

What were the types of attack used, or the circumstances in which attack most commonly originated? What are the chief accusations against Pope by his enemies, and what, at this distance, seem to be his salient traits as a fighter? A survey based on these questions may help to guide us in our further history of the campaigns against 'the English Homer', as our poet was now called.

We have seen Pope, apparently as the aggressor, attacking Elkanah Settle in a little-regarded poem, John Dennis in a few lines of the *Essay on Criticism*, Philips's *Pastorals* in *Guardian* No. 40, and Addison's *Cato* in an epigram said to be by himself and Rowe—doubtless the product of a half-hour in a tavern. So far as we know, he had not attacked Gildon, Welsted, Burnet, Duckett, or the authors of such anonymous pamphlets as *Aesop at the Bear-Garden*. It seems apparent that, in part, both Pope and his opponents were victims of something like 'gang warfare', and that individual responsibility is consequently hard to place. The Little Senate, on the one hand, may be partly blamed for Addison's growing hostility to Pope, and it is certain that Pope was at times the victim of his friendship with Swift, Arbuthnot, and Gay, whose works were more than once ascribed to him. We have seen Dennis ascribing to him Wagstaffe's *Letter from the Facetious Doctor Andrew Tripe, at Bath* (1714), and the wits at Button's insisting on his responsibility for the *What D'ye Call It*.[1] Many of

[1] Cibber told Spence the following story:
Mr. Pope brought some of the 'What d'ye call it', in his own handwriting

Gay's works of 1714–16 show a fighting bias in favour of
Pope, and Pope must accept some responsibility in such
cases. So also of course must Addison in the case of his
followers. Gay's attacks on Philips are works of art, but
they may have hurt the more because of their quality.
Lacking, apparently, abundant ammunition against Pope,
the Buttonians made use of the political and religious issues
of the time: they love to remind the public that Pope is a
Catholic, and as such a Non-juror and potential traitor.

Because of a habit of taking his victims by surprise
whenever he chose, Pope early acquired a reputation for
treacherous attack. The decorum of surprise in attack,
whether in games, in war, or in satire, is difficult to prescribe.
Pope's victims are fundamentally surprised to find themselves such. Their attitude is summed up in the reputed
exclamation of Philips: 'I wonder why the little crooked
bastard should attack me, who never offended him either in
word or deed.'[1] They never realize that inferior writing or
pretentious claims to fame are crimes for a littérateur. We
have seen Dennis totally at a loss to understand why Pope,
who hardly knew him, should repeat the criticisms made
by others who knew him well. Probably Addison was likewise at a loss to understand why Pope should make free with
so beautiful a work as *Cato*. Hence grew up the idea that
Pope was actuated by unaccountable malice. His own portrait was conceived to be drawn by himself in the picture
of Thersites in the second Book of his *Iliad*. Such an
interpretation of Pope depends essentially on an assured
belief by his victims in their own superior merit. It was
inconceivable to Dennis that he was a type of irritable
poet; and yet if Pope had never written, the evidence of
Dennis's irritability would be ample. It was inconceivable
to Philips, apparently, that one should question his right

---

to Cibber, the part about the miscarriage in particular, but not much beside.
When it was read to the players, Mr. Pope read it, though Gay was by.—Gay
always used to read his own plays. After this, upon seeing a knife with the name
of J. Gay upon it, Cibber said: 'What, does Mr. Pope make knives too?' Spence,
p. 348.
[1] J. Nichols, *Illustrations*, vii. 713.

to be ranked with Theocritus and Spenser; and Addison could brook no facetiousness with regard to his noble Roman tragedy. To these men it seemed that only malice could prompt unfavourable opinions. Their very attitude shows the need of some attempt to make them realize their fallibility. Pope's efforts, contaminated with politics and other accidental issues, were unhappy, but one may well doubt if his lines on Dennis, his essay on Philips's *Pastorals*, or the reflections on *Cato* in his epigram or in the *What D'ye Call It* were unduly severe. So far he seems well to have preserved the Horatian and Addisonian spirit of *ridentem dicere*. The 'Atticus' portrait, to be sure, shows a more serious mood.

We have already seen Dennis's fairly early list of accusations against Pope.[1] It may be profitable to set down here a later bill of complaints from a post-Dunciad pamphlet, *Pope Alexander's Supremacy* (1729), written by Duckett and Dennis, if Pope was rightly informed. The passage has a double interest as a bill of complaints and as a summary of the years now under discussion:

I find, that upon his first coming to Town, out of pure Compassion for his exotick Figure, narrow Circumstances and humble Appearance, the late Mr. *Wycherley* admitted him into his Society, and suffer'd him, notwithstanding his Make, to be his humble admirer at *Will's*; and afterwards finding in him a glimmering of Genius, recommended him to some People of Rank, and introduc'd him to the most eminent Men of Letters; which Courtesy he soon after repaid with a satyrical Copy of Verses on his Benefactor: This put an End to their Correspondence some Time before Mr. *Wycherley* dy'd. His Acquaintance by this Means being made with Sir *Richard Steele*, and Mr. *Addison*, they likewise, in Compassion to his unhappy Form, and destitute Condition, endeavour'd to procure him a Support under both, by setting on Foot a Subscription in his Behalf; it was, indeed, for a Work, which (as has since appeared) they must have known he was not equal to; but they hoped, with their friendly Assistance, to have supply'd his Defects. However, his Subscriptions were no sooner full, when the little mischievous Urchin, no longer able to contain his Malice,

[1] *Supra*, p. 105.

wrote a Satyr upon both these Gentlemen, (as he did afterwards an abusive Libel on one of them;) and as many Things which had pass'd in private Conversation at *Button*'s Coffee-house, came to be known by the Lord O[xford] of which Infidelity *Scriblerus* was suspected, he was obliged to absent himself for some Years from thence. After this, he listed openly in the *Tory* Service, and every Week publish'd scandalous Invectives on those very *Whigs*, who had been his amplest *Subscribers*. He was in this honourable Occupation, when the late Queen dy'd; and our Poet soon changing his Note, found Means to be introduc'd to some of the young Ladies of the Court. Four of these, who were his best Friends and Patronesses, (as they are to any Thing that carries the Face of Wit or Learning) he abused in a Scurvy Ballad, for which any other Man would have received Correction; but in his Case, these generous Ladies contented themselves with shewing a Contempt of his Malice, and banishing him their Company. This did not hinder him from writing a second Lampoon, wherein he spared not the most exalted Characters, though under feigned Names; and adding Treachery to Ill-Nature, he threw the scandalous Imputation of having wrote this Libel, on a Lady of Quality, whose Wit is equal to her Beauty, and whose Character might have suffer'd by this impudent Forgery of his.[1]

It will be noted that the specific charges here are all made vaguely, and consequently it is difficult to examine them with assurance; but it seems safe to say that not one of the seven specific charges made was ever proved or ever supported either by valid evidence or by a shadow of probability. (1) There is no reason for believing that he satirized Wycherley; they were less intimate in the last five years of Wycherley's life, but they were friends most of that period. (2) Steele may have helped Pope's subscription for the *Iliad*, but apparently Addison did not. Pope never satirized Steele, so far as is known; his notices of *Cato* hardly answer the description given here of satire on 'both these gentlemen'. The Atticus lines may be called 'an abusive libel' certainly. (3) The charge that Pope was a spy for Oxford at Button's seems absurd, but his attempts to

---

[1] pp. 13, 14, of *Pope Alexander's Supremacy and Infallibility examin'd; And the Errors of Scriblerus and his Man William Detected* . . . J. Roberts . . . 1729.

frequent both the Little Senate and the Scriblerus Club might easily give rise to such a charge. On the face of it the charge is at least improbable, though it is interesting as suggesting the sense of self-importance of the Buttonians. It reminds one of Dennis's fear of Louis XIV's personal interest in him. (4) That he was a weekly writer for the Tories in 1714 is hardly possible. There is not the slightest evidence in favour of such a charge. It is probably based on a rank Curll pamphlet, *The Catholick Poet* (1716), which asserts that as soon as Pope's subscription for Homer was filled by 'Protestant Authors', the poet 'immediately betray'd all their private Conversations to the late Ministry, and at the same time wrote *Guardians* and *Examiners*'.[1] (5) The ballad on the maids of honour is probably 'The Challenge'—sometimes called 'A Court Ballad' (1717).[2] That this bit of persiflage was badly received by the ladies in question is certainly false. Mrs. Lepel—later Lady Hervey—was a visitor in the Pope household in 1720,[3] and Mrs. Howard was a friend during most of his later life. So also were the Misses Griffin and Bellenden. (6) That there was a second lampoon, which (7) Pope tried to ascribe to (probably) Lady Mary Wortley Montagu is possibly gossip of the time concerning 'Roxana, or the Drawing Room', one of the *Court Poems* for which Pope gave Curll an emetic, as we shall see, in 1716. The truth seems to be that 'Roxana' was actually by Lady Mary, and that Pope gallantly took the discredit for it.

The wild accusation of this passage is typical of what Pope faced throughout the rest of his life after 1715. Nothing (usually) is proved; the most sensational charges are made in the vaguest possible terms; and by reiteration the charges have been made to pass as an authentic source of light on Pope's character. The more general charges here

---

[1] p. 5.

[2] The assertions are equally false if they refer to the so-called *Court Poems* (for 'Roxana', which satirizes ladies who may have been maids of honour, is by Lady Mary Wortley Montagu) or to the *News from Court* (1719: very likely not by Pope).

[3] Elwin-Courthope, viii. 45.

made—those involving moral traits—assert his ingratitude, treachery, ill-nature, and malice. If the concrete accusations were proved, these traits could safely be imputed to Pope. On the small measure of truth contained in the vague accusations, what inferences can be made?

First, was Pope ungrateful? If he was ungrateful to Wycherley, it was probably the natural 'ingratitude' of a brilliant offspring to a (poetically) inferior parent. (Wycherley is here regarded solely as a poet, not as a dramatist.) Pope outgrew Wycherley as a poet: he possibly made to others slighting but true remarks about Wycherley's verses, which he was so long revising; but as for evidence of a more censurable ingratitude, there is none. With regard to Steele, whose mentions of Pope in the *Spectator*[1] were much more glowing than those by Addison, there is not the slightest evidence of ingratitude. Pope did not write the *Letter of Doctor Andrew Tripe*, and he seems always to have spoken of Steele as a friend might, and Steele has left no adverse comments on Pope. With regard to the maids of honour again the charge is absurd.

In the case of Addison the matter is debatable. Addison, like Wycherley, may have introduced Pope to many important persons: we must assume that he did, though Pope had many influential friends before he knew Addison. As for the *Spectator's* comment on the *Essay on Criticism*, it is an obvious service and a great one. At the same time, when Pope came to know Addison and to see how his critic's mind was always hedged about with reservations, it would be natural for Pope to feel less enthusiasm for the praise. It was hardly just for Addison to say the things he had said against Dennis in the *Spectator* and *Tatler*, and then to stigmatize the lines in the *Essay on Criticism* devoted to 'Appius' as 'strokes of ill nature'. Addison's services, and consequently Pope's ingratitude, have been much exaggerated. Pope's sins against Philips and against *Cato* have also been magnified. One may well wish that Pope had

---

[1] Cf. *Spectator*, Nos. 378, 532, 534, 555 (by Steele), with Nos. 253 and 523 (by Addison).

never committed even these faults; but one must doubt whether, if he had refrained, he could have escaped that Whig wrath that was inevitably to come upon such as were friends with Tory writers. After all, the outbursts against Gay's works were almost as violent as those against Pope; but no one has called Gay ingrate or traitor—though they have spoken of his 'impenetrable stupidity'.[1] The charge of Pope's ingratitude to Addison comes nearer being true than most of the accusations made by the Dunces; but it can hardly be taken very seriously. Doubtless Pope, knowing Addison, should not have been concerned in the epigram about the Tory Celia and *Cato*—especially since he had written the Prologue to the play; but since Rowe was his fellow criminal, it is pretty certain that the intention was to satirize Tories—or at least party vehemence—rather than to depreciate *Cato*.

The charge of treachery also will be commonly repeated. One of the astonishing things about Burnet's attacks on Pope in 1715 is the fact that apparently Burnet knew Pope but slightly. After Addison finally, in 1716, bade the wild contention cease between the Buttonians and Pope, Burnet wrote to Duckett:

> For my part Garth made Mr. Pope and myself dine together and would have us friends and Acquaintance; and to speak [truth] it is an ill natured little false Dog, but he does not want for a great deal of very diverting Satyrical Wit.[2]

'Ill natured little false Dog' might in 1716 be applied at Button's to almost any Catholic writer, but Burnet is giving the reputation, no doubt, that Pope there enjoyed. Again there is not much clear evidence for the reputation. The major facts would be that Wycherley disliked the treatment he had received from Pope; that Pope had written a Prologue for *Cato* and then had mildly attacked the play, and

---

[1] Addison evidently felt qualms about Gay. Early in 1716 he subscribed for ten copies of *Trivia* (R. E. Tickell, *Thomas Tickell*, p. 77); and there is the curious story of Addison's begging Gay's forgiveness for unnamed injuries on his death-bed. See Spence, pp. 149–50.

[2] *Letters*, ed. Nichol Smith, p. 99.

that he had written *Guardian* No. 40 surreptitiously against
Philips. Or perhaps the major 'fact' was that Whigs
regarded all Roman Catholics as deceitful and treacherous.
An important ground for the notion of Pope's slyness is the
charge made in the *Key to the What D'ye Call It* that he
fought behind the shelter of his friends. It is quite true that
he did this in some cases—notably that of Gay. But it is
further true that just as Steele took abuse for Addison's
strokes of ill nature on Dennis, so Pope frequently took
blame for works of Swift and Gay. Pope's whole psychology
was that of physical inferiority. He loved allies, and if his
battles were those of a 'gang warfare', he had to take the
disadvantages along with the advantages of that system. He
was certainly at times willing, as we shall see, to let others
shoulder the responsibility of his lampoons. What personal
satirist has not been thankful for such relief?

So general a charge as malice and ill nature can hardly be
argued. It can only be stated as a matter of opinion, not
likely to be keenly disputed, that of his satirical writings *so
far* only the *Narrative of Dr. Robert Norris* and the 'Atticus'
lines are likely to be accused of serious malice. There has
been a general assumption through the last 'romantic' century that the genesis of satire is ill nature, but this hardly
seems a sound view. At any rate, nowhere except in the
'Atticus' lines do we yet see the style or mood of the later
satirist.

A charge against Pope's muse that has so far been urged
(curiously enough) only against the *Rape of the Lock*, but one
that will in the future be recurrent, is indecency. There can
be small doubt that 'little Alexander, whom the women
laugh at', was at this time free in his morals and freer in his
language. As early as March 1713, Sir William Trumbull
had (if the letter is authentic) written to beg Pope to take
care of his health, and 'to get out of all tavern company, and
fly away *tanquam ex incendio*'.[1] The poet was by nature too
convivial to take such advice, and in 1715 he boasts of sitting
until the small hours over burgundy and champagne.[2] Even

---

[1] Elwin-Courthope, vi. 5.   [2] Ibid. vi. 228 (April 1715).

in his later years he at least occasionally drank too much.[1]
Carruthers regarded the period 1714–18 as perhaps the
gayest of Pope's life.[2] Probably in 1716 or 1717 occurred
something like the episode in 'a house of carnal recreation'
that Cibber in 1742 narrated in his *Letter to Mr. Pope*.[3]
Pope denied that Cibber ever thus rescued him from a
diseased bawd, but it was in an atmosphere of jokes about
unsanitary venereal experiences that the gentlemen of the
town then lived, and Pope, conscious of his physical
inferiority, put up a brave front at being a rake. He was at
the time occasionally in the company of the Earl of Warwick, a youth of about eighteen years, who according to
tradition was responsible for the attempted joke narrated
by Cibber.[4] Pope mentions Warwick in his 'Farewell to
London'. This poetic regret for the exchange of town life
for Binfield and the dull labour of translation is, in spite of
the lamentable implications of certain lines, one of Pope's
more spirited and light-hearted *jeux d'esprit*. Among its
stanzas come:

> Dear, damn'd, distracting town, farewell!
> Thy fools no more I'll tease:
> This year in peace, ye critics, dwell,
> Ye harlots, sleep at ease!
>
> .   .   .   .   .   .
>
> To drink and droll be Rowe allow'd
> Till the third watchman's toll;
> Let Jervas gratis paint, and Frowde
> Save threepence and his soul.
>
> Farewell, Arbuthnot's raillery
> On every learned sot;
> And Garth, the best good Christian he,
> Although he knows it not.
>
> .   .   .   .   .   .

---

[1] See letters of William Kent, the artist, in *Hist. MSS. Comm.: Second Report*
(1871), p. 19 (Spencer MSS.).
[2] Carruthers's *Life of Pope* (1857), p. 133.
[3] *A Letter from Mr. Cibber to Mr. Pope*, London, W. Lewis, 1742 (1st ed.?),
pp. 47–9.   [4] W. H. Dilworth, *Life of Pope* (1759), p. 111.

Why should I stay? Both parties rage;
    My vixen mistress squalls;
The wits in envious feuds engage:
    And Homer (damn him!) calls.

    .   .   .   .   .   .

Why make I friendships with the great,
    When I no favour seek?
Or follow girls, seven hours in eight?
    I us'd but once a week.

Still idle, with a busy air,
    Deep whimsies to contrive;
The gayest valetudinaire,
    Most thinking rake, alive.

    .   .   .   .   .   .

Luxurious lobster-nights, farewell,
    For sober studious days!
And Burlington's delicious meal,
    For salads, tarts, and pease!

Adieu to all, but Gay alone,
    Whose soul, sincere and free,
Loves all mankind, but flatters none,
    And so may starve with me.

The results of Pope's tavern hours were not all so happy as
this. The epigram on *Cato*, for example, is more typically
gross and less pleasant in its consequences on his career. Of
somewhat the same type of fashionable indecency are his
'Receipt to Make a Cuckold' (December 1713), and the
lamentable version of the first Psalm (June 1716).[1] Such
morsels, surreptitiously published at inopportune moments,
caused Pope considerable uneasiness and enabled hostile
persons to ascribe at will to his pen any anonymous indecencies. The period of translation was fertile in these bits
of verse and it is not altogether astonishing that Pope's
muse after weeks of labour in high heroics should refresh
herself in an epigram or in some informal excursion into
jocose scandal. The charge of indecency was added to those

---

[1] Griffith, pp. 53 and 548.

of ingratitude, treachery, and malice, and made to re-echo through the years that preceded the *Dunciad* as well as those that followed.

Though this last charge of indecency was stressed in the attacks on Pope during 1716, politics and religion were stressed more. There had been much excitement over the Jacobite uprising of 1715, and in 1716 there was still excitement over the trials of the unfortunates captured at Preston. A last day for Non-jurors to take the oaths of allegiance was 23 January 1716. Prior and many others availed themselves of this last chance, but not Pope. There was before Parliament a measure to require all Roman Catholics to register their estates, so that additional land-taxes might be levied on them. This caused much selling of real estate by Catholics and even the migration of many, among whom was Pope's friend Edward Blount.[1] Largely to avoid taxes, probably, the Popes sold their place at Binfield, and in April 1716, settled near the Earl of Burlington's villa on the waterside at Chiswick.[2] The larger result of this commotion concerning Catholics was, apart from the selling of property, &c., to stimulate vituperation of all such 'traitors' as might be expected to be awaiting another attempt by the Pretender. The personal effect of the removal to Chiswick was that Pope could now go to London almost daily if he wished: he could be in the thick of the fray.

For a time he was. During the unusual cold of January 1716, he lived in London at Jervas's house, though Jervas had gone to Ireland. The year for Pope, however, opened warm, with a ballad in the *Flying Post* for 5 January 1716. It was called 'The Raree-Show, or an Explication of the O——d A——c for the Year 1716. By Jeremiah Van Husen, a German Artist.' This consists of stanzas identifying various figures in a print, real or imaginary, on the 'Ormond Almanac'. (Ormond's flight to France and the Pretender in 1715 had been a notable sensation.) The central figure is naturally 'James the III', and about him

---

[1] Pope's letters to Edward Blount, Elwin-Courthope, vi. 374–5.
[2] Elwin-Courthope, vi. 241 (20 April [1716]).

are grouped Ormond, Sacheverell (or Trapp), Dr. Phipps, and then

> The next is,—or may my End be a Rope;
> That little High-Church Rhimer, Poet Po—;
> Or, that I may guess yet a little nigher,
> Hang me but it may happen to be Pri—.

Further, unimportant association of Pope with Jacobite hopes, fears, and superstitions resulted from a series of nights made portentous by displays of the aurora borealis. The *Weekly Packet*, 18 February 1716, quoted from Pope's *Iliad*, Book IV, lines 95–106, the description of Minerva descending like a comet to break the truce between the Greeks and the Trojans. The quotation of this passage, apropros of 'letters from Paris [that] tell of earthquakes and meteors in Italy, which scientists regard as portents of war', was quite possibly intended as a compliment; but it was unpleasant to be associated needlessly with Jacobite prophesies of further wars or uprisings. On 6 March the King 'gave the Royal Assent to *An Act for the speedy and easy Tryal of the* [Jacobite] *Rebels*', and the same evening followed more aurora borealis that seemed ominous to sympathizers with the rebels.[1] On 19 May appeared in a volume of *State Poems*, 'An Epilogue written for the late celebrated New Play called the *Drummer*, but not spoke'.[2] Addison's unsuccessful comedy the *Drummer* had its brief run beginning 10 March, and this discarded Prologue included party strokes that are somewhat obscure, in satire of these Jacobite superstitions concerning meteors and portents. The Prologue near its beginning makes mention of Pope's uneasiness at having his comets made Jacobite portents:

> If any *Briton* in this Place appears,
> A slave to Priests, or superstitious Fears,

---

[1] *The Historical Register . . . for the Year 1716*, pp. 117 and 217. On p. 217 is an account of further portents in the sky for 2 April. The capital made of these 'omens' is seen in a pamphlet called *A Dialogue between a Whig and a Jacobite . . . Occasion'd by the Phaenomenon in the Skie, March 6. 1715/16*. Printed for J. Roberts . . . 1716. This is a Whig pamphlet that ran to at least three editions.   [2] Ibid., pp. 20–3.

Let these odd Scenes reform his Brainsick Notions,
Or BYFIELD's ready—to apply his Potions.
Those Wits Excepted, who appear'd so wise,
To Conjure Spectres from the vap'ry Skies.
A very POPE (I'm told) may be afraid,
And tremble at the Monsters, which he made.
From dark misshapen *Clouds of many a Dye,
A different Object rose to every Eye:
And the same Vapour, as your Fancies ran,
Appear'd a Monarch, or a Warming-Pan.[1]

* The late Meteor.

Such talk of meteors was likely to occur in the days of satire
on astrologers and almanac-makers. At the end of 1716 we
shall find Pope again involved in some predictions made by
E. Parker, Philomath.

Along with these attempts to place Pope among the
Jacobites came various adverse mentions of his religion, and
of course there were slurs on the second volume of Homer—
though nothing like the campaign that the first volume had
undergone. There were also the usual bold and contemptible personalities, and these as well as the other sorts of
attack for the most part seem to come from one antagonist.
In 1715 there had been a 'gang warfare' between the Little
Senate and the remnants of the Scriblerus Club. In 1716
the spectacle is focused on the personal combat between
Pope and Edmund Curll.

It is unnecessary to sketch in detail the character or career
of this astonishing person.[2] His role in the first half of the
eighteenth century resembles nothing more than that of
some foul bird acting as scavenger for a literary battle-field.
But Curll could do more than a vulture: he could stimulate
the dying fight, and see that its carrion was preserved in
print. After all, we ought not to be too abusive of this man;
for his energy and his thoroughly modern journalistic spirit

[1] The last verse quoted refers to scandalous gossip—kept alive by Hanoverians
—to the effect that the Pretender was not of royal birth, but had been smuggled
into the queen's chamber in a warming-pan, and presented as a new-born,
royal heir.
[2] It has been done by Ralph Straus in *The Unspeakable Curll*, London, 1928.

of trying all chances for a good story have preserved for us
many a small piece of epigram or lampoon; and his brazen
impudence has preserved for us many a private letter by
some person of note, who had no desire frequently to have
his letters embalmed in printer's ink. It must be added too
that while for most celebrities Curll acted only as a surreptitious or even a piratical publisher, his initiative and
ability to sell—or some other qualities—won him the
chance to print apparently approved editions for virtuous
men like Addison, Blackmore, Richard Rawlinson, and
Edward Young.[1] His specialities, however, were his scandalous biographies, which, according to Arbuthnot, 'added
a new terror to death',[2] and his seditious and pornographic
pamphlets, which more than once put him in the pillory.
He kept, supposedly, a garret full of needy authors, who
wrote exclusively at his personal direction. William Pattison,[3] one of these authors, has left us a somewhat favourable
account of this 'literary' factory, and Henry Fielding in the
Author's Farce has given a very amusing account of it.

In Pope's career Curll is always surreptitious, though
Pope himself sometimes steals the role. Curll first entered
our poet's sphere as the 'snapper up of unconsidered trifles'
by Jonathan Swift. Throughout the period, in fact, he was
just as ready to print Swiftiana as Popiana—and he found
rather more of the former than of the latter: there was
enough of both sorts for all readers.

On 30 August 1716 Swift wrote in reply evidently to
some laments Pope had sent about numerous enemies:

And who are all these enemies you hint at? I can only think of
Curll, Gildon, Squire Burnet, Blackmore, and a few others, whose
fame I have forgot. Fools, in my opinion, are as necessary for a
good writer as pen, ink, and paper. And besides, I would fain know
whether every draper does not show you three or four damned

---

[1] It may be doubted if Addison employed Curll, but the others did. Addison
seems not to have objected to Curll's editions.

[2] Swift's *Correspondence*, ed. Ball, iv. 378.

[3] See Pattison's *Poetical Works* (1728), p. 44. Also for Curll's indecencies see
the 'leader' in (Mist's) *Weekly Journal: or, Saturday's Post*, 5 April 1718, and in
many other journals of the day.

pieces of stuff to set off his good one? However, I will grant that one thorough bookselling rogue is better qualified to vex an author, than all his contemporary scribblers in critic or satire, not only by stolen copies of what was incorrect or unfit for the public but by downright laying of other men's dulness at your door. I had a long design upon the ears of that Curll when I was in credit, but the rogue would never allow me a fair stroke at them, although my penknife was drawn and sharp.[1]

In the *Journal to Stella*, 14 May 1711, we have further evidence of Swift's animosity, which later in the lines 'On the Death of Dr. Swift' (1733) becomes merely irony:

> Now Curll his shop from rubbish drains:
> Three genuine tomes of Swift's remains!
>
> .   .   .   .
>
> He'll treat me as he does my betters,
> Publish my will, my life, my letters:
> Revive the libels born to die,
> Which Pope must bear, as well as I.

Pope's experience was to prove the truth of Swift's observation that 'one thorough bookselling rogue is better qualified to vex an author, than all his contemporary scribblers in critic or satire'. Curll, as Pope's biographer Dilworth mildly remarked, 'carried on the trade to lengths unknown before him'.[2] He used all the possible irritants in his power, and from the time early in 1714, when he seems to have begun on Pope, to the time in 1741 when he pirated the Pope-Swift correspondence, he was seldom idle. He nothing extenuated, and, to give him his due, he set down relatively little in especial malice: his objects were those of the true journalist—to give the public good hot stuff, and to make money. As Pope makes Mrs. Curll say, somewhat too neatly for her: her husband wanted daily books, and his family wanted daily bread.[3]

Early in 1714, Curll, through the shop of J. Roberts, had published *A new Rehearsal, or Bays the Younger*. This pamphlet, Charles Gildon's first known attack on Pope, is a

---

[1] Elwin-Courthope, vii. 15–16.   [2] *Life of Pope* (1759), p. 84.
[3] Elwin-Courthope, x. 470.

caustic satire particularly on Rowe and Pope. Pope is represented as insufferably conceited and brazen: the attack, so
far as Pope's works are concerned, centres on the *Rape of the
Lock*, but his ignorance of Greek and his incompetence as
translator of the *Iliad* are roundly asserted. Why Gildon at
this and other times attacked Pope is unknown. Evidently
Pope later thought the Whigs hired him, and if the Whigs
thought Pope could be thus deterred from party writing,
they doubtless in 1714 would have hired Gildon, or any one
else, to turn the trick. More likely Gildon's relations with
Wycherley stimulated him to hostility against Pope. In
1719, when blind and poverty-stricken, Gildon wrote to
Addison for help almost as if he thought the Whig party or
Addison himself owed him aid.[1]

At almost this same time another Whig writer in Curll's
employ exhibited for Pope two other typical bookseller's
tricks. In the second edition of Lintot's Miscellany[2] Pope
had first printed one of his tavern pieces, his 'Epigram upon
Two or Three'. Curll, or his agent Pemberton, got hold of
the poem, which was next printed in Oldmixon's Miscellany on 10 April 1714, with the more alluring title of 'A
Receipt to make a Cuckold. By Mr. Pope.'[3] Not content
with annoying Pope by such a title, Oldmixon gravely
apologized for the epigram in his Preface:

> I know of but one *Poem* that has crept into it, which I would
> have had kept still in *Manuscript*. 'Tis a very little One, and will
> be easily slipt over in so great a Number of Others that seem
> intended for the Press; which certainly that never was. Thus much
> was due to Justice, considering the Company it is in.

The volume also contained 'Advice to Mr. Pope, on his
intended Translation of Homer', which, while ostensibly
complimentary, stresses the mercenary objective—the true
one—of the translator. During this same year Curll put his
own name on the title-page of another Miscellany[4] that

---

[1] Manuscript letter in the British Museum, Egerton MS. 1971, fol. 33.
[2] See Griffith, p. 32, Book 32. The title-page is dated 1714, but the volume
was published 4 December 1713 (*Daily Courant*).
[3] See Griffith, p. 32, Book 31. Adv. on 6 and 10 April 1714, in the *Evening Post*.
[4] See Griffith, p. 34, Book 33.

contained the epigram 'Upon the Duke of Marlborough's House at Woodstock', a 'house' that caused much comment in 1714 when the nation's attitude towards Marlborough was shifting. Later in the year this piece was reprinted in Curll's *Elzevir Miscellany*, which had a second edition in 1715. This Miscellany also included the 'Epigram on a Tory Lady . . . at *Cato*', which had first appeared in the *Poetical Entertainer*, a Morphew production. Possibly, as Straus thinks, Morphew worked with Curll. If so, it may be that Curll's first service for Pope was to publish this squib at an unlucky moment.

During the hectic spring of 1715 Curll seems almost suspiciously absent from the front of the battle. Most of the attacks on Pope in these months were, to be sure, published by Roberts, Morphew, and Burleigh,[1] and if again Straus is right in assuming that they were frequently agents for Curll, he may have been in the fray after all. It is probable that in July Curll had a hand in procuring publicity for Gildon's *New Rehearsal*, which was sold with *Remarks on Mr. Rowe's Tragedy of the Lady Jane Gray*.[2] Some time during the year also his translator, Ozell, found a publisher, probably really Curll, for *The Works of the celebrated Monsieur Voiture. Done from the Paris Edition by Mr. Ozell, to which is prefixed the Author's Life and a Character of his Writings by Mr. Pope*.[3] This 'character' was a reprint,

---

[1] The mere fact that these publishers were active against Pope, or that Curll sometimes advertised their wares as for sale in his shop, seems insufficient proof that they were Curll's agents. In all but enterprise and unscrupulousness they were far Curll's superiors. Pope's *Full and True Account of a Horrid and Barbarous Revenge on . . . Curll* (1716) has on its title-page: 'Sold by J. Roberts, R. Burleigh, J. Baker, and S. Popping.' If these were Curll's customary confederates, as seems likely, the list has of course a satirical rather than commercial purpose. For the *New Rehearsal*, which bore only Roberts's name, Pope blames Curll (Elwin-Courthope, x. 466).

[2] Adv. in the *Weekly Packet*, 2 July 1715. The type was not reset. A new title, half-title, and 12 pages of comment on Rowe's play are prefixed to old sheets. This duodecimo work is not to be confused with an octavo pamphlet, also from Roberts, called *Remarks on the Tragedy of the Lady Jane Grey; in a Letter to Mr. Rowe.* [n.d.]

[3] I have seen only a bookseller's advertisement of this volume, not the book itself. Curll was advertising it late in 1716.

almost certainly pirated, of Pope's 'Epistle to a Lady with
the Works of Voiture'. Pope spent parts of August and
September 1715 at Bath; and in October Curll advertised
a sixpenny miscellany under the title,

> The Bath Toasts, for the Year 1715 (being Characters of the
> Ladies who were there this Summer) a Poem. Inscrib'd to Mr.
> Pope. To which are added exact Descriptions of the Bath and
> Tunbridge-Wells. Printed for E. Curll.[1]

The inscription 'to Mr. Pope' may have been complimentary, but one doubts it.[2] Later in the year Curll, so one
suspects, may have inspired an item of literary interest
printed in the *Weekly Packet* for 12 November 1715:

> We hear that Mr. Oldsworth of Hants, the celebrated Author
> of a Poem call'd *Muscipula*, which is admirably well translated into
> English Blank Verse lately by a Gentleman, is preparing Amend-
> ments and Corrections for Mr. Pope's Homer, the Errors of which
> are already pleasantly display'd in a Pamphlet call'd *Homer in a
> Nutshell*.

There is perhaps not much truth in this item. Edward
Holdsworth, author of *Muscipula*, was born in Hampshire,
but was a tutor at Oxford until 1715, when he left as a Non-
juror. His poem was printed repeatedly by Curll. William
Oldisworth,[3] collaborator with Ozell and Broome, in the
prose (blank verse!) translation of Homer, and also a Curll
writer, might seem, however, more probably to be writing
against Pope's *Iliad*. But Oldisworth was a Jacobite, had
written for the *Examiner*, and would be writing for a
dinner rather than for spite if he were attacking Pope.

All these were, however, relatively casual and desultory
engagements; the real encounter between Pope and Curll
was to commence in 1716. Things then began tamely
enough with Curll advertising the *Bath Toasts* again in

---

[1] Adv. in the *Monthly Catalogue*, ii (October 1715), 33. No copy of the book
is known.

[2] It seems possible, in view of Duckett's 'Epilogue for Punch' in the *Homerides*
of 1715, that Pope and Duckett had been at Bath at the same time in 1714. It
was Pope's first visit. See Elwin-Courthope, vi. 218–19 (25 September [1714]).

[3] Curiously enough, the father of Oldisworth, a clergyman, held two of the
Hampshire livings that Pope's grandfather had held.

February.[1] The next month he published the first volume of Sir Richard Blackmore's virtuous *Essays upon Several Subjects*, which contained even a bit of praise of Pope's *Iliad*;[2] but Blackmore was no friend of Arbuthnot, nor of Swift, whom, in his 'Essay upon Wit', he called 'an impious buffoon'.[3] Blackmore on wit was too good a joke to pass without notice, and Gay with speed defended Swift in 'Verses to be placed under the Picture of England's Arch Poet'.[4] Thus Pope and Gay passed into the large class of 'impious buffoons' destined later to be the theme of Blackmore's pious fulminations.

On 24 March the second volume of the *Iliad* appeared. It was favourably received by every one who at the moment really counted; but by Curll and his hungry authors—supported by some few others possibly—it was treated with scorn. For just at this moment Pope, evidently not knowing his man, decided to rid himself of the nuisance that was Edmund Curll. The occasion that stung him to this decision was obvious enough, but Pope's reasons for regarding the occasion as serious are less clear. The occasion was the unauthorized publication by Curll of a volume which had as its first title-page the following:

Court Poems. Viz; I. The Basset-Table. An Eclogue. II. The Drawing Room. III. The Toilet. Publish'd faithfully, as they were found in a Pocket-Book taken up in Westminster-Hall, the Last Day of the Lord Winton's Tryal. London: Printed for J. Roberts, near the Oxford Arms in Warwick-Lane. MDCCVI. Price Six-Pence.[5]

The brazenness of such a title is obvious: what can one do with a bookseller who avows that he publishes poems from lost pocket-books? But that part of the advertisement is a 'faithful' lie; for, as Curll himself later admitted, he got the poems some weeks before publication from John Oldmixon—who in 1714 had published 'A Receipt to make a Cuckold'. But the title could not be particularly irritating, and at first sight the poems seem fully as presentable as

---

[1] *Evening Post*, 21 February 1716.   [2] p. vi.   [3] Ibid., pp. 217 ff.
[4] G. Faber in his edition of Gay's *Poetical Works* (Oxford, 1926), p. xxv, thinks the work not Gay's; but see Elwin-Courthope, viii. 22 (Pope to Jervas, 14 November 1716).   [5] The date is a misprint for MDCCXVI.

the 'tavern pieces' that Pope would keep on writing. What then did enrage him? We get a clue from the 'Advertisement' on pages i–iii of the thin octavo:

The *Reader* is acquainted, from the Title-Page, how I came possess'd of the following Poems. All that I have to add, is, only a Word or two concerning their *Author*.

Upon Reading them over at St. *James's* Coffee-House, they were attributed by the General Voice to be the Productions of a Lady of Quality.

When I produc'd them at *Button's*, the *Poetical Jury* there brought in a different Verdict; and the Foreman strenuously insisted upon it, that Mr. Gay was the *Man*; and declar'd, in Comparing the *Basset-Table*, with that Gentleman's Pastorals, he found the *Stile*, and *Turn of Thought*, to be evidently the same; which confirm'd him, and his Brethren, in the Sentence they had pronounc'd.

Not content with these Two Decisions, I was resolv'd to call in an Umpire; and accordingly chose a Gentleman of distinguish'd Merit, who lives not far from Chelsea.[1] I sent him the Papers; which he return'd to me the next Day, with this Answer:

Sir, Depend upon it, these Lines could come from no other Hand, than the Judicious Translator of Homer.

Thus having impartially given the Sentiment of the *Town*; I hope I may deserve Thanks, for the Pains I have taken, in endeavouring to find out the *Author* of these Valuable Performances; and every Body is at Liberty to bestow the Laurel as they please.

At any rate this was good advertising. The poems were by one of two of the best poets of the day or by the most brilliant female wit of the time, Lady Mary Wortley Montagu. All three would share in any discredit that might accrue, and since the poems embody scandals in high life that were recognizable, harm might come of it. For Gay, especially, who still hoped for a place at Court, 'The Drawing Room',[2] with its satire on court personages, might, if

---

[1] This should be Addison; but Curll is evidently trying to involve Addison and his group, and hence no credit need be given to this implication that Addison ascribed the poems to Pope.

[2] Roxana in this poem represents the Duchess of Roxburghe and Cockatilla the Duchess of Shrewsbury. The satire is also keen on the Princess of Wales. It may be to this poem that Dennis refers as Pope's satire on the maids of honour; but this is Lady Mary's. See the *Curliad* (1729), p. 21.

fastened upon him, lock for ever the doors of preferment. That doubtless angered Pope; but the wrath of Lady Mary, the real author of the poems,[1] moved him more. Pope had known her probably less than a year, but he was already the victim of that unlucky fondness that was to occupy his mind for the next few years. One assumes that her anger was the moving force with Pope, because, contrary to his custom, he took vengeance into his own hands. Gay, who was three times Pope's size, might have acted since he was equally offended as author; but for him to act would have been construed as an admission of authorship—and in any case Pope might naturally wish to be the hero of any revenge taken for Lady Mary's sake.

Since Pope was too puny to give Curll the physical chastisement that all the world would have approved, and that Hogarth has depicted in 'The Distressed Poet',[2] he prosecuted (with the aid of Arbuthnot and Lintot) a medical revenge: he gave Curll an emetic. Then he went home, wrote a history of the case, and published it as *A Full and true Account of a Horrid and Barbarous Revenge by Poison on the Body of Mr. Edmund Curll.* According to this thin folio pamphlet the *Court Poems* appeared on Monday, 26 March;[3] the emetic was administered the ensuing Wednesday; and the pamphlets giving the story of the revenge doubtless were in print almost at once.[4] The story is in part as follows:

Now on the Wednesday ensuing, between the hours of ten and eleven, Mr. Lintot, a neighbouring bookseller, desired a conference with Mr. Curll, about settling a title-page, inviting him at the same time to take a whet together. Mr. Pope, who is not the only

---

[1] 'The Toilette' may be Gay's (he included it in his *Poems* [1720]); but the other two are almost certainly Lady Mary's. On her claim to the 'Basset Table' see *Notes and Queries,* 7 S. ix. 225, 515; 9 S. ii. 141. And see also p. 204 of this present work.

[2] See R. H. Griffith, in the *Manly Anniversary Studies* (Chicago, 1923), pp. 190–6.

[3] Elwin-Courthope, x. 462. The statement accords closely with newspaper advertisements. See *Evening Post,* 27–9 March, &c.

[4] Griffith, pp. 51, 53. The first of these antedates 3 April 1716, when Oldmixon advertised in reply to it in the *Flying Post.*

instance how persons of bright parts may be carried away by the instigation of the devil, found means to convey himself into the same room, under pretence of business with Mr. Lintot, who, it seems, is the printer of his Homer. This gentleman, with a seeming coolness, reprimanded Mr. Curll for wrongfully ascribing to him the aforesaid poems: he excused himself by declaring, that one of his authors (Mr. Oldmixon by name) gave the copies to the press, and wrote the preface. Upon this Mr. Pope, being to all appearance reconciled, very civilly drank a glass of sack to Mr. Curll, which he as civilly pledged; . . . common sack, yet it was plain, by the pangs this unhappy stationer felt soon after, that some poisonous drug had been secretly infused therein.[1]

We need not give further details. Much of the pamphlet is disgusting, though there are amusing moments, as, for example, when *in extremis* Curll excepts from general damnations one of his authors: 'Only God bless Sir Richard Blackmore! you know he takes no copy-money.'[2]

In the *Full and True Account* Pope had ascribed the Preface of the *Court Poems* to John Oldmixon. Probably merely to advertise the poems, Oldmixon denied the accusation in an advertisement in the *Flying Post*, 3 April 1716:

Whereas Mr. *Lintot*, or Mr. *Pope*, has publish'd a false and ridiculous Libel, reflecting on several Gentlemen, particularly on myself: and it is said therein, that I was the Publisher of certain Verses call'd *Court Poems*, and that I wrote the Preface; I hereby declare, that I never saw a great part of those Verses, nor ever saw or heard of the Title or Preface to them till after the Poems were publish'd.   J. Oldmixon.
Witness, E. Curll

The purpose of this lying advertisement, if not publicity, must have been to prevent any one from giving Oldmixon unwanted medical attention. Some light, either on the veracity of Oldmixon's statement or on Curll's truthfulness, was thrown in 1735 in the prefatory letter addressed 'To Mr. Pope' in Curll's *Mr. Pope's Literary Correspondence. Volume the Second*[3] (pp. vii–viii):

. . . upon your sending for me to the *Swan-Tavern* in *Fleet-street*,

---

[1] Elwin-Courthope, x. 463.   [2] Ibid., p. 465.
[3] Griffith, pp. 308–10, Book 386. Cf. the *Curliad* (1729), p. 20.

in Company with Mr. *Lintot*, and enquiring into the Publication of that Pamphlet [the *Court Poems*], I then frankly told you, that those Pieces, were by Mr. *Joseph Jacobs*, a Dissenting Teacher, given to Mr. *John Oldmixon*, who sent the same to be published by Mr. *James Roberts* in *Warwick-Lane*; and that my Neighbour Mr. *Pemberton*, and *myself*, had each of us a Share, with Mr. *Oldmixon*, in the said Pamphlet. For this you were pleased to treat me, with half a Pint of Canary, antimonially prepared. . . .

Even in 1735 Curll could still remember the emetic; but he forgot that the later story contradicted one that he had stood witness to in the *Flying Post* of 1716.

An episode, hardly connected with Pope, but keenly felt by Curll in this year of his many tribulations, should perhaps be noted, so that one may better estimate his status in society. On 8 July the celebrated preacher Dr. South had died, and not many days later[1] Curll was advertising the *Posthumous Works of Dr. South*. South's executrix protested[2] that such a publication was unauthorized, but it was nevertheless on sale. In it Curll included a Latin funeral oration, spoken by John Barber, Captain of Westminster School and son of Pope's friend 'Alderman' Barber—who being a printer, doubtless had strong opinions concerning Edmund Curll. The sequel appears in the *Original Weekly Journal*, 4 August 1716:

King's College, Westminster, Aug. 3, 1716

Sir,

You are desired to acquaint the Publick, that a certain B—er near Temple-Bar (not taking warning by the frequent Drubs that he has undergone for his often Pyrating other Mens Copies) did lately (without the Consent of Mr. JOHN BARBER, present Captain of Westminster School) publish the Scraps of a Funeral Oration, spoken by him over the Corps of the Reverend Dr. *South*. And being on Thursday last fortunately Nab'd within the Limits of *Dean's Yard* by the Kings Schollars, there he met with a College Salutation: For he was first presented with the Ceremony of the Blanket, in which, when the Skeleton had been well shook, he was

---

[1] Curll's advertisement is in the *Evening Post*, 19 July 1716. See the *Weekly Packet*, 21 July 1716, for an account of South's funeral.
[2] *London Gazette*, 4 August 1716.

carry'd in Triumph to the School; and after receiving a Gram-matical Correction for his false Concords; he was Reconducted to *Dean's Yard*, and on his Knees, asking Pardon of the aforesaid Mr. BARBER for his Offense; he was kick'd out of the Yard, and left to the Huzza's of the Rabble,

I am Sir, Yours, T. A.

This punishment illustrates the belief that Curll had to be dealt with in fashions extraordinary—though evidently it is more permissible for schoolboys to 'rag' a bookseller than for a great poet to give him an emetic. Samuel Wesley, head usher in Westminster School, published a lampoon on the occasion called *Neck or Nothing*.[1] In it he suggested jocosely that Pope might make an epic on Curll.

This whole story of the emetic is amazing; and it is per-haps the least dignified in all Pope's career. But strange as it may seem to the present century, in the eighteenth it counted little against the poet, except among uneasy enemies. Certainly no one would feel any pity for Curll; to most of his contemporaries he was exactly what Straus has called him: unspeakable. One hates to think that Pope set an acceptable fashion in revenges; but the *Weekly Journal; or, British Gazetteer*, 8 September 1716, narrates a somewhat similar punishment which the Tory journalist Abel Roper received at a military coffee-house:

This Week Mr. Roper being sent for to young Man's Coffee-House at Charing Cross, was decently chastiz'd by a worthy Gentle-man, who he had aspersed in one of his late written News Letters, that he roar'd at both Ends, and afterwards was left to the Discre-tion of the Porters and Chairmen, that usually ply thereabouts.[2]

It was thus that one might treat persons too contemptible even for a caning. If Pope's pitiful conduct to Curll is to be at all extenuated, it can be so by remembering two facts: first, that this bookseller was widely regarded as beneath even the dignity of a beating; and, secondly, that the age had a childish delight in practical jokes. It is not accident

---

[1] *Neck or Nothing: A consolatory Letter from D-nt-n to Mr. Curll* (Sold by Charles King in Westminster-Hall. MDCCXVI), p. 28.

[2] In 1713 also attempts were made (by Whigs?) to waylay and beat Roper. See *Post Boy*, 28 April 1713.

nor merely a literary tradition that led Fielding to fill *Joseph Andrews* and Smollett to stuff all his novels with tales of practical jokes. The age loved them; the Duke of Montagu played them on distinguished foreigners like Montesquieu;[1] and the weakling Pope conveniently followed the spirit of the age. That he felt no shame for his crude joke is shown by the two pamphlets[2] that trumpeted and amplified it abroad.

One imagines that if Swift had been at hand to advise, he might have prevented this piece of indecorum, not as indecorous but rather as useless. Clearly Curll was not to be silenced, unless by law and the loss of his ears. The immediate consequence of this excitement, which came within a fortnight after the publication of the second volume of the *Iliad*, was to provoke expressions of scorn for the translation.

There had been some difficulty again in choosing a day of publication. As Arbuthnot wrote to Parnell, the appearance of the volume had been delayed so that excitement over the trials of the Preston rebels might die down.[3] Pope recognized that at such a juncture his religion and Jacobite sympathies would be subjected to comment. He urged Parnell to send on his *Life of Zoilus*, a defence of the translation, prepared before volume i appeared. The *Flying Post*, for which Oldmixon was a writer,[4] was ready with the political-religious innuendoes that Pope expected. On 7 April it advertised:

This Day is publish'd,

The Second Part of Mr. Pope's *Popish* Translation* of Homer. The Subscribers having made great Complaint that there were no Pictures in the First Part: This is to give Notice, that to this Second Part there is added a spacious MAP of the *Trojan* Tents and Rivers, finely delineated. Translated into Copper from the Wooden Original as you have it in the Learned Dr. Fuller's *Pisgah*

---

[1] J. Churton Collins, *Voltaire, Montesquieu, and Rousseau in England* (1908), p. 170. From Francis Hardy's *Memoirs of the Earl of Charlemont* (1812), i. 65.

[2] The title of the second was *A Further Account Of the most Deplorable Condition of Mr. Edmund Curll . . .* 1716. See Griffith, p. 53, Book 56.

[3] Elwin-Courthope, vii. 460.

[4] Cibber [R. Shiels], *Lives of the Poets* (1753), iv. 202.

Sight; being the True Travels of Moses and the children of *Israel*, from the Land of Goshen to the Land of Canaan. With an exact Scale. Sold by E. Curll, at the Dial and Bible against St. Dunstan's Church in Fleetstreet. Where may be had Mr. Pope's Court Poems, price 6d.

  * N. B. Mr. Pope has translated one Verse of *Homer* thus:
        The *Priest* can pardon, and the God appease.

Next Week will be publish'd An Excellent New Ballad call'd *The Catholick Poet*, or Protestant *Barnaby's Lamentation*. To the Tune of, *Which no body can deny*.

        Tho of his Wit the Catholick has boasted,
        Lintot and *Pope* by turns shall both be roasted.

This beginning of revenge on Curll's part was followed by another advertisement three days later in the same journal, which recalls that about 'Mr. Oldsworth of Hants':

  To prevent any farther Imposition on the Publick, there is
        now preparing for the Press by several Hands,

Homer defended: Being a Detection of the many Errors committed by Mr. *Pope*, in his pretended Translation of *Homer*, wherein is fully prov'd that he neither understands the Original, nor the Author's Meaning, and that in several Places he has falsified it on Purpose. To which is added, a Specimen of a Translation of the first Book of the Odyssey, which has lain printed by Mr. Lintott some Time, and which he intends to publish, in Order to prejudice Mr. *Tickell*'s excellent Version. Any Gentlemen who have made Observations upon Mr. *Pope's Homer*, and will be pleas'd to send them to Mr. Curl, at the Dial and Bible against St. Dunstan's Church in Fleet-street, shall have them faithfully inserted in this Work.

Of these two advertisements the second represents a project to be held *in terrorem* against Pope: it never eventuated as a single pamphlet. The fragment of the *Odyssey* seems pure fiction. In the first advertisement the charge that the pictorial map of Troy was a mere plagiarism from Fuller's *Pisgah Sight* (1650) is similarly false. There is not even a striking resemblance between it and the engravings in Fuller's volume. Of the *Catholick Poet* we shall hear more presently.

The next bit of enterprise on Curll's part was to publish on 1 May, a satire by Pope with the title *To the Ingenious Mr. Moore, Author of the Celebrated Worm-Powder. By Mr. Pope.*[1] At the foot of the verso of this broadside, after the customary 'Printed for E. Curll' . . . came: 'N. B. Speedily will be Publish'd, some more of Mr. Pope's Pieces, and all his Writings for the Future, except Homer, will be Printed for E. Curll.' By this time, one imagines, Pope saw the error of his emetic. That the publication of the *Worms*, as the lines to Moore were commonly called, in the heat of a campaign in which the Buttonians were seemingly quiescent, was unauthorized, one deduces from the *Postman*, 5 May 1716, where another Curll advertisement suggests that Pope as 'Peter Pencil' desired to know how Curll got hold of his copy of the poem:

> This Day is published the 2d Edition of The Worms: A Satire, Written by Mr. Pope. . . . Mr. Curll hereby gives Notice, that he received a Letter on Wednesday last [2 May], sign'd Peter Pencil; If the said Peter will send Word how a Letter may be directed to him, he shall receive a satisfactory Answer to his Epistle.[2]

Curll reprinted the *Worms* in various pamphlets all somehow associated with Pope, and the poem had an interesting effect on Pope's reputation. It was built on the metaphor: all men are worms. That seems an antique and harmless idea, even if one reads an indecent stanza not reprinted in late editions. The last two lines contain the sting (such as it was) of the poem:

> Ev'n Button's wits to worms shall turn,
> Who maggots were before.

The poem was not, however, frankly assailed as a satire on the Little Senate: it was criticized as an undiscriminating satire against all mankind; and such satire was thought impossible except by impious buffoons, thoroughly atheistical, men such as the Earl of Rochester or perhaps Swift. The poem is more than once called Pope's 'satire against

---

[1] Griffith, p. 52, Book 53.
[2] Quoted from A. E. Case, 'Notes on the Bibliography of Pope', *Modern Philology*, xxiv (1927), 300–1.

mankind'. Here, then, he first met the dilemma of satire in his day: personal satire was lampoon, and the result of spite; general satire was indiscriminating and the result of venomous and impious misanthropy.

The publication of the poem gave Addison a chance to be magnanimous. It is, of course, possible that he was also prompted by the fact that Pope had sent him the 'Atticus' lines. At any rate, a week after the *Worms* appeared Addison in the *Freeholder* No. 40 (7 May 1716) commended English translation of the classics, and held forth an olive branch to Pope:

> The illiterate among our countrymen, may learn to judge from *Dryden's Virgil* of the most perfect epic performance: and those parts of *Homer*, which have already been published by Mr. *Pope*, give us reason to think that the *Iliad* will appear in English with as little disadvantage to that immortal Poem.

This was small amends for what had passed, but it was graciously done. That there was more behind it, we learn from Thomas Burnet's letters; for Addison exercised his influence not merely to render a forthcoming pamphlet[1] on Homer by Burnet and Duckett innocuous to Pope, but even persuaded Burnet, much to Duckett's disgust, to insert a more glowing compliment than Addison himself had paid:

> ... the afore-mention'd Poet [Pope] has been so careful of doing justice to his Original, that he has nothing in his whole Poem that is not Homer's, but the Language. And I think one may say of his Translation, as one wou'd of a Copy by *Titian* of one of his own Pictures, That nothing can be better, but the Original.[2]

This is generous, and such praise makes it almost ungenerous to point out a detail that Addison did not efface from the same page of the pamphlet—a small gibe at Pope's religion in the ironic statement that in his (Burnet's) burlesque of Homer, here printed, the reader 'will find but one

---

[1] *Homerides: or, Homer's First Book Moderniz'd. By Sir Iliad Doggrel.* This volume, published 29 May 1716, is not the same as the *Homerides* of 1715.

[2] p. v.

Popish Saint in the first Book'. Burnet defended the compliment to Pope by his announcement to Duckett that 'Addison and the rest of the Rhiming Gang' were no longer actively hostile to Pope.[1] It was rather an armed truce that succeeded between the Buttonians and Pope, and a truce that was more than once violated.

Though Curll's attempt to draw the wits at Button's into the fray by printing the *Worms* was a failure, he himself did not despair of the battle.[2] Roberts published for him about the middle of May a thin volume called *State Poems*, which included the *Worms* and other products of Curll's shop, but nothing new except the 'Epilogue for the *Drummer*'.[3] On the last day of May appeared the *Catholick Poet* and *A True Character of Mr. Pope and his Writings*,[4] which are two of the most virulent attacks upon Pope that Curll ever procured.

The Catholick Poet is a very rare folio of six pages, the first two of which contain a 'ballad', while pages 3–6 contain a burlesque 'humble Petition of Barnaby Bernard Lintott

---

[1] *Letters*, ed. Nichol Smith, p. 99.

[2] An item by R. Burchett, Esq., *Strife and Envy since the Fall of Man*, published 3 May 1716 (*Daily Courant*), sounds like a reply to the *Worms*. I have never seen a copy.

[3] pp. 20–3, 'An Epilogue written for the late celebrated New Play called the Drummer, but not spoke'. See *supra*, pp. 160–1.

[4] *Flying Post*, 31 May 1716. The tone of the advertisement makes reprinting perhaps worth while:

> For the Diversion of the Town, this Day is publish'd,
> Two Pamphlets,
>
> 1 THE Catholick Poet; or Protestant Barnaby's Sorrowful Lamentation, an excellent new Ballad. To the Tune of, *Which no Body can deny*. Price 3d.
> 2. A True Character of Mr. Pope, and his Writings. In a Letter to a Friend. Price 3d.
>
> > *A Lump Deform'd and Shapeless was he Born;*
> > *Begot in Love's Despight, and Nature's Scorn.*—Roch.
> >
> > *In* Scandal *busy, in* Reproaches *bold:*
> > *Spleen to* Mankind *his envious Heart possess'd,*
> > *And much he hated All, but most the Best.*—Homer, Book 2.
>
> Sold at the News Shops, and by all the Booksellers in England, Dominion of Wales, and Town of Berwick upon Tweed. Where may be had the WORMS, a Satyr, by Mr. Pope, price 2d.
> N. B. These Town Diversions will be continued Weekly, so long as the Pope-*ish* Controversy is on foot.

. . . to all Gentlemen, Authors, Translators, or Translating Poets, who are Protestants, and well affected to the . . . House of Hanover.' The two efforts represent well the poverty of material to be found against Pope. Lintot is joined with him, not merely because he was Pope's publisher but because he served as a 'decoy' in the episode of the emetic.[1] The central theme is the failure of Pope's Homer, both to please and to sell. The effect of the charge, absurd on the face of it, is nullified by the bold advertisement of an intended piracy in a 'new *Dutch Elzevir* Letter, in two neat Pocket Volumes. Price 5s.'[2] If the work would not sell, why bring out a cheap reprint of it? Apart from the stale comment on Homer we find Pope accused of trying 'with vile smut' to charm 'pretty Bell. Fermor', and, of course, of being a Jacobite and a 'hunch-back'd Papist'. This work Pope ascribed to Mrs. Centlivre, whom he had mentioned in his *Full and True Account*[3] as a particular favourite of Curll's among his authors. Curll, however, said later that it was wholly by John Oldmixon.[4]

The other attack, *A True Character of Mr. Pope and his Writings*, was in the Appendix to the *Dunciad* ascribed to John Dennis, and without doubt correctly: it is done *Dennisissime*! It has also been ascribed to Gildon.[5] Its choicest passage asserts about Pope:

> That he is one, whom God and Nature have mark'd for want of Common Honesty, and his own Contemptible Rhimes for want of Common Sense, that those Rhimes have found great Success with the Rabble, which is a Word almost as comprehensive as Mankind; but that the Town, which supports him, will do by him, as the Dolphin did by the Shipwrack'd *Monkey*, drop him as soon as it finds him out to be a Beast. . . .[6]

---

[1] Elwin-Courthope, x. 462–8.

[2] Lintot may have been the happier to see Curll get his emetic if Curll helped to sell the pirated *Iliad* imported from Holland (published at The Hague by T. Johnson), which cut the profits of Lintot. See *infra*, p. 188, and J. Nichols, *Literary Anecdotes*, i. 78 n.

[3] Elwin-Courthope, x. 468.   [4] Ibid. x. 474 and note.

[5] As collaborator with Dennis. See *Dunciad* (4to, 1729), p. 91.

[6] p. 4.

He is a Professor of the worst Religion, which he laughs at, and yet has most inviolably observ'd the most execrable Maxim in it, *That no Faith is to be kept with Hereticks.* A wretch, whose true Religion is his Interest, and yet so stupidly blind to that Interest that he often meets her, without knowing her, and very grossly Affronts her ... some Men of good Understanding, value him for his Rhimes, as they would be fond of an *Asseinego*, that could sing his part in a Catch, or of a *Baboon* that could whistle *Walsingham*.[1]

But if any one appears to be concern'd at our Upbraiding him with his Natural Deformity, which did not come by his own Fault, but seems to be the Curse of God upon him; we desire that Person to consider, that this little Monster has upbraided People with their Calamities and their Diseases, and Calamities and Diseases which are either false or past, or which he himself gave them by administring Poison to them; we desire that Person to consider ... that there is no one Disease, but what all the rest of Men are subject too [*sic*]; whereas the Deformity of this Libeller, is Visible, Present, Lasting, Unalterable, and Peculiar to himself. 'Tis the mark of God and Nature upon him, to give us warning that we should hold no Society with him, as a Creature not of our Original, nor of our Species. And they who have refus'd to take this Warning which God and Nature have given them, and have in spight of it by a Senseless Presumption, ventur'd to be familiar with him, have severely suffer'd for it, by his Perfidiousness. They tell me, he has been lately pleas'd to say, *That 'tis Doubtful if the Race of Men are the Offspring of* Adam *or of the* Devil.* But if 'tis doubtful as to the Race of Men, 'tis certain at least, that his Original is not from *Adam*, but from the *Divel.*[2]

*The WORMS, a Satire, Stanza 4.

The insane glitter in this passage has been met before in Dennis's attacks on Pope, and it is hardly necessary to present the more speciously rational parts of the pamphlet. The charges of perfidiousness were discussed at the beginning of the chapter, and the only additional case to be mentioned is Pope's attack on Blackmore. Blackmore had complimented the English Homer, and consequently, it is asserted, he 'had laid very great Obligations on' Pope.[3] But it is neatly fallacious to say that among his 'benefactors'

---

[1] p. 5.   [2] pp. 9–10.   [3] p. 15.

Pope had 'attack'd no one so often, or with so much ridiculous, impotent Malice, as Sir *Richard Blackmore*'. Pope might have replied that he had *not* often attacked Blackmore (though he was to do so later), and that in any case a compliment is not insurance against criticism.

Other charges are that the poet is servilely imitative: 'Whenever he Scribbles, he is emphatically a *Monkey*. . . . Thus for fifteen Years together this Ludicrous Animal has been a constant *Imitator*.' His recent 'Imitation of Horace' is called 'the most execrable of them all'.[1] In translating Homer the qualities to be secured are 'the Beauty of his Diction, and the various Harmony of his Versification. But 'tis as Ridiculous to pretend to make these Shine out in *English* Rhimes, as it would be to emulate upon a *Bag-pipe*, the Solemn and Majestick Thorough Basse of an Organ.' Pope is elsewhere compared with Horace and found utterly lacking in judgement and taste.[2] In general the criticism of his personality is that formulated on the basis of Pope's lines on Thersites, which appear on the title-page:

> Aw'd by no Shame, by no Respect control'd,
> In Scandal busie, in Reproaches bold:
> Spleen to Mankind his envious Heart possesst,
> And much he hated All, but most the Best.[3]

These lines were regarded as accidental self-portrayal on Pope's part, and the notion is so picturesque that reputable critics to the present day have accepted an interpretation of Pope's character very like that of this raving pamphleteer. As we shall see, Pope's friends in general included the ablest and most interesting men of his day; they never found him the monster that Dennis pictured him.

The next blow aimed at Pope after the *Catholick Poet*—

---

[1] pp. 6, 7. Pope was doing no known Imitations of Horace so early as this, and there seems to be no plausible identification of the poem mentioned unless we go back to April 1714, and assume that Dennis is awarding to Pope Swift's *John Dennis, the Sheltering Poet's Invitation to Richard Steele, the secluded Party-Writer and Member, to come and live with him in the Mint. In Imitation of Horace's 5th Epistle, Lib. I.* (Adv. by Morphew in the *Post Boy*, 27 April 1714, as 'just published'.)

[2] p. 17.   [3] From Pope's *Iliad*, ii. 257-8, 267-8.

and again very likely a blow due to Curll's enterprise—was the publication of *A Roman Catholick Version of the First Psalm; for the Use of a Young Lady. By Mr. Pope. Printed for R. Burleigh.*[1] This tavern piece of truly impious buffoonery seemed to justify much that Pope's enemies had been saying about the mixture of sacred and profane in his Muse. The insertion of *Roman Catholick* in the title was the normal attempt to discredit Pope's religion, odious as it was for political reasons. The *Psalm* was, of course, never intended for publication, and the poet was so abashed by its appearance that he attempted to disclaim it in the *Postman*, 31 July 1716, and in the *Evening Post*, 2 August:

> Whereas there have been publish'd in my Name, certain scandalous Libels, which I hope no Person of Candor would have thought me capable of, I am sorry to find myself obliged to declare, that no Genuine Pieces of mine have been printed by any but Mr. Tonson and Mr. Lintot. And in particular, as to that which is entituled, A Version of the first Psalm; I hereby promise a Reward of three Guineas to any one who shall discover the Person or Persons concerned in the Publication of the said Libel, of which I am wholly ignorant.
>
> A. Pope.

One must, as Professor Case suggests, 'agree with Pope's remark in his letter of August 7, 1716, to Martha Blount, that he had "equivocated pretty genteelly" in this advertisement'.[2] The poem was reprinted in Curll's various Pope miscellanies, and at the end of August appeared a loyal Hanoverian poem, which glanced at Pope and his unfortunate poem only in the title: *An English Psalm: or, a Hymn on the late Thanksgiving-Day. Being a Protestant Version of the Second Psalm.* Much more disheartening than Dennis's lurid assertion is this genteel equivocation, in which Pope shows uncanny rhetorical ability.

The season was now over, and since pamphleteering was

---

[1] Adv. in the *Flying Post*, 30 June 1716. The conclusion of the advertisement is: 'To which is added, *Barnaby's* Petition—*Bella horrida Bella*. Pr 3d. Sold by all Booksellers. *N. B.* The *Pope*-ish Controversy continues.'

[2] *Modern Philology*, xxiv (1927), 301.

unprofitable for the most part, in the long vacation, it is natural that fewer things should appear in print.

In a better temper and in better taste than the pamphlets of the Curll battle are certain squibs that obscurely concern Pope. One broadside is very likely either by Pope or Arbuthnot. It is called *God's Revenge against Punning. Showing the miserable Fates of Persons addicted to this Crying Sin, in Court and Town.*[1] Among the judgements of Heaven here cited against punsters one may note the mention of a Devonshire wit, who, in the act of making an atrocious pun, fell from his horse—and broke his snuff-box. Since Pope wrote to Teresa Blount on 7 August, 'Mr. Gay has had a fall from his horse, and broken his fine snuff-box', one assumes that *God's Revenge* was written within the family, so to speak. If so, what shall we make of *An Heroi-comical Epistle from a certain Doctor to a certain Gentlewoman, in Defense of the most antient Art of Punning*?[2] This appeared in November. It urges the antiquity and dignity of punning: Jesus punned on St. Peter's name; James I made celebrated puns, and, in short, the good-humoured conclusion is that this opposition to punning is another *Popish* plot.

> Dear *Nanny*, all the World is running
> Stark mad against our vein of *Punning*;
> But I regard not their *James Baker*
> So much as barking *Cur* or *Quaker*;
>
> .   .   .   .   .
>
> But, dearest Nann, I smell the bottom
> Of all our *Anti-punsters* (rott'em;)
> It is a *Popish-Jesuit* Plot,
> By *Tore Jacobites* begot. . . .

This is good fun after Curll's stuff, and so are the end-of-the-year predictions of E. Parker, Philomath., in *Mr. Joanidion Fielding His True and Faithful Account of the Strange and miraculous Comet which was Seen by the Mufti of Con-*

---

[1] This is included in the Pope-Swift, &c., *Miscellanies*, iii (1732), 52–6.

[2] Could the 'certain Gentlewoman', here called 'Nanny', be 'a certain Doctor's' daughter, Ann Arbuthnot? The Doctor called his daughter 'Nanny' at times.

stantinople. Such New Year prophecies were popular in these days, and while they occasionally savour of Curllicism, they are fairly innocent. Among the prophecies three are of interest:

Mr. *Curll* shall be Vomited the second Time, Tost in a Blanket the Third, and Cudgel'd the Ninth Time, for Printing the Will of Sir J—— Baker, by the Executors of the said Sir J——.[1]

Mr. *Moor* shall die of a Dose of the same Powder by which he liv'd.

If the Pope be not Eat up by Pun-aises, for Anathemas that he never denounc'd, he shall at least be Tickled to Death, or receive a Phillip from St. Ambrose.

And so a mad year ended in good humour. Pope was, according to his custom, rambling during the late summer. He visited Binfield in August, after Lady Mary had sailed away to Constantinople. He was in Yorkshire with Lord Burlington in October, after which he went to Bath for his annual visit.[2] Later in the autumn he returned to Chiswick and London. It is interesting to note that in the autumn[3] Lewis Theobald was bringing out a cheap translation of Ovid's *Metamorphoses* 'by several hands' for a group of publishers that included Curll. It was doubtless designed to rival the Garth-Tonson expensive version of the same poems, in which Pope's *Fable of Dryope* was included. Somehow the publisher of the cheap edition got permission to use Pope's *Vertumnus and Pomona*; and so Book XIV was put down as translated 'by Mr. Pope and Mr. Theobald',[4] probably their only case of collaboration, though they were perhaps friends at this time.

By the end of this lamentable year there were certain lessons that Pope had learned or ought to have learned. One of the most important, and the one that he learned

---

[1] p. 5. The sly prophecy of Sir James Baker's death, as well as that of Moor (the apothecary whom the *Worms* celebrated), reminds one of the Partridge hoax. Baker was probably the chief butt in all this anti-punning campaign. He wa concerned in the publication of the *White-Hall* and *St. James's Journals.*

[2] For these various rambles see Elwin-Courthope, ix. 364 and note, and 485 see also x. 205 ff. for the famous ride to Oxford with Lintot.

[3] 27 October 1716; see Griffith, p. 551, Book 59 b.

[4] *Ovid's Metamorphoses. In Fifteen Books. A New Translation,* i. [312].

best, was to keep his small pieces under cover. How Oldmixon and Curll got hold of the *Court Poems*, the *Worms*,
and the *First Psalm*, no one knows; but it was very likely
through Pope's allowing friends to have copies. After
1716, or at least after 1717, the supply stopped. In the
conversation narrated by Curll as having passed while he
drank his emetic, Pope is represented as saying 'that Satires
should not be Printed'. To which Curll with a realist's
mind had replied, 'They should not be wrote, for if they
were they would be Printed.' Curll was doubtless right:
Pope's idea that small lampoons might pass from hand to
hand privately was a sad error, and one that the experience
of 1716 taught him to correct by more rigidly controlling
the circulation of his unprinted pieces. Thus the satire on
Addison was successfully suppressed until 1722, and other
things until 1727. After 1717 Curll had a lean decade so far
as Popiana went.

Pope should also have learned that it was easy and useless
to acquire enemies. Those active in 1716 are distinctly
inferior to those of 1715. When we get to Curll, Oldmixon,
and possibly Gildon, we have reached the hireling class,
who had no personal acquaintance with Pope and who
wrote simply for their daily bread. Any attack on such
people would be resented because it might tend to deprive
them of their livelihood. Because of their lack of social
position and their lack of much personal knowledge of Pope,
these venal quills were recklessly abusive and untruthful.
Pope's replies, the *Worms* and even some of the pamphlets
about Curll, are more amusing, more dignified, and more
truthful than the attacks upon him. One cannot forgive
his setting up as a practising apothecary; but one must conclude that his few retorts, and those of his allies, are not
remarkable for ill nature and malice. The obvious truth,
however, is that he should have been above retort. The
one good thing the emergence of these hirelings did was to
drive most of the gentlemen out of the field. The Buttonians had to withdraw or place themselves in a class with
Curll's hacks, Oldmixon or Gildon, which some of them

remained to do. Pope should have learned the Addisonian aloofness to attack. He did learn a certain amount of caution, which a natural recklessness would at various moments overcome; but he failed to learn the fundamental lesson of manners and morals: 'This same pitch defileth.'

VII

ROUTINE AND UNREST

OBVIOUS self-contradiction in Pope's character may be seen perhaps at almost any point in his career, but it becomes notable in various forms during the later years in which he was translating the *Iliad*. We have seen even earlier that from his 'regular' poetic labours he stole holidays and wrote disreputable squibs: first his *Messiah*, jeered his enemies, and then his burlesque *First Psalm*. Another release from the tedium of translation came increasingly at Chiswick through social amusements, and still another when late in 1718 he removed to Twickenham, and could there indulge modestly his love of building and gardening. And it must not be forgotten that, totally apart from his creative work, Pope was preoccupied with books and reading.

> The soul uneasy and confined at home
> Rests and expatiates in the life to come,

he later wrote; and the couplet applies aptly to his bodily confinements when he read at home and wished to be abroad conversing with friends. It is impossible to tell what forces pulled strongest, whether retirement, books, and his garden, or society, conversation, and the world of affairs. The vile antithesis of sickness and health cuts across all attempt to evaluate spontaneous motives.

But through it all operated the necessary and terrible tedium of translation. Years later Pope (after the relatively easy methods of doing the *Odyssey*) minimized to Spence the oppressiveness of this burden:

What terrible moments does one feel, after one has engaged for a large work!—In the beginning of my translating the Iliad, I wished any body would hang me, a hundred times.—It sat so heavily on my mind at first, that I often used to dream of it, and do sometimes still.* [* He used to dream that he was engaged in a long journey, puzzled which way to take; and full of fears that he should never get to the end of it.—Spence.]—When I fell into the method of translating thirty or forty verses before I got up, and piddled with it the rest of the morning, it went on easy enough; and when I was thoroughly got into the way of it, I did the rest with pleasure.[1]

The pleasure no one can doubt who reads Pope's *Iliad*, but the tedium cannot be doubted by any one who reads his letters. He was not a free man. He was like a small boy who must stay indoors at his lessons while his fellows are at play. He had to work, but he could not resist the temptations and invitations of polite society, which more and more taxed his strength and took him from his labours. Very early his preference of society to translation is clear. From Binfield he writes with only semi-artificial gallantry to Martha Blount at Mapledurham:

This letter may very possibly be the only thing that hinders you from a total forgetfulness of me. I would to God I could as easily forget Maple-Durham is within ten miles of me. I am just in the condition of the poor people in purgatory: Heaven is in sight, and the pain of loss the greatest I endure.[2]

And a year later he tells her: 'I am here studying ten hours a day, but thinking of you in spite of all the learned.'[3] In similar tone he writes Digby, 2 June 1717, to tell of his retirement to work on Homer:

Adieu! I am going to forget you: this minute you took up all my mind; the next I shall think of nothing but the reconciliation with Agamemnon, and the recovery of Briseïs. I shall be Achilles's humble servant these two months (with the good leave of all my friends). I have no ambition so strong at present, as that noble one of Sir Salathiel Lovel, recorder of London, to furnish out a decent and plentiful execution of Greeks and Trojans. It is not to be expressed how heartily I wish the death of all Homer's heroes, one after another. The Lord preserve me in the day of battle, which is just approaching! Join in your prayers for me, and know me to be always. Your, &c.[4]

---

[1] Spence, p. 218.   [2] Elwin-Courthope, ix. 258–9 (3 June [1715]).
[3] Ibid. ix. 264.   [4] Ibid. ix. 68.

Business cares came with the cares of translation itself. 'The minute I can get to you,' he writes Caryll (6 August 1717), 'I will, though Lintot's accounts are yet to settle, and three parts of my year's task to do.'[1] As this indicates, the mere labour of publication was considerable. At first Pope had to distribute at his own cost copies to such subscribers as did not call for their books at Lintot's shop. Before the second volume came out, he made new arrangements, embodied in a document now preserved in the British Museum.[2] According to it, Lintot was to receive the subscription money for the second volumes (one guinea each), and was to distribute all except 120 copies to subscribers. He was also to furnish Pope with 120 copies and pay him 400 guineas in addition to the 200 already stipulated as copy money for each volume.[3] The 120 copies, which 'on demand' Lintot was to deliver to Pope himself were, according to an endorsement on the document, for Pope's 'own use for some particular Subscribers, ye double ones, &c.' The document specifies that 'so many of such said One hundred & Twenty second volumes (and so many only) shall be printed on Royall paper of the first and second sort as will answer the number of so many of the first volumes as have been already delivered to any of the Subscribers printed on such Royal paper.' Pope seems to have paid Lintot something like 134 guineas for distributing 534 subscription copies of this volume for him. It may be that such generosity was due in part to Lintot's losses through the piracy of T. Johnson, who from The Hague shipped cheap copies to London. In his *Journal literaire de l'année M.DCC.XVIII* Johnson boldly advertises, facing page 1:

Il [Johnson] debite aussi les Oeuvres Mêlées de Mr. POPE, très excellent Poëte Anglois, & sa belle Traduction en vers de l'Iliade d'Homére, avec des Dissertations & des Remarques Savantes & Curieuses, proprement & correctément imprimées en divers Volumes petit 8°, il les vend à 24 sols le Volume, qui est environ la sixiéme partie de ce qu'on les vend en Angleterre.

---

[1] Elwin-Courthope, vi. 248.   [2] Egerton MS. 1951.   [3] Griffith, pp. 41, 42.

Lintot's profits depended not on the subscription but on
the public sale, which must have been spoiled by Johnson's
cheap reprint. Whether Pope's arrangement for the second
volume was continued for other volumes one may doubt.[1]
If it was, it testifies to his desire to free himself from business
details.

Not merely the business arrangements and the labour of
translation (with the good leave of all his friends) were
oppressive: annotation had to be provided. At the very
first, Parnell helped; but business called him from Binfield,
where he had been with the poet, and Pope sent frantic
entreaties for a speedy return:

The minute I lost you, Eustathius with nine hundred pages, and
nine thousand contractions of the Greek character, arose to my
view! Spondanus, with all his auxiliaries, in number a thousand
pages, (value three shillings,) and Dacier's three volumes, Barnes's
two, Valterie's three, Cuperus, half in Greek, Leo Allatius, three
parts in Greek, Scaliger, Macrobius, and (worse than them all)
Aulus Gellius! All these rushed upon my soul at once, and whelmed
me under a fit of the headache. I cursed them all religiously,
damned my best friends among the rest, and even blasphemed
Homer himself. Dear Sir, not only as you are a friend, and a good-
natured man, but as you are a christian and a divine, come back
speedily, and prevent the increase of my sins. . . .[2]

But Parnell had to return to Ireland, and William Broome
undertook the task of excavating notes from Eustathius,
a labour which he carried on through the third volume,
that is, through half the *Iliad*. Then, either weary of his
task (which was a friendly service, not remunerated), or
engrossed in the rich widow whom he married in July
1716, he ceased for a time to work on these notes. In 1717
(6 July) Pope wrote to Parnell begging for aid, apparently
in vain. Pope's friend Dr. Evans of St. John's College seems
to have procured for the translator the assistance of an
Oxonian, Mr. Peachy, 'a very learned & ingenious man',[3]
and through Dr. Thirlby of Cambridge, after some service

---

[1] Elwin-Courthope, viii. 25; x. 107.
[2] Ibid. vii. 451-2.   [3] Ibid. x. 106.

from an unnamed Cambridge man, Pope secured the assistance of John Jortin, then an undergraduate but later a
distinguished scholar.[1] It is possible that Fenton, Arbuthnot, and even Gay may have lent a hand also. In general
Pope's friends seemed anxious to help; a notable case was
that of his old Binfield friend, Thomas Dancastle, who even
after the Popes removed to Chiswick and Twickenham
continued to transcribe the copy for the printer[2] from the
odd bits of paper upon which Pope 'composed'.

With all these aids and with his 'system' of thirty lines
each morning Pope, though feeling always behindhand in
his task, managed to get every volume out on time until
1719, when he was sadly in arrears. The publication of the
first four volumes fell on or about the following days:
6 June 1715, 22 March 1716, 3 June 1717, and 28 June
1718.[3] When 1719 came around Pope advertised in the
Evening Post, 19 May 1719 (and very likely in other places):

> Whereas the Original Proposal for Mr. Pope's Translation of
> Homer, was, that the said Work should be finished in 6 Years, and
> one Volume of it deliver'd annually; which has hitherto been done
> according to the said Proposal: This is to advertise, that the 5th
> Volume of that Translation now lies finished at the Press: But the
> said Mr. Pope having made a greater Progress in the Remainder
> than he expected, or promised; hereby gives Notice, that he shall
> deliver the whole to the Subscribers by the Beginning of the next
> Winter, and that they may then receive the two last Volumes
> together, paying the Subscription, which is now due, at that time.
> Printed for Bernard Lintot between the Temple-Gates; where may
> be had the 1st, 2d, 3d, and 4th Volumes of Mr. Pope's Homer, and
> his Miscellaneous Poetical Works in large and small Paper, Folio.

Volume v included Books XVII–XXI (the only volume to
contain five Books), and since an apparently trustworthy
letter from Dancastle indicates that Book XXI was still in

---

[1] See Jortin's 'Critical Remarks on Modern Authors', in his *Works* (1790),
xiii. 519 ff.
[2] Elwin-Courthope, ix. 485, 490. Dancastle made a beautiful transcription if
one may judge from several leaves preserved in the manuscripts of the *Odyssey*
(B.M. Add. MS. 4809). Pope used the backs of some of the sheets of the transcription of the *Iliad* for paper on which to translate parts of the *Odyssey*.
[3] Griffith, pp. 40, 49, 64, 76.

manuscript when he wrote (27 July [1719]),[1] it seems
doubtful if the newspaper advertisement is quite veracious
in saying that in May 1719 'the 5th Volume . . . now lies
finished at the Press'. Books XVII–XX may have lain there
in quires,[2] and the decision to bind Book XXI with them
may have been made later (to leave more room for 'appara-
tus' in the last volume); but the pretty certain fact is that
the poet had really fallen behind in his task. Volumes v
and vi finally appeared in May 1720. No protest over this
delay seems to have been made.

Once translated, annotated, and published, the translation had to be defended. The attacks fell off decidedly
after 1716. During the campaign against *Three Hours after
Marriage*, to be sure, there appeared in February 1717
one attack that Pope had long awaited. This was from the
inevitable Dennis and was called *Remarks upon Mr. Pope's
. . . Homer*. Here Dennis reasseverates the utter lack of
worth in Pope's work. He attacks Lewis Theobald, who in
the *Censor* No. 3 had praised the translation, and he denies
any ground of commendation for the work:

. . . the Truth of the Matter is, that there is in this Translation
neither the Justness of the Original, even where the Original is
just; nor any Beauty of Language, nor any variety of Numbers.
Instead of the Justness of the Original, there is in this Translation
Absurdity and Extravagance. Instead of the beautiful Language
of the Original, there is in the Translation Solecism and barbarous
English.[3]

Pope's reply to Dennis, who was getting to be an old story,
had been waiting for two years, and in May 1717 duly
appeared. It was Parnell's 'Life of Zoilus' prefixed to his
translation of the *Batrachomuomachia*. This work, which
Pope saw through the press, is less interesting as a retort
on Dennis than it is in its Preface as a defence of Pope's
methods, particularly in such matters as versification. In

---

[1] Elwin-Courthope, ix. 490.
[2] The inscription on the window at Stanton Harcourt (see *infra*, p. 216) about
the completion of vol. v in 1718 might well refer to Books XVII–XX.
[3] *Remarks*, p. 10.

a conversation with the translator the author of the Preface says:

The next Point I ventur'd to speak on, was the Sort of Poetry he intended to use; how some may fancy, a Poet of the greatest Fire wou'd be imitated better in the Freedom of Blank Verse, and the Description of War sounds more pompous out of Rhime. But, will the Translation, said he, be thus remov'd enough from Prose, without greater Inconveniences? What Transpositions is *Milton* forc'd to, as an Equivalent for Want of Rhime, in the Poetry of a Language which depends upon a natural Order of Words? And even this wou'd not have done his Business, had he not given the fullest Scope to his Genius, by choosing a Subject upon which there could be no Hyperboles. We see (however he be deservedly successful) that the *Ridicule* of his Manner succeeds better than the *Imitation* of it; because Transpositions, which are unnatural to a Language, are to be fairly derided, if they ruin it by being frequently introduced; and because Hyperboles, which outrage every lesser Subject where they are seriously us'd, are often beautiful in Ridicule. Let the *French*, whose Language is not copious, translate in Prose; but ours, which exceeds it in Copiousness of Words, may have a more frequent Likeness of Sounds, to make the Unison or Rhime easier; a Grace of Musick, that attones for the Harshness our Consonants and Monosyllables occasion.[1]

If this passage is compared with Pope's letter to Atterbury (an ardent advocate of blank verse) on 8 September 1718,[2] one will see that Pope's opposition to blank verse was not so insuperable as has sometimes been thought. He wishes the bishop to concede rhyme some merits, and he will in return 'promise your Lordship, as soon as Homer is translated, to allow it [rhyme] unfit for long works, but to say so at present, would be what your *second* thoughts could never approve of, because it would be a profession of repentance and conviction, and yet a perseverance in the sin'.

Doubtless attacks on his translation as well as the routine labour involved kept Pope occupied. It was a steadying influence for years. But other forces continually pulled

---

[1] *Homer's Battle of the Frogs and Mice. With the Remarks of Zoilus. To which is Prefix'd, The Life of the said Zoilus. . . .* London, Bernard Lintot, 1717. See leaf A4 *r* and *v*.   [2] Elwin-Courthope, ix. 14.

him into varied activities. The great cause of unrest in early 1717 was the farce, already mentioned, *Three Hours after Marriage*.[1] Published as by Gay, the piece was admittedly the result of collaboration with Dr. Arbuthnot and Pope. To Pope, interestingly enough, was imputed most of the scandal of the piece.

This scandal lay not in its alleged obscenity but in its absurdity and its personalities. In the play Fossile, an elderly quack, marries a young woman of the town whose lovers use various disguises, in true farcical style, in attempts to get into the house of the jealous bridegroom. As a crowning absurdity the two lovers are introduced disguised respectively as a mummy and a crocodile, both apparently objects naturally found in laboratories of the day. A further absurd figure is Fossile's niece, Phoebe Clinket, who is so ardent a playwright that her maid precedes her everywhere with a writing desk at her back, so that no gem of thought from Mrs. Clinket's brain may be lost. Absurdities such as these were not so popular as the comedy of manners, but they were accepted, and would have been accepted in this case had it not been for the personalities of the piece.

Some of these are certain, others merely alleged. There can be no doubt that in Fossile Dr. John Woodward, Arbuthnot's professional enemy, is satirized. The Scriblerean tradition might account for an interest on the part of Gay and Pope in satirizing this early geologist, but the chief stimulus must have been Arbuthnot's personal dislike. The critic, Sir Tremendous, was clearly John Dennis; and the animus here would come from Pope, whose ally against Dennis Gay had been more than once. Colley Cibber played the role of an actor-manager, and was made thus to utter lines that satirized himself. Such satire on Cibber was not unknown by 1717; after the *Non-Juror* it was very common indeed. These personalities can all be determined from internal evidence: the characters more than once talk like their published works, and talk of

[1] For a more detailed account than is here given see *Modern Philology*, xxiv (1926), 91–109.

well-known hobbies of the persons burlesqued. Working on
the same basis, one would conclude Phoebe Clinket to be
Mrs. Susannah Centlivre, and Mrs. Townley would seem to
have no individuality except as a woman of the town. The
fact remains that at least three attacks on the play[1] identified Mrs. Townley as the wife of Dr. Mead (Mead was also
hostile to Woodward, and friendly to the authors of the
farce: Woodward was a bachelor), and Phoebe Clinket as
the Countess of Winchilsea. The identifications of these
two ladies come from the same witnesses, who are obviously
malicious in their attempts to make Pope appear to attack
his friends. No one has accepted the identification of
Townley as Mrs. Mead, but the identification of Clinket
as Lady Winchilsea has been generally accepted. The
external evidence is as good for one as for the other:
internal evidence gives no warrant for either. Since both
the Meads and Lady Winchilsea remained friendly with the
three authors after the farce was acted, they tacitly expressed disbelief in the identifications, which are interesting as illustrating how Pope's enemies built up a notion
widely accepted after the *Dunciad* that the poet was a
treacherous friend. It was his enemies rather than his
friends who pretended to think so.[2]

[1] See *Modern Philology*, xxiv. 94. Mrs. Mead could hardly have had a trait in
common with Townley. At least the Meads had several children, and presumably
Mrs. Mead was domestic and no longer very young.

[2] Pope (15 December [1713]) wrote Caryll: 'I was invited that day to dinner
to my Lady Winchilsea, and after dinner to hear a play read, at both which I sat
in great disorder with sickness at my head and stomach.' It has been *assumed*,
naturally perhaps, that the play was by the Countess; and the letter has been
thought to indicate Pope's attitude towards her. The passage is largely, as the
context shows, an excuse for having failed to meet Caryll afterwards. There is
not much reason for thinking Pope hostile to the Countess. Certainly she was
not made hostile to him by *Three Hours*; for within six months after it was acted
she entertained him in her home, she contributed to the obscure *Poems on Several
Occasions* that Pope edited for Lintot (published July 1717), and she prefixed
commendatory verses to his *Works* in June 1717. The fact that these last verses
were not reprinted in 1736 or in the later *Works* may have some meaning (Lady
Winchilsea died in 1720). But clearly the retiring Countess, who never sought
to have her plays staged, has little in common with that inveterate playwright,
Phoebe Clinket, whose aim in life was to get her plays acted. It is noteworthy
that in the *Further Account of the most Deplorable Condition of Mr. Edmund Curll*

The play had a stormy reception. Before it was acted, Tom Burnet had written Duckett: 'Pope is coming out with a Play, in which everyone of our modern Poets are ridiculed.'[1] The coming shadow exaggerated the event, and doubtless aroused the Buttonian wits to their last organized attack on Pope. Beginning 16 January, the play had an unusual run of seven consecutive nights in spite of a strong attempt to 'damn' it at its first performance. Two or three of the performances were riotous, and it was asserted at the time that only presents to the actors kept the play going, though the theatre, according to all reports, was crowded. Broadsides, newspapers, and pamphlets all expressed loud disapproval of the play and especially of its authors. Doubtless some attacks were motivated by friendship to Dr. Woodward, but most of them seemed desirous of avowing hostility to Pope. Over a dozen of them have been noted, which would date between 22 January and 30 April, and which must have given Pope a notion of what to expect in the spring of 1728 when the *Dunciad* appeared. They came from the bookshops of Curll and his associates, and from authors stimulated by Curll or by the wits at Button's. The most interesting attack is by Curll's author Breval ('Joseph Gay') in whose *Confederates* one can find a picturesque if partisan history of the play. Some of the anonymous attacks as well as Charles Johnson's Prologue to the *Sultaness* (acted 25–8 February) and Welsted's *Palaemon to Celia, at Bath* are Buttonian in origin. Sir Richard Blackmore (friendly to Woodward) avenged Gay's defence of Swift by a comment on the play and on Pope in the second volume of his *Essays*[2] (published 26

(Elwin-Courthope, x. 472) Pope had already derided the 'similes' of Mrs. Centlivre in the same way that Phoebe Clinket's are assailed in *Three Hours*. In making their identification with Lady Winchilsea, Pope's enemies, with obvious malice, picked an authoress of position, known to be intimate with Pope. Curll's other writers were unlikely to mention Mrs. Centlivre in the matter, for she was their associate. Their identifications had no immediate effect on Lady Winchilsea —or on the Meads.

[1] *Letters*, ed. Nichol Smith, p. 119.
[2] Preface, pp. xlvii–l, on *Three Hours*, and 'An Essay upon Polite Writing', pp. 269–70, on the 'First Psalm'.

March), and a possibly pseudonymous 'E. Parker, Philomath.', contributed a *Complete Key to the New Farce* (2 February).[1] There were others, many malicious, all caustic, and all depressing to the 'English Homer'. Early in 1717 Pope wrote to Parnell:

> I have been ever since December last in greater variety of business than any such men as you (that is, divines and philosophers) can possibly imagine a reasonable creature capable of. Gay's play, among the rest, has cost much time and long suffering to stem a tide of malice and party, that certain authors have raised against it. The best revenge upon such fellows is now in my hands, I mean your Zoilus, which really transcends the expectation I had conceived of it. I have put it into the press. . . .[2]

The last important echo of this turmoil came as late as 1742, when Cibber in his first *Letter from Mr. Cibber to Mr. Pope* gave his well-known account of the reasons for Pope's frequent fondness for seeing Mr. Cibber's name in his satires.[3] A fortnight after *Three Hours* was withdrawn, Cibber revived the *Rehearsal* (7 February), and to the astonishment of his erstwhile playwrights inserted a gibe at their discarded farce. According to Cibber's *Letter*, this gibe

> . . . was so heinously taken by Mr. *Pope*, that, in the swelling of his Heart, after the Play was over, he came behind the Scenes, with his Lips pale and his Voice trembling, to call me to account for the Insult: And accordingly fell upon me with all the foul Language, that a Wit out of his Senses could be capable of—How durst I have the Impudence to treat any Gentleman in that manner? &c, &c. . . . When he was almost choked with the foam of his Passion, I was enough recover'd from my Amazement to make him (as near as I can remember) this Reply, *viz.* 'Mr. *Pope*—You are so particular a Man, that I must be asham'd to return your Language as I ought to do: but since you have attacked me in so monstrous a Manner; This you may depend upon, that as long as

---

[1] In 1716 the name of this author had appeared on the title-page of *Mr. Joanidion Fielding His True and Faithful Account of the . . . Comet.* See *supra*, pp. 182–3.

[2] Elwin-Courthope, vii. 463–4. Parnell's volume was published in May. See *Postman*, 9 May 1717, 'next week will be published . . .'.

[3] pp. 17–19.

the Play continues to be acted, I will never fail to repeat the same
Words over and over again.'[1]

The printed attacks on the play do not mention this
dramatic episode (in which Cibber makes his own self-
control contrast so admirably with the foaming fury of
Pope), but they do give accounts of a meeting between
Gay and Cibber in the nature of fistic encounter. The
bout was short and the winner uncertain; some of the
attacks on the play award the decision to Gay,[2] but a
contemporary letter printed in 'George Paston's' *Mr. Pope*
favours Cibber:

... I don't know whether you heard, before you went out of town,
that *The Rehearsal* was revived, not having been acted before these
ten years, and Cibber interlarded it with several things in ridicule
of the last play, upon which Pope went up to him and told him
he was a rascal, and if he were able he would cane him; that his
friend Gay was a proper fellow, and if he went on in his sauciness
he might expect such a reception from him. The next night Gay
came accordingly, and, treating him as Pope had done the night
before, Cibber very fairly gave him a fillip on the nose, which made
them both roar. The Guards came and parted them, and carried
away Gay, and so ended this poetical scuffle.[3]

Cibber in his *Letter* continues with the allegation that the
offensive remark (or remarks), repeated 'over and over
again', during the rest of the season, was the origin of
Pope's hostility to him, which eventually made him the
King of the Dunces. Evidence of some earlier hostility or
contempt is seen in the lines put into the mouth of Plot-
well (acted by Cibber) in the play, but doubtless the
Rehearsal intensified the animosity, and thus *Three Hours*
served to win Pope additional enemies, from whom he was
never again to be free.

There is one pleasanter side to the episode. The uproar

[1] Ed. of 1742 (sold by W. Lewis), pp. 18–19.
[2] *Modern Philology*, xxiv. 106–7.
[3] George Paston, *Mr. Pope* (1909), i. 197. This letter should have been cited
by me in *Modern Philology*. It obviously corrects certain positions taken in the
earlier account of the play.

at performances came largely from the pit; the boxes, where sat the aristocracy, were more complaisant. Breval in his *Confederates* alleges that the maids of honour of the Princess of Wales were particularly pleased with what he chose to call the 'smut' of the performance, and he tells how a purse of gold was sent Gay by

> three Ladies known full well;
> Their Names are G——n, B——ne, L-p-l.

The Misses Griffin, Bellenden, and Lepel had for some time admitted Gay and Pope to their intimacy; they and especially another of the maids of honour, Mrs. Howard, later Countess of Suffolk, remained friendly to the authors long after *Three Hours* was almost forgotten. That the three ladies mentioned by Breval were kind to Gay's farce is perhaps implied in a poem that Pope addressed to them at this moment, and which was published almost certainly without authorization by Pope before the end of January, as the *Court Ballad*. Later Pope (?) called it the *Challenge*. The lines are hilarious in the extreme, and seem so frank and even free in tone that one assumes that neither the poet nor the ladies would be anxious to see them in print. Dennis, as we have seen, accused Pope of libelling these ladies immediately after their kindness to him, but Dennis was, probably honestly, misled by the appearance in January 1719 of an imitation of the *Court Ballad*, called *News from Court* . . . By Mr. Pope.[1] This imitation is so inferior that its authorship must be questioned; it was never acknowledged or collected into Pope's *Works*. In any case the ladies continued friendly, and in such trifles as the lines on prudery[2] addressed to Miss How or those 'On a Certain Lady at Court' (Mrs. Howard) the poet attains a playful elegance which is most felicitous. Such moods of harmless gaiety contrast favourably with those of

---

[1] Griffith, ii. 562.

[2] First printed, so far as is known, in the *Weekly Packet*, 18 October 1718. It is introduced as follows: 'Mrs. Lepell, and Miss How, two Maids of Honour to the Princess, ask'd Mr. Pope what *Prudery* is. [He making Use of that Expression in Conversation.] His ANSWER' (the ten lines follow).

his earlier 'tavern-pieces'. The maids of honour did Pope good, and we may trust that he did them no harm.

These diversions from Homeric austerity might well take on this pleasant tone; for after the episode of *Three Hours* attacks on Pope declined remarkably for some years. The cause was in part his wise withdrawal to the country where he laboured at Homer and visited his friends. A more potent cause, however, would be the fact that Grub Street, tiring of one victim, turned its attention to others. The noisy Bangorian controversy (17 March 1717 and later) gave it a chance to turn several dishonest pennies from jocose pamphlets. The astonishing arrest of Count Gyllenborg, the Swedish envoy, in January 1717 (which involved the arrest of one of Pope's friends, Charles Caesar)[1] gave added matter for printer's ink. The Whig schism of April 1717, through which Addison rose to be Secretary of State, affected Grub Street even more profoundly; for now the Buttonians all expected their fortunes to be made. Many of them were dissatisfied with Addison's efforts in their behalf, and presently, by the summer of 1718, they were indulging in a sniping civil war against each other. Oldmixon and Tickell (who had secured places) were the chief ones attacked. Even Steele and Addison were somewhat estranged, apparently, and fell to blows on opposite sides of the Peerage Bill of 1719.

Another diversion of satire came at the end of 1717 when Cibber's Whig comedy of the *Non-Juror* was acted. The clumsiness of this partisan effort called forth attacks on Cibber from the most diverse quarters. In the crowd Pope tried to slip an attack into town anonymously through the hands of Edmund Curll himself. Curll, however, was shrewd as usual; he published the pamphlet, and advertised it as follows:

This Day is publish'd the two following Books,

I. The PLOT DISCOVER'D; or, a Clue to the Comedy of the Non-Juror. With some Hints of Consequence relating to that Play. In a Letter to N. Rowe, Esq; Poet-Laureate to his Majesty. To

[1] *Weekly Journal, or British Gazetteer,* 2 February 1717, p. 643.

which is subjoin'd some Verses written by Mr. Rowe, pr. 6d. [The Manuscript of this Pamphlet was sent to me on Tuesday last, and I was this Morning given to understand, that this signal Favour was conferr'd on me by Mr. Pope, for which I hereby return my most grateful Acknowledgment for the same. E. Curll.] . . .[1]

Another probably later issue of this pamphlet uses the sub-title as title: *A Clue to the Non-Juror, or, the Plot discover'd, containing some hints of Consequence relating to that Play*; and there is still another issue of the same sheets with a new title-page, 'the second edition' of the *Plot Discover'd*. This last has on the verso of the title-page a rhyme entreating Pope to be 'generous' and own the work. There is some evidence that the work actually was Pope's. Certainly it comes nearer than does any other to satisfying Cibber's muddled description of Pope's attack, the title of which he had, so he said, forgotten. He perhaps naturally confused the attack with Pope's *Key to the Lock*; for the *Plot Discover'd* uses a technique similar to that of Pope's earlier allegorical interpretation of his *Rape of the Lock*. Cibber writes of Pope's work on the *Non-Juror*:

The Purport of this odd Piece of Wit was to prove, that *The Non-Juror* in its Design, its Characters, and almost every Scene of it, was a closely couched Jacobite Libel against the Government: And, in troth, the Charge was in some places so shrewdly maintained, that I almost liked the Jest myself; at least, it was so much above the Spirit, and Invention of the Daily-Paper Satyrists, that all the sensible Readers I met with, without Hesitation gave it to Mr. Pope.[2]

The pamphlet ingeniously turns the play into a satire on the Bishop of Bangor (Woodvil-Orgon) and the converted Jesuit of his household, M. de la Pillonière (Wolf-Tartuffe). It was of course easy to expose the awkward political implications in Cibber's adaptation of *Tartuffe*. Attacks by others on the play were succeeded by attacks on the management of Drury Lane. These included various pieces from Dennis, whose vitriol for some time now was largely concentrated against Steele and Cibber.

---

[1] *Evening Post*, 18 February 1718.
[2] *Letter to Mr. Pope* (1742: sold by W. Lewis), p. 26.

All these excursions and alarums, to which should be added Richard Bentley's troubles at Cambridge and, above all, the South Sea Bubble with its tumultuous reverberations, preoccupied Grub Street and left Pope in a relatively happy state of peace. The five years 1718–23, ending with the appearance of his edition of the Duke of Buckingham-shire's *Works*, formed one of the most tranquil periods in Pope's life. It was not unmarked by attacks, but the attacks were sporadic and, for the most part, were patiently endured and wisely ignored. An example is Aaron Hill's 'plain-dealing Preface' to his *Northern Star* (1718). Lintot submitted this poem to Pope, and reported to Hill, some-what ramblingly, Pope's opinion that a poem praising the Czar might be taken ill by the Government at a moment when Russia seemed to be forsaking its alliance with George I for an *entente* with Sweden and the Pretender. Hill evidently thought Pope jealous of the poem, and in the Preface attacked him violently. By 1720 this breach had been temporarily healed, but again in 1728 Hill was offended at finding in the *Bathos* the initials 'A. H.'[1]—which might have referred to Anthony Hammond, Anthony Henley, or perhaps others. Pope's forbearance with Hill, whose excitability was not endearing, deserves to be remembered.

Freedom from attack allowed Pope's reputation to aug-ment itself. The great agent in this process was the *Iliad*; but in June 1717 appeared the first collected volume of his *Works*, and such a volume is always a landmark in a poet's career. Pope's volume was more than a collection of pieces already known: it included several new poems, some of which were of first importance. There was a brilliant Preface and a 'Discourse on Pastoral Poetry', the 'Fable of Dryope from Ovid', 'Two Choruses to the Tragedy of Brutus, not yet publick', 'Verses to the Memory of an Unfortunate Lady', 'To a Young Lady [Teresa Blount]. On her leaving Town after the Coronation', 'On a Fan of

---

[1] Elwin-Courthope, x. 1, 2, and note. See also the *Dunciad* (4to, 1729), Book II, line 285, and note.

the Author's Design', 'Epitaph' [for Sir William Trumbull], 'Epilogue to Jane Shore', [Lines] 'Occasion'd by some Verses of his Grace the Duke of Buckingham', and, finally, 'Eloisa to Abelard'. The fable from Ovid appeared a month later in the sumptuous translation of the *Metamorphoses* made 'by the most eminent hands' and published under the supervision of Sir Samuel Garth. Apparently as a *jeu d'esprit* on Garth's Ovid, Pope wrote 'Sandys' Ghost', first published, so far as is known, in 1727. The other pieces show at least his varied social connexions, and two of them reveal Pope's highest achievement in elegiac poetry. The first of these, the 'Verses to the Memory of an Unfortunate Lady', seems probably inspired by Pope's interest in tragedy, stimulated in part by his friendship for Nicholas Rowe. The style is plainer and more nervous than Pope's had been elsewhere; the imagery seems tragic in the purely theatrical sense of that word—the midnight gloom, the ghost, the dagger, all suggest the stage. But his readers in the eighteenth century took the poem earnestly. The problem for them was to identify the Unfortunate Lady. In the standard edition of the poet's works, Elwin and Courthope[1] have presented so many candidates as to reduce the problem to an absurdity; for obviously no candidate fits the poem. They, however, settle upon Mrs. Weston, a lady who like many others was hardly used by her family. She was befriended by Pope and Caryll, but not much to any one's advantage so far as we know. She did not, however, like the Unfortunate Lady, enter a convent or stab herself. An almost conclusive argument against Mrs. Weston comes from the pen of Caryll, who knew her story thoroughly. Apparently she did not occur to him as a possibility; for he wrote Pope six weeks after the poem appeared: 'But pray, in your next, tell me who was the unfortunate lady you address a copy of verses to. I think you once gave me her history, but it is now quite out of my head. But now I have named such a person, Mrs. Cope occurs to my mind.'[2] It seems probable that the woes of

[1] ii. 201–5; v. 130–4.   [2] Ibid., vi. 247.

various ladies with brutal parents or husbands may have been sublimated into the tragedy of Pope's lady, but no one alone among all those suggested notably parallels her woes.

The truth is that he was during these years much thrown into the society of women, and thus came to sympathize with feminine sorrows. His contemptible physique made any admiration of women on his part practically futile so far as love was concerned, and made him feel keenly such frustration of that passion as he depicts in these two elegiac poems, which constitute his most successful attempts at pathos. The second of the two, 'Eloisa to Abelard', is in the manner of Ovid's *Heroides*, and is perhaps as good an example as exists in English of what may be called Roman pathos. Its appeal to a person of the Latin races is still strong; it seems, however, to be definitely out of the English tradition, and to belong rather to a tradition like that of 'grand' opera, which has never naturalized itself among English-speaking peoples, and the excellence, at least the naturalness, of which in consequence arouses some question.

So far as a biographical background for 'Eloisa to Abelard' is concerned, one is on slightly less difficult ground than in the case of the Unfortunate Lady. To Martha Blount he wrote in a fashion to imply that love for her inspired him; and somewhat later he paid the same compliment to Lady Mary Wortley Montagu.[1] Pope got pleasure from imagining that he was in love with both these ladies; but so far as 'Eloisa' is concerned, the romantic reviling of marriage and the theme of love in absence:

> Condemned whole years in absence to deplore,
> And image charms he must behold no more—

indicate that Lady Mary had the greater influence. Pope had made her acquaintance by the summer of 1715;[2] he had been at once dazzled by her wit, daring, and social position, and was evidently allowed to exchange witty bits of gallantry with her.

[1] Ibid., ix. 264, 382.   [2] Ibid. ix. 263, note 2.

The first public episode in their acquaintance came when in 1716[1] Curll published the so-called *Court Poems*. Pope took the onus of these effusions from the shoulders of Gay or Lady Mary. According to Pope's note in the 1729 *Dunciad* to Book II, line 54, Curll 'meant to publish [this volume] as the work of the true writer, a Lady of quality; but being first threaten'd, and afterwards punish'd, for it by Mr. *Pope*, he generously transferr'd it from *her* to *him*, and has now printed it twelve years in his name.'[2] When Pope wrote this note he was openly hostile to Lady Mary, but it seems probable that she was the 'true writer' of the two poems in the volume that were dangerous as satires, and that Gay wrote the third. At any rate the two poems in question had been circulating as Lady Mary's before they were printed. James Brydges, Earl of Carnarvon (later first Duke of Chandos), in an unpublished letter to Colonel Bladen dated 26 January 1715/6 comments on 'Roxana' and Lady Mary's reputation for satire:

Lady Mary is almost recover'd & her sickness [small-pox] has given occasion for a Pun amongst Ladies. They say, she was very full & yet not pitted, but she'l live to be reveng'd on some more of her Sex. Have you seen her verses on y[e] Dutchess of Roxburgh & her comparison by way of Eclogue between y[e] pleasure of Basset & Love. If you have not I'l send them you, for they are very entertaining.[3]

Three weeks later the Earl forwarded one of the poems to General Cadogan,[4] ascribing it to Lady Mary; and on 20 February he sent the group to Bladen, with the comment:

I know you have but little time for such curiosities, but they are entertaining enough, & their being wrote by a Lady, renders them no less agreable. I can assure you for my own part she is one whose wit I admire much more than her Person. . . .[5]

The Earl was intimate with Dr. Arbuthnot, and acquainted with Gay; his gossip consequently is valuable evidence here.

---

[1] *Supra*, pp. 167–9. [2] *Dunciad* (4to, 1729), p. 27 n.
[3] *Chandos Letter Books: Letters to Several Persons*, xii. 255 (Huntington Library MSS.). [4] Ibid. xii. 278. [5] Ibid. xii. 281.

It is a testimonial to the high regard Pope's editors have had for Curll that at least one of these poems continues to be ascribed to Pope. The whole episode suggests a dangerous basis for solid friendship between Pope and the lady.

During her absence in the Orient, where, 1716–18, Mr. Wortley Montagu was ambassador to Turkey, Pope wrote her very ardent letters. In 1720 or 1721 after their return to England, the Wortley Montagus came to be his neighbours at Twickenham, and at this time he may have written the *Lines* to Lady Mary celebrating her 'beauty and wit', which Curll so often printed, and which Thomas Burnet claimed as his own.[1] The friendship gradually cooled, doubtless from many causes, but the change from intimacy to hot enmity, which took place before 1727, has never been explained, though there are several plausible hypotheses.

The two that seem most adequate are those offered by the principals in the case. Lady Mary is said to have ascribed Pope's fury to the fact that once when he attempted a declaration of love she laughed in his face.[2] Lady Mary told Spence that Arbuthnot represented Pope as saying that 'Lady M. and Lord Hervey had pressed him once together (and I don't remember that we were ever together with him in our lives), to write a Satire on some certain persons, that he refused it: and that this had occasioned the breach between us.'[3] This last explanation comes from fairly near the source, and has vaguely intrinsic plausibility. Lady Mary and Pope were bound together by a common love of wit, gossip, and satire. Both, in fact, were active satirists; but Lady Mary's friends were mostly Whigs, and Pope's chief ties were with the Tories. Satires by the one might frequently hit friends of the other, and joint authorship would be fraught with difficulty.

Lady Mary was not popular with her own sex, more than

---

[1] *Manly Anniversary Studies* (Chicago, 1923), pp. 173–4. Pope never did own these lines, I believe, but his later dislike of Lady Mary may be what prevented him from so doing.

[2] *Letters and Works of Lady Mary Wortley Montagu*, ed. Wharncliffe (1893), i. 92.   [3] Spence, p. 235.

one of whom she lampooned. During her Twickenham residence she was involved in a quarrel with her (and apparently Pope's) friend Mrs. Joanna Baillie Murray.[1] In 1721 and later Mrs. Murray was in the public eye because a footman of her father's household entered her chamber at night and was prevented from criminal assault only by her presence of mind. Upon this episode (which Lady Mary thought most amusing), she wrote and owned 'An Epistle from Arthur Grey in Newgate to Mrs. Murray'. Lady Mary was accused by Mrs. Murray in 1725 of writing also a ballad on the same subject printed as a broadside called *Virtue in Danger: Or Arthur Gray's last Farewell to the World. Written by a Gentleman at St. James's.* In the face of Mrs. Murray's charge, Lady Mary represents herself as simply defying Mrs. Murray to prove her authorship of this broadside; she seems almost to admit to the Countess of Mar a certain complicity.[2] The piece was included in the 1776 *Additions to the Works of . . . Pope,*[3] and was there ascribed to Lady Mary.

There is no evidence that Lady Mary attempted to shift responsibility for this indelicate effort to the shoulders of Mrs. Murray's friend Pope though possibly when he was in Jervas's house the curious title of 'a Gentleman at St. James's' might suggest him. Lady Mary had shifted such responsibilities in the case of the *Court Poems* of 1716, and early in 1723 she wrote to her sister:

Mrs. Murray and all her satellites have so seldom fallen in my way, I can say little about them. Your old friend Mrs. Lowther is still fair and young, and in pale pink every night in the Parks; but, after being highly in favour, poor I am in utter disgrace, without being able to guess wherefore, except she fancied me the author or abettor of two vile ballads written on her dying adventure, which I am so innocent of that I never saw [them]. *A propos* of ballads, a most delightful one is said or sung in most houses about our dear beloved plot, which has been laid firstly to Pope, and

---

[1] She was a cousin of Pope's friend the third Earl of Marchmont, and was called by Lady Hervey (Molly Lepel) one of 'my dearest, oldest friends'. See Lady Hervey's *Letters* (1821), p. 221 (11 September 1756).

[2] *Letters and Works,* ed. cit. i. 482–3.   [3] i. 176–82.

secondly to me, when God knows we have neither of us wit enough to make it.[1]

It has been thought that the ballad on the plot was Swift's 'Upon the Horrid Plot discovered by Harlequin the Bishop of Rochester's French Dog'. In that case it must have been flattering to any lady to have the works of the greatest geniuses ascribed to her pen, and it may have been convenient at times to ascribe one's works to one or another of them in return.

The ballad *Virtue in Danger* seems to have antagonized Mrs. Murray in the winter of 1725, and if Lady Mary tried to impute it to Pope, the attempt would account neatly for the first open attack on Lady Mary by Pope or his allies. This appeared in the 'last' volume of the *Miscellanies* (March 1728; dated 1727). It is a poem by Swift called 'The Capon's Tale'. In it Swift writes of a Yorkshire hen with too many chickens, for some of which she gets a deluded capon to act as mother. One would hardly recognize Pope as the capon, incapable of satirical offspring, but the conclusion of the poem clearly charges Lady Mary (who came from Yorkshire) with leaving her chicks on the doorsteps of others:

> Such, Lady *Mary*, are your Tricks;
> But since you hatch, pray own your chicks.

This first shot was followed later by much rougher treatment of the lady. The barbed couplets that Pope in his Horatian period bestowed on her may have been undeserved; but she herself was robust and hard-mouthed rather than delicate in taste or sensitive in moral matters. Her beauty waned; in fact, a disfiguring sore on her face, together with untidiness in dress, must have made her distinctly unattractive. It probably made her glad to live abroad for some years with itinerant eccentrics such as Molly Skerritt and Lady Pomfret. Lady Mary's later years were a sad decline after the brilliant, reckless days when she ran with Pope, who was the acme of wit, and the Duke of

---

[1] *Letters and Works*, ed. cit. i. 466.

Wharton, who charmed all ladies with his reputation for wickedness.[1] These later years, however, were far off from the days when Lady Mary inspired fervour in the words of Eloisa. Before 1725 or 1726 the only warmth between Lady Mary and Pope was the gradually cooling ardour of a more or less imaginary passion. To the end of his life Pope kept portraits of Lady Mary on his walls—a portrait 'in the best room fronting the Thames' and a drawing 'in the great parlor'.[2]

Hardly a month after 'Eloisa' appeared in the *Works* of 1717, a more obscure volume was published by Lintot, in which Pope had a considerable interest. It was called *Poems on Several Occasions: By His Grace the Duke of Buckingham, Mr. Wycherly, Lady Winchelsea, Sir Samuel Garth, N. Rowe, Esq; Mrs. Singer, Bevil Higgons, Esq; And other eminent Hands. London: Printed for Bernard Lintot between the Temple-Gates,* 1717. This octavo, apparently now very rare, was unknown to students of Pope until in 1926 Professor Arthur E. Case called attention to the fact that it contained several poems by Pope not reprinted between 1717 and 1926.[3] Pope was very likely the editor of the volume; for Case shows from the poet's letters that Pope got Broome and an unknown friend[4] to contribute and that he was responsible for the inclusion of verses by Parnell's friend the Rev. James Ward.[5] The more distinguished names on the title-page read like a list of Pope's friends. His own verses here published include only small pieces, five of which after some revision he preserved

---

[1] James Brydges (later Duke of Chandos), who was ordinarily not at all malicious, wrote to his friend Colonel Bladen, 28 December 1715:

Poor Lady Mary Wortley has ye small pox, just as it began (to her great joy) to be known she was in fav^r with one whom every one, who looks on, cannot but love. Her Husband too is inconsolable for ye disappointment this gives him in ye carrier [career?] he had chalkt out of his fortunes, for ye Ladies who know every minute of ye day, what her distemper takes, say she hath them exceedingly full & will be very severely markt. *Chandos Letter Books: Letters to Several Persons,* xii. 223–4 (Huntington Library MSS.).

[2] *Notes and Queries,* 6 S. v. 363–5.

[3] *London Mercury,* x. 614–23. Fresh discoveries are announced in Mr. Norman Ault's *Pope's Own Miscellany* now in the press.

[4] Elwin-Courthope, viii. 36, 38.   [5] Ibid. vii. 464.

in his later works.[1] The whole group are imitations or
translations, and are frankly juvenilia. Of six 'Verses in
imitation of Waller. By a Youth of thirteen' Pope preserved
later only one: 'Of her singing to a Lute'; of three in
imitation of Cowley he preserved only one, 'Weeping', and
that after much revision. Other juvenilia in the volume,
which were later owned by Pope are his Imitation of
Martial, Book 10, Epigram 23, sent early to Sir William
Trumbull, and the first printed form of a piece which,
later improved, became one of Pope's best small poems,
'Solitude. An Ode.' The subsequent disregard for pieces
labelled 'By the same Hand' as these acknowledged verses
by Pope is probably due to their juvenile and unoriginal
character. They are nevertheless placidly charming, and
reflect well the quieter moods of Pope's life when free from

> The rage of courts, the noise of towns.

But if they illustrate this love of quiet, their very existence
suggests the opposite of quiet: Pope's diverse and excessive
activities in many sorts of literary work, some of which he
never regarded again.

'The life of a wit', he had said, 'is a warfare on earth',
and from all this turmoil and fighting Pope had many
moments of strong revulsion. He talked of giving up poetry
altogether, and when depression strengthened, he took
more and more refuge in his villa and his grotto, and in the
hospitality of his many aristocratic friends. In view of the
fact that he was not by birth a gentleman, it must be
granted that Pope had attained an unusual social position.
Prior, Young, and Thomson also in his time acquired fame
in poetry, but none of them reached the position in society
to which Pope easily rose.

By the time the *Iliad* was appearing in print Pope's
social life, like his literary labours, had achieved a checkered
routine. The deviations from routine were not marked by
an oscillation between high and low society, but were due
to variations in the poet's health or in that of his mother.

---

[1] The rest are reprinted by Case in the *London Mercury*, x. 617-23.

After 1714 Pope's times and seasons (health permitting) accorded with the habits of the *beau monde*. The winters were spent in the country: in cold weather Pope naturally clung closer to the chimney corner than most men of his years; the spring and early summer (at least until Parliament rose) might be spent in London; two months of the summer were devoted to translation, or to fashionable visits; and in the autumn he might spend a few weeks at Bath.

It is not true that Pope was no traveller. Hazlitt neatly (but not too accurately) remarked that 'His Muse never wandered with safety, but from his library to his grotto, or from his grotto into his library back again'; but Pope himself loved to wander. Beginning with 1707 when he journeyed to Abberley to visit Walsh, the summer ramble was almost a habit with Pope. His health kept him from crossing either to France or to Ireland, and he had little interest in seeing Scotland or Wales; but England he covered in his various rambles with more thoroughness than most gentlemen of his day with no estates to visit. The family somehow had acquired a rent charge on land near Ruston in Yorkshire, which they wished to sell, and it is possible that Pope's speedy trip to York in 1716, when he writes to Lady Mary, 'I have been at York and Bath in less than a fortnight,' had a business purpose.[1] Practically all of his rambles, however, were visits to friends, not business trips. In the summers of 1711 and 1712 he visited the Carylls at Ladyholt; in 1713 he remained in London; and in 1714, 1715, and 1716 he journeyed to Bath. In 1717 his rambles were more numerous though not more extensive than in other years. For that year it happens that from his letters we can trace his movements more minutely than in some other summers.

Caryll, as usual, put in an early plea for a visit, and on 7 June Pope replies hopefully:

I may now think of seeing Ladyholt, though not a line of my next year's task is writ. . . . I am really in St. Paul's condition, distracted

---

[1] Elwin-Courthope, ix. 364.

with many businesses. I expect this instant Mr. Harcourt, who is
to pass some days with me. Mr. Edward Blount and Sir Henry
Bedingfield follow next. I am engaged to Mr. Stonor's afterwards
(there, you have all my Catholics at once, except the Mrs. Blounts,
who have me always); then my Lord Burlington and Duchess
Hamilton, upon ten or twenty parties. I had made one with Lord
Jersey last week to have run away and seen the Isle of Wight and
Stanstead. He thought it a mere ramble; but my design lay deeper
to have got to you. But the late sitting of Parliament hindered
this project. In short, if I stay at home I shall do nothing. I must
go abroad to follow my business, and if Ladyholt's shades afford
me protection, it is there Homer's battles must be fought.

> O quis me in vallibus Æmi
> Sistat—et ingenti ramorum protegat umbra![1]

But for one reason or another Pope stayed near or at home,
spending his time not in Homer's battles but in the great
houses of his 'neighbours'. On 6 August he wrote Caryll
explaining his delay:

That you may see I have no common obstacles hitherto, besides
the neighbourhood of your fair cousins, I have been indispensably
obliged to pass some days at almost every house along the Thames
—half my acquaintance being, upon the breaking up of the Parliament, become my neighbours. After some attendance on my Lord
Burlington, I have been at the Duke of Shrewsbury's, Duke of
Argyle's, Lady Rochester's, Lord Percival's, Mr. Stonor's, Lord
Winchelsea's, Sir Godfrey Kneller, who has made me a fine present
of a picture, and Duchess Hamilton's. All these have indispensable
claims to me, under penalty of the imputation of direct rudeness,
living within two hours' sail of Chiswick. Then am I obliged to
pass some days between my Lord Bathurst's, and three or four
more on Windsor side; thence to Mr. Dancastle, and my relations
on Bagshot Heath. I am also promised three months ago to the
Bishop of Rochester for three days on the other side of the water.
Besides all this, two of my friends have engaged to be here a week;
and into this computation I do not reckon Dr. Arbuthnot and others
in town, who have an immediate jurisdiction over me. In a word,
the minute I can get to you, I will. . . .[2]

The visit was destined not to take place. We can follow
the poet's movements on some of his successive rambles in

---

[1] Ibid., vi. 244-5.   [2] Ibid. vi. 248.

badly edited letters sent to the Misses Blount. On a Saturday (7 September?) he went by water to Hampton Court, where he enjoyed a dinner with his friends (*pace* Dennis!) the Princess's maids of honour. His comment is:

I can easily believe, no lone House in Wales, with a Mountain & a Rookery, is more contemplative than this Court; and as a proof of it I need only tell you Mrs Lepell walk'd all alone with me three or 4 hours, by moonlight; and we mett no Creature of any quality, but the King, who gave audience all alone to the Vice-chamberlen, under the Garden-wall. . . .

I was heartily tired; & glad to be gone by 8 aclock next morning; hir'd two damnd Horses, gallopd to Staines, lost leather, kept Miss Griffin from Church all ye Sunday, & lay at my Brothers near Bagshot that night. . . .

I arrived at Mr Dancastles [Binfield] on Tuesday-noon, having fled from the face (I wish I could say from the horned face) of Mr Weston, who dined that day at my Brother's. I have seen my Farmer, yea and the Gold-ring which I forgot, on his finger. I have sent to Sr W. Compton, & past the rest of the day in those Woods where I have so often enjoyd—an author & a Book; and begot such Sons upon the Muses, as I hope will live to see their father what he never was yet, an old and a good Man. I made a Hymn as I past thro' these Groves; it ended with a deep Sigh, which I will not tell you the meaning of. . . .

On Thursday I went to Stonor, which I have long had a mind to see since the romantic description you gave me of it. The Melancholy which my Wood, and this Place, have spread over me will go near to cast a cloud upon the rest of my letter, if I don't make haste to conclude it here. . . .[1]

As a sequel to this letter, which is carefully dated 13 September 1717, Pope printed in 1735 an undated letter to the Misses Blount. There are difficulties in the way of referring these two letters to the same year when one sees the full texts in manuscript. The letter just quoted was written on a Friday, and in a part of a letter to his father, dated the 17th, the poet represents himself as having

---

[1] Elwin-Courthope, ix. 274 and note. The passages from this letter as well as from the next are here printed from rotographs of the manuscripts. There are notable verbal changes even from the edition of Bowles, which gives the best text of the Mapledurham letters.

reached Oxford on 'Friday last'. If this is a slip for Thursday, and if 'this place' in the last sentence just quoted from his letter of the 13th means 'this place just mentioned' and not 'this place where I now am', the sequel printed by Pope may properly continue his travels of 1717. There seems to be no more plausible year for the second letter, which, in any case, continues effectively the tone of the first letter as well as its journey:

I came from Stonor (its Master not being at home) to Oxford the same night. Nothing could have more of that Melancholy which once us'd to please me, than that days journey: For after having passd thro' my favorite Woods in the forest, with a thousand Reveries of past pleasures; I rid over hanging hills, whose tops were edgd with groves, & whose feet water'd with winding rivers, listening to the falls of Cataracts below, & the murmuring of winds above. The gloomy Verdure of Stonor succeeded to these, & then the Shades of the Evening overtook me, the Moon rose in the clearest Sky I ever saw, by whose solemn light I pac'd on slowly, without company, or any interuption, to the range of my thoughts. About a mile before I reachd Oxford, all the Night bells toll'd, in different notes; the Clocks of every College answerd one another; & told me, some in a deeper, some in a softer voice, that it was eleven a clock.

All this was no ill preparation to the life I have led since; among those old walls, venerable Galleries, Stone Portico's, studious walks & solitary Scenes of the University. I wanted nothing but a black gown and a Salary, to be as meer a Bookworm as any there. I conform'd myself to the College hours, was rolld up in books & wrapt in meditation, lay in one of the most ancient, dusky parts of ye University, and was as dead to the world as any Hermite of the desart. If anything was awake or alive in me, it was a little Vanity, such as even those good men usd to entertain when the Monks of their own order extolld their Piety & abstractedness. For I found my self receivd with a sort of respect, wch this idle part of mankind, the Learned, pay to their own Species; who are as considerable here, as the Busy the Gay and ye Ambitious are in your World. Indeed I was so treated, that I could not but sometimes ask myself in my mind, what College I was founder of,[1] or what Library

---

[1] Ibid. ix. 275–6. The founder of Trinity College, Oxford, was Sir Thomas Pope, of whom the poet regarded himself a descendant. The sentence in the letter makes one wonder if university friends encouraged in the poet the mistaken belief that he was related to these Oxfordshire Popes.

I had built? Methinks I do very ill, to return to the world again. . . .

After some ten days spent in this hospitable and congenial environment and in brief visits to Stanton Harcourt, Cornbury, and Blenheim, Pope returned home by way of Reading.[1] On 6 October he is in London,[2] ready to start for Ladyholt if Caryll is at home; by the 18th the expected invitation has not yet arrived. Somewhat more than the autumn floods and the 'great cold' conspired to forbid this journey to Sussex: in the night of 23/4 October the poet's father unexpectedly died—'without a groan, or the sickness of two minutes,' as the son wrote John Gay—'in a word, as silently and peacefully as he lived.'[3]

The effect of this event upon the poet was manifold. The tie between father and son had been unusually close; and from his father the poet had acquired interests that coloured his whole life. 'I have lost one whom I was even more obliged to as a friend than as a father',[4] he wrote Caryll, and we know he was deeply insulted when six months later Gildon in his *Memoirs of William Wycherley* sneered at 'the Decease of his [Pope's] Rustick Parent'.[5] The event bound Pope more closely than ever to his aged mother. It did not at once stop his rambles; for in February 1718/19 he wrote Broome, 'I have at this present writing no less than five houses, in different counties, through which I make a tour every summer';[6] but such tours now had to depend upon the health of his mother. Until 5 November 1725 the family included the poet's nurse Mary (or Mercy) Beech; but after her death on this date,[7] the household, except for mother and son, must have been quite changed from that of the regretted Binfield days. It was Pope's tenderest duty to keep these changes from weighing his mother with melancholy. To his Anglican friends, especially the Bishop of Rochester and perhaps Swift, the death of the elder Pope seemed to relieve the son of the

---

[1] Elwin-Courthope, ix. 478.   [2] Ibid. vi. 251.   [3] Ibid. vii. 420.
[4] Ibid. vi. 253.   [5] p. 16.   [6] Elwin-Courthope, viii. 42.
[7] Ibid. i. ix: 'Nutrix mea fidelissima M. Beech, obiit 5 Novem. 1725, aet. 77.'

necessity of remaining a Roman Catholic; but to letters urging the advantages of conversion the poet returned the reply that such a change would grieve his mother, and that since he had no civic ambitions, he saw no point in making the change.[1]

The most obvious result of the father's demise was probably to hasten a removal from Chiswick. Binfield had always been regretted. The new friends acquired about Chiswick were people of fashion rather than (if the Earl of Burlington be excepted) intimates; life thereabouts was hardly more than a damnable iteration of visits to great houses. Time and physical energy as well were exhausted; and about a year after the death of his father the poet leased the villa at Twickenham, his home for the rest of his life. Chiswick he speaks of as in the country, and Twickenham might even more justly be so called. In fact, two centuries after Pope's removal to his celebrated villa the outlook across the river from its well-chosen site was still distinctly rural. The village in Pope's day was a favourite residence of folk who wished to be near the court, but in the days of the first two Georges fewer people wished that than one might imagine. Pope had considered moving to London itself, which his father's rigid observance of the laws against Catholics had probably precluded; but Lord Bathurst dissuaded the poet from building in town on account of the expense.[2] Pope spent the summer of 1718 (when the decision against living in town was made) in the country, and probably that fact was an influence in the decision.

Chiswick was impossible; for the poet was falling behind in his labours on Homer, and in Chiswick he had no time to himself. So he wrote to Caryll in 1718, declining an invitation to Ladyholt on the ground that he must work.

The consciousness of this has made me resolve to be alone for some months. As I cannot be so at Chiswick, nor long absent from my mother, and necessarily engaged to study, I am going near Oxford, the seat of the Muses, and at this time of vacation solitary enough.[3]

---

[1] Ibid. ix. 10–12. [2] Ibid. viii. 325 (14 August 1718).
[3] Ibid. vi. 263.

Earlier in the summer he had visited Oxford, Stanton-Harcourt, and Lord Bathurst's seat at Cirencester with Gay and Erasmus Lewis. He now persuaded his mother to go to Stanton-Harcourt,[1] and he and Gay divided their time during the whole summer between that place and Cirencester. Here he translated, meditated building projects, and sent to various friends his lines on John Hewet and Sarah Drew.[2] On 8 September he wrote to Atterbury:

> I have lived, where I have done nothing but sinned, that is rhymed, these six weeks. I dare not approach you till the fit is over. I thank God, I find the symptoms almost gone. . . .[3]

On a pane of glass at Stanton-Harcourt was inscribed: 'In the year 1718, Alexander Pope finished here the Fifth Volume of Homer.'[4] As late as October he was in the country playing and working with Lord Bathurst at Cirencester and writing the Misses Blount from his 'bower' in Oakley Wood. The letter shows the influences that led him to choose a residence where more gardening would be possible than in London:

> I am with Lord Bathurst, at my bower; in whose groves we had yesterday a dry walk of three hours. It is the place that of all others I fancy; and I am not yet out of humour with it, though I have had it some months: it does not cease to be agreeable to me so late in the season; the very dying of the leaves adds a variety of colours that is not unpleasant. I look upon it, as upon a beauty I once loved, whom I should preserve a respect for in her decay; and as we should look upon a friend, with remembrance how he pleased us once, though now declined from his gay and flourishing condition.
>
> I write an hour or two every morning, then ride out a hunting upon the Downs, eat heartily, talk tender sentiments with Lord B., or draw plans for houses and gardens, open avenues, cut glades, plant firs, contrive water-works, all very fine and beautiful in our own imagination. At night we play at commerce, and play pretty high: I do more, I bett too; for I am really rich, and must throw away my money if no deserving friend will use it. I like this course

---

[1] Elwin-Courthope, viii. 321–4. To Bathurst, 5 July 1718.
[2] Ibid. ix. 284–6, 398–9; vi. 266.   [3] Ibid. ix. 14.   [4] Ibid.

of life so well, that I am resolved to stay here till I hear of some-
body's being in town that is worth coming after.[1]

Three weeks after writing this letter he was back in Chiswick with his mother and his sister, Mrs. Rackett. The last-
named lady found comparisons between Bagshot Heath
(her place of residence) and Chiswick unfavourable to the
latter,[2] and one infers that she advocated a residence in her
own vicinity. Of the actual removal to Twickenham Pope's
letters give us small history. A letter to Broome, if dated
properly, and it seems so to be,[3] indicates that it took place
towards the end of 1718.

[1] Ibid. ix. 289–90.   [2] Ibid. ix. 489.
[3] Ibid. viii. 40–1 (31 December [1718]). A letter to Jervas, obviously misdated
12 December 1718 [Elwin-Courthope, viii. 36], and probably a composite of
more than one letter, speaks of the 'transplantation' as accomplished a year before
the letter was written. In another letter, to Aaron Hill [ibid. x. 1], dated 2 March,
and placed in the year 1720 by the editors, Pope says he has not lived at Chiswick
'this twelvemonth'.

VIII

'A MERE EDITOR'

'I MUST again sincerely protest to you that I have wholly given over scribbling, at least anything of my own, but am become, by due gradation of dulness, from a poet, a translator, and from a translator, a mere editor.' So Pope wrote Caryll in October 1722.[1] Early inspired by the tradition of the *bel esprit* and by such doctrines concerning critics as those found in *A Tale of a Tub*, Pope had learned contempt for 'word-catchers', and academic scavengers, who meddled with commas and other textual minutiae. He was, however, a born reviser of others' works, and he took a keener interest in antiquarian learning, especially of a literary sort, than he would have admitted to the Scriblerus Club. In later years he told Spence, 'I once got deep into Graevius, and was taken greatly with it: so far as to write a treatise in Latin, collected from the writers in Graevius on the Old Buildings in Rome.'[2] Spence, who was more than an amateur in archaeology, respected Pope's knowledge. In the poet's early letters to Walsh, and especially in those to Cromwell, he had exhibited a considerable tendency towards bookishness, and he continued throughout his career an interest in the history of English poetry.[3] He had revised the verses of Wycherley and other contemporary bards; he had edited the 'remains' of Betterton—modernizations of Chaucer—and in 1717–18 he became much interested in the Rev. Aaron Thompson's translation of Geoffrey of Monmouth. To this he made at least one small poetic contribution,[4] and his interest in the translation was probably an early stimulus towards the project of his epic on the subject of Brutus.

---

[1] Elwin-Courthope, vi. 281.   [2] Spence, p. 204.
[3] Ruffhead (*Life of Pope*, 8vo ed., 1769, pp. 424–5) prints Pope's plan for a 'discourse on the rise and progress of English poetry'. See also Spence, pp. 19–23, 144, 172–4, &c.   [4] Griffith, p. 559 (Add. 90 c).

After a half-dozen years of labouring at the *Iliad*, it is natural that Pope should speak of the due gradation downward from poet to translator and editor. It is clear, however, that his creative instincts were always paralleled by critical or historical tendencies; and it is also clear that his creative activity had, during the years of translation, notably subsided. Pope loved history; and he loved tinkering with phrases, whether his own or those of others. He came to feel somewhat injured if the works of deceased friends (Wycherley, for example) were not submitted to his care. In two cases during the years under consideration it was his fortune to render this service: he edited the works of Parnell, who died in the autumn of 1718, and those of his patron and friend, John Sheffield, Duke of Buckinghamshire,[1] who died in February 1720/1. He also advised the Earl of Oxford on the poetic remains of Prior, and, incidentally, seems to have wished to print 'Jinny the Just'[2] in the *Miscellanies* of 1727–8.

The task of bringing out (December 1721) Parnell's *Poems on several Occasions* was relatively simple. Pope had no pedantic notion that he ought to print all that his friend had written. In a letter to Jervas, who was then in Ireland, Pope enumerates his recent losses:

Poor Parnell, Garth, Rowe! You justly reprove me for not speaking of the death of the last: Parnell was too much in my mind, to whose memory I am erecting the best monument I can. What he gave me to publish, was but a small part of what he left behind him; but it was the best, and I will not make it worse by enlarging it.[3]

The story of Sheffield's *Works* is more complex, and since it became involved in the major 'scholarly' activities of Pope in these years—the edition of Shakespeare and the translation of the *Odyssey*—it will be well to present in some

---

[1] More commonly styled 'Buckingham' in his own day. The shorter form of the name will be hereafter used in these pages.

[2] Elwin-Courthope, viii. 232. What else could the 'Epitaph on Jenny' be?

[3] Ibid. viii. 28. A note here says that the suppressed poems were printed in 1758, and that Gray thought badly of them.

detail the trials arising from these three projects of the early 'twenties. The fact must be emphasized that from 1718 to 1723 Pope lived in a comparatively peaceful state. 'I have carefully avoided,' he writes to Swift (in August 1723), 'all intercourse with poets and scribblers, unless where by great chance I find a modest one. By these means I have had no quarrels with any personally, and none have been enemies, but who were also strangers to me.' . . .[1] This happy state was drawing to a close when Pope wrote. Political troubles over Sheffield's *Works* and bad faith with the public over the *Odyssey* led to attacks, which may be said to culminate in the explosion of his reputation as a Shakespearian editor by Lewis Theobald.

John Sheffield, Duke of Buckingham, had been praised by Pope in lines 719–24 of the *Essay on Criticism*, and had been asked to criticize the translation of the early books of the *Iliad*. To the 1717 edition of Pope's *Works* His Grace had prefixed complimentary verses, some of which the poet prized:

> And yet so wond'rous, so sublime a thing
> As the great Iliad, scarce could make me sing,
> Unless I justly could at once commend
> A good companion, and as firm a friend.
> One moral, or a mere well-natur'd deed
> Can all desert in sciences exceed.

And the complimentary verses of the Hon. Simon Harcourt in the same volume celebrate Sheffield as the 'old Chiron' who had formed Pope's genius.[2] In return for this ducal patronage Pope wrote four couplets of glowing praise and gratitude, first printed in his own *Works* of 1717 and later prefixed to his edition of Sheffield's *Works* (1723).[3] Probably in 1718 His Grace addressed to Pope an essay-letter 'On the late dispute about Homer', which constitutes a testimonial of esteem. Pope's *Works* also included two choruses that he had contributed to the duke's tragedy of *Brutus*, which was first printed entire in 1723. These choruses were

---

[1] Elwin-Courthope, vii. 40. [2] Ibid. i. 20, 31; iv. 65.
[3] Ibid. iv. 454.

probably most known in January of that year, when they were performed at a magnificent 'consort and ball' at Buckingham House (now Buckingham Palace), in honour of the young Duke Edmond's seventh birthday. The singers included Pope's friend Mrs. Robinson, 'Mrs. Barbier, and another singer Mrs. Clark.'[1] The choruses had probably their only separate publication on this occasion of the second duke's birthday.

All these compliments on both sides imply a constant if somewhat formal friendship. Prior also was a favourite of the duke's, who liked to have poets gather at Buckingham House. An undated note from Pope to Charles Ford says: 'I write this to give you timely notice that the Duke of Buckingham having heard of Mr. Prior's and our meeting desires it may be at his Grace's house. . . . I beg you to pre-engage Mr. Gay, as for my own part, I shall goe to London on purpose that day.' . . .[2]

It was natural, then, that after the duke's death Pope, who had advised him (and Atterbury) concerning Dryden's monument in the Abbey, should also advise the duchess concerning her late husband's monument (since monuments, inscriptions, epitaphs, were among Pope's specialities at this period), and also concerning the publication of the duke's works. Sheffield had forestalled Pope's efforts as a writer of epitaphs by leaving one composed by himself. In fact, the first inkling of how the newspapers were likely to receive any posthumous writings by this pompous Jacobite leader might have come from comments on this epitaph. The lines as placed on his monument certainly constitute a 'document':

> Dubius, sed non Improbus, Vixi.
> Incertus morior, non Perturbatus;
> Humanum est Nescire et Errare,

---

[1] See *Book Prices Current* for 1919, pp. 552–3. See also the *London Journal* for 12 and 19 January 1723.

[2] Sotheby Catalogue for the sale of 18 February 1899, lot 60. This dinner probably occurred in June 1720, when Prior wrote to the Earl of Oxford of dining at Buckingham House, calling the occasion 'a sort of *convivium poeticum*, for Pope and Gay are the other two guests'. See W. Legg, *Matthew Prior*, p. 263.

Deo confido omnipotenti Benevolentissimo.
Ens Entium miserere mei.

Pro Rege saepe, pro Republica semper.[1]

Upon early rumours concerning the epitaph Pope wrote
Caryll:

Several idle reports about the Duke of Buckingham's epitaph,
with very various and misrepresenting copies, are spread about the
town. I remember only this, that what His Grace two years ago
repeated to me as his intended inscription had nothing exceptionable in it, in any fair or christian construction.[2]

In the *Daily Journal*, 22 January 1721/2, Edmund Curll
advertised 'That the Works of the late Right Honourable
John Sheffield Duke of *Buckinghamshire*, in Prose and Verse
with his Life (compleated from a Plan drawn up by his
Grace) by Mr. Theobald, and a True Copy of his last Will
and Testament, will speedily be published, by E. Curll.' ...
The House of Lords promptly ordered Curll to appear
before it on the 23rd, and explain by whose permission he
was publishing the book. Finding, naturally, that Curll
had nobody's permission, the Lords on the 31st ordered
'That if, after the Death of any Lord of this House, any
Person presume to publish in Print, his Works, or any Part
of them, not published in his Life time, or his Life or last
Will, without the Consent of his Heirs, Executors, Administrators, or Trustees, the same is a Breach of the
Privilege of this House.'[3]
Whereupon Curll checked his bold design, but being
himself did not abandon it. He dropped Theobald's life,
omitted the will, but put on sale a moderate-sized octavo
of the duke's *Works*, with a careful advertisement on the
verso of the title-page (dated 1721) to the effect that these
works had all been published during the duke's lifetime,
and that they had even been revised by the duke himself
and turned over to Charles Gildon for publication. How

---

[1] Here quoted from the frontispiece reproduction in Pope's edition of the
Works (1723). Other versions were published.

[2] Elwin-Courthope, vi. 277.

[3] *Notes and Queries*, 2 S. ii (1856), 442.

much truth there was in this last statement one may
question, but of course Gildon had enjoyed the duke's
patronage and perhaps even his friendship. Since Gildon
was blind in 1719, one doubts if Buckingham gave him
works to publish after that time. The dedicatory poem in
Curll's edition of these *Works* was addressed to the Duke of
Argyll and signed by John ['Orator'] Henley. Such a
constellation as Curll, Henley, Gildon, and Theobald,
indicates the forces that were already shaping the *Dunciad*.

After Pope had, in 1735, secured for Curll a 'return
engagement' before the House of Lords in connexion with
the alleged breach of privilege in publishing letters from
lords to Pope, Curll (who in 1735 came off uncensored)
jeered back at the poet: 'But you have met a *Second* Defeat
before the most August Assembly, as you did in your *first*
Attack, relating to the Duke of *Buckingham's* Works.'[1] If
in 1722 Curll blamed Pope for activity against him with
regard to the duke's *Works*, probably Pope felt new or
renewed hostility to Curll, Gildon, Henley, and Theobald
in the matter. And they doubtless felt likewise towards
him. The episode may account for the fact that Theobald,
who had been Pope's admirer, did not offer any aid on
Pope's edition of Shakespeare. Finally, one may wonder
if this same sly Curll was, in turn, active against Pope
when, in 1723, Pope's edition of Buckingham's *Works* was
suppressed.

Shortly before Curll's volume had been announced Pope
had assumed the position of 'official' editor of the deceased
nobleman's papers. In February 1722 he sent the duke's
two tragedies to Lord Edward Harley for a very private
inspection, and late in 1722 he announced his editorship to
Caryll: 'I have the care of overlooking the Duke of Buckingham's papers, and correcting the press,' he writes. 'That will
be a very beautiful book, and has many things in it you will
be particularly glad to see in relation to some former reigns.'[2]
This last phrase indicates Pope's probable knowledge of

---

[1] *Mr. Pope's Literary Correspondence. Volume the Second. . . .* Printed for
E. Curll, 1735, p. x.   [2] Elwin-Courthope, vi. 280.

the Jacobite tendencies of some pieces included in the two volumes. This phase of the matter led him for a time, even before August 1722, when Atterbury was sent to the Tower on a charge of treasonable complicity in a Jacobite plot, to wish to dissociate himself from the publication of Buckingham's *Works*. On 3 September [1721] he wrote Tonson from Oxford, saying in part:

As to the Duke of Bucks' works: I have resolved upon further thoughts, to give up the business of the impression entirely out of my hands, and have no concern in the profits at all. The Bishop and her Grace, I find, inclined to employ Mr Barber in the whole matter, so that I shall have nothing to do but with the trouble, in which I'll have no view but to oblige her Grace. In this I'm sure I can't be in the wrong, nor accountable, or liable to any misconstruction, or thought of any interest in it. I know this will seem romantic to a bookseller, even to You that are least a bookseller. But you must allow a little madness to poets.[1]

Bishop Atterbury and her Grace evidently led Pope to change his mind, and he added the drudgery of 'correcting the press' to the 'trouble' of editing the papers. Long before publication a royal licence to print had been granted in April 1722 to Alderman Barber, a Tory printer and a friend of Pope's, and finally the two elaborate quarto volumes were published on Thursday, 24 January 1723, about a fortnight after the 'consort and ball' already mentioned. Then fell the thunderbolt! On Sunday the 27th they were 'seiz'd by some of his Majesty's Messengers, as it is said, because in some Part of these Volumes great Reflections are cast upon the late happy Revolution'.[2] Pope, as editor, might be held responsible for any seditious or Jacobitical passages, and he was much worried, partly for his personal safety (after all, Atterbury was one of his most intimate friends!) and more for possible injury to his major projects of the moment, the edition of Shakespeare and, above all, the translation of the *Odyssey*. The *Works* of Buckingham had seemed innocent enough; but of course

[1] See Appendix I, p. 307.
[2] The *British Journal*, 2 February 1723, p. 5.

(so Pope would remember) Tickell and other Buttonians were subordinates in the office of the Secretary of State, which caused the suppression. Proposals for the *Odyssey* subscription were ready for circulation, but Pope wrote to Harley announcing their postponement:

I find such a cry upon me, however unreasonable, about the duke's books, and from persons, from whose education and quality one might expect a more sensible proceeding, that I am advised by Lord Harcourt, to defer pushing this Subscription till a more seasonable time. . . . If our governors are displeased at me, I am not fond of being the slave of the public against its will, for three years more. Let the Odyssey remain untranslated, or let them employ Mr. Tickell upon it.[1]

The cry upon Pope is traceable in the newspapers, especially in *Pasquin* (possibly by George Duckett), which printed in No. xii (13 February 1723) and No. xiii (20 February) ironical letters purporting to be addressed by Pope to the deceased duke. The first of these epistles, signed 'A. P.' and addressed 'To his Grace the late D. of B—, London, Feb. 8, 1722' [i.e. 1723], stresses the scandal of the duke's epitaph, and contrasts ironically Buckingham and Marlborough. Pope is made to 'declare . . . upon the Word of a *Poet* and a *Christian* (like yourself)' that he has never celebrated Marlborough nor helped Gay to do so. The second letter makes Pope confess that he secured a patent for printing the *Works* by the subterfuge of showing only inoffensive writings, but that once the patent was secure, he inserted other things against the public interest such as the 'Account of the Revolution' and 'The Feast of the Gods'. The tone in which Pope's enemies represent him as writing to the duke is significant:

You can't imagine, my Lord, how I have been censured for this artifice, by some *Tories* as well as *Whigs*, who call it a vile *Prevarication*; but your *Grace* knows that I am obliged *to keep no Faith with Hereticks*; in which Article of my Religion (as much as I have ridiculed most others) I have constantly been very punctual: Could the strongest human Obligations have prevailed upon me to

<hr>

[1] Elwin-Courthope, viii. 191–2.

dispense with it. I ought certainly to have done it towards Mr. *ADDISON*, Sir *RICHARD STEELE*, and the whole Fraternity at *Button's*.

The accusation of such trickery, whether true or false (and as usual we have only the accusation, no evidence), touched Pope keenly. Evidently *Pasquin* was not the first to accuse; for before this issue of 20 February appeared, Pope wrote to Lord Carteret as follows:

I am told (and in print too by some of the Party Scriblers) that I've been suspected of putting that vile thing a Trick upon you, in being the procurer of your Licence to the Duke of Buckingham-shire's Book. When I had the honor of waiting on your Lordship, I did not dream there was any need of speaking on this Article. But I now think myself obliged to assure you, that I never look'd into those papers or was privy to the contents of them, when that Licence was procured by Mr. Barber, to secure his own property.[1]

These statements have been stigmatized also as a 'vile prevarication'. It must be noted, however, that Barber and not Pope secured the licence, which was evidently applied for in April 1722 partly to prevent further piracies by such as Curll. All Pope says is that when the licence was procured, he had not examined the duke's papers; and this might possibly be true. The sentence is indeed equivocal but not surely mendacious. It must be remembered that the offensive pieces in the duke's works were not very obviously offensive. It is even possible that the assistants of Lord Carteret did not read all the copy submitted or did not read with sufficiently suspicious care.

The later history of Buckingham's *Works* is obscure. Six weeks after the seizure of the offending sheets of the volumes, the *London Journal* (9 March 1723) with typically cautious indirectness prints the following news item:

One of the foreign Prints, in the Article from London, says, 'That Mr. P—— the Editor of the Works of the late D—— of B—— is making all possible Interest that the publick Prohibition may be

---

[1] Elwin-Courthope, x. 139. The occasion when Pope 'had the honor of waiting on your Lordship' does not refer to the procuring of the licence, but to a more recent interview, in which, as the rest of the letter shows, Carteret had urged the continuance of the work on the *Odyssey*.

taken off from the same, and offers to expunge all those Passages which have given Offence. 'Tis further said his Grace has treated with great License the major Part of the sovereign Princes of Europe, whom he has distinguished by different Names from the fabulous Divinities, whose real Names are express'd in his Marginal Notes; which has given great Umbrage to the foreign Ministers. 'Tis added, that neither his Grace, nor the Editor of his Works, have explain'd how his Conduct can be reconciled with the Principles of Honour and Conscience in regard to the late K. William, Q. Mary, and Q. Anne, of whom he receiv'd Pensions, and acknowledged to be his lawful Sovereigns; when at the same time, if Judgment may be made from his Writings, he regarded them in another Light.'

We may judge from Pope's letter to Carteret that he was 'making all possible Interest to have the publick Prohibition removed,' and the fact that copies of the quarto *Works* of 1723 are fairly common with the excised leaves reprinted on a different paper, with a different water-mark, seems to indicate that the prohibition was removed even from the pieces that had been declared offensive. No other edition in 1723 is known; and since not later than the spring of 1724 Tonson rendered Pope an accounting for the *Works*, in which he announced profits[1] of £197 9s., it is evident that the edition was on sale before that time. The *Works* were advertised in the *Evening Post*, 29 February 1724, under the caption 'This Day is Republish'd', and the advertisement probably followed reasonably soon after the prohibition was removed.[2] Apparently in the later part of 1724, when the proof-sheets of Shakespeare were in hand, Pope was eager that Tonson should make every effort to sell

[1] Elwin-Courthope, ix. 546. The editor's date of 1722 for this letter is impossible. The original letter is on the verso of fol. 92 of the manuscript of Pope's *Odyssey* (Add. MS. 4809), which is a part of Book X. Pope was doing Book IX in July 1723 (Elwin-Courthope, viii. 66), and he probably finished Book XIII about the end of April 1724 (ibid. viii. 77, and cf. the date of the letter on fol. 116 of the *Odyssey* MS.). Tonson would seem to have rendered this accounting, then, possibly in the autumn of 1723.

[2] Wilford's *Monthly Catalogue* for February 1724 lists the *Works* among 'New Books', as two volumes, quarto, 'Price Two Guineas in Sheets to Subscribers.' In the *Evening Post*, 7 July 1724, Curll advertises an edition in one volume, octavo.

copies of the duke's *Works*. 'I need not repeat,' he writes in an undated letter, 'how much I depend on your assistance in this point.'[1]

So far as Pope himself is concerned his anxiety over the suppression of these *Works* was increased by the fact that the second *Pasquin* letter about him (20 February 1723) implied a connexion between him and a Jacobite plot recently discovered. Hoping to take advantage of popular dissatisfaction resultant from the South Sea Bubble, Bishop Atterbury and others had been in active correspondence with the Pretender and were plotting a revolution in his favour. Pope had friends in all parties, but a great many of his friends were sympathetic towards 'James III'. Atterbury had been arrested on the capital charge of high treason in August 1722 and taken to the Tower. Evidence against him was less convincing than against his accomplice Layer, and so the bishop came to trial only after a considerable delay in May 1723. In the trial before the House of Lords Pope was called as a sort of character witness, to testify that during the years under question he had seen Atterbury constantly, and had never heard him talk of politics or treason. Pope worried considerably beforehand, expecting questions about his adherence to the Church of Rome.[2] His evidence obviously was somewhat discredited in advance by the disaffection implied in his edition of Buckingham's *Works*. That the experience of testifying was unpleasant one gathers from the account given by Pope years later to Spence:

When I was to appear for the Bishop of Rochester, in his trial,

---

[1] See Appendix I, p. 311.

[2] Elwin-Courthope, x. 199 (letter to Harcourt, 5 May 1723). In part he writes: 'I resolve to take any opportunity of declaring (even upon oath) how different I am from what a reputed Papist is. I could almost wish I were ask'd if I am not a Papist? Would it be proper in such a case to reply, that I don't perfectly know the import of the word, and would not answer anything that might, for ought I know, be prejudicial to me, during the bill against such, which is depending. But that *if to be a Papist be to profess and hold many such tenets of faith as are ascribed to Papists, I am not a Papist; and if to be a Papist be to hold any that are averse to or destructive of the present Government, King, or Constitution, I am no Papist.'*

though I had but ten words to say, and that on a plain point, (how that bishop spent his time whilst I was with him at Bromley) I made two or three blunders in it: and that notwithstanding the first row of lords, (which was all I could see) were mostly of my acquaintance.[1]

A sort of 'official' summary of Pope's evidence was given in William Wynne's printed *Defense of Francis, late Lord Bishop of Rochester* (London, Jonah Bowyer, 1723):

We have likewise shewn your Lordships by Mr. *Pope*, who has been for these Two or Three last Years, the most constant Companion of his Lordship's Hours; Two or Three Days, he says, almost in every Week, and an hour or two almost in every of those Days: That his Lordship generally sat in one Room, which I think was his Bed-Chamber; that he was admitted to him at all Hours, and into all Companies, and never found the Discourse change at his coming in. That his Lordship never in the least discover'd any Thoughts or Intentions like those now charged upon him; but had heard occasionally many Things drop from the Bishop of a Tendency directly contrary: and to this we might have called many others, if it were necessary.[2]

The publication of the *Stuart Papers* (Roxburghe Club, 1889) has established what the prosecution could not prove in 1723, the complete guilt of Atterbury. In view of this guilt and of Pope's possible Jacobite sympathies, one wonders whether his testimony was perjured or whether Atterbury had used him as a literary 'blind' during the hatching of the plot. The newspapers assumed Pope's perjury. *Pasquin* No. xxxvi (20 May 1723) continues its jeers by making Atterbury say:

As a farther Proof of my Innocence, I have produced the worthy Mr. *P—pe*, a professed *Roman Catholick*, who has deposed that he used frequently to visit me, and that I never mentioned this *Scheme* to him; but constantly entertained him with agreeable Panegyricks upon the *Protestant Religion*, and the *Church of England* as by Law established.

Pasquin was always violently anti-Catholic, and is here indulging in sarcasm. The trial of Atterbury lasted from

[1] Spence, p. 156. [2] p. 41.

the 6th to the 11th of May; the evidence failed to warrant execution, but he was deprived of all his ecclesiastical honours, and banished for life. Layer, however, was executed a week after the Atterbury trial closed; hence one may assume that a belief in Atterbury's complete guilt was fairly common. After dramatic farewells in the Tower to Pope and others, Atterbury sailed away to France in June. It was unlawful to correspond with him in his exile, but Pope did so at infrequent intervals.

All of these entanglements with Jacobitism and the consequent unfavourable publicity in the journals of the day made the first part of 1723 the least settled of any time in Pope's life since 1717. The situation illustrates the feverishness of the poet's existence. His mother was ill; he had Buckingham's suppressed *Works* to look after; he had Atterbury to defend; he had Shakespeare to edit, and he had two coadjutors to stimulate to industry and secrecy in the translation of the *Odyssey*. Work enough, certainly, for any invalid!

The fact that he worried over the effects of these entanglements on the *Odyssey* rather than on his edition of Shakespeare is significant. The subscription to the *Odyssey*, proposals for which were being deferred on account of the outcry over Pope's Jacobitism, was for the benefit of Pope and his 'two friends', Fenton and Broome. The subscription to Shakespeare was for the benefit of Tonson, the publisher. Pope and his assistants in this edition were paid stated sums for their labours, and had nothing, so far as is known, to do with the subscription. Money, it may be noted, was desired by Pope since in 1723 further special taxes were levied upon Roman Catholics, and there is probably nothing like heavy taxation to make persons of comfortable incomes feel poor.

The editing of Shakespeare was begun before the arrest of Atterbury and before the commencement of work on the *Odyssey*. The project of translation, to be sure, is mentioned by Pope in a letter[1] that might seem at first

---

[1] Printed in the *Athenaeum*, 17 May 1884, p. 631.

sight to date as early as 1719. Its probable date, however, is 12 February [1723]. It acknowledges to a subordinate, somehow attached to the Foreign Office, the kindness of Sir Luke Schaub, the English ambassador at Paris, in sending Pope a copy of Mme. Dacier's hostile remarks on Pope's Preface to the *Iliad*. These had been published in 1719, but Curll did not publish them in England until 1724; and hence one may assume that they were not known in London as early as one might have expected. Pope's letter also alludes, apparently, to his troubles with Carteret's Office (through which Schaub's present had passed) over Buckingham's *Works* in 1723. Pope regrets Mme Dacier's sarcasms on his political possibilities 'at this time, when I am told people blame me for having seen a Book. And such a Book (God knows) as I had no more thoughts of Correcting than of Homer himself.' He continues, after this probable allusion to Buckingham's *Works*:

I believe you have heard I had thoughts of translating ye Odyssey. I won't tell you whether tis my mortification at Madam Dacier's, or at any other's displeasure that has made me put a sudden stop to my Friends' eagerness in ye affair. But I desire you to tell Mr. Tickel, I was three times to wait on him to ask if he had no view of that design himself, before I could actually ingage in it. And I yet will certainly desist from it, if he will Faithfully promise for himself, or if his Superiors will but ingage for him that he will do Homer this justice? I wish you could exhort him hereto, for ye honour & safety of ye Protestant Religion & Establishment, which otherwise (according to M. Dacier) a Papist may do much damage to.

Since Schaub was ambassador from March 1721 to May 1724, this letter must belong to 1722 or 1723 (for 1724 is too late), and in tone and substance it seems to fit in with letters to Harcourt and Carteret written in February 1723. One may doubt if Pope himself had translated any of the *Odyssey* by this time, though his collaborators were at work in 1722. The letters upon the backs of which Pope translated his early Books of the Poem are in general dated after February 1723.

Upon Shakespeare he had worked before this time.[1] One assumes, of course, that nothing had been done on this task until after the last of the *Iliad* had been published in 1720. On 5 May of that year Pope wrote to Fenton, an assistant later both on Shakespeare and in the *Odyssey*, as follows:

I am a little scandalised at your complaint that your time lies heavy on your hands, when the muses have put so many good materials into your head to employ them. As to your question, what I am doing, I answer, just what I have been doing some years—my duty; secondly, relieving myself with necessary amusements, or exercises, which shall serve me instead of physic as long as they can; thirdly, reading till I am tired; and lastly, writing when I have no other thing in the world to do, or no friend to entertain in company.[2]

Pope was frequently uncommunicative about works in process, but this paragraph at least must indicate that Fenton was not yet a partner in any project. One suspects that Atterbury's letter to Pope of 2 August,[3] in which he is so eloquent as to the need of a commentary on the text of Shakespeare, is a response to some announcement of Pope's decision to undertake an edition. In October 1721 Atterbury promises to bring to Twickenham Pope's Folio of Shakespeare.[4] He comments:

Shakespear shall bear it [Pope's Pastorals] company, and be put into your hands as clear and as fair as it came out of them, though you, I think, have been dabbling here and there with the text.

---

[1] In the *Dunciad* printed for Gilliver and Clarke as vol. iv of Pope's *Works* (8vo), 1736, Pope writes in a note to Book III, line 328 (line 332 in Elwin-Courthope) as follows: 'He began the Iliad in 1713 and finish'd it in 1719. The *Edition of Shakespear*, (which he undertook merely because he thought nobody else would) took up near two years more, in the drugery of comparing Impressions, rectifying the Scenary, &c. and the translation of half the Odyssey employ'd him from that time to 1725.'   [2] Elwin-Courthope, viii. 46.   [3] Ibid. ix. 26.

[4] What has been thought to be Pope's copy of the third Folio is now in the Folger Shakespeare Library. It was described in *Notes and Queries*, 5 S. iii (6 February 1875). The marginalia in this Folio are certainly not in Pope's hand, but it is barely possible that they are in the hand of some unidentified assistant. More probably, however, since they are written smoothly, without such signs of hesitation as might mark the process of composition, they were copied from Pope's printed edition, and were not preliminary to it. Dr. Joseph Q. Adams of the Folger Library and Mr. R. Flower of the British Museum have helped investigate this matter.

I have had more reverence for the writer and the printer, and left every thing standing just as I found it. However, I thank you for the pleasure you have given me in putting me upon reading him once more before I die.[1]

This suggests that Pope's work on Shakespeare either had already advanced with systematic effort or had sprung from desultory reforming of the text in his casual reading. At any rate the 'dabblings' noted by Atterbury, if not so designed, were destined to be used in an edition of Shakespeare. That the project was under way before the edition of Buckingham's *Works* was proof-read is clear from an undated letter to Caryll, which must fall late in 1721, though dated 1722 by the editors.[2] The public was informed of the work in the autumn of 1721 when Pope advertised in the *Evening Post* (21 October 1721) for help and when the doubtfully friendly *Weekly Journal, or Saturday's Post* (18 November) announced: 'The celebrated Mr. Pope is preparing a correct Edition of Shakespear's Works; that of the late Mr. Rowe being very faulty.'[3]

As in the case of the *Iliad* Pope sought the aid of friends. One doubts if he got much from Atterbury, who though keenly interested in early English literature, was now occupied with his 'Scheme' (so the plot was called) to bring in the Pretender. By February 1722 Pope had got in touch with the Jonathan Richardsons (father and son) and was asking

that you will tell your friend Mr. Chiselden I shall be obliged to him if he will put upon a paper those conjectures of some passages of Shakespeare which he mentioned to Dr. Arbuthnot, or any others that may have occurred to him. The edition of that author being reprinted, and from all hands (especially from a man of his good will and abilities) information or elucidation being welcome to me. Pray send me these as soon as you can. . . .[4]

This letter very likely marks the beginning of the friendship with Chiselden, the famous surgeon, who at times attended

---

[1] Elwin-Courthope, ix. 31–2.   [2] Ibid. vi. 280.
[3] T. R. Lounsbury, *The Text of Shakespeare* (1908), p. 81.
[4] Elwin-Courthope, ix. 492.

Pope professionally, and who figures in various anecdotes of Pope's last hours. To Chiselden, in the Huntington Library MS. of the *Anecdotes*, Spence ascribes the Shake-spearian echo to the effect that (in his last hours) Pope's mind was 'like a fine ring of bells, jangled out of tune'.[1] By about the beginning of 1722 Fenton, Broome, and Pope had agreed to translate the *Odyssey*, and Pope felt free to write to both of them about Shakespeare as well. Fenton was to render especial assistance in the editing, and Broome was to do more than Fenton on the *Odyssey*.[2]

The question how much Pope knew about Shakespeare and how hard he worked on the edition cannot be answered satisfactorily. Evidently he had both paid and unpaid assistants. He himself received £217 12s. From notes abstracted, one judges, from Tonson's account books it seems evident that for helping Pope Fenton received £30 14s., and Gay received £35 17s. 6d.[3] From a letter to Tonson (3 September [1721]) we learn that Fenton received £25 in addition to this payment entered in Tonson's account books, and it becomes apparent that £35 were paid, as Pope requested, to 'a man or two here at Oxford to ease me of part of the drudgery of Shakespeare'.[4] Pope would be paid for the prestige of his name as well as for work done: Fenton, Gay, and the men at Oxford very likely did much of the work. Since Tonson paid each of these helpers something like the total sum paid Rowe (£36 10s.) for editorial work, one can only infer that they eased Pope of a considerable amount of drudgery.

From one of the Tonson letters, again—a letter written probably in 1724 and certainly written in a manner difficult to interpret—it is possible to surmise that Tonson tried to persuade Pope not to advertise that he had no benefit from the Shakespeare subscription. One may also *suspect* from Pope's excessive protestations of wounded honour that

---

[1] Spence, p. 320. Huntington Library MS., *HM 1271*, p. 518.

[2] Elwin-Courthope, viii. 48–9, 57, &c.

[3] *Gent. Mag.* lvii (1787), 76; also in Nichols's *Literary Anecdotes*, v. 597. Theobald (1735) got £652 10s.

[4] See Appendix I, p. 307.

A Bill for Mr: Pope

June th. 8

for 5 cg: my Mr:phers serman to my Lord Bollor Corong	0 — 2
ṣ and B: Unifornite serman each a Guino	
10 for B: a Letter for my Mr:phor	0 — 2
11 for carr: a Letter to my Lords to my Mr:phor	0 — 2
for B: th3 Copey and Jas	
2 for sending a Letter to Luson Street going Staver	0 — 2
ṣ one to my Lord Bollos Corons and B: a purse back	0 — 6
4 for carr: my Mr:phor and the sanbeg to Bollinton	
ṣ and to Jffddsworth and each a Guin	
8 for carr: my Mr:phor to London	54 — 0
for carr: a Parfoll to Mr: Ganford	4 — 0
for going to Mr: Congroves	0 — 2
for carr: a Letter to Mr: Starlings Jn Hg:burn	0 — 2
for going to the Taylor Jn Mr:lmouth Street	0 — 2
15 for carr: a Proofs of Clarke:	0 — 2
19 for going to the Taylor a Guin	0 — 2
10	0 — 2

A BILL FROM POPE'S WATERMAN, 8 JUNE [1724]

(Add. MS. 4809, f. 127v)

possibly after all he did receive such benefits and that
Tonson had been reproaching him for his advertised denial
of the fact.[1] In general these letters show Pope and Tonson
on pleasantly amicable terms.

Work on Shakespeare was actively under way by the
autumn of 1721. In 1722 and 1723 it engrossed such of
Pope's time as was not taken up by Buckingham's *Works*
or by the *Odyssey*. From the letter of 3 September [1721]
to Tonson it is apparent that the task of establishing the
division of scenes was by that date already undertaken, and
not by Pope himself. It is evident that Pope worked to
improve Shakespeare's diction and metre, but in so far as
such improvements depended on collation of early copies
of the plays, the method was amusingly informal and un-
scientific. In the spring of 1722 Pope writes Tonson:

... my affairs have hurried me to and from London, interchangeably every day; the last part of the planting season taking me up
here, and business which I think less agreeable, there. I'm resolved
to pass the next whole week in London, purposely to get together
parties of my acquaintance every night, to collate the several editions of Shakespeare's single plays—five of which [whom?] I have
engaged to this design.[2]

Apart from Atterbury's remarks as to Pope's marginal notes
in his Folio, this passage is about the most definite indication we have of Pope's methods of working on the text of
the plays. From the letters to Tonson of 1723–4, we learn
that Pope had hoped to get the edition into five volumes
but that six were finally preferred, and we further learn
that the sheets of the fifth volume were to be read by
Fenton and those of the sixth by Pope. Further distribu-
tion of the labour can be only sketchily traced. On
12 August [1722] Pope wrote to Broome:

Be pleased also to inform Mr. Fenton, that he may refer all the
historical plays of Shakespeare to volume three, into which division
we have contrived to bring them.[3]

'We' very likely refers to Pope and Gay. From Fenton we

---

[1] See Appendix I, pp. 311–12.   [2] See Appendix I, p. 308.
[3] Elwin-Courthope, viii. 57.

learn that making the Index was part of his task,[1] and that he completed it before 19 June 1724. By 31 October of the same year Pope could write: 'Shakespeare is finished. I have just written the preface, and in less than three weeks it will be public.'[2] The work was not published, however, until 12 March 1725.

In view of Pope's receptiveness with regard to readings suggested by Chiselden and others, it is quite possible that Pope's contribution consisted of dabblings in the text accumulated over a period of years, and now supplemented by changes advised by various friends. Pope's conception of the proper duties of the textual editor is set forth in his Preface, and the conception is, on the whole, surprisingly just. In the Preface he gives an account of the history and state of the text, which, if superficial, is at least a pioneer statement of the case. He tells what he has done to improve the text, and if the performance had actually followed the profession, the results would have been admirable:

In what I have done I have rather given a proof of my willingness and desire, rather than of my ability, to do him [Shakespeare] justice. I have discharged the dull duty of an Editor, to my best judgment, with more labour than I expect thanks, with a religious abhorrence of all innovation, and without any indulgence to my private sense or conjecture. The method taken in this edition will show itself. The various readings are fairly put in the margin, so that every one may compare them: and those I have preferred into the text are constantly *ex fide codicum*, upon authority. The alterations or additions which Shakespear himself made, are taken notice of as they occur. Some suspected passages which are excessively bad (and which seem interpolations by being so inserted that one can entirely omit them without any chasm, or deficiency in the context) are degraded to the bottom of the page; with an asterisk referring to the places of their insertion. The scenes are marked so distinctly that every removal of place is specify'd; which is more necessary in this author than any other, since he shifts them more frequently: and sometimes without attending to this particular, the reader would have met with obscurities. The more obsolete or unusual words are explained. Some of the most shining passages

---

[1] Elwin-Courthope, viii. 82.   [2] Ibid. viii. 88.

are distinguished by commas in the margin: and where the beauty lay not in particulars but in the whole, a star is prefixed to the scene. This seems to me a shorter and less ostentatious method of performing the better half of criticism (namely the pointing out an author's excellencies), than to fill a whole paper with citations of fine passages, with *general applauses*, or *empty exclamations* at the tail of them. There is also subjoined a catalogue of those first editions by which the greater part of the various readings and of the corrected passages are authorised. . . .

Performance of these professions, however, was very defective. So far was Pope from abhorrence of innovation that he emended and excised capriciously; his explanations of obsolete and obscure words are at times purely imaginative. Even Pope's severest critics, however, have granted him credit for various textual improvements, chiefly metrical, which are likely to be permanently accepted as readings. Granting the best of intentions, one sees that Pope while understanding to some extent the nature of his duties was too inexperienced and too ignorant to fulfil those duties. Fenton was by temperament and training slightly more competent, but probably (since Pope was to have any credit that might arise) was less responsible than Pope. From any modern point of view the technique and results of the editing cannot be taken seriously, and apparently in Pope's lifetime only his friends had a high opinion of his work.

Pope's performance is excusable only on the grounds of incompetence. He seems to have been supplied astonishingly well with early editions, though he erred in his evaluation of them. On 10 February [1722] he wrote to Broome:

The play you mention will be of no use, nor any other whose date is not earlier than 1616. The oldest edition in folio is of 1621, which I have, and it is from that almost all the errors of succeeding editions take rise.[1]

His error in the date of the first folio may of course be a slip merely; the fact that Pope had a copy to use (which

---

[1] Elwin-Courthope, viii. 48–9.

Theobald had not) is notable, though his lack of respect for its text indicates how far removed he was from anything like modern method. If one can trust the list at the end of volume vi of the edition, Pope and his helpers consulted also a second folio, and twenty-seven quartos printed before 1620. They saw quartos of all the plays published before the first folio, except *Much Ado* and *Pericles*, and of the *Taming of a Shrew* (1607). Of seven plays they had more than one quarto.

In the pioneer days in which Pope worked, information concerning early editions was hard to obtain. It is only fair to assume that certain advertisements in the newspapers express a sincere desire for information as well as a desire to keep the project before the public. The first announcement of the work in the press was such an advertisement by Pope inserted in the *Evening Post*, 21 October 1721:

Whereas a new Edition of SHAKESPEAR has been for some Time preparing for the Press; any Person therefore who is possessed of any old Editions of single Plays of His, and will communicate the same to J. Tonson in the Strand, such Assistance will be received as a particular Obligation, or otherwise acknowledged in any Manner they shall think proper.

About six months later Pope inserted a new and more specific request for aid in the *Evening Post*, 5 May 1722:

The new Edition of Shakespear being now in the Press; this is to give Notice that if any Person has any Editions of the Tempest, Mackbeth, Julius Caesar, Timon of Athens, King John, and Henry the 8th; printed before the Year 1620, and will communicate the same to J. Tonson in the Strand, he shall receive any Satisfaction required.

The advertisement suggests that fairly early in the work Pope and his assistants had access to most of the quartos in their printed lists. Not having found any for the plays mentioned (no such quartos are known to have been printed), they advertised.

What results came from these requests no one knows. The man who in the years preceding Pope's edition had written most about Shakespeare,[1] and who was doubtless best read in Elizabethan literature, was Lewis Theobald. Pope had some acquaintance with this attorney, poet, and scholar, who had commended the translation of the *Iliad* in the *Censor* (5 January 1717), and who had been allowed to print Pope's *Vertumnus and Pomona* in his Ovid's *Metamorphoses* (1716/17). Yet after the suppression of the Theobald life of Buckingham, Pope could hardly have hoped for an alliance with Theobald on Shakespeare. Upon the publication of Pope's edition Theobald found it so bad that he was led to expose its deficiencies in his *Shakespeare Restored* (1726), which in turn stimulated (but did not originate) the *Dunciad*. In a note to the *Dunciad Variorum*, Book I, line 106, we read:

During the space of two years, while Mr. *Pope* was preparing his Edition of *Shakespear*, and published Advertisements, requesting all lovers of the Author to contribute to a more perfect one; this Restorer (who had then some correspondence with him, and was solliciting favours by Letters) did wholly conceal his design, 'till after its publication. Probably that proceeding elevated him to the Dignity he holds in this Poem. . . .[2]

Pope had, of course, no right to expect Theobald to share with him the results of years of reading, or to charge him with 'concealing his design'; but naturally he could not help hoping Theobald might aid him, or feeling disappointment and anger at the devastating use to which Theobald turned his reading in 1726. In fact, what Pope asked for in his advertisement was early editions, and in those Theobald was probably not rich. His strength lay in his reading of Elizabethan literature, and Pope seemed unaware of the necessity of a wide knowledge of Shakespeare's period.

With an elaborate advertising campaign, the edition was published 12 March 1725. It was received by the 'belly-critics' in the newspapers none too favourably; for Pope had few friends among the journalists, and Tonson, being

---

[1] He had hardly 'crucified poor Shakespear once a week', as Pope asserted in the *Dunciad* (Book I, l. 154 in 1728; l. 164 in 1729), but either in the *Censor* or in (Mist's) *Weekly Journal* he had written frequently of the great dramatist.
[2] p. 11 (quarto ed.).

a bookseller, was probably no more dear to Grub Street than was Pope. Since the subscription was for the benefit of Tonson, it was not expected that Pope and his friends would solicit subscribers, and consequently the list is somewhat less distinguished than that prefixed to the *Iliad* or to the *Odyssey*. Subscriptions for the benefit of publishers carried no high aristocratic tone. In the *Daily Post*, 18 November 1724, Tonson advertised:

> Mr. Pope's Edition of Shakespear in Six Vols. in Quarto, is now very near finish'd, and there being but a small Number Printed, such Persons who are willing to subscribe for the same, are desir'd to send their Names and first Payments to Jacob Tonson in the Strand, before the 16th Day of December next, at which Time the List of Subscribers will be printed off, and the Books (if any left) will then be raised One Guinea above the Subscription Price.[1]

Evidently Tonson found it both possible and advantageous to postpone closing the subscription, and we find him welcoming late-comers more formally in the *Daily Courant*, 18 January 1725:

> Proposals by JACOB TONSON for Mr. POPE'S
> Edition of SHAKESPEAR.

> I. This Work will consist of Six Volumes, printed upon Royal Paper in Quarto, each Volume containing not less than 70 Sheets.
> II. The Six Volumes are proposed until the 10th Day of February next, (at which Time the Subscription will be closed) at Five Guineas in Quiers, Two Guineas to be paid in Hand, and the other Three on Delivery of the Book.
> III. This Work will be delivered to the Subscribers before the End of February next at farthest, it being all printed off except the Preface, the Life of the Author, and the Index, which are now in the Press.
> N. B. If any Names are omitted in the List of the present Subscribers now printed and made publick, they shall be inserted upon the first Notice to J. Tonson in the Strand.[2]

Ultimately 411 subscribers took 417 copies of the six volumes.[3] According to Dr. Johnson 750 sets were printed,

---

[1] Reprinted ibid., 9 December.   [2] Ibid., 12 February, also.
[3] Griffith, p. 120.

and of these 140 remained unsold in 1767 when they brought only 16*s*. each instead of five guineas.[1] These statements (if authentic) hardly indicate the low regard for Pope's editing that Johnson asserts; they rather indicate a preference for the octavo and duodecimo editions which followed the quarto during the years 1728–35.

Adverse criticism of the edition at first concerned the cost of it. The criticism, naturally, was aimed at Tonson and not at Pope, though the same criticism was presently to be made of Pope's *Odyssey* when its first volumes appeared six weeks after the Shakespeare. The feeling behind this criticism of Tonson lies in part in a dissatisfaction with his claim of a perpetual copyright in Shakespeare. Other booksellers and editors would have been glad to do a better and cheaper job. In March a society was formed to combat 'the encroachments of booksellers and players'[2] upon the rights of authors. The mouthpiece of this movement was the *Weekly Journal, or Saturday's Post*, a Jacobite and Tory organ published by Nathaniel Mist and written by whatever Grub Street hack could do it and evade the arrest that frequently came to Mist's authors. Who succeeded Daniel Defoe on this journal after his quarrel with Mist in November 1724 is unknown. Pope later tried to accuse Theobald of 'cackling to the Tories'[3] by writing for Mist, and the charge annoyed Theobald extremely; for he did not wish to be associated with either Jacobites or Tories. Pope offered no evidence: there was usually small evidence when it came to convicting a man of writing for Mist; but two articles about the edition of Shakespeare that were published in the issues of 20 and 27 March sound as if they were written by a man who would gladly edit Shakespeare if the copyright of Tonson did not forbid such editing. The first of these articles is a leader addressed ostensibly as a letter to Mr. Mist himself; the second is a leader, ostensibly by

---

[1] *Lives of the Poets* (ed. Hill), iii. 138. Cf. *Gent. Mag.* lvii (1787), 76.

[2] The inclusion of players is probably an echo of the recent outcries against the managers of Drury Lane, especially Cibber.

[3] *Dunciad* (quarto, 1729), Book I, l. 192.

Mr. Mist himself, but avowedly by the same author as the
leader of 20 March. Both are doubtless by the same staff
writer. The tone and substance may be gained from the
following:

> Indeed, some Persons may object, that if another Bookseller had
> been the Publisher of this *Shakespear*, he might have sold it, ready
> bound, that is, with a plain binding, for about forty Shillings, have
> been able to pay Copy-Money out of that, and yet have gain'd
> a good Bookseller's Profit by it.—But let your slovenly Scholars
> and poor Rogues, who buy Books only to read, complain and make
> this Remark. The People of the *Beau Monde* look upon Books no
> otherwise than as the neat Furniture of a Closet, and are of
> Opinion, they are not to be esteem'd according to their intrinsick
> Worth, but like Toys, bear a Value and a Price according to the
> Shop they come from. . . .
>
> I am very well inform'd, that the Benefits of this extravagant
> Subscription are not design'd for the ingenious Gentleman who
> revises the Work; nay, he has himself publickly declar'd it, and,
> indeed, he has Merit of his own to support him; and, I believe,
> would scorn to take in Subscriptions for the Labours of another.[1]
>
> ——As to the Bookseller, if he should be pleas'd to give us a more
> correct Edition of *Shakespear* than has yet been printed, we should
> be obliged to him, provided it was at a reasonable Price; and tho'
> he should pay handsomely for revising it, the Thing it self would
> reward him in the Sale. . . .

And the leader closes as follows:

> . . . we take this Opportunity of inviting you, to be a Member of
> a Club or Society of Authors, which is to meet once a Week, or
> oftner, as Occasion shall require, to consider of Ways and Means
> for keeping up and maintaining the Privileges of Authors, and de-
> fending our Rights and Properties against the Incroachments of
> Booksellers and Players.

[1] Pope's Proposals for his *Odyssey* were published in the *Daily Courant*,
25 January 1725, and had been privately circulated earlier. There is very likely
a slur here on his use of help from Broome and Fenton as well as an allusion to
the 'labours' of Shakespeare, from which Pope scorns to profit. *Printed* Proposals
had not been circulated long before the project was advertised in the journals
if we are to accept the date given them by Pope in the 'Testimonies of Authors',
in the quarto *Dunciad* of 1729 (p. 10), where he says they were 'printed by
J. Watts, Jan. 10, 1724'. The year is given in 'old style' of course, and is really
1724/5.

Possibly this society of embattled Grub Street is the 'Concanen Club', whose hostility to Pope was later denounced by Savage.[1] If so, it is evident that from the start Pope was an object, though not the chief object, of their animosity.

The second leader (27 March) starts, 'In my last I took some Notice' and goes on to defend subscription editions as a substitute for patronage such as French authors still enjoy. A subscription by a bookseller for his own benefit, however, is another thing; he is certainly unwarranted in taking in extravagant Subscriptions for old copies [i.e. copyrights?], as it manifestly breaks in upon the Rights of Authors; and by swelling the Prices of Books, affects the Interest of all those who buy Books to read.

Besides, I conceive there cannot be the least Pretence for advancing upon us in the Price of *Shakespeare*; for the Bookseller owes the Publick a good Edition of that Work, since the last publish'd by him, and which he sold dear enough, was, by much, the most incorrect and faulty that ever yet came out.

But if a silly Notion should prevail, that a Book receives any real Merit from the Hand which sells it, or the Person who has the Copy, I speak in vain.—If People will be *duped*, I can't help it.

The *Weekly Journal, or Saturday's Post* repeatedly expressed its pride in such views as these, and letters were addressed to Mr. Mist such as the following one in the issue of 19 June 1725:

You, who have . . . drawn your Pen with such uncommon Warmth and Impartiality upon a potent Bookseller, for his exorbitant Demands in the Publication of another Man's Works, must needs . . . countenance me in animadverting upon a Country Theological Author, who exposes to Sale his own Divine Compositions . . . at an unreasonable Rate. . . .

---

[1] See Savage's *Author to be Let* (1729), The Publisher's Preface; see also R. F. Jones, *Lewis Theobald* (New York, 1919), pp. 101, 135–6. The Club is frequently mentioned during the period April to June 1725 in (Read's) *Weekly Journal or British Gazetteer*. See especially the issue of 19 June, which expresses surprise at this new coalition of Grub Street writers, calling themselves Whigs, and Mist. This or another club became publicly known for hostility to Pope and Swift in 1728 according to a letter from Edward Young to Thomas Tickell, published in E. Tickell's *Thomas Tickell* (1931), pp. 145–6.

Aaron Hill's *Plain Dealer* No. 116 (3 May 1725) joined in the attack by complaining that the seventh volume (Shakepeare's non-dramatic works, edited by George Sewell) had to be purchased separately:

. . . I have been inform'd, That this Volume . . . has not by some of the Wits in *Leading-Strings*, been look'd upon with equal Favour; because this Edition of it was not midwif'd into the World, by *great Names* that have condescended, for the Emolument of the Publick, to shine in the Title Page of the First Six Volumes. . . .

In 1726 Concanen was on the staff of the *London Journal*, but that did not prevent continuing the alliance of his Whig group with the Tory Mist. Concanen contributed a letter of his own on Shakespeare to (Mist's) *Weekly Journal*, 7 May 1726, and one by Theobald he inserted with a eulogistic introduction in the *London Journal*, 3 September 1726.[1] Until after the *Dunciad* appeared these two journals were actively hostile to Pope.

With these last letters criticism of the edition enters a new phrase. One doubts if many members of the Concanen Club spent six guineas (the price for non-subscribers) for Pope's Shakespeare, but by 1726 the journalists were talking less of the cost than of the textual defects of the edition. It was an age when the brilliant example of Richard Bentley encouraged wholesale emendation of everything from Hesychius to Milton, and the ablest of Bentley's imitators was the attorney-poet Lewis Theobald, who doubtless guided the textual reforms made by Concanen and others of the group. In March 1726 Theobald brought out a quarto volume of approximately two hundred pages entitled:

SHAKESPEARE restored: or, a SPECIMEN of the Many ERRORS, as well *Committed*, as *Unamended*, by Mr. *POPE* In his Late EDITION of this Poet. DESIGNED Not only to correct the said Edition, but to restore the True READING of *SHAKESPEARE* in all the *Editions* ever yet publish'd. By Mr. THEOBALD.

[1] See Lounsbury, *The Text of Shakespeare*, pp. 178, 180–2, 249, 280, *et passim*, for mentions of these attacks.

Theobald has been called a modest, unassuming scholar, but this title-page and various passages in the volume would seem to indicate a certain amount of confidence—even assurance. Not that the volume is ever opprobrious in matter or manner. Theobald is genuinely more interested in amending Shakespeare than in correcting Pope. He is very complimentary to Pope the poet, but is devastating to the work of Pope the editor.

The volume begins with a Dedication to John Rich, the manager of the Lincoln's Inn Fields Theatre, who, as Theobald confesses in his first sentence, had gone a great way towards shutting Shakespeare out of the theatre in favour of pantomime. An introduction of eight pages follows, in which Pope's poetry is commended and an early satisfaction with Pope's proposal to edit Shakespeare is alleged. The lack of original manuscripts of the plays and the evil effects of copyright on editing are lamented. Theobald's position is that he is 'assuming a task here, which this learned *Editor* [Pope!] seems purposely (I was going to say, with too nice a Scruple) to have declined'. In other words, he finds Pope's 'religious Abhorrence of Innovation' is really 'downright Superstition'. As the title of the volume indicated, it is what is 'unamended' by Pope that in large part occupies Theobald, who regards the task of 'amending' as practically untouched. To show what a really able editor can do, he offers formally ninety-seven (there are really more of them) specimen emendations of Pope's text of *Hamlet*. Then in an appendix of sixty pages he emends passages in various other plays. The whole is offered, as both title-page and text indicate, as a specimen.

There can be no doubt of Theobald's superior knowledge and technique as compared with Pope's, but it may be urged that modern attempts to exalt Theobald's reputation have exaggerated somewhat the merits of *Shakespeare Restored*. About a third of its corrections are based on appeal to early texts—a 1632 folio, a 1637 quarto, and Hughes's edition of 1703. More than another third are conjectural emendations, and many are corrections in pointing and printing. These last probably annoyed Pope most; for many of them simply make the text slightly easier to read, but do not change the meaning in the least: they at times merely represent the eighteenth-century love of many commas. The corrections most commonly accepted by later editors are those based on 'various readings' of texts neglected by Pope. Of the first fifty emendations about twenty are conjectural in nature, and seventeen of these have *not* been accepted by recent editors. Some of these are almost as absurd as Pope's howlers; others would irritate a *bel esprit* by their excessive technique. No. xxviii, for example, wishes to emend Hamlet's questioning of the ghost (I. iv. 54–5) who makes:

> night hideous and WE fools of nature
> So HORRIDLY to shake our disposition. . . .

by inserting *us* for *we* and changing *horridly* to *horribly*. Theobald recognizes that there is no warrant in Shakespeare's usage for changing the pronoun, and yet he wishes the great poet to use 'good English'. *Horribly* is, he thinks, etymologically better than *horridly*; and, for no reason at all, he cites similar cases where Shakespeare uses *horrible*, and even drags in five passages where *terrible* occurs.[1] Later when he wishes the ghost to be 'confined to ROAST in fires' (I. v. 11) instead of 'to FAST in fires', though he can find no warrant for his preference in the early readings, he becomes dogmatic and announces: 'The Poet certainly, in my Opinion, intends to mix the old *Pagan* System here with the more modern Notion of a local Purgatory.'[2] More than once Theobald's changes are quite gratuitous. One may so consider No. 1. The passage (II. ii. 449–54) is quoted from Pope's edition as follows:

> . . . unequal MATCH'D,
> *Pyrrhus* at *Priam* drives, in rage strikes wide;
> But with the whif and wind of his fell Sword
> Th' unnerved father falls[.] THEN SENSELESS [ ] Ilium
> Seeming to feel this blow, with flaming top
> Stoops to his base, &c.

---

[1] pp. 39–44.   [2] p. 45.

Theobald would have it read:

>   ... Unequal Match!
> *Pyrrhus* at *Priam* drives; in Rage strikes wide;
> But with the Whif and Wind of his fell Sword
> Th' unnerved Father falls DOWN SENSELESS. . . . Ilium
> Seeming to feel this Blow, with flaming Top
> Stoops to his Base, &c.[1]

Some of Theobald's changes in this passage have been adopted by a few recent editors—whether upon more evidence than Theobald had, is doubtful; in general his changes here seem to be 'cracking the wind of a poor phrase'[2] and 'wronging' it as well. For the most part Theobald is saner than this, and these passages have been quoted as specimens that might explain Pope's reaction rather than illustrate Theobald's ability. In most of his emendations he uses his reading and his parallels as evidence for changes. At times he is exasperated with Pope's superficiality until he implies more than once what he blurts out on page 75:

There are many Passages of such intolerable Carelessness interspers'd thro' all six Volumes, that, were not a few of Mr. Pope's *Notes* scatter'd here and there too, I should be induced to believe that the Words in the Title Page of the *First* Volume, . . . COLLATED *and* CORRECTED *by the former* EDITIONS, *By Mr. POPE*, . . . were plac'd there by the *Bookseller* to enhaunce the *Credit* of his *Edition*; but that he had play'd false with his *Editor*, and never sent him the Sheets to revise. . . .

Throughout the book Theobald's attitude is that Tonson owed the world a better edition of Shakespeare than Pope's: he was doubtless right, but one may wonder if he was quite disinterested in urging the point. His suggestions and emendations in *Shakespeare Restored* were frequently adopted in the second edition of Pope's Shakespeare (1728), often the poor emendations as well as the good; but the review of Pope's work by Theobald struck a mortal blow at Pope's reputation as editor, and, as every one knows, Pope eventually took his revenge in the *Dunciad*.

---

[1] pp. 71–2.   [2] p. 25.

IX

THE ETHICS OF COLLABORATION

POPE'S irritation at *Shakespeare Restored*, natural in itself, was intensified by annoyances arising from his other large project of the moment, the translation of the *Odyssey*. The first half of the translation (volumes i–iii) was published six weeks after the edition of Shakespeare. Subscriptions to the Shakespeare (for Tonson) and to the *Odyssey* (for Pope) were advertised in the newspapers in January 1725, and the size and importance of the undertakings, together with the supposed large remuneration to Pope, caused much comment, some of it envious and some of it critical of his ability.

Pope's *Odyssey* raises classic problems in the morals of book-making, especially with regard to collaboration. From the point of view of the public the question arises, how explicitly must collaboration be announced? and from the point of view of one's collaborators the problem is, how much remuneration in fame or in money should be allowed to assistants? These problems can be easily resolved in a categorical doctrine of complete and explicit avowal of collaboration to the public and in very generous acknowledgements to one's helpers. But that is not the way of the world. Men of reputation are always accepting unacknowledged assistance from paid or unpaid subordinates; the world hears rumours of the methods used, and is seldom censorious of them. There seems to be more inclination to censure concealed collaboration in a work of art than in a work of utilitarian purpose. So collaboration in a poetic translation of Homer is more reprehensible than it is in an edition of Shakespeare. It was worse to let Fenton or Broome be the author of unacknowledged translation than of unacknowledged footnotes. Literary factories such as those of Smollett, Dumas, or Edgar Wallace have seldom aroused antagonism on the part of the public; but the greater the genius, apparently, the greater the outcry. The sin lies ultimately in concealment or in lack of acknowledgement. Since the days of Scriblerus and the work on the *Iliad* Pope had thoughtlessly used the labour of friends. Broome had been responsible, without much acknowledgement, for many of the notes to the *Iliad*. Dancastle and others had transcribed for Pope, and, in general, intimate friends had put their learning at his disposal. So Pope drifted into a use of assistance of many sorts. In the case of the *Odyssey* he doubtless justified his acceptance of secret aid by the fact that he revised all the work of his collaborators until he had made it so much his own that the joint authorship has never been aesthetically obtrusive.[1] Why, then, he might ask, should the public object? The objection is, from aesthetic standards, inconsiderable; but morally it is sound and fundamental. The real wrong in the case of the *Odyssey* seems to lie in the attempts of Pope to deceive the public. He has, however, been scolded rather more often for using his collaborators badly.

As a matter of fact, they had small grounds for complaint. They evidently undertook the collaboration in anticipation of fame rather than fortune; for the financial details of the partnership were unsettled—through diffidence of the collaborators, not at Pope's desire—until after the work was completed and published. The project started (however it may have ended) in a friendly and informal fashion. Exactly when it started we do not know, but in August 1720 Atterbury had 'Chapman' (presumably the translation of Homer) 'clasped up' ready to send to Pope,[2] and it is possible that the project was already taking form. Early

---

[1] We do not know how much Pope did by way of revision of the work of Broome and Fenton. At the end of the notes to Book XXIV Broome says Pope revised 'every sheet' of the translation. The manuscripts of the poem, preserved in the British Museum (Add. MS. 4809), lack all the Books done by Broome and one of the four translated by Fenton. The manuscripts of Books done by Pope are the first draft, and many revisions appear. Not many corrections appear on the manuscripts of Books done by Fenton; but these Books very likely represent a final copy (made for the printer), into which Pope's revisions of Fenton's work may already have been incorporated—a copy to which Pope added a few last-moment revisions.   [2] Elwin-Courthope, ix. 19.

in 1722 it emerges into the daylight of the (authentic) correspondence of the collaborators.[1] There we can read of friendly competition for favourite Books to translate, and can follow the actual progress of the work Book by Book. We learn that in April 1722 it was designed to publish Proposals about Michaelmas, and to have the first volume appear 'March next' (1723).[2] In November Pope thought the time unripe for the Proposals, and in February 1723 the recent outcry concerning Buckingham's *Works* led not merely to further delay, but to fears lest the time would never be ripe for Pope to appear as translator. The dated letters, on the backs of which Pope translated, indicate that his labours began not earlier than May 1723.

The collaborators had thus far worked together quite happily. Fenton was none too strenuous in his labours, and went presently to work on his edition of Waller; but Broome was indefatigable. In 1723 Pope urges him: 'Pray keep the utmost secrecy in this matter';[3] and injunctions on this head mark a gradual change of relations. Cupidity (as some insist) or at least a natural dread of the new taxes on Catholics, was the *radix malorum* at this stage. Pope wrote Caryll regarding the tax bill under consideration: 'Yet if this bill passes, I shall lose a good part of my income.'[4] At any rate Pope wanted the collaboration kept secret because if known it would probably make subscribers less easy to secure, and it was through subscribers that they were to 'find their account' in the *Odyssey*. While no financial arrangements with Broome and Fenton had yet been made, it is probable that the general plan was to divide, in proportion to the work done, the copy-money paid by the bookseller (Lintot), and to allow each author to have the subscription money from whatever subscribers he personally secured.[5] Hence, before the Proposals were published, Pope and Broome had secured subscribers privately. This procedure was due, in part at least, to the tardy

---

[1] Elwin-Courthope, viii. 48 ff.   [2] Ibid. viii. 52.
[3] Ibid. viii. 66 (6 April). An earlier passage (viii. 60) may possibly refer to the same matter.   [4] Ibid. vi. 283.   [5] Ibid. viii. 84.

publication of the Proposals on account of Pope's connexion with Jacobite scandals. It was naturally easy for Pope to pile up subscriptions with his large circle of aristocratic acquaintance and with the desire of owners of his *Iliad* to have also his *Odyssey*. It would be less easy for Fenton and Broome in any case; but if they might not avow the real nature of their partnership with Pope the number of their subscriptions would naturally be small. They seem, indeed, to have made little effort to get subscriptions; for Fenton got none, and Broome a total of only 14.[1] In general they relied on Pope supinely so far as finances were concerned.

In a letter to Broome, written in November 1724, Pope offered a choice, not only of avowing or concealing the partnership, but also a choice between 'a certain though small gratuity' and a share in the proceeds from the *published* Proposals. Pope writes:

I shall forthwith publish the proposal to the town; and, as I before told you, if you make it your choice, you shall fairly divide what profit shall arise from the future subscribers; for I have done with those procured by my personal interest, and will push my particular friends no farther. Therefore you are to divide whatever comes above my present list; and for any that your own interest can make, or already has made, you are to look upon them as wholly your own, unless you prefer a certain though small gratuity, as I first proposed by Mr. Fenton to you two years ago. Take your choice. I think I need not recommend to you further the necessity of keeping this whole matter to yourself, as I am very sure Fenton has done, lest the least air of it prejudice it with the town. But if you judge otherwise, I do not prohibit you taking to yourself your due share of fame. Take your choice also in that.[2]

The implication is that if Broome wishes a share in the public subscription, it will be to his interest to let the public think Pope the translator. Broome must have replied asking Pope to adjust financial arrangements as he might think best. Apparently with regard to finances and to avowal of authorship Broome wished Pope 'to proceed in

---

[1] Ibid. viii. 96.
[2] Ibid. viii. 89. Elwin misinterprets this letter.

the affair of Homer as if there were no person concerned in it but' Pope himself.[1] Such conduct with regard to the authorship Pope presently concluded to be impossible. The long delay in issuing the Proposals had given Broome opportunity to talk of his task, and Pope saw, doubtless with regret, the necessity of at least hinting in the Proposals the aid he had received. This is apparent in the letter which he addressed to Broome on 4 December 1724:

Had our design, which I will call ours, since it was intended to promote your reputation in one respect more than my own, and to do what you express a great desire of, to let the public at first mistake your work for mine,—had, I say, our design been made a secret as to the particular parts we were each engaged in, as much by you, as it really was by Fenton and me, there had been no harm in it, nor any ill consequence from it, which I could have reclaimed against or scrupled, as long as I did not to my private friends make any secret of it, further than you yourselves enjoined. But, to be honest with you, you have betrayed your own secret to so many people, that it would be dishonourable and unjust for me to seem, though it were no more than by connivance or silence in the point, to take to myself what does not belong to me. If, therefore, the fortune or fame of the work receive any prejudice from the partial opinion of the town on my side, preferably to what it ought to have on yours, I am not to blame. But when I am to propose to the public the undertaking, it would be dishonest to do it as purely my own. To common acquaintance indeed there was no necessity or obligation upon me to give a particular account. But it is you yourself who have altered the case. I must therefore give the world the hint, that it is not obliged to me only for this undertaking, *coute qui coute.* All I can do in honour is not to let them into the particulars, what parts of it are, or are not mine. That I leave to you, at your own time to do; but, to deal plainly with you, I think, for your own interest, you have chosen a wrong one, in being so early in it.[2]

Evidently Pope's design (he may be disingenuous in calling it 'ours') had been to publish the whole translation as his own, and when the public had been 'trepanned' into doing the whole 'justice',[3] he would reveal the fact that half

---

[1] Elwin-Courthope, viii. 91.   [2] Ibid. viii. 91–2.   [3] Ibid. viii. 90.

of it was done by Broome and Fenton. The joke would be on the critics, and Broome and Fenton would be exalted to Pope's level. That original plan was now impossible, and the public subscription would doubtless suffer. The fault was Broome's, but Pope was still (so he conveniently thought) bound in 'honour' not to particularize the work of each collaborator since Fenton had his original promise against so doing. It is probably by putting Broome thus in the wrong that Pope got him to write the account of the collaboration printed at the end of the translation—of which more anon.

Soon after the beginning of 1724 the early books were in press. There had been difficulties in getting a bookseller. Attempts had been made to interest Tonson in the matter. Fenton wrote to Broome (9 January 1723/4):

Tonson does not care to contract for the copy, and application has been made to Lintot, upon which he exerts the true spirit of a scoundrel, believing that he has Pope entirely at his mercy.[1]

Sir Clement Cotterell tried to aid these negotiations with Lintot, and anticipated (with justice!) many difficulties 'from such a suspicious, wrong-headed fellow as my friend Lintot'.[2] Pope speaks of Lintot about the same time (28 December [1723]) as 'such a fool'.[3] It was doubtless the collaboration that made the publishers hesitate. The terms Lintot gave Pope have been variously reported. Johnson says they were the same as for the *Iliad* except that the copy-money was £100 instead of £200 a volume.[4] There were five volumes, and 610 subscribers took 1,057 sets.[5] Courthope gives other figures.[6] Nichols seems to give the sums actually paid Pope and the books actually furnished:[7]

Copy-money for the Odyssey, Volumes I. II. III.;
    and 750 of each Volume printed on Royal Paper,
    4to   615   6   0
Copy-money for the Odyssey, Volumes IV. V.; and
    750 of each Volume, Royal 425 18   7½

---

[1] Ibid. viii. 73.   [2] Ibid. viii. 73 n.   [3] Ibid. viii. 72.
[4] *Lives of the Poets* (ed. Hill), iii. 142.   [5] Griffith, pp. 121–2.
[6] Elwin-Courthope, v. 199, 204.   [7] Nichols's *Literary Anecdotes*, viii. 300.

However these entries are interpreted, it is clear that the 750 volumes represent a value in addition to the sums paid by Lintot. If the payments are for copy-money only, Pope got slightly more than £200 a volume, but far from £100 a Book.

There is, however, some reason to suspect that all the various accounts cited here or current in other lives of Pope are erroneous. The figures given by Nichols command respectful attention for obvious reasons, but it will presently appear that the entries as transcribed are contradicted by other evidence. The indenture signed by Pope and Lintot (and by Pope's legal advisers, Bickford and Fortescue) on 18 February 1723/4 is still preserved in the British Museum.[1] It may be that this indenture was later superseded by another; but it is difficult to imagine how Pope having signed this document could later persuade Lintot to grant better terms. And the terms of this document are far from being what Dr. Johnson and Pope's other biographers have represented them. According to it, Lintot paid Pope £52 10s. earnest money before the indenture was sealed. He in the indenture agreed to pay Pope just before publication of volumes i–iii the sum of £157 10s. and to pay a like sum before the publication of volumes iv and v. The total, then, agreed upon for copy-money was £315—far less than it has been supposed Pope got. Lintot further agreed to furnish 'for the sole use and benefit' of Pope 200 copies in quarto on 'the best writing Royal paper' (a specimen attached and attested) and 550 copies in quarto on 'the best printing Royal paper'. Pope got, then, the 750 copies specified by Nichols; but the sums of money given by Nichols as paid Pope by Lintot are far greater than the indenture demands. One assumes that Lintot must have collected some of the subscriptions, and is paying the money over to Pope in the sums noted by Nichols. In that case, however, the sums are not copy-money. Pope was to pay certain costs in connexion with engraved plates and ornaments, and presumably that fact explains the odd sums

[1] Egerton Chart. 130. Transcribed and printed here as Appendix II.

involved in the account books. Unless a later, more favourable, agreement was reached with Lintot, Pope got £52 10*s*. for signing the contract; got £315 for copy-money, and got the amounts paid (whatever they may have been) for subscriptions secured by him. The total of sets subscribed for was 1,057, at least 14 of which were for Broome's subscribers. Each set subscribed for should bring the poets five guineas, according to the Proposals.

Quarrels with Lintot attended various stages of the publication. One of the difficulties that arose is indicated in a letter of 13 February [1725] from Pope to Broome:

You cannot imagine what a scoundrel Lintot is in all respects; pray send not to him for anything, or on any account correspond with or answer him. I will take care to convey the books to you for your subscribers.[1]

Lintot already had objected, one surmises, to furnishing free copies for Broome's subscribers, and Pope is assuring Broome that he shall have them. On 5 March Pope again writes:

Lintot, I perceive, will give me what silly uneasiness he can, and if I were as great a fool as he, he might. I once more desire, for very good reasons, that whatever he may write to you, you will return him no sort of word in answer. I am sorry you ever writ to him, for I know he has ill designs. I hope you said nothing as to your part in the work.[2]

Lintot probably did not know how much of the work Broome was doing, but if he corresponded with Broome, he must have known of the collaboration; and since a law-suit was meditated to interpret the contract, it was advisable not to furnish any written evidence. The lawsuit did not eventuate.

Lintot seems not merely to have refused free copies for Broome's subscribers but also to have worked against the public subscription. The public phase of the subscription opened in January 1725. The Proposals were dated the tenth. A fortnight later they were inserted in the newspapers; and Lintot was brazen enough to set up a rival subscription for his own benefit. Pope's advertisement reads:

Proposals by Mr. Pope,
For a Translation of Homer's Odyssey.

This Work consists of the same Number of Books as the Iliad, (viz. twenty four) and of as large a Body of Notes and Extracts. It is printed in the same Manner, Size, Paper, and Ornaments.

It is proposed to the Subscribers at a Guinea less namely at five Guineas. The first three Volumes (Viz. fourteen Books) are already printed; in consideration of which, three Guineas are to be now paid, and the remaining two upon the delivery of them.

The greatest Number of the Impression being already subscribed for, those [who] would have the book are desired to send their Names and Payments to Mr. Lintot at the Cross-Keys between the Temple Gates in Fleet-street; who will deliver Receipts for the same till the last Day of February next, when the Subscription will be closed.

The day after this advertisement was printed in the *Daily Courant* of 25 January 1725,[1] Lintot in the *Evening Post* (26 January) advertised that persons subscribing for *his* benefit might have cheaper and easier rates. His 'modest proposal' reads:

Proposals by Bernard Lintott for his own Benefit, for Printing
a translation of Homer's Odyssey by Mr. Pope.

This Work consists of the same Number of Books as the Iliad, and of as large a body of Notes and Extracts. It is printed in five Volumes in large and small Paper Folio in the same Manner, Size and Paper. The large is proposed to the Subscribers at two Guineas per Sett less than the Iliad, namely at four Guineas. The small Paper at Ten Shillings less, namely at Fifty Shillings per Sett, half to be paid upon Subscribing, the Remainder upon the Delivery of the two last Volumes. Two hundred and fifty Setts only are printed for those Gentlemen who have the Iliad in Folio, who are desired to send in their first Payments by the last Day of February next, to the Proprietor, Bernard Lintott at the Cross Keys between the Temple Gates in Fleet-street, when the Subscription will be closed.

N. B. The Edition in Twelves of Mr. Pope's Odyssey, with the

---

[1] See also the issues for 27, 28, and 29 January; also the *Daily Post*, and doubtless other journals.

Notes printed at the Bottom of each Page, with Cuts, will be published in one Month after the Subscription Books are deliver'd.[1]

Such behaviour would have caused any author to shout 'rascal'. Lintot's advertisement blandly announced that if subscribers wished quarto copies with their names printed in the subscription list, they would have to pay a guinea more to Pope than they would to Lintot for a large folio (without their names presumably: that is not made clear). All knew that either a large or a small folio (and the small folio sold for half the price of Pope's quartos) could be trimmed to match quarto *Iliads*, if one possessed such. Pope, furthermore, required payment in advance for all volumes—for the first three, like Lintot, upon subscribing; for the last two upon delivery of the first three. Lintot's subscribers could pay for volumes iv and v upon delivery. Of course Lintot's 'subscription' was merely an unscrupulous advertisement of his trade editions, and one might urge that Pope after getting his thousand subscriptions ought to have been generous and unconcerned over Lintot's attempts. But if Pope was depending on the public subscription to gratify Broome and Fenton, who had been negligent about getting subscribers, Lintot's probable wrecking of the public subscription was undoubtedly annoying. The bookseller (so Pope would think) had acted in this fashion only because for some reason he thought 'Pope entirely at his mercy', as Fenton had put it.[2] And the cause of his suspicions was Broome's excessive love of communication. If the collaborators during these weeks and thereafter spoke of each other with less affection than their correspondence had hitherto manifested, much must be set down to the various exasperations arising from charges of Jacobitism, charges of editorial incompetence with regard to Shakespeare, and now, last of all, the mess in which, with Lintot's aid, sly collaboration in the *Odyssey* had resulted.

[1] In the *Daily Post*, 25 May 1725, Lintot advertises his editions as follows: 12mo, 2s. the volume in quires; large folio, 17s. the volume in quires; small folio, 10s. the volume in quires. [2] Elwin-Courthope, viii. 73 (9 January 1724).

This was the mood in which work on the *Odyssey* terminated, and we must remember these various circumstances when we come to the financial settlement between the three. Fenton, while the task was on, was little interested. At the crucial period in December 1724 he wrote to Broome: 'I have seen Pope but twice, in passing, since I came to town. How the great affair goes on I know not, nor am inquisitive.'[1] A year later, however, he thought it high time for Broome to come to town 'that we may settle [financial] affairs with Mr. Pope'.[2] Broome demurred:

I leave, my dear friend, that part to you; at least let those accounts sleep till spring. I fancy Mr. Pope will forgive us for letting the money rest in his hands. But to deal plainly, I expect a breach rather than peace from that treaty. I fear we have hunted with the lion, who, like his predecessor in Phaedrus, will take the first share merely because he is a lion; the second because he is more brave; the third because he is of most importance; and if either of us shall presume to touch the fourth, woe be to us. This perhaps may not be the case with respect to the lucrative part, but I have strong apprehensions it will happen with regard to our reputations. Be assured Mr. Pope will not let us divide—I fear not give us our due share of honour. He is a Caesar in poetry, and will bear no equal.[3]

Fenton declined to act in Broome's absence, even though Pope offered him the money.[4] Eventually, in this atmosphere of suspicion, there was a settlement. It was not a generous one, perhaps, on Pope's part. Certainly it has not been so regarded; but one must now recognize the apparent fact that Pope got far less in copy-money than has been generally supposed. And if one recalls that the correspondence between Pope and Broome indicates the intention to let each get his profits through subscriptions, and remembers that neither Broome nor Fenton made any serious attempt to obtain subscribers, Pope stands somewhat excused. As for the second source of profit, the copy-money, Pope acted generously there. He received less than £50 a book, but he gave that sum to his collaborators—

---

[1] Elwin-Courthope, viii. 93.   [2] Ibid. viii. 103.
[3] Ibid. viii. 105–6.   [4] Ibid. viii. 108.

Fenton had £200 for four books, and Broome had £500 for eight. Broome got 70 guineas in subscription-money of his own, and from the public subscription he must have made about £25 if Pope speaks accurately in a note to the 1729 *Dunciad*, Book III, line 328, where he says Broome got £500 'and a present of all those books for which his own interest could procure him Subscribers, to the value of *One hundred more*'.[1] For half the work Pope's collaborators got £800, while Pope reserved for himself the lion's share, which may be estimated (with various expenses deducted) as over £5,000. The only justification for Pope is the fact that most of this sum came from subscriptions that he or his friends (other than his collaborators) solicited. One doubts if Broome and Fenton were ever better paid for verses than they were when hunting with a lion who was worthy of Phaedrus' fable.

The immediate grievance of Broome (if not of Fenton) was that the collaborators were deprived of honour due to them for their poetry. And yet it was Broome's own hand that publicly did this wrong. Pope was caught in another dilemma. With Grub Street already organized against him on Shakespeare and crying out against the first volumes of the *Odyssey*, he dared neither acknowledge nor deny the collaboration. Characteristically he compromised, and acknowledged a bit less than half of it—through Broome! One of Pope's uncanniest gifts was his ability to get others to do for him the most improbable services. It is impossible to imagine how he persuaded Broome to affix at the end of the notes to the *Odyssey* a poem extravagantly (and doubtless insincerely) eulogistic of Pope and a statement signed 'William Broome' that deserves partial quotation:

I have sometimes used Madam *Dacier* as she has done others, in transcribing some of her Remarks without particularizing them; but indeed it was through inadvertency only that her name is sometimes omitted at the bottom of the note. If my performance has merit, either in these, or in my part of the translation (namely in the sixth, eleventh, and eighteenth books) it is but just to

---

[1] p. 77.

attribute it to the judgment and care of Mr. *Pope*, by whose hand every sheet was corrected. His other, and much more able assistant, was Mr. *Fenton*, in the fourth and twentieth books. It was our particular request, that our several parts might not be made known to the world till the end of it: And if they have had the good fortune not to be distinguished from His, we ought to be the less vain, since the resemblance proceeds much less from our diligence and study to copy his manner, than from his own daily revisal and correction. . . .

I must not conclude without declaring our mutual satisfaction in Mr. *Pope's* acceptance of our best endeavours, which have contributed at least to his more speedy execution of this great undertaking. If ever My name be numbred with the learned, I must ascribe it to his friendship, in transmitting it to posterity by a participation in his labours.[1]

This astonishing statement must have been practically dictated by Pope; but how he cajoled Broome into signing it and how Broome could at the end of such a statement burst into a paean of heroic couplets in Pope's praise is beyond present-day understanding. Broome implies that he did three books of the translation, whereas from his correspondence with Pope and from his later statements it is clear that he did eight: II, VI, VIII, XI, XII, XVI, XVIII, and XXIII. To Fenton he ascribes two books, though Fenton actually did four: I, IV, XIX, XXII. Not content with this abnegation, he contrives to ascribe all the merit to Pope's abilities. He even takes the blame for all concealment, which is ironical in view of his inability to conceal. There is, of course, some evidence that warrants his acceptance of this blame. He had wished Pope to proceed as if Pope alone were doing the *Odyssey*,[2] and Fenton wished to remain concealed even after the work was done.[3]

Pope accepted complacently the lies which he pretty certainly made Broome tell. In what he calls 'a long critical postscript' to the *Odyssey* he spoke of the collaboration as follows:

My errors had been fewer, had each of those Gentlemen who join'd

---

[1] Pope's *Odyssey* (folio, 1726), v. 260–1.
[2] Elwin-Courthope, viii. 91.   [3] Ibid. viii. 121.

with me shown as much of the severity of a friend to me, as I did
to them, in strict animadversion and correction. What assistance
I receiv'd from them, was made known in general to the publick
in the original Proposals for this work, and the particulars are
specify'd at the conclusion of it; to which I must add (to be
punctually just) some part of the tenth and fifteenth books.[1] The
Reader will now be too good a judge, how much the greater part
of it, and consequently of its faults, is chargeable upon me alone.
But this I can with integrity affirm, that I have bestowed as much
time and pains upon the whole, as were consistent with the indispensable duties and cares of life, and with that wretched state of
health which God has been pleased to make my portion.[2]

Pope never showed himself to less advantage than in this
hypocritical and dishonest utterance. It ought, however,
to be recorded that later he quietly (very quietly) corrected
the mis-statements that Broome and he had made at the
end of the *Odyssey*. At first there was, to be sure, some
sparring. On various pages of his *Poems on several Occasions*[3] (1727) Broome showed how easily he could have
blurted out the truth. Pope countered by slipping some
of Broome's lines into the 'Bathos',[4] and in the *Dunciad
Variorum* (1729) showed how easy it would be to take
revenge on Broome if he told:

> Hibernian Politicks, O Swift, thy doom,
> And Pope's, translating three whole years with Broome.[5]

The poet added, to be sure, in a footnote, that whoever
imagined this was a sarcasm on Broome was 'greatly mistaken' and that 'the author only seems to lament, that he
was imploy'd in Translation at all'.[6] In the summer of 1730
Fenton died, and after some years of more or less acute
estrangement Broome was reconciled to Pope in 1735. At

---

[1] See A. Warren, in the *Review of English Studies*, viii (1932), 77–82. Unknown
to Broome and Fenton, Henry Layng had helped Pope on parts of these Books.
[2] *Odyssey* (4to, 1726), v. 306–7.   [3] pp. 1, 3, 98, 194, &c.
[4] Elwin-Courthope, viii. 162.   [5] p. 77 (4to, 1729).
[6] In the edition of the *Dunciad* printed for Gilliver and Clarke in 1736 as
volume iv of the *Works* the poet revised the couplet so that Broome's name no
longer appeared in it. In the note to the couplet he speaks of his share in the
translation as 'half the *Odyssey*' (*Works* [8vo, 1736], iv. 224–5). The Gilliver
8vo *Dunciad* of 1736 has the couplet unrevised and a somewhat different note.
See Griffith, pp. 323 and 344, and Elwin-Courthope, viii. 178.

the end of that year on leaf A 4 of his quarto *Works*
Pope specified as among his writings 'twelve books of
the *Odyssey*, with the Postscript (not the Notes)'.   When
Broome reprinted his *Poems* in 1739, he with equal casual-
ness claimed 'eight Books of the *Odyssey*' and in a footnote
ascribed four to Fenton.[1] Truth in the matter was tardily
being told.

So much for the intrigues of the collaborators. Fully as
important, though less interesting, is the reception the
translation got from the public. Much of the unfavourable
comment on it must have appeared in the newspapers. On
Christmas Day, 1725, Pope wrote Caryll vaguely of 'railing
papers about the *Odyssey*', and on 20 November of the same
year Fenton had written to Broome, 'We have been but
coarsely used this last summer, both in print and conversation.'[2] A specimen of the blunt accusations hurled against
Pope because of his slyness in the collaboration may be
found in the *London Journal*, 17 July 1725, in a letter 'To
the Author of the *London Journal*', signed 'Homerides'.[3]
This attack is exactly what the translators had to expect
under the circumstances. The author exposes various
artifices of 'modern' writers, and then adds:

And yet, I fear there is a Practice of this sort coming into
Fashion, of more mischievous Consequence than any of the former;
which is that of an eminent Poet's taking in *Subscriptions* for any
Work, for the sake of *Lucre*, and getting it done by *Hackney-Hands*
for the sake of *Idleness*, and at length publishing it in his *own Name*.

In short, what gave occasion to these Reflections, is the late
Translation of *Homer's Odyssey*, which was published by Subscrip-

---

[1] pp. [xxiv] and 47 n. In the 1727 edition his Advertisement facing page 1
had been vague; in 1739 he added to it the four words here given in brackets:
'The Author has not Inserted into this Collection any part of his Translation of
[the eight Books of] the *Odyssey*, published by Mr. *Pope*: he thought it an
Imposition on the Public to swell this Volume with Verses taken from a Work
that is already in the Hands of almost every Reader.'

[2] Elwin-Courthope, viii. 104.

[3] Other attacks occur in such morsels as Thomas Cooke's *Battle of the Poets*,
which appeared first in May 1725, and should not be (as it usually is) confused
with the dramatic 'Battle of the Poets' inserted in 1730 (?) in Fielding's *Tom
Thumb*. This last 'Battle' is almost certainly *not* by Cooke.

tion, and proposed to be done by the Translator of the *Iliad*; but it is confidently reported, that other Persons have had the chief Hand in it, and that They do not pretend to deny it themselves. I own, that, upon perusal of some Part of it, I had a Jealousy of this Nature; and I was strengthened in my Suspicions, upon comparing the *Patents* which are prefixed to both these Works. In that before the *Iliad*, it is recited that

——*Whereas our trusty and well-beloved* Bernard Lintot, *of our City of* London, *Bookseller, hath, by his Petition, humbly represented unto us, that he is now preparing for the Press a Translation of the* Iliad *of* Homer, *by Mr.* Alexander Pope, *Gent.* &c.

In the other it runs thus,

Whereas Bernard Lintot, *of our City of London, Bookseller, hath, by his Petition, humbly represented unto us, that he is now printing a Translation, UNDERTAKEN by our* trusty *and* well-beloved Alexander Pope, *Esquire, of the* Odyssey *of* Homer, *&c.*

Methinks the Word *Undertaken*, in the latter, savours strongly of *Jesuitical* Prevarication, and very much confirms these Suspicions. However, it is in the Power of that ingenious Gentleman to do himself Justice, by publicly declaring, that he has *bonâ fide* translated it all himself; in which case I will as publicly acknowledge, that I was mistaken in my Surmises as to this Particular, whatever I may think of the Performance it self. But if he does not think fit to do this, I must take the Liberty, as an Enemy to all Imposition, to advertise the Publick not to look upon him as the *Translator*, but only the *Publisher*; or, as it is expressed in his Patent, the *Undertaker* of this Translation.

We have frequently heard of celebrated Poets, who have published their light unfinished Pieces, under some subordinate Name; in which Case the Publick is agreeably deceived: But I thought the natural Pride of a Good Author would not suffer him, upon any Account, to father the Works of one less famous than himself; and for that Reason, I thought we were safe from any such Imposition: But if once *Avarice* gets the better of *Pride* in this Point, we may live to see the most eminent Writers keep half a Dozen Journeymen a-piece, and vend their hireling Labours, as *How* did his *Knives*, by putting his own Name upon them all.

I shall not say any thing concerning the Persons who are supposed to be our *Poetical Undertaker's* Deputies in this Affair, because were they as able to translate *Homer* as even their *Taskmaster* himself, yet to have one or more Authors obtruded upon us, without our Knowledge or Consent, under the Name and Character of another to whom we have subscribed, is *Quackery* and *C—licism* in the greatest Perfection.

I have a great veneration for this admired Poet, and also for his ingenious Bookseller; but I hope they will not always expect to impose *extravagant Prices* upon us, for *bad Paper, old Types,* and *Journey work Poetry.*

I am SIR, | Your humble Servant, | HOMERIDES.[1]

Apart from this natural criticism of Pope as an 'undertaking poet'[2] who let collaborators do the work, the comment doubtless followed the obvious lines laid down by critics of the *Iliad.* There would be criticism of the use of rhyme instead of blank verse and criticism of the decorative elegance of the version—designed to please the *beau monde.* One of the best-tempered expressions of this view of the *Iliad* came in 1719 in the frequently reprinted, anonymous *Three Satires. Most humbly inscribed and recommended to that little gentleman, of great vanity, who has just published, A Fourth Volume of Homer.* In the first of these three, 'On the English Translators of Homer', would-be translators pass in review, and in due place

> Gay *P—pe* succeeds, and joins his skill with these,
> He smoothes him o'er, and gives him grace and ease,
> And makes him *fine,*—the *Beaus* and *Belles* to please.

Earlier in the same poem Pope has been called 'an unfledg'd author'

> Who the gay trifling croud with tinkling chimes
> Has skill to please, and fash'onably rhimes.

The facts that successful translation is always popularization, and that Pope's subscription list contained many names of aristocrats, would make such observations as these inevitable.

---

[1] The same issue of this journal contains also an epigram, 'To Mr. *P—PE*, on his second Subscription to *Homer*', which accuses Pope of bad faith and of avarice.

[2] Gibes on the word *undertaker* must have been common. See, for example, the title-page of the *Stamford Toasts*, a thin octavo of verses by Thomas Pope of Peterborough, which Curll brought out in 1726 as 'By Mr. Pope; not the *Undertaker*'.

Other unfavourable criticisms are equally obvious. Pope is accused of being incompetent[1] and mercenary[2] and doubtless many other unpleasant things. In post-*Dunciad* times the tone of asperity was more marked, and in response to *Sober Advice from Horace*, Thomas Bentley, nephew to Dr. Richard Bentley, wrote *A Letter to Mr. Pope* (1735), which speaks caustically of the poet's aversion to the great classical scholar:

You are grown very angry, it seems, at Dr. *Bentley* of late. Is it because he said (*to your Face*, I have been told) that your HOMER was *miserable stuff*? That it might be called, HOMER *modernised*, or something *to that effect*; but that there were very little or no *Vestiges* at all of the *old Grecian*. Dr. BENTLEY said right. Hundreds have said the same *behind your Back*. For HOMER *translated, first* in English, *secondly* in Rhyme, *thirdly* not from the Original, but *fourthly*, from a French Translation, and that in *Prose*, by a *Woman* too,[3] how the Devil should it be *Homer*? As for the *Greek* Language, everybody that *knows* it and has compared your Version with the Original, as I have done in many Places, must *know* too that you *know* nothing of it. I my self am satisfied, but don't expect to make anybody else believe so, that you can but barely construe *Latin*. . . . You have not that compass of human Learning, always thought necessary to a true Poet. . . . Let me advise you as a Friend (for a Friend I am, and adore your very Foot-steps as a polite Writer) don't hurt your self by your own Writings; have it always before your Eyes, That no Man is demolished but by himself.[4]

If at the moment of writing this friend and adorer knew more reasons why Pope's Homer was all wrong, he evidently could not remember them. This sort of thing was an old story before 1735.

Kinder comments came from the poet's actual friends, and it is pleasing to record the beginning of one of Pope's most satisfactory friendships as dating from the publication of the *Odyssey*. A young Fellow of New College, Oxford, a friend of Christopher Pitt (who was among Pope's helpers

---

[1] Jo. Hervey, *A Collection of Miscellany Poems* . . . (Edinburgh, 1726), p. 8.
[2] *Whartoniana* . . . (London, E. Curll, 1727), i. 144.
[3] Mme Dacier.   [4] p. 14.

on the *Odyssey*),[1] brought out an elaborately eulogistic essay upon the translation. This young man was Joseph Spence, of whom Christopher Pitt said: 'Mr. Spence is the completest scholar, either in solid or polite learning, for his years, that I ever knew. Besides he is the sweetest tempered gentleman breathing.'[2] Spence, who was apparently quite unknown to Pope in 1725, presently attached himself to the poet, much as Boswell later did to Johnson, and all biographers of Pope have acknowledged a major indebtedness to the *Anecdotes* of Spence, which were first printed in 1820. The devotion of a man of Spence's amiable character is one of the strongest proofs of the personal magnetism and worth of Alexander Pope.

Spence's comment on the *Odyssey* appeared, like Pope's translation, in two instalments; the first, early in June 1726, and the second in August 1727.[3] Under the title *An Essay on Mr. Pope's Odyssey* he presented five 'evenings', or dialogues in 'the old Platonick way', between Antiphaüs and Philypsus. The former hates 'glitter' and 'glare', as his name might suggest; and the latter, similarly, is fond of elevation:

The enlarged Genius of *Philypsus* always led him to dwell upon the most beautified Parts of a Poem with the greatest Pleasure; while *Antiphaüs*, who has a very clear Head, and has given much into a strict way of thinking, is taken most with just Descriptions, and plain natural Ideas: The one was so possest with the Pleasure which he felt from fine Thoughts and warm Expressions, that He did not take a full Satisfaction in low Beauty, and simple Representations of Nature; the other, on the contrary, had such an aversion to *glitterings* and *elevation*, that he was distasted at any the least appearance of either. If the latter was prejudiced for the Ancients, from the Purity and Justness, which we find in most of their Works; *Philypsus* had his *foible* too, and was sometimes caught by the Flourish and Colouring of the Moderns.[4]

---

[1] Elwin-Courthope, x. 127.

[2] Spence's *Anecdotes* (Singer ed.), p. xviii.

[3] So listed in the *Monthly Catalogue*, June 1726 and August 1727. A second edition, called 'improved', is listed in the *Gentleman's Magazine*, August 1737.

[4] pp. 2–3.

The aesthetic problem posed is, how far may a translator 'heighten' or otherwise modify the tone of his original. Before this time the generally accepted doctrine had been that which Denham expressed in neat metaphor in the Preface to his 'Destruction of Troy':

. . . Poesie is of so subtile a spirit, that in pouring out of one Language into another, it will all evaporate; and if a new spirit be not added in the transfusion, there will remain nothing but a *Caput mortuum*. . . .[1]

Spence's general position is in favour of fidelity to the spirit of the original; but while he offers trenchant criticisms of Pope's work, his natural generosity and his sincere enthusiasm for the translation make the combination of stricture and compliment at times bewildering. The first three dialogues present (1) the objections of Antiphaüs to Pope's tendency to 'heighten' the style of the *Odyssey* in English, (2) the answers of Philypsus in favour of the tendency, and (3) the question of rhyme versus blank verse. The last two dialogues, published over a year later, deal with general matters of (4) language and (5) style.

During the interval between the publication of the two sections of Spence's *Essay* Pope had apparently sought out Spence, and their friendship began. The manuscript of the last two dialogues was read by Pope before publication, and Pope's marginal comments on it have been preserved for us.[2] These indicate his ability, so often seen elsewhere, to admit himself in the wrong, and they also show a natural tendency to protest against criticisms that he believed unfounded. He apparently exercised no undue 'influence' in modifying before publication the opinions of Spence.

The method of the classical dialogue is used with admirable skill to accuse the poet of faults and to soothe with flattery. At the end of his first instalment Spence epitomizes his points by saying of Pope: 'His faults are the faults of a Man, but his beauties are the beauties of an Angel.'[3]

---

[1] Denham's *Poetical Works* (ed. Banks, 1928), p. 159.
[2] *Notes and Queries*, 1 S. i (1850), 396. But where is the original manuscript now? [3] p. 156.

In spite of flattery the strictures are keenly made. Not merely is rhyme repeatedly depreciated as a vehicle for translation, but there is also a reiterated charge of artificiality, over-ornamentation, and lack of fidelity to the original. He is excused, but not absolved, for these faults. 'It is next to impossible,' Antiphaüs asserts, 'in so long a Translation, especially as it is in *Rhime*, not to give sometimes into Sound and Ornament; when to crown all, the Vogue of the World goes so strong for both.'[1] More than once the excuse of writing for the taste of his own generation is partly allowed Pope. Philypsus, the Modern, hard beset by the proposition that 'too much finery is always affectation', argues in the first dialogue:

I allow, to use your own thought, that a profusion of Lace and Embroidery wou'd be a disguise upon an Old Hero; but they are so far from being improper, that they are becoming on the Heroes of our Age.[2]

But he is overwhelmed instantly by the apostle of true simplicity, who retorts:

. . . if you view a real modern Hero in a true light, those fineries do not set well upon him: and I think, I never saw any thing more truly ridiculous, than the Piece we were laughing at the other Day, in your Picture-Gallery.—Good Heaven! The Duke of *Marlbrough* in the heat of an Engagement, with a full-bottom'd Wigg, very carefully spread over his Shoulders![3]

Faced with so uncomplimentary an *impasse* in the argument, Spence either changes the subject (as in this case) or resorts to extreme laudation. The latter method is seen characteristically in the discussion of rhyme during the dialogue of the third evening:

When they [posterity] read Mr. *Pope's Iliad* or *Odyssey*, they will often applaud the greatness of his thoughts; and often admire the happiness of his diction, as far as the present Language shall be preserv'd to them. They will honour his remains, and when they look toward his Ashes with veneration, 'There (will they say) lies the Great Man, who in ancient Days, is said to have shewn the noblest Genius to Poetry in the World: what beauties do we dis-

---

[1] p. 19.   [2] p. 21.   [3] p. 22.

cover in him, thro' all this rust of time, and so much obsolete
language? He is every way to be commended as far as any of our
ancient Poets are; Only he fell into the common fault of those
Ages; and always shews that trifling labour of making the last syl-
lable of every alternate line, sound like the close of the foregoing:
Bating this insignificant taste of those times, how much is he to
be praised, and how much to be admired?'[1]

Spence is certainly more convincing on the subject of finery
than on that of rhyme, but this last passage indicates how
Pope, supposedly suspicious and irritable in the face of
criticism, swallowed charges of fustian and artifice and made
a close friend of the critic. These dialogues, with all their
excessive praise, still embody the most incisive and just
criticism of Pope's *Odyssey*. Their mild and equable tone
warrants Dr. Johnson's verdict that in Spence 'Pope had
the first experience of a critick without malevolence, who
thought it as much his duty to display beauties as expose
faults; who censured with respect, and praised with
alacrity.'[2] In view of Spence's later collection of anecdotes
about Pope, one may surely say that if Pope had never
received a guinea for the *Odyssey*, he would yet have ' found
his account' in it through gaining Spence as a friend.

[1] p. 134.
[2] *Lives of the Poets* (ed. Hill), iii. 143. Lounsbury in his *Text of Shakespeare*,
pp. 192–4, is severe on Spence for praising Pope and on Johnson for praising
Spence.

X

LIFE AT TWICKENHAM

A MAN like Spence, amiable and inoffensive, could without a smile call the world of letters 'that serene Republick'.[1] It was probably a weariness of warfare in this same republic, together with a real appetite for gardening, that led Pope about the end of 1718 to accept Lord Bathurst's advice against building a *palazzotto* in London[2] and to settle at Twickenham, or Twitnam, as he loved to spell it. His relations with the capital were, however, not much altered by this decision; for he still made his town head-quarters at the house of Jervas. As late as 1725 and 1726 subscribers to the *Odyssey* were asked to send to him for their copies 'at Mr. Jervas's, Principal Painter to his Majesty, next Door to the Right Hon. the Lord Viscount Townshend's, in Cleveland-Court, St. James's.'[3] Sometimes he stayed with Lord Peterborough or Lord Edward Harley (second Earl of Oxford); but Jervas's house was his usual town address for years before and after the settlement at Twickenham.

For almost a decade after this settlement, literature had hardly more interest for the poet than had gardening and the country houses of a few friends. The taste, in fact, was not new; but with the leasing of his villa it became dominant. It is astonishing how in this period the poetic impulse diminished. Apart from the translations of Homer no poetic work of first importance was printed during the years 1719–26. He wrote new things, but they were chiefly *jeux d'esprit* to which he gave little thought, epitaphs for deceased friends, one or two epistles of the Horatian type, or prose squibs of little importance. All grew casually from his social relationships rather than from deliberate cultivation of the Muse.

[1] *An Essay on Pope's Odyssey*, Preface, leaf a 3 *v.*
[2] Elwin-Courthope, viii. 325 (14 August 1718).
[3] *Evening Post*, 15 April 1725 and 14 June 1726.

Possibly from this statement exceptions should be made in favour of the *Epistle to Addison*, prefixed to Tickell's edition of Addison's *Works* in September 1721 and in favour of the *Epistle to Oxford*, which similarly adorned Pope's edition of Parnell's *Poems* in December of the same year. The lines to Addison, in spite of the somewhat malicious arguments of Elwin and Courthope,[1] were very likely written some years before publication, and were printed as public evidence of a reconciliation with Tickell after Addison's death. The *Epistle to Oxford*, also very likely written before the removal to Twickenham, is a superb example of Pope's firm dignity of tone in what is really elegiac verse; it illustrates his desire to be known as a friend to worth even when it was in disgrace. His muse is ready to attend the fallen minister

> or to the scaffold, or the cell,
> When the last lingering friend has bid farewell.
> Ev'n now she shades thy evening walk with bays
> (No hireling she, no prostitute to praise);
> Ev'n now, observant of the parting ray,
> Eyes the calm sunset of thy various day;
> Through Fortune's cloud one truly great can see,
> Nor fears to tell that Mortimer is he.

But these two epistles, while studied and polished, are strictly 'occasional'. They are the most important products of their years.

Among slighter things there are some, such as the epitaph 'intended for Mr. Rowe', amplified later for the Abbey monument by another hand,[2] and the lines to the Duke of Argyll upon receiving the added title of Duke of Greenwich, which were published by Pope himself. Others came into print less certainly under the care and intention of the author. Among these would be the *News from Court*, 1719, the lines to Lady Mary Wortley Montagu (pub-

[1] iii. 201.

[2] See Alfred Jackson, 'Pope's Epitaphs on Nicholas Rowe', *Review of English Studies*, vii (1931), 76–9. It may be added that the *Universal Spectator*, 25 June 1743, prints the longer form of the epitaph and makes no mention of Pope as author.

T

lished by Curll as 'The Second Eve' in March 1720), and the lines 'To Mrs. M. B. [Martha Blount] on her Birthday', which escaped into the world via the *British Journal*, 14 November 1724, apparently about a year and a half after they were written. Furtive but perhaps authorized was the publication in December 1722 of a small prose thing called *Annus Mirabilis*. This was ascribed to Pope by the *London Journal*, 5 January 1723, which says the work 'is a Performance full of Wit, and has met with a Reception from the Ingenious not in the least Inferior to its Merit'. The piece is marked by indecency as well as by wit; and its medical details suggest, but do not establish, collaboration with Arbuthnot. The publication of Pope's letters to Henry Cromwell in Curll's *Miscellanea* (dated on the title-page 1727 but published in the summer of 1726) is a celebrated case of unauthorized printing.

It is problematical if the appearance of two other pieces was countenanced by Pope—probably it was not. These are the 'Atticus' lines, later famous in the *Epistle to Dr. Arbuthnot*, and the *Memoirs of the Life of Scriblerus*, 1723.

Circumstances surrounding the publication of both these items are bafflingly obscure. The lines on Addison appeared first (so far as is known) in the *St. James's Journal*, 15 December 1722, as part of a correspondence contributed by 'Dorimant'. This consisted of four letters published in this *Journal* between 22 November 1722 and 20 April 1723,[1]—letters dealing with the controversy over Steele's *Conscious Lovers*, which was being violently attacked by Dennis and others and being defended with equal warmth by allies of Steele. In this controversy Pope, so far as we know, took no interest. He had worries of his own with Atterbury in the Tower, and with Buckingham's *Works*, Shakespeare's *Works*, and the *Odyssey* all on his hands. Furthermore, he had in the spring of 1721 made peace

---

[1] Three of these have been reprinted in *P.M.L.A.* xxix (1914), 236–55, and ascribed to Pope, simply because the lines on Addison are included in one of the three. The author of the letters, however, makes no claim to authorship of the lines, rather the contrary, in fact. The letter of 20 April is not reprinted, but a letter signed Townley (printed 15 November) is included and ascribed to Pope.

with Dennis,[1] and the publication of his *Epistle to Addison* implies a burying of the hatchet also with regard to the Buttonians. December 1722 is an improbable time for Pope to join in the attack on Dennis and to revive his enmity with Addison's friends. It is also true that the 'Dorimant' letters show a knowledge of and interest in theatrical affairs that Pope lacked. The lines are appended to a letter from 'Dorimant', dated 'Button's, 12 Decemb. 1722,' in a brief postscript that says, 'The following lines have been in good reputation here, and are now submitted to publick censure.'[2] One may suspect that they were injected into the Dennis-Steele controversy as a tub thrown to divert a whale—injected by some Steele partisan who valued the lines for the satire on Dennis with which they began, and hoped to deflect the pen of that critic towards Pope. If so, he failed; for the lines attracted practically no attention. In 1723 Jeremiah Markland (?) printed them in Curll's *Cythereia* from an inferior manuscript, with no mention of previous publication; and in the *Dunciad* of 1729 Pope himself said that the lines were 'never made publick till by *Curl* . . . in his miscellanies, 12*mo* 1727'.[3] It was only after the *Dunciad* that these lines became generally famous.

Another work about which too little is known was published in February 1722/3,[4] with the title:
MEMOIRS / of the / LIFE / of / *SCRIBLERUS*. /—/ *Scalpellum, Calami, Atramentum, Charta, Libelli.* /—/ By *D. S*——*t.* /—/ [Ornament] /—/ *LONDON:* / Printed from the Original Copy from / *Dublin*; and Sold by *A. Moore* near / St. *Paul*'s. MDCCXXIII.
Almost the only sure facts about this publication are that A. Moore, the publisher, was notorious for dubious or false

[1] Elwin-Courthope, x. 111–12, and Dennis, *Remarks upon Mr. Pope's Dunciad* (1729), p. 40, where Pope's letter is printed with comment.

[2] It may be worth while to add that the first line of the satire appended to the letter speaks of Gildon's 'venal quill', and hence there is no warrant for the elaborate malice that Elwin and Courthope built up around the supposition that *venal* was a later insertion. See Elwin-Courthope, iii. 235. On the publication in *Cythereia* see the *Bodleian Quarterly Record*, v (1928), 301, and *supra*, p. 127 n.

[3] *Dunciad* (4to ed.), p. 12 of the 'Testimonies of Authors'.

[4] Adv., 'this day published', in the *Post Boy*, 19 February 1723.

attributions to Swift, and that the author of the pamphlet knew, though apparently in no great detail, the earlier plans of the Scriblerus Club for writing memoirs of their hero Martinus. The statement, 'Printed from the Original Copy from Dublin,' may be taken with scepticism: it was the usual device of Grub Street when fathering a work upon Swift. Even the advertising of the work must arouse suspicion. The *Post Boy*, 9 March 1723, describes the work as:

Memoirs of the Life of *Joachim Scriblerus*, and his seven Sons. The Father, a Learned Divine, who flourish'd in the 13th and 14th Centuries, and wrote an immence Quantity of very valuable Books in Divinity. Six of the Sons were turn'd out into the wide World, and Tim the Seventh (alias J—n D——s) run Mad with writing Criticisms, &c. Written by Dr. S—ft. Reprinted from the Dublin Copy; price 6d.

Evidently the advertiser had not read his muddled pamphlet too carefully; for he makes Joachim the hero, makes Joachim the father instead of the ancestor of Tim (the actual hero), and represents Tim as being John Dennis, the critic. In the text 'Tim' is chiefly Swift himself, with curiously added traits taken from Dennis and Bentley. The following passage attaches to Swift Dennis's favourite profanity and his well-known 'true taste for the sublime':

It happen'd unluckily about this Time that Tim fell sick of a Fever that settled in his Head, and he would run up and down in Alleys and Corners affronting every Body: In this Mood a Friend of mine met him one Day, and Tim accosted him with a great Oath, Z—ds, Sir, Don't you know me? Not I indeed, Sir, quoth my Friend, very civilly. No, Sir, I am J—n S—t Sir, the only Man alive that has a true Taste of the Sublime. Sir, your most humble Servant, says my Friend, then you are not the Man I took you for. To convince you that I am, quoth Tim, stooping down to the Kennel, take that, and throws a great Handful of Mud all over his Cloaths.[1]

Presently Tim is discoursing on the Letters of 'Mr. Bull',

---

[1] *Satires and Personal Writings by Jonathan Swift*. Edited with Introduction and Notes by W. A. Eddy (Oxford University Press, 1932), p. 150. Eddy believes that this pamphlet is by Swift, who here 'scores his own literary activities' (ibid., p. 142). The satire, however, is hardly limited to Swift's 'literary activities'; it includes his personality and his religion.

obviously the Epistles of Phalaris, and such discourse is
more appropriate satire on Swift than is talk of the sublime;
but within a page Tim is an irate Master of a College, and
in that role one recognizes Bentley.

The satire is thus made a somewhat inept jumble.
Brief flashes may show genius worthy of the begetters of
Martinus; but for the most part the satire seems too confused and pointless (except as a satire on the Dean) to come
from such as Swift, Pope, Arbuthnot, or Gay. Suppose the
pamphlet was written to satirize Dennis and remade by the
agency of the unscrupulous Moore into a satire on Swift.
Only Pope of the group might be supposed hostile to
Dennis, and Pope had recently made peace with the critic.
At the moment Pope was not likely to attack any one; for
about two weeks before the pamphlet appeared his edition
of Buckingham's *Works* had been suppressed, and it was
consequently no time for Pope to arouse sleeping dogs.
Or suppose that Swift himself is the author and that in the
Memoirs he 'scores his own literary activities'. Certainly
none of the defunct Club would play him such a trick.
Would Swift play such a trick on himself? It seems very
doubtful whether if wishing to 'score his own literary
activities' he would advertise, as the pamphlet does, his
love of abuse and indecency or would jeer at himself by
saying that the world knew 'that his Talent lay more in
sound Divinity than Repartee'. It is probable that some
needy writer, who had heard vaguely about the Club's
project for memoirs of 'Scriblerus', 'forged' this pamphlet
and got Moore to publish it. Without more evidence any
attempt to explain the provenience of the work is mere
guessing.

Such productions are in any case fairly negligible: certainly Pope can hardly be suspected of this advertised
attack on Dennis, which is really an attack on Swift.
Equally negligible if considered aesthetically might seem
to be the epitaphs written by Pope, many of which date
from the early years at Twickenham. The epitaphs, however, enforce the fact, already stated, that most of Pope's

poetry of this period rises out of his varied social connexions. In these years epitaphs and elegiac verses were composed for many deceased friends: Parnell he memorialized in the *Epistle to Oxford*; for Rowe he wrote an epitaph, used later in an expanded form in Westminster Abbey; for friends like the Hon. Simon Harcourt (died June 1720) and Secretary Craggs (died January 1721) and for his distinguished neighbour, Sir Godfrey Kneller (died October 1723), Pope composed dignified and decorous mortuary verses. The epitaph for Sir Godfrey (placed in the Abbey, where Sir Godfrey would not be buried) was, indeed, the result of a death-bed promise, which, so Lady Kneller insisted, included a promise to pull down the monument to Pope's father so as to make room in Twickenham Church for a magnificent monument to Sir Godfrey. Lady Kneller took the matter into the ecclesiastical courts in 1725, but Pope was vindicated and his father's monument left *in situ*. About this time also were composed some beautiful lines for a monument in St. Margaret's, Westminster, for Lady Hotham's daughter, Miss (called Mrs.) Elizabeth Corbet, who died in France, March 1725.[1] Prior (died September 1721) fortunately left his own epitaph, which saved Pope embarrassment, since the Earl of Oxford would have expected one from Pope—and the Duchess of Buckingham and Atterbury would have been annoyed had he written one for Prior. In his later years Pope wrote epitaphs for Fenton, Gay, Atterbury, and other friends. The most concise and celebrated of these efforts is the well-known epigram on Sir Isaac Newton:

> Nature and Nature's laws lay hid in night:
> God said, *Let Newton be!* and all was light.

Pope made a reputation for himself not merely as the author of epitaphs but as one who had a pretty taste in monuments and in epitaphs by others. So he 'corrected' the lines that his friend Miss Judith Cowper wrote for her uncle the Lord Chancellor (died October 1723).[2] He

---

[1] See *Daily Journal*, 11 March 1725.   [2] Elwin-Courthope, ix. 432–3.

advised with Buckingham and Atterbury on the monument to Dryden that the duke planned for the Abbey (1720),[1] and he probably advised Alderman Barber concerning the monument which Barber in 1721 erected in the Abbey to the author of *Hudibras*;[2] he assisted the Duchess of Buckingham with the duke's monument,[3] and in 1727 helped Mrs. Knight with regard to the monument of her brother,[4] Secretary Craggs. Later there were other notable services of this sort, which included membership in the committee (of which Burlington was chairman) on the Abbey monument to Shakespeare.[5] Work on such monuments of public esteem testifies to Pope's reputation as a man of taste; his services to personal friends suggest the remark that if so many came to him for advice in times of bereavement, they probably knew him as a sympathetic friend and not merely as a dangerously witty person.

These employments were not very taxing so far as time or effort was concerned; they were hardly trifling occupations, but they are certainly not major interests. Gardening, on the other hand, became in these years a major interest and employment both at Twickenham and elsewhere. 'Of late', writes Gay concerning Pope in 1723, 'he has talked only as a gardener.'[6] Such talk indicated no suddenly acquired hobby. The skill of his father, at least in practical gardening, may early have influenced the poet; before the removal from Binfield at any rate and very likely before forming any intimate acquaintance with well-known 'gardeners' Pope had shown an interest in the subject in *Guardian* No. 173 (29 September 1713). Ten days before the essay appeared Pope wrote Caryll: 'I am just returned from the country, whither Mr. Rowe did me the favour to accompany me and to pass a week at Binfield.'[7] The first paragraph of the essay seems to reflect this visit,

---

[1] Ibid. ix. 18–19 (August 1720).
[2] The *Weekly Packet*, 1 and 8 July 1721.
[3] Elwin-Courthope, x. 153.   [4] Ibid. ix. 442.
[5] *Gent. Mag.* xi (February 1741), 105.
[6] *Correspondence of Swift* (ed. Ball), iii. 154. Letter of Gay to Swift, 3 February 1723.   [7] Elwin-Courthope, vi. 194.

and suggests the influence of modest, rural Binfield on Pope's conception of what a garden well might be:

> I lately took a particular friend of mine to my house in the country, not without some apprehension, that it could afford little entertainment to a man of his polite taste, particularly in architecture and gardening, who had so long been conversant with all that is beautiful and great in either. But it was a pleasant surprise to me to hear him so often declare he had found in my little retirement that beauty which he always thought wanting in the most celebrated seats (or, if you will, villas) of the nation. This he described to me in those verses with which Martial begins one of his epigrams:—
>
> > Baiana nostri villa, Basse, Faustini,
> > Non otiosis ordinata myrtetis,
> > Viduaque platano, tonsilique buxeto,
> > Ingrata lati spatia detinet campi;
> > Sed rure vero barbaroque laetatur.[1]
>
> There is certainly something in the amiable simplicity of unadorned Nature that spreads over the mind a more noble sort of tranquillity, and a loftier sensation of pleasure, than can be raised from the nicer scenes of art.[2]

Whether Binfield or Martial inspired this doctrine, it was the sort Pope was to preach throughout his lifetime with reference to gardening. When he went on to announce that 'all art consists in imitation and study of Nature',[3] he was saying nothing that would flutter the eyelashes of his contemporaries, but his swift use of the principle in attacking the sculptured evergreens so dear to London and Wise, the royal gardeners of the day, was more startling. It becomes evident at once that if certain tendencies in Pope's early poetry were towards the artificial, other tendencies, in his theory of gardening, were quite averse from that style. In his later pronouncement on gardening and architecture, in the *Epistle to the Earl of Burlington* (1731), he reiterates the ideas expressed in this *Guardian*

---

[1] Martial, 3. 58. 3.   [2] Elwin-Courthope, x. 530.
[3] Ibid., p. 532.

essay, with illustrations which were just but which were unhappily and wrongfully taken as personal.

Horace Walpole[1] has been generous in according Pope credit for important reforms in gardening, and there is perhaps justice in doing so; but Pope had certain notable friends whose views accorded strikingly with his, and the reforms are possibly due to interchange of ideas rather than merely to Pope's originality. It is true, however, that these acquaintances manifested their tastes only at a date later than Pope's paper in the *Guardian*. Among the wealthy patrons of building and gardening who were early friends were Burlington, Bathurst, and Cobham. Acquaintance with Burlington (begun in 1716 or earlier) very likely strengthened Pope's belief in 'amiable simplicity'; for Burlington had come back from an early residence in Italy precociously enthusiastic over the severely plain work of Palladio. Pope and he seem to have agreed in an admiration for Palladio and Inigo Jones as compared with the more elaborate and ornamental manner of Wren. In 1716 his lordship rebuilt Burlington House in a style more austere and distinguished than was common at the moment, and Pope approved. We find him the same summer at Oxford, where Dr. George Clarke showed him Inigo Jones's designs for Whitehall.[2] Pope was already Burlington's neighbour at Chiswick (1716–18), a fact which must have prompted an interchange of ideas on gardening and building. The intimacy of the two is further attested by the fact that Burlington was one of the three noble lords who condescended to become the publishers of the *Dunciad*. Finally, it was to Burlington in 1731 that Pope addressed the epistle 'Of Taste' that dealt notably with building and gardening. Burlington and Pope must have influenced each other as they certainly did the public taste, but Burlington's influence was rather in building and Pope's in landscaping.

A second friend, who possibly should come first, was Allen Bathurst, who in 1712 was one of the Tory dozen raised to

---

[1] 'On Modern Gardening', Walpole's *Works*, ii (1798), 535 ff.
[2] Elwin-Courthope, viii. 23 (29 November 1716).

the peerage.[1] Lord Bathurst's seat at Cirencester was at sight a joy to Pope. He divided the whole summer of 1718 between Stanton Harcourt and Cirencester, and seems at this time to have fallen in love with Bathurst's park. It lacked water, but the high timber was praised as 'the finest wood in England'.[2] The 'bower' in Oakley Wood became speedily known as the poet's favourite spot. In 1720 he wrote to his friend the Hon. Robert Digby of Sherborne (whose seat he later viewed with such delight)[3] of 'the Elysian groves of Cirencester, whither, I could say almost in the style of a sermon, the Lord bring us all, &c. Thither may we tend, by various ways, to one blissful bower'.[4] A year later he writes to Lady Mary Wortley Montagu 'of the noble scenes, openings, and avenues, of this immense design at Cirencester. No words, nor painting, nor poetry (not even your own), can give the least image proportionable to it.'[5] It is probable that during this visit of 1721 Pope and Bathurst exchanged ideas on the improvements of the latter's park which were then in process.[6] In general his love of Cirencester indicates a love of prospects seen at the end of shaded vistas and a fondness for natural disposition of shade rather than for arrangements of formal alleys and square, balanced effects.[7]

The friend whose building and planting was most magnificent was Sir Richard Temple, who in 1718 was created Viscount Cobham in recognition of sound Whig principle and of military distinction. Cobham's real achievement was the house and magnificent gardens at Stowe. Plans of Vanbrugh, Gibbs, Bridgeman, Kent, and 'Capability' Brown assisted him, and the result placed Stowe at the very acme of fame in its day. In his *Epistle to Burlington* Pope urges upon that peer the necessity of consulting the 'genius

---

[1] Since he was Baron Bathurst until 1772 (then Earl), he is in this work called 'Lord Bathurst', as all of his friends in Pope's time styled him.

[2] Elwin-Courthope, ix. 80. [3] Ibid. ix. 300–1. [4] Ibid. ix. 75.

[5] Ibid. ix. 415.

[6] Ibid. ix. 30 (27 September 1721).

[7] Pope talked interestingly to Spence about gardens; see Spence, pp. 12, 209–10, 260, &c.

of the place', of being moderate in adorning nature, and
compliments Stowe for its dazzling quality:

> Still follow sense, of every art the soul,
> Parts answering parts shall slide into a whole,
> Spontaneous beauties all around advance,
> Start ev'n from difficulty, strike from chance;
> Nature shall join you; Time shall make it grow
> A work to wonder at—perhaps a Stowe.[1]

As this passage indicates, Stowe was to Pope a *ne plus ultra*.
'If anything under Paradise', he wrote to his friend John
Knight,[2] 'could set me beyond earthly cogitations, Stowe
might do it.' Probably it was not so much the numberless
statues, columns, arches, obelisks, or towers sprinkling
Cobham's woods and lawns that delighted Pope as it was
the endless variety of pictorial effect in which monumental
stone and natural verdure blended with careful art. Stowe
had the lakes that Cirencester lacked; in fact, Stowe had
everything. This estate confirmed Pope in the doctrine
that from the start he had preached: landscape was to be
picturesque and not too obviously formalized; this effect
was to be secured by more or less irregular arrangement of
lawn and shrubbery or wood interspersed with contrasting
ornament of stone or bronze. Obviously in Pope's own
practice the scale must differ in magnificence from that
on which his noble friends built and planted, and it is
not impossible that the multiplicity of effects at Stowe
influenced Pope to a regrettable multiplicity of miniature
effects at Twickenham.

Among the professional landscape gardeners and archi-
tects with whom Pope was intimate must be named Charles
Bridgeman and William Kent. It is possible also that when
in 1718 Pope contemplated building in London, James
Gibbs was his chosen architect.[3] Bridgeman he knew first,
and, according to Walpole, it was through Bridgeman that
Pope's ideas gained currency. In 1725 Bridgeman and
Pope visited the Earl of Oxford at Down Hall, and Pope

---

[1] Lines 65–70. [2] Elwin-Courthope, ix. 448.
[3] Ibid. ix. 291 n., 518.

opposed Gibbs's plans for remodelling the house, which
Oxford had acquired at Prior's death. Bridgeman and
Kent both advised Cobham at Stowe, and probably aided
Bathurst as well. Kent was brought back from Italy by
Burlington in 1719, and the Earl was his patron from that
time on. Pope to the end of his life was intimate with Kent,
who developed the gardening principles of Bridgeman even
to the point of mannerism. Kent's 'ruling principle', wrote
Walpole, 'was, that *nature abhors a straight line*'.[1] And it
was in reaction against such views that Walpole exclaimed:
'Methinks a straight canal is as rational at least as a mean-
dering bridge.'[2] One judges from the *Plan of Mr. Pope's
Garden*, 1745, that Pope's antipathy to straight lines, while
noticeable, was by no means so extreme as Kent's.

These peers and gardeners form the environment in
which Pope worked; whether they influenced him more
than he them is possibly doubtful. In his own application
of his or their principles to his grounds at Twickenham
Pope was forced above all to consult in no esoteric fashion
the 'genius of the place'. His house had two stories, with
a central hall or gallery, on each side of which were two
small parlours. It faced the Thames, and being situated
on a bend of the river commanded a fine view both up
stream and down. Between the river and the house was an
unadorned lawn—floods made any 'gay parterre' imprac-
ticable on this front. Close behind the house ran the high-
road from Hampton Court to London, and on the upper
side of this road lay the five acres that were to be Pope's
gardens. From this division of the 'estate' came as a convenience the passage under the road, which Pope called
his 'grotto'. In the language of Dr. Johnson: 'Pope's
excavation was requisite as an entrance to his garden, and,
as some men try to be proud of their defects, he extracted
an ornament from an inconvenience, and vanity produced
a grotto where necessity enforced a passage.'[3]

Work on such various 'improvements' must have started

---

[1] Walpole's *Works*, ii (1798), 539.   [2] Ibid., p. 533.
[3] *Lives of the Poets*, ed. Hill, iii. 135.

as soon as Pope leased the villa. Talk of himself as a retired poet was joined with plans for his garden. Of certain friends he writes to Broome, 16 February 1718/19:

They will find me a mere old fellow at their return hither, pursuing very innocent pleasures, building, planting, and gardening. Study and amours are two vanities I have utterly left off.[1]

Months later he seems to have written to Jervas—though the letter as printed by him is an amalgam, and is misdated —of his transformation into an architect.

But I must own, when you talk of building and planting, you touch my string; and I am as apt to pardon you, as the fellow that thought himself Jupiter would have pardoned the other madman who called himself his brother Neptune. Alas, sir, do you know whom you talk to? one that has been a poet, was degraded to a translator, and, at last, through mere dulness, is turned an architect. You know Martial's censure, *Praeconem facito vel architectum.* However, I have one way left to plan, to elevate, and to surprise, as Bayes says. The next news you may expect to hear, is that I am in debt.

The history of my transplantation and settlement, which you desire, would require a volume were I to enumerate the many projects, difficulties, vicissitudes, and various fates attending that important part of my life: much more, should I describe the many draughts, elevations, profiles, perspectives, &c., of every palace and garden proposed, intended, and happily raised, by the strength of that faculty wherein all great geniuses excel, imagination. At last, the gods and fate have fixed me on the borders of the Thames, in the districts of Richmond and Twickenham. It is here I have passed an entire year of my life, without any fixed abode in London, or more than casting a transitory glance (for a day or two at most in a month) on the pomps of the town. It is here I hope to receive you, sir, returned from eternizing the Ireland of this age. For you my structures rise; for you my colonnades extend their wings; for you my groves aspire, and roses bloom.[2]

About the time this passage should have gone to Jervas, Pope wrote to Caryll of his vast deal of labour with masons and gardeners and of his difficulties over the taxes on

---

[1] Elwin-Courthope, viii. 42.   [2] Ibid. viii. 26–7.

Catholics.[1] The spring of 1720 found him remodelling the house and rejoicing in its surroundings:

Our river glitters beneath an unclouded sun, at the same time that its banks retain the verdure of showers; our gardens are offering their first nosegays; our trees, like new acquaintance brought happily together, are stretching their arms to meet each other, and growing nearer and nearer every hour; the birds are paying their thanksgiving songs for the new habitations I have made them: my building rises high enough to attract the eye and curiosity of the passenger from the river, where, upon beholding a mixture of beauty and ruin, he inquires what house is falling, or what church is rising? So little taste have our common Tritons of Vitruvius; whatever delight the poetical gods of the river may take, in reflecting on their streams, my Tuscan porticos, or Ionic pilasters.[2]

The autumn—after the South Sea Bubble had burst!—found him still 'encompassed by workmen',[3] and December brought a flood that quite covered his grass plot before the house.[4] During it he wrote the sprightly Teresa Blount that his house was 'exactly like Noah's ark, in everything except that there is no propagation of species in it.' He continues:

The prospect is prodigiously fine. It is just like an arm of the sea; and the flood over my grass-plot, embraced between the two walls whose tops are only seen, looks like an open bay to the terrace. The opposite meadow, where you so often walked, is covered with sails; and, not to flatter you, I believe the flowers in it next spring will be rather attributed to the production of the waters, than of your footsteps, which will be very unpoetical after all. We see a new river behind Kingston, which was never beheld before; and that our own house may not be void of wonders, we pump up gudgeons, through the pipe in the kitchen, with our water.[5]

The celebrated grotto, parent of so many similar artificialities, was ready for visitors in the summer of 1722. He wrote of it to Broome in July and in the autumn sent Mrs. Judith Cowper some sentimental verses about it.[6] This toy was constantly his care until in his later years he had made it something like a geological museum (shades of

---

[1] Elwin-Courthope, vi. 271.   [2] Ibid. ix. 72.   [3] Ibid. vi. 273.
[4] Ibid. vi. 275.   [5] Ibid. ix. 299.   [6] Ibid. viii. 56; ix. 420–1.

Dr. Woodward!). Its earlier state is most fully described in a letter to Edward Blount, 2 June 1725:

Let the young ladies [Blount's daughters] be assured I make nothing new in my gardens without wishing to see the print of their fairy steps in every part of them. I have put the last hand to my works of this kind, in happily finishing the subterraneous way and grotto. I there found a spring of the clearest water, which falls in a perpetual rill, that echoes through the cavern day and night. From the river Thames, you see through my arch up a walk of the wilderness, to a kind of open temple, wholly composed of shells in the rustic manner; and from that distance under the temple you look down through a sloping arcade of trees, and see the sails on the river passing suddenly and vanishing as through a perspective glass. When you shut the doors of this grotto it becomes on the instant, from a luminous room, a *Camera obscura*, on the walls of which all the objects of the river, hills, woods, and boats, are forming a moving picture in their visible radiations; and when you have a mind to light it up, it affords you a very different scene. It is finished with shells interspersed with pieces of looking-glass in angular forms; and in the ceiling is a star of the same material, at which when a lamp, of an orbicular figure of thin alabaster, is hung in the middle, a thousand pointed rays glitter, and are reflected over the place. There are connected to this grotto by a narrower passage two porches with niches and seats,—one towards the river of smooth stones, full of light, and open; the other towards the arch of trees, rough with shells, flints, and iron-ore. The bottom is paved with simple pebble, as the adjoining walk up the wilderness to the temple is to be cockle-shells, in the natural taste, agreeing not ill with the little dripping murmur, and the aquatic idea of the whole place. It wants nothing to complete it but a good statue with an inscription, like that beautiful antique one which you know I am so fond of:—

> *Hujus Nympha loci, sacri custodia fontis,*
> *Dormio, dum blandæ sentio murmur aquæ.*
> *Parce meum, quisquis tangis cava marmora, somnum*
> *Rumpere; sive bibas, sive lavere, tace.*

> Nymph of the grot, these sacred springs I keep,
> And to the murmur of these waters sleep;
> Ah, spare my slumbers, gently tread the cave!
> And drink in silence, or in silence lave!

You will think I have been very poetical in this description, but it is pretty near the truth. I wish you were here to bear testimony how little it owes to art, either the place itself, or the image I give of it.[1]

One can hardly help thinking that if the 'little, dripping murmur' soothed the poet, 'the aquatic idea of the whole place' must have been bad for his rheumatism. That seems to have been Dr. Johnson's feeling. For Pope, however, his grotto was his pride. As late as 1741 he invited Sarah Duchess of Marlborough, then aged 81, to 'see (for you must see) my grotto'.

What then does your Grace think of bringing me back in your coach about five, and supping there, now the moonlight favours your return. . . .[2]

But the grotto was not the only source of satisfaction in Pope's grounds. The long description, just quoted, indicates that already the 'wilderness' which secluded the garden from the highway and the shell temple at the end of the walk from the grotto were in existence. Another 'feature' added early (and later apparently removed) is recorded in March 1726 in a letter to Oxford in which Pope announces: 'I have just turfed a little Bridgmannic theatre myself. It was done by a detachment of his [Bridgeman's] workmen from the Prince's, all at a stroke, and it is yet unpaid for, but that is nothing with a poetical genius.'[3] Other ornamental details were introduced before 1726, and except for his mother's monument and the 'mount', very probably the place looked in 1726 much as it did in 1745 when the 'Plan' was published. From Pope's description of the grotto as well as from the 'Plan' one can see the curious blend of the 'natural', the 'rough', and the artificial that his taste had evolved. The 'little Bridgmannic theatre' illustrates his love of miniature, toy-like effects, which, with his delight in 'pleasing intricacies', introduced much of artifice into his grounds. That he had some realization

---

[1] Elwin-Courthope, vi. 383-4.   [2] Ibid. v. 410.
[3] Ibid. viii. 222.

of this vice is apparent in his playful account to the Earl of Strafford:

> I am as busy in three inches of gardening as any man can be in threescore acres. I fancy myself like the fellow that spent his life in cutting ye twelve apostles in one cherry stone. I have a Theatre, an Arcade, a Bowling-green, a Grove, & what not? in a bit of ground that would have been but a plate of sallet to Nebuchadnezzar, the first day he was turnd to graze.[1]

Obviously gardening was for Pope a source of self-expression and joy, and he succeeded in being 'different' from other gardeners of his day: in talking even of his vegetable garden one spoke of such 'hard names to spell' as 'brocoli' and 'fenochio'.[2] With success came reputation and requests from friends for assistance on their gardens. From 1718 Bathurst and Pope had conversed on their individual projects; in 1719 Pope was consulted about the gardens of the Prince of Wales at Richmond Lodge[3]— gardens which Bridgeman was laying out and which, so Walpole says, imitated or paralleled Pope's effects. There was at least a grotto. Another achievement for Pope (with Bathurst's aid this time) was the garden of Marble Hill, the villa which royalty was erecting for Mrs. Howard (the Countess of Suffolk) in Twickenham. While at Sherborne, enjoying Digby's grounds, Pope wrote to Martha Blount:

> . . . do not let any lady . . . imagine that my head is so full of any gardens as to forget hers. The greatest proof I could give her to the contrary is, that I have spent many hours here in studying for hers, and in drawing new plans for her.[4]

In September (1724) he says, 'My head is still more upon Mrs. Hd and her works, than upon my own.' At Christmas, 1725, Pope and Bridgeman were visiting the Earl of Oxford to advise him on the improvement of Down Hall.[5] Other gardens, specified by Walpole[6] as imitative of Pope's grounds, are those of the Prince of Wales at Carlton House

---

[1] Ibid. x. 183. [2] Ibid. ix. 87. [3] Ibid. viii. 328.
[4] Ibid. ix. 304–5, 102. [5] Ibid. viii. 216–17. [6] Op. cit. ii. 538.

and those of General Dormer at Rousham. These were the work of Pope's friend Kent. Since Pope's planting became thus a model for gardens of modest size the chances are that his influence was even more widespread than this account indicates. His reputation in this field was at its height when Bolingbroke in 1725 returned from exile to settle at Dawley Farm, Uxbridge, where for about a dozen years he posed as the farmer-philosopher. It would be interesting to know if Pope's and Martial's admiration for *rus verum barbarumque* affected the gardens at Dawley.

The pleasantest occupation Pope had in the trying years when his literary labours included the astonishing array of projects realized in the years 1722–7, was gardening. It was an elegant as well as engrossing amusement, and brought many distinguished visitors to his house—though fewer than found their way in later decades to near-by Strawberry Hill. It kept the poet in contact with the 'best people', and out of conflict with the scribblers of Grub Street.

The social environment of Twickenham was pleasant and varied. Although few of Pope's closest friends lived there, he had there for a brief period the companionship of Craggs; Fortescue was at Richmond within walking distance; and after 1724 Mrs. Howard was at Marble Hill, where Martha Blount paid frequent visits. In the same year that saw Marble Hill rise, Bolingbroke settled a few miles away at Dawley Farm, where he resided intermittently until 1739. There were other interesting neighbours in Twickenham itself, with whom Pope was at least casually acquainted. Such were the Duke of Wharton ('the scorn and wonder of our days'), Sir Godfrey Kneller, Sir Clement Cotterell[1] (Master of Ceremonies, and a notable antiquarian), Nathaniel Pigott (the Catholic attorney), Secretary James Johnstone (a cousin of Bishop Burnet, and a practical gardener, who very likely smiled at Pope's toy-garden), and the Countess of Seaforth, who was the mother of Lady Mary Caryll.

[1] Sir Clement was brother-in-law to Sir William Trumbull.

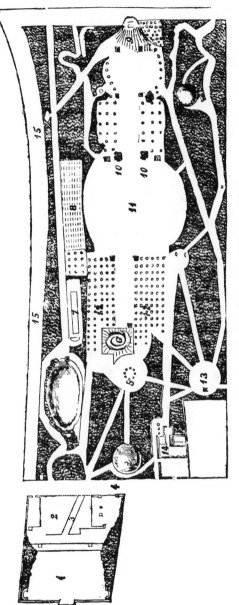

THE PLAN OF POPE'S GARDEN AND GROTTO

by J. SEARLE, his Gardener

1. The Grass Plat before the House next the Thames.
2. The House.
3. The Underground Passage or Grotto.
4. The Road from Hampton Court to London.
5. The Shell Temple.
6. The Large Mount.
7. The Stoves.
8. The Vineyard.
9. The Obelisk in Memory of his Mother.
10. Two Small Mounts.
11. The Bowling Green.
12. The Grove.
13. The Orangery.
14. The Garden House.
15. Kitchen Garden.

The situation of the village in convenient proximity to either Richmond or Hampton Court, brought to it many transient residents, place-holders or place-seekers, hangers-on at Court of all sorts. Among these were Gyllenborg, the Swedish ambassador, and, for a few years after their return from Constantinople, the Wortley Montagus. The air of the village was thought salubrious, and in 1720 attracted thither, as a guest of Pope and his mother, the beautiful and then convalescent Molly Lepel. It was evidently a popular place for summer residence; for in October 1730[1] Pope writes of the departure of his 'fair-weather friends of the summer', and we know that in the summer of 1721 three of the most luminous 'stars' from the opera lived there—Buononcini, Senesino, and Anastasia Robinson. The last was certainly a friend of Pope's, and one judges that he also esteemed Buononcini, since among the subscribers to that musician's *Cantate*, 1721, we find the poet's name and that of the Duchess of Buckingham, which last Pope had put down without consulting her Grace.[2] Many other friends of Pope are among the subscribers. His 'great room' or gallery was doubtless the scene of more than one concert that summer. Presently in September he rambled off to Cirencester without having transferred a harpsichord, promised to Lady Mary Wortley Montagu, from his gallery to her house. In fact, finding that he was not permitted to lend it to her from his house, he suggests that she hold her concerts in his room, which he hopes he may be permitted to lend. He apologizes ingenuously as 'a beast'; but Lady Mary had evidently counted on that harpsichord.

Concerts and gaieties were probably the exception in Pope's villa. His parties, for many reasons, would not be like Prior's, for example, about one of which Prior wrote to Harley: 'It was a conversation about five o'clock, a disputation towards seven, and a bear-garden about ten.' The presence of his mother would restrain old friends; for, according to tradition, a single excessively gross remark by

[1] Elwin-Courthope, vii. 441.   [2] Ibid. x. 154.

the distinguished stranger, Voltaire,[1] drove her from the table. Usually we should imagine Pope entertaining in the elegant fashion later praised by Lord Orrery:

... he treated his friends with a politeness that charmed, and a generosity that was much to his honour. Every guest was made happy within his doors. Pleasure dwelt under his roof, and elegance presided at his table.[2]

Perhaps the great seasons in this first part of Pope's career were 1726 and 1727, when Jonathan Swift himself was a guest; but in 1726 the deafness of Swift, the rheumatism of Pope, and the illness of his mother conspired against sociability. 'There is nobody with me', he writes Fortescue, 'but the Dean of St. Patrick's, who would hardly be here if he were not the best-natured and indulgent man I know; it is so melancholy a way of passing his time.'[3] In 1727, after a long visit, Swift wrote: 'I am very uneasy here, because so many of our acquaintance come to see us, and I cannot be seen; besides Mr. Pope is too sickly and complaisant, therefore I resolve to go somewhere else.'[4] There were, meanwhile, reunions at least with Arbuthnot, Bolingbroke, Congreve, and Gay, and much talk of projects past and to come. Upon his sudden return to Ireland in 1726 the Dean takes to dreaming:

... I can every night distinctly see Twitenham and the Grotto, and Dawley, and Mrs. Blount, and many other et ceteras, and it is but three nights since I beat Mrs. Pope.[5]

One pictures the Dean and his eighty-six-year-old opponent —would it be at backgammon? At any rate her revenge was, so he said, to pray for his conversion to the Roman Church. 'I pray God bless her,' is his return, 'for I am sure

[1] E. Audra, L'Influence française dans l'œuvre de Pope (Paris, 1931), p. 76.

[2] John Earl of Orrery, Remarks on the Life and Writings of Dr. Jonathan Swift (2nd ed., 1752), pp. 145–6.

[3] Elwin-Courthope, ix. 108 (16 May [1726]).

[4] Swift Correspondence (ed. Ball), iii. 410 (12 August 1727).

[5] Elwin-Courthope, vii. 72. The dates of the Pope-Swift letters of 1726 and 1727 were evidently inaccurately set down. In 1741 this letter was printed with the date 'Oct. 30, 1727'. Elwin-Courthope and Ball (Swift Correspondence, iii. 334) would date the letter August 1726.

she is a good Christian, and, which is almost as rare, a good woman.'

Not all the details of Pope's life were so tranquil as these days spent diversely among his garden, his friends, his books, and his illnesses. There were discordant elements rising sometimes from his literary ventures and increasingly from his personal reputation. One seems to note in his letters that the deeper he gets into the mire about the *Odyssey*, the more he protests the tenderness of his honour and honesty. These protests may arise from sense of guilt, but one imagines his honour was really touched, for example, by gossip about himself and 'Patty' Blount. It is possible that even from Binfield days the grandparents (Englefields) of Martha and Teresa had some reservations concerning the intimacy of the girls with Pope, but these could hardly have been serious. After 1718 Pope's relations with the sisters were somewhat clarified, and it was understood that Martha and not Teresa was the object of his deepest affection. If Pope's 'carcase' had not been so crazy and insignificant and if Martha Blount had not been so tall and stately, one imagines they might have married. The poet evidently felt that marriage would simply make them both ridiculous, and he was very likely right in so thinking. In 1717 when Lord Harcourt suggested a match between the poet and a beautiful, if impecunious, relative of his lordship's, Pope replied that 'it was what he [Harcourt] could never have thought of, if it had not been his misfortune to be blind; and what I could never think of, while I had eyes to see both her and myself'.[1] It is significant that the person to whom he writes thus is Martha Blount herself. Whether she was Pope's mistress is now nobody's business; no evidence of the slightest validity, apart from the unusualness of their friendship, has ever been adduced to indicate such a relationship. Of course they lived in the eighteenth century, but that fact is hardly evidence.

This affair becomes our business only because it was gossip in this period of Pope's life and later. In September

[1] Elwin-Courthope, ix. 277.

1722 Pope denies to Broome rumours of his approaching marriage:

Your report of my quitting, or being in the least inclined to quit, the easy, single state I now enjoy, is altogether groundless; as idle, as the news which people invent, merely because they are idle.[1]

Three years later rumours still persisted; for we find two ladies corresponding at that time, one of whom says: 'The marriage of Mr. Pope and Patty Blount (who, I fancy, you must remember about town) [I] was a little surprised at, till I heard he was rich.'[2] That this harmless but annoying story of a secret marriage persisted for the rest of Pope's life is evident from a letter of his early friend, Molly Lepel, who as Lady Hervey was naturally less friendly after Pope quarrelled with her husband. After Pope's death she commented, in this letter, on the 'illegal delicacy' of his will, referring, it is thought, to the fact that he left his property to *Miss Martha Blount* when the person intended was legally Mrs. Alexander Pope.[3]

Inevitably not all the gossip about this affair would include matrimony. In a letter to Caryll, 25 December 1725, Pope gives a summary of this viler gossip, which it is only fair to quote at some length. He has been talking of slanders about the *Odyssey*, wishes he had nothing to trouble him more, makes some reflections upon scandal-mongers, and then continues:

I have had an occasion to make these reflections of late, much juster than from anything that concerns my writings, for it is one that concerns my morals, and,—which I ought to be as tender of as my own,—the good character of another very innocent person, who I am sure shares your friendship no less than I do. You, too, are brought into the story so falsely, that I think it but just to appeal against the injustice to yourself singly, as a full and worthy judge and evidence too. A very confident asseveration has been

---

[1] Elwin-Courthope, viii. 59.

[2] *Hist. MSS. Comm.: First Report* (1870), p. 51. Carruthers in his *Life of Pope* (1858: p. 388) quotes a letter from Mr. L. Schrader (tutor to the Prince of Wales) to Martha Blount. On the matter of this supposed match between Pope and Miss Blount, Schrader wrote: 'You once told me that no such thing could ever happen.'

[3] *Letters of Mary Lepel, Lady Hervey* (London, 1821), p. 68.

made, which has spread over the town, that your god-daughter, Miss Patty, and I, lived two or three years since in a manner that was reported to you as giving scandal to many; that upon your writing to me upon it, I consulted with her, and sent you an excusive alleviating answer, but did, after that, privately and of myself, write to you a full confession how much I myself disapproved the way of life, and owning the prejudice done her, charging it on herself, and declaring that I wished to break off what I acted against my conscience, &c.; and that she, being at the same time spoken to by a lady of your acquaintance at your instigation, did absolutely deny to alter any part of her conduct, were it ever so disreputable or exceptionable. Upon this villainous lying tale, it is farther added by the same hand, that I brought her acquainted with a noble lord, and into an intimacy with some others, merely to get quit of her myself, being moved in consciousness by what you and I had conferred together, and playing this base part to get off.

You will bless yourself at so vile a wickedness, who very well, I dare say, remember the truth of what then passed, and the satisfaction you expressed I gave you (and Mrs. Caryll also expressed the same thing to her kinswoman) upon that head. God knows upon what motives anyone should malign a sincere and virtuous friendship. I wish those very people had never led her into anything more liable to objection, or more dangerous to a good mind, than I hope my conversation or kindness are. She has in reality had less of it these two years past, than ever since I knew her; and truly when she has it, it is almost wholly a preachment, which I think necessary, against the ill consequences of another sort of company which they [her mother and sister?], by their good will, would always keep; and she, in compliance and for quiet's sake, keeps more than you or I could wish.[1]

'The truth of what then passed' in 1722 or 1723 when Caryll and his wife spoke plainly or inquiringly to Pope and Miss Blount about their relations would be far more interesting than this account of what some individual had written by way of scandal about the affair. Fortunately at Mapledurham is preserved what seems certainly to be Mrs. Caryll's letter in reply to Martha Blount's defence of her conduct. It is a letter addressed to Miss Blount in

[1] Elwin-Courthope, vi. 287–8.

Bolton Street, Piccadilly, signed E. Caryll, and dated 'March 15', with no year. The part concerning the affair in question is as follows:

> Nothing Could be more kind then ye way of y^r expressing my takeing no notice of what had given you so much trouble, and uneasynes. I owne to you I had heard a good deal of what the pratting part of ye world had Babbled about, but never gave any more ear to itt, then to ye Wind, but when I found my owne Dear, tooke Something to heart, in good Earnest, y^t related to ye two in ye world he heartily Loves, and wishes so well to, I began to examine more about it. Then he told me all y^t his friend had imparted to him, wch was so highly to y^r Credict [*sic*], and Co-m̄endation, that itt Caused no Change in my thoughts about the matter, and I realy was glad that you had had such a friend in ye world, nor can I ever hope, that any thing should Change him from ever being so to you. I am so far convinced of his honour, and worth, joined wth his good understanding, that should all ye peevish, ill will or passionat mallice in ye world invent all y^t Lay in them it would in no kind ever make me have ye least thought of what I could wish othere wayes as to y^r friendships. I am heartily sorry itt has given you so much uneasynes, and hope you may enjoy ye Comfort of being happy friends, w^thout any grounds for ye most malicious to Lay hold on. . . .

This letter certainly shows the satisfaction on Mrs. Caryll's part that Pope mentions in his letter just quoted, and tends to support the face value of that letter.

The hand that penned 'this villainous lying' tale has not been identified.[1] It is true that Pope's 'morals' had been impugned and that Eliza Haywood had in one of her scandal chronicles tried to tarnish the name of Miss Blount, but the particular libel described by Pope remains to be uncovered. Two other pamphlets, however, may serve to indicate (with Pope's letter) the trend of the scandal. The first is the *Life of the late Celebrated Mrs. Elizabeth Wisebourn, Vulgarly call'd Mother Wybourn*, which was advertised for sale by A. Moore in May 1721. The Publisher's Preface to *An Author to be Let*, 1732, ascribes the work to

---

[1] It may be gossip rather than printed libel to which Pope refers, but the phrase 'the same hand' *implies* a written attack.

Richard Morley.[1] Mother Wybourn was apparently an actual bawd who had died in 1720, and this *Life* is a veiled scandal against many prominent persons (chiefly Tories?) who are represented as having frequented her establishment. Two passages relating to Pope will serve to show the absurd vileness of Morley's methods. Monavaria, described as natural born, her husband not dead a year, may stand for the Duchess of Buckingham. This newly made widow is alleged to have an affair with her Doctor.[2]

The *Doctor's* only Rival, if (which is much doubted) he has really any, is a Poet, who is as eminent for his Person as his *Genius*; his *Form* is the best Index of his *Mind*; nor can the Drawings of Sir *Godfrey Kneller*, or *Dahl*, give one so just an Idea of the former, as *that it self* does of the latter: If *Monavaria* does now and then scatter some of her Favours upon him, it must be only to appease the *Manes* of her Husband; he was his *Friend* when he was living, and therefore ought to be consider'd as his *Representative* now he is dead.[3]

One other typical passage may be quoted concerning a nameless member of Mother Wybourn's 'Society':

Perhaps it would be thought an Injustice to her Memory, to pass over unspoke of, so shining an Ornament of this Society as that Lady once was, who stabb'd herself in the *Nunnery*, into which she was forc'd by the *Cruelty* of her *Relations*, for the Love of Mr. *P—pe*, whom I have already mention'd in the Account of *Monavaria* and the *Doctor*; as he himself relates it in a Poem of his, under the Title of *Verses to the Memory of an unfortunate Lady*: However, the Cause of her Death, I will venture to say, almost atones for the Sin of it; his *Person* is as amiable as his *Muse* and certainly not to be seen by *any of the Sex* without some fatal effect; especially if big with Child, as this Lady was before she enter'd into a Vow for the *Conservation* of her Chastity.[4]

This pamphlet shows the general impugning of Pope's morals; a work that comes closer to the supposed Pope-Blount affair is Eliza Haywood's *Memoirs of a certain Island*

[1] By 'Anodyne Tanner, M.D.', according to the title-page. Pope (or Savage) ascribes it to Dick Morley in *An Author to be Let*, 8vo ed., leaf [C³]ʳ. Morley also wrote, we are told here, for the 'Weekly Journals'.

[2] Dr. Chamberlen was said to be the Duchess's lover: she put up a monument to him in the Abbey.   [3] p. 33.   [4] p. 44.

adjacent to the Kingdom of Utopia, volume i of which was dated 1725 but published in September 1724.[1] This shameless scandal chronicle tells among other tales the 'Story of the Enchanted Well'; that is, of the South Sea Bubble. In this story Marthalia (indicated in the Key as 'Mrs. Bl—t') is the mistress of, among others, Lucitario (= Craggs). She was, the story goes, formerly in tatters and quite shameless and despised. Now she has married 'an old servant of the Necromancer's'; he is diseased, and she manages his estate.[2]

. . . she is now caress'd by those, whose Servants once despised her, and the Footman, who could not formerly be prevailed on to take her in his Arms, sees her now in his Master's, and lights him to that Bed, he would not once have ventured to go into himself—so strangely does a little Pomp influence the Minds and Affections of Mankind!—But there are some who of late have severely repented trusting themselves in her Embraces, and cursed the artificial Sweets and Perfumes, which hindred them from discovering those Scents, that would have been infallible Warnings of what they might expect in such polluted Sheets.—But I can no longer endure to look upon her—the Object is too foul . . . .[3]

Such a story involving Mrs. Marthalia Bl—t and Craggs, who is Lucitario the Necromancer, and the 'old servant of the Necromancer's' (could Pope be intended?) is wild enough to be disregarded, but vile enough to outrage the sensibilities of any lover, however Platonic. *Memoirs of a certain Island*, had it been Mrs. Haywood's only offence against Pope and his friends, would have demanded punishment from him. Three years later came the revenge in Book ii of the *Dunciad*; a revenge merciless and indecent; but one must admit a certain propriety in talking to such authors in the language in which they think. More pity has been wasted on Mrs. Haywood than her character

---

[1] Volume ii is advertised in the *Evening Post*, 26 October 1725—with a new edition of volume i. Not all copies contain the Key. It is in the British Museum copy, at the end of volume i (press-mark 12613 g. 18).

[2] Sir John Blount was a South Sea director, and his wife might be partly the object of this slander; but her name was neither Martha nor 'Marthalia'. Nor would she be called 'Mrs.' properly in the Key.

[3] p. 13.

warrants; for no one has ever believed that the lady to whom Pope in 1723 addressed the 'preachment' called 'To Mrs. M. B. on her Birthday' did or could ever give cause for such a libel as Mrs. Haywood's.

Again Pope faced substantially the same life-problem that had bothered him in the years at Chiswick. Should he sever diplomatic relations with this raucous, jeering republic of letters and devote himself to being an *honnête homme*, a celebrated gardener, amateur architect, and genteel antiquarian, or should he sound his trumpets, march valiantly against the walls of Dullness and Scandal in full faith that in any direct encounter genius must triumph over stupidity? One could tolerate, had tolerated, attacks on one's works and on one's person, but ought attacks by thoroughly worthless people on one's morals, and attacks involving one's dearest friends, to be allowed to perpetrate themselves with no retort?

The answer to such questioning was possibly as obvious as it now seems, and during his first few years at Twickenham Pope at least inclined to the plan of retiring from the noise and smoke of literature. He had examples of retirement in Congreve and in Bolingbroke, and there was in him at this time an anticipation of the principle of Candide: *Il faut cultiver notre jardin*—and shun all scribblers. There was an element of pose in this attitude, which many Tory friends had assumed plaintively after the catastrophe of Queen Anne's death. The pose became rather more apparent when Bolingbroke somewhat surprisingly adopted it upon his pardon in 1723. Swift comments (20 September 1723) on the affection of Pope and Bolingbroke for the retired life somewhat bluntly:

I have no very strong faith in you pretenders to retirement. You are not of an age for it, nor have gone through either good or bad fortune enough to go into a corner, and form conclusions *de contemptu mundi et fugâ saeculi*,—unless a poet grows weary of too much applause, as ministers do of too much weight of business.[1]

Pope had received early training in lip-service to retirement

---

[1] Elwin-Courthope, vii. 45–6.

through association with Sir William Trumbull, and even from his father; in the case of Bolingbroke the ideas, though now fixed, must have been somewhat less familiar. It is consequently amusing to find St. John retorting in kind upon the Dean two years after Swift's letter:

Pope and you are very great wits, and I think very indifferent philosophers. If you despised the world as much as you pretend, and perhaps believe, you would not be so angry with it. The founder of your sect,[1] that noble original whom you think it so great an honour to resemble, was a slave to the worst part of the world, to the court. . . . I should blush alike to be discovered fond of the world, or piqued at it.[2]

The pique of Pope and Swift seems, however, fully as natural as, if less rational than, this somewhat too lofty indifference of Bolingbroke. As he admits, Pope and Swift 'perhaps believed' that their contempt of society, or of phases of society, was sincere.

Some of Pope's expressions of love for retirement seem so little warranted or credible that he certainly would not have stated them so baldly if he had not *at the moment* sincerely felt them. As early as 1714, when in the eyes of the world his career was but beginning, he writes Caryll that 'long habit and wearisomeness of the same track' will, when Homer is done, cause his retirement: 'Homer will work a cure upon me.'[3] This is the same sort of *naïveté* that caused him in boyhood to notify his friends of his approaching demise. His bad health was, of course, another force in making quiet attractive, and he early recognized an incompatibility between his physique and that of the town.

I should make you a very long and extraordinary apology for having so long been silent, if I were to tell you in what a wild, distracted, amused, hurried state both my mind and body have been ever since my coming to this town. A good deal of it is so odd, that it would hardly find credit; and more so perplexed that it would move pity in you when you reflect how naturally people of my turn love quiet, and how much my present studies require

---

[1] Seneca [Pope's note].   [2] Elwin-Courthope, vii. 67–8.
[3] Ibid. vi. 214.

ease. In a word, the world and I agree as ill, as my soul and body, my appetites and constitution, my books and business.[1]

There is always this antagonism: his constitution demands quiet, but his appetites are too various and importunate. When the demands of his constitution triumph, he retires to Twickenham, 'water gruel, and Palladio.'[2] His appetites were social, and they kept his constitution only too busy. 'Two fits of the headache make me a philosopher at any time',[3] he writes to Broome. In June 1716 he is most philosophical about the new-found tranquillity of Chiswick;[4] six weeks later he boasts of and regrets at once his active life:

I have been here in a constant course of entertainment and visits ever since I saw you, which I partly delight in, and partly am tired with; the common case in all pleasures. I have not dined at home these fifteen days, and perfectly regret the quiet indolence, silence, and sauntering that made up my whole life in Windsor Forest.[5]

These are quite natural reactions, and one should hesitate to assert that either one is purely a pose.

In fact, though Pope's poetry shows relatively little of it, there can be no doubt that he had a genuine love for country scenes and country quiet, as well as for London. His gardening and his letters both indicate an unsuspected love of landscape and what we call the 'beauties of nature'. Even when in town living with Jervas, one of the things he enjoyed most was 'our evening walks in the park'.[6] He writes to Caryll, 'I have been just taking a solitary walk by moonshine in St. James's Park, full of the reflections of the transitory nature of all human delights'.[7] He walked with Miss Lepel 'by the moon' at Hampton Court; and later in his life, as we have seen, urged the Duchess of Marlborough to sup in his grotto by moonlight.[8] His varied descriptions of his gardens are filled with fervour, and our

[1] Ibid. vi. 234–5; letter to Caryll, at the end of 1715.
[2] Ibid. ix. 76.   [3] Ibid. viii. 31 (30 May 1714).   [4] Ibid. vi. 243.
[5] Ibid. ix. 485. To Thomas Dancastle, 7 August 1716.
[6] Ibid. viii. 27. Cf. ix. 395.   [7] Ibid. vi. 194.
[8] Ibid. v. 410.

more modern enthusiam for the savage, the untilled, the 'sublime' in nature must not prevent justice to Pope's love of the gentler scenes, which alone his England afforded.

This love of nature is, of course, more philosophic than sensuous. Landscape induces moral reflection rather than aesthetic ecstasy. Like the philosophers of Greece and Rome Pope felt the need of 'the mean and sure estate'. If he at times lived in 'a glut of company', he must have for himself 'some thinking hours . . . to employ (since they are not so many) in thoughts of more serious importance than versifying deserves.'[1] When, however, these thinking hours are employed in learning to 'despise the ways of the world' and in exclaiming

> Oh keep me innocent, make others great![2]

they seem less essential than the poet affects to believe. When addressed to a real disciple of retirement, however, such observations occasionally acquire an attractive and convincing tone. In 1726 he writes to Hugh Bethel:

Nor ought you to decline writing to me, upon an imagination, that I am much employed by other people. For though my house is like the house of a Patriarch of old standing by the highway side, and receiving all travellers, nevertheless I seldom go to bed without the reflection, that one's chief business is to be really at home: and I agree with you in your opinion of company, amusements, and all the silly things which mankind would fain make pleasures of, when in truth they are labour and sorrow.[3]

'One's chief business is to be really at home!' If this is true in any symbolic sense, Pope perhaps failed; for he could not lay down stable principles of action and abide by them. After a headache, company and amusements were silly; on other days they were one of his greatest joys. When, however, he keeps his eyes off the emptiness of the world and voices only his genuine (if occasional) love of quiet of mind, he sounds truly sincere. In 1724 he writes to Bolingbroke, again after an illness:

Whatever expectations my own vanity, or your partiality, might give me of a better fate than my predecessors in poetry, I own

---

[1] Elwin-Courthpoe, vi. 280.   [2] Ibid. ix. 44.   [3] Ibid. ix. 149.

I am already arrived to an age which more awakens my diligence
to live satisfactorily, than to write unsatisfactorily to myself; more
to consult my happiness, than my fame; or, in defect of happiness,
my quiet. Methinks quiet serves instead of happiness to philosophers, as vanity serves instead of fame to authors, for in either
case the art of contentment is all. But when men grow too nice
and too knowing, the succedaneum will not do to such delicate
constitutions, and the author becomes miserable to himself in the
degree that he grows acceptable to others. What you call a happy
author is the unhappiest man, and from the same cause that men
are generally miserable,—from aiming at a state more perfect than
man is capable of.[1]

Such reflections lived and grew into the *Essay on Man*, a
fact which may serve to remind us that intellectual con-
sistency, while possibly expected of philosophers, can only
be desired of poets.

Love of quiet was stimulated by ill health, by a real love
of the country, and by the philosophy conventional since
the days of Seneca or earlier. But the greatest stimulus to
retirement was probably the abuse Pope got from Grub
Street. This has been 'written large' throughout these
pages, and here need not be recapitulated. At almost any
moment during his career he might have written as he did
to Parnell in 1717:

The present violent bent to politics and earnest animosities of
parties, which grow within one another so fast, that one would
think even every single heart was breeding a worm to destroy itself,
—these have left no room for any thought but those of mischief
to one another. The muses are all run mad and turned bacchanals,
and a poet now may be like Amphion and sing with the stones about
his ears.[2]

Pope disliked to think of singing with the stones about his
ears; he loved to dream of days that might

> slide soft away
> In health of body, peace of mind,
>   Quiet by day,

---

[1] Ibid. vii. 399.   [2] Ibid. vii. 466–7.

Sound sleep by night; study and ease,
Together mixt; sweet meditation;
And Innocence, which most does please
               With meditation.

The achievement of such a state clearly demanded a sound
body and a relatively good-natured age to live in. Pope
was blessed with neither; and if he dreamed, it was with
little expectation that his dreams would come true.

In fact, the decision really had been made when this
undersized offspring of elderly parents was born into a
Roman Catholic home and into an environment where to
be a Catholic was to be suspected of treason and other
crimes. Much of Pope's life had been defensive. He had
endured all sorts of attack from sources known or unknown.
He believed in retorting in kind; but his aristocratic friends
did not, and so *usually* he had thus far remained quiet. It
was certainly not his habit to reply in the haste of a white
heat of rage. Usually he waited, sure of a moment when
some mis-step would lay the Dunce particularly open to
ridicule.

Whoe'er offends, at some unlucky time
Slides into verse, and hitches in a rhyme,

he later wrote. His was not a watchful waiting: it was
confident and off-hand, bred of a feeling that in the long
run stupidity would collaborate with him in making itself
absurd.

During the first decade of his publishing career he had
retorted relatively seldom upon the numerous persons who
attacked him. From 1719 to 1727 he published very little
in the satiric vein. But he was at work, and interlarded his
reflections upon quiet of mind with notions of gaining such
quiet through the annihilation of his enemies. 'This poem',
he wrote before publishing the *Dunciad*, 'will rid me of
these insects';[1] and it is apparent that he was sufficiently
self-confident to believe so blissful a consummation possible. He never understood men well, though he could
strike out valid reflections upon man. It was perhaps the

---

[1] Elwin-Courthope, vii. 124 (23 March 1728).

a priori rationalism of his day, as well as a fair conceit of himself, that led him to believe that in any direct encounter genius could conquer dullness—that he could silence the bad poets, pedants, and journalists of his day. They were not worth attacking severally and individually; execution must resemble a massacre. Such ideas came gradually, perhaps; but during some years he harboured them, and they eventuated in the *Dunciad*. The story of that poem belongs to the satiric half of his career; here we need only mark certain steps of transition towards it.

Near the end of 1725 he wrote to Swift:

I am sorry poor Philips is not promoted in this age; for certainly if his reward be of the next, he is of all poets the most miserable. I am also sorry for another reason; if they do not promote him, they will spoil a very good conclusion of one of my Satires, where, having endeavoured to correct the taste of the town in wit and criticism, I end thus:

But what avails to lay down rules for sense?
In [George]'s reign these fruitless lines were writ,
When Ambrose Philips was preferred for wit![1]

At this time he had recently suffered annoyance over Buckingham's *Works*, over the difficulties attendant upon collaboration in the *Odyssey*, and over the gossip about himself and Miss Blount. There had been some criticism of his edition of Shakespeare, but *Shakespeare Restored* was not yet published. At such a juncture (if not earlier) we must assume that the first tentative redaction of the poem that was to be the *Dunciad* was already on paper. The comment on Phillips is merely a reply to gossip about that pastoral bard (who was just entering his 'Namby-Pamby' stage) in Swift's last letter; there is no reason to assume that Philips was more than a major 'ornament' in this first 'state' of the poem.

It is true that in a note to the first line of the 1743 edition of the *Dunciad* we are told that 'This poem was written in 1726,' and it is equally true, as we see from Pope's

[1] Ibid. vii. 57.

letters, that he worked busily on it during the months from June 1727 to March 1728. The footnote is not particularly important; for few authors can be sure exactly when their masterpieces were written, and Pope got dates wrong almost as often as he got them right. He must have begun work on the *Progress of Dulness*, as the poem was first called, as early as 1725; and small topical allusions to earlier events make sometime about 1720 a plausible date for certain lines. Some of these small events would be largely forgotten by Pope himself in 1725. Why, for instance, the action should be supposed to take place on the day (29 October 1719) when Sir George Thorold became Lord Mayor of London is a mystery.[1] That pageant could hardly mean much to Pope, one would imagine, since on the day after the event he wrote:

I am in a very odd course for the pain in my side: I mean a course of brickbats and tiles, which they apply to me piping hot, morning and night; and sure it is very satisfactory to one who loves architecture at his heart, to be built round in his very bed.[2]

One judges Pope did not see the 'broad banners and broad faces' of the procession of 1719. There is an allusion to another small scandal in Book ii, line 202, to His Grace's secretary, Edward Webster, who, according to Budgell, won the favour of the Duke of Bolton in 1718 by disreputable means.[3] Settle's death (12 February 1724) was an event more significant organically to the poem, but animosity to this aged and harmless Whig partisan could hardly have influenced Pope or his public very much in 1726 or 1727. The real stimulus came from the long and intermittent series of attacks that Pope had endured, mainly from persons of no importance. Small events 'hitched into rhyme' incidentally as the accumulation of a decade; most of the passages, for example, quoted in the *Bathos* (1727) were chosen several years before they were

---

[1] *Dunciad*, Book I, l. 85 (1728 eds. l. 73).

[2] Elwin-Courthope, ix. 293. Of course there is always the possibility that the letter is misdated.

[3] See Budgell's *Letter to the Lord ****, 1718, pp. 15, 17, 18.

used in that treatise. The whole trouble with Pope's projects against the Dunces was that they did not 'come off;' they lacked point; and so they lay idle until Swift in his visits of 1726 and 1727 gave the necessary fillip to Pope's ingenuity, and the satirist definitively emerged.

He had, of course, been known as a satirist before. The *Rape of the Lock* one almost forgets to call satire, but the *Worms*, the lines on Addison, and numerous small things had given Pope a reputation for biting and furtive potentialities in the genre. These small pieces were, however, firecracker squibs such as a clever schoolboy might produce. In the 'twenties it is clear Pope began to have more serious thoughts of reforming the age after the theory of classical satire. In the *Monthly Packet of Advices from Parnassus*, October 1722, we find the author (Matthias Earbury?) writing of the state of wit despondently:

Pope, indeed, keeps up the Face of an *English* Poet. Oh! could he write what he thinks, in Numbers sweet as those he has already sent into the World; then he would, like *Oldham*, scourge a wicked Age, and trace the Muses Miseries to their Fountain Head.[1]

Within a few years after this passage appeared, Pope made it clear that he could write what he thought, and he began not merely 'to correct the taste of the town in wit and criticism' but to enter the broader and (to him) more inviting field of moral and political satire. He entered, in other words, upon a more brilliant and important phase of his career.

[1] p. 28.

APPENDIX I

LETTERS OF POPE TO JACOB TONSON

(British Museum, Add. MS. 28275, fols. 228–42)

1. Fol. 231^r.

To Jacob Tonson

Sunday night [1721?]

Sir

Whenever ye weather permits, & y^r Leisure joins wth it, you will now find me at Twitnam. I hope you will quicken Fenton now & then by a letter. I have not had a word from him.

I must desire ye favor of y^u to send me but for a day or two, a book calld, ye Life of K. William ye Third, printed in large octavo ab^t 12 years ago. I'm told ther is in it a Speech of ye late Duke of Buck's: wch I never heard of. In this you'l oblige Y^r very affect. Servt.   A. Pope

2. Fol. 234^r; 235^v.

To Jacob Tonson

From St. James's Square

Sir

I coud be very glad if you had a Day & a Night's leisure to spend y^t time wth me at Twitnam, upon some necessary affairs in relation to our undertaking. I wish to morrow w^d agree wth your conveniency. I'm going wth Ld Burlington to Chiswick, from whence I take a Chaise to night, home; & shall stay there till Friday morning. I'd be glad to fix a party with Mr Carpenter & y^{r}Self, but of this when we meet.

     I am

       Y^r humble Servt.

       A. Pope.

Saturday

I desire a word by ye bearer.

   Address (on 235^v): To/Mr. Tonson.

3. Fol. 237^{r+v}; 238^{r+v}.

To Jacob Tonson

Oxford. Sept. 3 [1721]

Sir

I sent twice to speak with you, ye day I left London, before my Journey. I was with ye B^p of Rochester, but you forgot to send me your Waller, in wch I will do you w^t service I can. I have also ingagd Mr Kent to draw ye Outline of Mr Addison upon ye Copper plate itself. You must therfore get a Plate prepard to etch upon, that I may send it him for y^t purpose.

Pray let ye Division of ye Scenes in Shakespear be finishd wth all speed: it will else greatly retard ye Index.

As to ye D. of Bucks' works: I have resolvd upon further thoughts, to give up ye business of ye Impression intirely out of my hands, & have no concern in ye profits at all. The Bishop & her Grace, I find, inclined to imploy Mr Barber in ye whole matter, so y^t I shall have nothing to do but with ye Trouble, in wch I'l have no View, but to oblige her Grace. In this I'm sure I can't be in ye wrong, nor accountable, or lyable to any Misconstruction, or Thought of any Interest in it. I know this will seem Romantic to a Bookseller, even to You that are least a Bookseller. But you must allow a little madness to Poets.

I have a favour to ask of you, that if (as I'm told) poor Mr Craggs's Library comes into y^r hands to be disposed of, you will lay y^r hands upon an odd Volume of Barrows Sermons, which I lent him a week before he dyed, ye loss of which will spoil me a whole Sett. You'l easily know it, for he had no other; it is bound in a Cover with a Table in it, ye Leaves sprinkld with red & green.

I have got a man or two here at Oxford to ease me of part of ye drudgery of Shakespear, If you'l let me draw upon you (as you told me) by parcells, as far as sixty pd^s as they shall have occasion. I shall be at my Lord Bathursts at Cirencester in three days where y^r Com̃ands will find/Y^r humble Servt./

A. Pope.

Lord Harcourt went yesterday/to London.

[*On* 238^r *is written in Tonson's hand*:]

Ir

35 paid To Mr Popes ord^r } both Sums paid To M^r
25 D^o To E: Fentons ord^r } Popes Waterman

60

The 2 Notes for these Sums I gave up to Mr Pope as being no part of the 1st agreem^t but what I agreed to allow Mr Pope furth^r that he might not want help

JT

answer^d

Address (on 238^v): To/Mr Tonson at Shakesper's/head neer Somerset house/in the Strand/London
Frank: Geo. Clarke
Postmark: 5/SE.

4. Fol. 232^{r+v}; 233^v.

To Jacob Tonson

Twitenham, Wednesday

S^r

My ill fortune so orderd it, that I had three people who came and took possession of all ye Beds in my house last week. I sent to acquaint y^u with it, depending otherwise upon y^r promise of passing a night or so here. Since that time, my affairs have hurryd me to & from London, interchangeably every day; the last part of ye Planting Season taking me up here, & business which I think less agreeable, there. I'm resolvd to pass ye next whole week in London, purposely to get together Parties of my acquaintance ev'ry night, to collate ye several Editions of Shakespear's single Plays, 5 of which I have ingaged to this design. You shall then hear of me: till when too, I'm forced (much agst my inclination) to put off our meeting at Mr Carpenter's. I wish you'd inform Sr Godfry how busy I have been. I think it three Ages since I saw him and if my Features are altred, in proportion to ye length of Time wch it has seemd to me since I saw him, my Picture at next Sitting, will be as old as Nestor. So tell him, & tell y^r self that I am

S^r

Y^r very humble
Servt
A. Pope.

Address (on 233^v): To Mr Tonson, at Shakes-/pear's head ov^r agst Catha/rine street in the/Strand/London.

5. Fol. 236^{r+v}.

To Jacob Tonson

[written on the cover of a letter addressed to Pope at the top of 236^r in a large flowing hand as follows:]

To Alexander Pope Esqr at/his house in/Twickenham/Middlesex./ Free/Tem: Stanyan.

Sr. The Indisposition y^t continues much upon me hinders my coming to town as yet. I dare say you'l not find ye Volumes too thick, dividing ye whole into five, as I sent a direction. Pray let me have That copyd out. Unless we settle this, Fenton must stop in ye Index, & much time will be lost, I fear.

Address (on 236^v): To Mr Tonson, at Shakesp^{rs}/head ov^r agst Catharine street,/in the Strand,/London.
Postmark (on 236^v): 6/AV.

6. Fol. 240^r; 241^v.

To Jacob Tonson

Sir,   Tuesday night.
    Mr Gay & myself think it absolutely necessary that you should cancel that Leaf in which ye Epilogue is printed, or if it falls out wrong, cancell both leaves rather than fail; It must necessarily be inserted, after ye Title *EPILOGUE* [*Sent by an unknown Hand.*] Whatever charge this Cancelling will cost, shall be paid. It is yet time, I am very sure, to do it, before ye general publication on Thursday. This must be done to oblige him, &
                          Y^r most humble/Servt/A. Pope.

I must go out before ten/& shall be glad to see y^u (upon ye other affair) before nine.

Address (on conjugate 241^v): To/Mr Tonson ov^r agst/Catharine street in y^e/Strand.

7. Fol. 229.

To Jacob Tonson

S^r   [1723]
 I had writ to Mr Lintot just as I left ye Town, but at my coming
hither I find yours. Pray give my services to Mr Lintot, & acquaint
him that I shall make him ye Compliment which you desire, of
accepting one Royal for ye other, so y^t ye work need not to be
retarded. Since you assure me that is as good, tho somewhat less
Expensive.
 I must desire a favor of you, in return to this, which is also to
redound to ye credit of Mr Lintot. I mean in regard to ye beauty
of ye Impression, that you will use y^r interest wth Mr Watts, to
cause y^m to work off ye Sheets more carefully than they usually do;
& to preserve ye blackness of ye Letter, by good working, as well as
by ye best Ink. The Sheets I've seen since ye first Proof, are not so
well in this respect as ye first. I beg y^r Recommendation as to this
particular. There's nothing so mu[ch] contributes to ye Beauty and
credit of a Book, wch m[ay] be equally a reputation to Mr Lintot
& to me.
 Wright has writ to me for Prints of ye Dukes Monum^t. I have
no such thing, & suppose you have them: so be pleasd to acquaint
him. Pray (as y^u know I am ignorant of ye whole matter) tell me
what Booksellers are concernd in ye Shares of ye Dukes Book, now
Re-publishd, besides yrself, Mr Taylor & Innys? Why shou'd not
Lintot be admitted among 'em if there's any thing to be got? Y^u
know I must be concernd in his interests, now he is again my Bookseller.   Y^{rs} A. Pope.

 Address (on verso): To Mr Tonson, ov^r agst/Catharine street
in ye Strand.

8. Fol. 230^r.

To Jacob Tonson

Dr Sir   Twitnam, Wensday [1724]
 I calld twice & mist of you. I have prevaild upon Mr Fenton to
correct ye sheets of one volume, ye first of wch is Timon of Athens
wch I send you to begin ye Fifth Volume. Let ye Sixth be under
my care, & continue to send ye sheets of Cymbeline to me. I shall
be at Bolton Street agen on Friday.

By what Mr Wright tells me; I don't find y^u have got in any Bookseller (besides y^{r}self) to ingage in ye affair of his master the night y^u met with him & Innys, I conclude you have, or will, tho y^u did not bring any body else to that meeting. I remember y^u mentiond Taylor & some others to me as whom you had a personal influence upon. I need not repeat how much I depend upon y^r assistance in this point. In any thing in my power y^u shall ever command & in commanding oblige

Y^r faithfull affect. Servt A. Pope

[Conjugate with fol. 230^r and following it comes:]

Pray shew Mr Fenton this letter. I've chose these plays for him, because y^y will be infinitely less troublesome than ye other volume, When he is weary, he shall be discharg'd.

Address (on the verso of the postscript): To Mr Tonson

9. Fol. 239^r.

To Jacob Tonson

Sr. Sunday night

You are so perfectly in ye right in your Correction of *Containing* to *Consisting of*, that I think when I print any thing of my own I must get y^u to do for me, what you make me do for Shakespear, and Correct in my behalf. I think now ye Title is very well. I could have been very glad (not now only, but at any time) to see you; being really, with a sense of y^r many civilities to me, Ever

Y^r affect. humble Servt.
A. Pope.

I thank y^u for ye paper.

10. Fol. 242^{r+v}.

To Jacob Tonson

I assure y^u I have considerd & reconsider'd this matter, & would give y^u all ye Proofs possible that I w^d please you, wch are consistent with my reason & honour. I am absolutely oblig'd to mention ye business of Shakespear, (it is Requird directly of me, besides, by those whom I cannot disobey). But you see I comply to ye utmost wth you, in leaving out all your Three objections. The saying before y^t I c^d not *deny it at your Request* was meant meerly to express our Friendship, wch y^u seemd, as well as myself, to desire. Tho indeed ye putting you down as a Receiver of ye Subscriptions for me, was enough to demonstrate upon what good terms we stood. You'l see, by this wondrous Lett^r inclosd, how highly Lintot takes it, in that very light. I sh^d be glad y^u c^d call at Ld Peterborows as soon as y^u go out this morning. As to ye other particular I thank y^u for your advice, wch I'm sure is well meant, & I believe partly Right, but I don't think it so honourable a part to conceal ye least branch of a Truth till an Interest is servd: Tis fairer to do it at first, & that's all my reason. You may depend on my taking every thing right of you, & upon my being sincerely, (without any views, for you'l find I have none) Y^r affect. humble Servt./A. Pope.

[*On the verso is written an address, partly cut away:* Mr Pope at the/l of Peterboroughs/Piccadilly. *This indicates that Pope is using the cover of a letter received by him for paper upon which to write Tonson.*]

11. Fol. 228^r.

To Jacob Tonson

To Mr Tonson: Jan. 20th 1726/7
My Lord Oxford desires you to give the Bearer twelve of Dr Arbuthnots Books, and pray send with them, one to me.
Y^r humble Servt.
A. Pope.

[*Added below in Tonson's hand:*] D^d. Wm Williams—sent to my Ld Oxford

ODYSSEY INDENTURE

(18 *February* 1723)

(British Museum, Eg. Ch., 130)

𝕿𝖍𝖎𝖘 𝕵𝖓𝖉𝖊𝖓𝖙𝖚𝖗𝖊 made the Eighteenth day of February in the Tenth Year of the Reign of our Sovereign Lord George by the Grace of God of Great Britain ffrance and Ireland King Defender of the ffaith &cᵃ Annoq̃ Dnī One thousand Seven hundred and twenty three 𝕭𝖊𝖙𝖜𝖊𝖊𝖓 Alexander Pope of Twickenham in the county of Middlesex Gentleman of the one part and Bernard Lintott Stationer and Citizen of London of the other part 𝖂𝖍𝖊𝖗𝖊𝖆𝖘 the Said Alexander Pope hath undertaken a Translation of Homer's Odysses by Subscription in five Volumes with notes 𝕬𝖓𝖉 𝖂𝖍𝖊𝖗𝖊𝖆𝖘 it is agreed between them the Said Alexander Pope and Bernard Lintott that he the Said Bernard Lintott and his Assignes Shall for the Considerations[1] hereafter mentioned Have the Sole Right of Printing Selling and Publishing the Said Book consisting of the Said five volumes as far as He the Said Alexander Pope can grant the Same 𝕹𝖔𝖜 𝖂𝖎𝖙𝖓𝖊𝖘𝖘 𝖙𝖍𝖊𝖘𝖊 𝕻𝖗𝖊𝖘𝖊𝖓𝖙𝖘 that He the Said Alexander Pope for and in Consideration of the Sum of fifty two pounds and ten Shillings by Him the Said Bernard Lintott unto him the Said Alexander Pope in hand paid at or before the Sealing and Delivery of these presents and for and in Consideration of the farther Sum of three hundred and fifteen pounds by Him the S[aid] Bernard Lintott his Executors Admʳˢ or Assignes to be paid unto Him the Said Alexander Pope his Executors or Administrators in Such manner an[d] at Such times as is hereinafter mentioned and Expressed touching and concerning the Same And for and in Consideration of the Several Covenants Conditions and agreements Hereinafter mentioned by Him the Said Bernard Lintott to be kept Executed and performed 𝕳𝖆𝖙𝖍 Granted Bargained Sold and Assigned and by these presents 𝕯𝖔𝖙𝖍 Grant Bargain Sell and Assign unto the Said Bernard Lintott his Executors Administrators and Assignes the Copy of the Said Book in five volumes or of Such of the Said five Volumes as Shall be finished in the Life time of the Said Alexander Pope in

---

[1] The archaic -c̄on is here and elsewhere printed -*tion*.

case the Said Alexander Pope Shall dye any of the Said five Volumes being unfinished and the Sole Right of Printing Publishing and Selling thereof together with all the Right Title and Interest of Him the Said Alexander Pope in the Same 𝕋𝕠 𝕳𝖆𝖛𝖊 𝖆𝖓𝖉 𝖙𝖔 𝕳𝖔𝖑𝖉 unto the Said Bernard Lintott his Executors Administrators and Assignes from the day of the Publishing the Same for and during the Term of fourteen Years fully to be Compleat and Ended; and for and during all and every Such farther time and times Term or Termes as He the Said Alexander Pope by any Act or Acts of Parliament or otherwise Howsoever is Enabled to Grant and Assign the Same 𝕬𝖓𝖉 it is concluded and agreed by and between the Said Alexander Pope and Bernard Lintott and the Said Bernard Lintott Doth for himself his Heirs Executors Administrators and Assignes Covenant Promise and Grant to and with the Said Alexander Pope his Executors and Administrators by these presents That He the Said Bernard Lintott his Executors Administrators or Assignes Shall and will pay or Cause to be paid unto the Said Alexander Pope his Executors or Administrators the Sum of One hundred fifty Seven pounds and ten Shillings of good and Lawful money of Great Britain being the Moiety of the Said Sum of Three hundred and fifteen pounds at or before the Publication of the ffirst, Second, and Third Volumes of the Said Book and Shall pay or Cause to be paid unto the Said Alexander Pope his Executors or Administrators the farther Sum of One hundred fifty Seven pounds and ten Shillings being the Remainder of the Said Sum of three hundred and fifteen pounds at or before the publication of the ffourth and ffifth Volumes of the Said Book 𝕬𝖓𝖉 𝖋𝖋𝖆𝖗𝖙𝖍𝖊𝖗 that He the Said Bernard Lintott his Executors Administrators or Assignes Shall and will Print or cause to be Printed at his or their own Costs and Charges as well for Paper as Printing but for the Sole use and benefit of Him the Said Alexander Pope his Executors or Administrators Seven hundred and fifty of each of the Said five Volumes in manner and form following That is to Say Two hundred of each of the Said five Volumes with Notes or of So many of the Said five Volumes as Shall be finished in the Life time of the Said Alexander Pope in case the Said Alexander Pope Shall dye any of the Said five Volumes being unfinished in Quarto on the best writing Royal Paper Such as is hereunto annexed and five hundred and fifty of Each of the Said five Volumes, or So many of them as Shall be finished in the Life time of the Said Alexander Pope He dying as aforesaid in Quarto on the best Printing Royal paper Such as is hereunto annexed and Shall and will deliver or Cause to be Deliver'd unto the Said Alexander Pope his Executors Administrators or Assignes the Said Seven hundred and ffifty of each of the ffirst, Second, and Third Volumes or Such of them as Shall be finished in the Life time of the Said Alexander Pope he dying as aforesaid, Printed on Such Paper and in such manner as is aforesaid and without any Cost or Expense of Him the Said Alexander Pope his Executors or Administrators the Space of one week or more before the Publication of Each of the ffirst, Second, and Third Volumes or Such of them as Shall be finished at the time of the Death of the Said Alexander Pope He dying as aforesaid And Shall and will Deliver or Cause to be Delivered unto the Said Alexander Pope his Executors Administrators or Assignes without any Costs Charge or Expenses of Him the Said Alexander Pope his Executors Administrators or Assignes the Said Seven hundred and fifty of Each of the Said ffourth and ffifth Volumes or Such of them as Shall be finished in the life time of the Said Alexander Pope He dying as aforesaid, Printed in Such manner as is aforesaid, the Space of one week or more before the publication of the Said ffourth and ffifth Volumes, or Such of them as Shall be Printed in the life time of the Said Alexander Pope He dying as aforesaid **And** that He the Said Bernard Lintott Shall not Print or Cause to be Printed any other Book or Bookes Volume or Volumes of the Said Translation of Homer's Odysses in any Quarto Volume nor on the Same Sort of paper, nor with the Same plates Head peices Tail peices Initial Letters or other Ornaments whatsoever or any of them as the Seven hundred and fifty of Each of the Said Volumes of the Said Book which are above mentioned to be Printed for the Sole Use of the Said Alexander Pope as aforesaid or any of them Shall be printed within the Space of Ten Years next imediately after the date hereof **And ffarther** that the Said Bernard Lintott or his Assignes Shall not Publish the ffirst, Second, and Third Volumes of the Said Book or any of them within one week after the ffirst, Second, and Third Volumes or Such of them as Shall be finished in the Life time of the Said Alexander Pope as aforesaid Shall be deliver'd to the Said Alexander Pope or his Assignes and Shall not Publish the ffourth and ffifth Volumes of the Said Translation or any of them within one Week next after the Said ffourth and ffifth Volumes Shall be deliver'd unto the Said Alexander Pope or his Assignes **And** it is farther Covenanted Concluded and Agreed by and between the Said Alexander Pope and Bernard Lintott that

the Said Alexander Pope Shall be at the whole Expense and Charge of the Copper Plates for the Head peices, Tail peices and Initial Letters, **Except** only the Charge of working the Same at the rolling Press which Charge He the Said Bernard Lintott Shall be at **And farther** that the Said Copper Plates Shall always after remain to Him the Said Bernard Lintott and his Assignes **But** that notwithstanding the Said Bernard Lintott or his Assignes Shall at any time or times permit the Said Alexander Pope or his Assignes to have the Use of the Said Copper Plates for the Printing of any other Book or Books which He the Said Alexander Pope Shall think fit **He** the Said Alexander Pope or his Assignes being at the charge of touching up the Said Plates if Occasion Shall So require **And** He the Said Alexander Pope Doth for Himself his heirs Executors and Administrators Covenant Promise and Grant to and with the Said Bernard Lintott his Executors Administrators and Assignes That He the Said Bernard Lintott and his Assignes Shall and may under the conditions Covent[s] and Agreem[ts] aforementioned quietly Have Hold and Enjoy the Said Copy in Such manner as is before mentioned against Him the Said Alexander Pope and his Assignes **In witness whereof** the Said parties to these presents their Hands and Seales Have Set the day and Yearst [*sic*] first above written.
Alex[SEAL] Pope

Endorsed on the verso: Sealed & Delivered/(being first stampt wth three six penny stamps) in the presence of

Edm[d] Bickford
W Fortescue

Articles between/M[r] Pope & M[r] Lintot,/for y[e] Odyssey.

On a sheet of paper accompanying the indenture is the following:

This is the Writing Royal I approve of w[ch] Mr Lintot shall print y[e] 200 Books upon if it be any way in his power to procure it: If not, upon y[e] other writing royal hereunto annex'd./A. Pope. I do hereunto agree./Bernard Lintot

Witness Hereunto
W Fortescue
Edm[d] Bickford

INDEX OF NAMES

[Titles of printed books are given in the case of periodical publications and of other works the authorship of which is unknown or debatable.]

Pope, Alexander (the poet). (For biographies see under the names of their
authors.) Ancestry, 27–30. Parents,
29–36. Birth and childhood, 34,
37–8. Education, 38–42. Painting
and drawing, 39, 102–3. Physique
and health, 13, 42–4, 99, 210. BIN-
FIELD: life there, 17, 34, 36–8, 40,
62, 78, 116, 157, 159, 278, 291;
friends made there, 45–50, 190;
friends entertained there, 53, 70, 72,
94, 111, 125, 277; visited (after 1716),
183, 187, 212; Pope's early rusticity,
46. His summer 'rambles', 55, 99,
210–17, 280, 289; visits to Bath, 79,
125, 142, 166, 183, 210. His use of
Jervas's house in London, 69, 102,
270. Frequents Will's and Button's
coffee-houses, 46, 47, 51, 60, 62–4,
66, 67, 69, 115. His reputation as an
enemy, 149–56, 178–80. Binfield
sold, 70, 159. CHISWICK, life at, 159,
186, 211, 215, 299. TWICKENHAM,
removal to, 215, 217; life there, 277,
282–91. Tedious years of translation,
186–90 (see also under Homer). Views
on blank verse, 192. Relative freedom from attack (1718–22), 184,
201, 220. Troubles over Buckingham's Works, 220–8. Atterbury's
trial and exile, 228–30. (For the
edition of Shakespeare, see under
that author.) Gossip about Pope and
Martha Blount, 291–7. His skill in
epitaphs, 271, 275–7. His manipula-
tion of his letters, 20–3, 51. Financial
affairs, 132, 227, 234, 250, 253–9.
His funeral, 2.
PERSONALITY AND INTELLECTUAL
INTERESTS: Unpleasant traits of
character, 93, 158–9, 181, 184–5,
226, 234–5, 261. His character
attacked, 105, 161, 164, 178–80.
Amiable traits, 7, 43–5, 209. Free-
thinking tendencies, 61–2, 95–6.
Religion, 35–7, 62, 69, 174, 176–7,
214–15, 225, 228 n. Politics, 67,
69–70, 100–2, 228–30. Tendency
towards satire, 80–2, 302–5.
Thoughts of retirement, 209, 220,
270, 297–302. His antiquarianism,

218–19. His interest in architecture, 278–83; in monuments, 221;
in gardening, 35, 216, 270, 277–88.
His love of nature, 213, 216, 299–300.
WORKS: Unpublished juvenilia,
83–4. Tonson's Miscellany (1709),
51–3, 85. Pastorals, 10, 51–3, 55–9,
66, 85, 88, 119–20, 201. Essay on
Criticism, 17, 56, 60, 65, 69, 71, 74,
86–96, 104, 109–10, 154. Sappho to
Phaon, 97, 98. Messiah, 65–6, 97,
186. Miscellaneous Poems and Translations (Lintot, 1712), 97–9. To the
Author of a Poem entitled 'Successio',
84, 98, 117. Windsor Forest, 60, 67,
71, 88, 101, 117. Prologue to Cato,
101–2, 105, 122. Hadrian's verses to
his soul, 100. The Rape of the Lock,
67, 97, 98, 99, 122, 125, 156, 164, 305.
Ode for Musick, 103. Early epigrams
(on Cato), 63, 123–4, 165; Receipt to
Make a Cuckold, 125, 164; on
Blenheim Palace, 165. The Temple
of Fame, 135–6. Memoirs of Martinus
Scriblerus, composition of, 66, 76–81.
Memoirs of P.P. Clerk of this Parish,
81. A Prayer to God (Universal
Prayer), 61. A Farewell to London,
61, 157. A Key to the Lock, 80, 135,
138, 200. (See under HOMER for
Pope's Iliad and Odyssey.) The lines
on Addison, 126, 127 n., 145–8,
151–2, 176, 272 (see also under
Addison.) Pope's version of the
First Psalm, 63, 181, 184. God's
Revenge against Punning, 82, 182.
Poems addressed to the Misses
Blount, 98, 166, 201, 272, 297. The
Challenge, 153, 198. Court Poems,
153, 167–71, 174, 184, 204, 206. The
pamphlets about Curll's emetic,
169–71, 173 n., 178, 194 n. The
Worms, 175–7, 184, 305. Three Hours
after Marriage, 81, 193–9. A Court
Ballad, 153, 198. News from Court,
153 n., 198, 271. Pope's collected
Works (1717), 194 n., 201–2, 220.
Verses to the Memory of an Unfor-
tunate Lady, 201–3, 295. Eloisa to
Abelard, 97, 202, 203–8. Poems on
Several Occasions (Lintot, 1717), 84,